WRATH OF
ANGELS

WRATH OF ANGELS

THE AMERICAN ABORTION WAR

James Risen & Judy L. Thomas

BASIC BOOKS

A Member of the Perseus Books Group

Published by Basic Books,
A Member of the Perseus Books Group

Designed by Jessica Shatan

Library of Congress Cataloging-in-Publication Data

Risen, Jim.
     Wrath of angels : The American abortion war / Jim Risen and Judy L.
Thomas.—
     1st ed.
          p.   cm.
     Includes bibliographical references and index.
     ISBN 0-465-09272-1 (cloth)   ISBN 0-465-09273-X (pbk.)
     1. Pro-life movement—United States—History.   2. Pro-life movement—
Moral
     and ethical aspects—United States.   3. Abortion—Government policy—
United
     States.   4. Abortion services—United States.   5. Bombings—United States.
     I. Thomas, Judy.   II. Title.
     HQ767.15.R57   1998
     363.46'0973—dc20   97-45936

98 99 00 01 02 ❖/RRD   10 9 8 7 6 5 4 3 2 1

To Penny

To Tracy

Contents

PART IV WRATH

Acknowledgments

Wrath of Angels would not have been possible without the commitment of our editors, Susan Rabiner and Gail Winston, who fervently believed in our project and whose enthusiasm carried us through the longest and most difficult days. Our agent, Judith Riven, was also a constant source of guidance and support, and served as a determined advocate who refused to rest until this book became a reality. Our researcher, Robin Cochran, was also a marvel, enthusiastically investing her own time to dig for facts. Marcia Thurmond did yeoman's duty transcribing endless hours of taped interviews conducted by the authors.

James Risen would also like to thank Doyle McManus, Washington Bureau chief of the *Los Angeles Times,* for his great support, encouragement, sympathy, and forbearance throughout the making of this book. Doyle truly was the father-confessor of *Wrath of Angels.*

In addition, Risen would like to thank his editors in the Washington Bureau of the *Los Angeles Times,* who displayed tolerance and understanding, including Tom McCarthy, Joel Havemann, Drex Heikes, and Warren Vieth. Many friends and colleagues also offered support along the way; among many others were Tom Rosenstiel, Richard Serrano, and Robert Rosenblatt.

Above all is Penny Risen, who has always stood by her husband with unquestioning love. This book is dedicated to her. Like their mother, Thomas, William, and Daniel Risen showed remarkable patience for their father's long hours of "book work." They always showered their father with sorely needed encouragement and love. This book is also a tribute to the memory of the late William and Frances Risen, who always nourished and encouraged their son's dreams.

Judy L. Thomas would also like to thank her editors at the *Kansas City Star*—Randy Smith, Bill Dalton, Mark Zieman, and Arthur Brisbane—who allowed her the time off needed to write and trek from coast to coast on numerous research trips. Several colleagues at the *Star* provided a support network as well, including Michael Mansur, Donna McGuire, and Matthew Schofield, who listened patiently and offered much needed feedback and advice.

Others who deserve credit are Thomas's parents, Robert and Carolyn Lundstrom, who instilled in their daughter a love of knowledge and have stood by her through even the most difficult periods; in-laws Eleanor Thomas and Henry and Mariruth Thomas; and friends, especially Janet McRae, whose undying support and generous and frequent offers to baby-sit made travel possible and much less stressful.

There are three more people Thomas would like to mention, knowing that without them this book would not exist. Tracy Thomas, to whom this book is dedicated, provided steadfast guidance and countenance along the way, never once complaining about the extra burden it placed on him. And young Justin and baby Nathan Thomas were a constant source of inspiration, whose smiles and hugs kept their mother going even through the toughest of times.

Finally, we are both indebted to the more than two hundred people—leaders from both sides of the abortion battle and their families and friends, rank-and-file activists, law enforcement officials, attorneys, politicians, journalists, academics, and other experts—who graciously shared their stories with us. Many extended their cooperation past the normal limits of endurance in the interests of history and truth. We can only hope that we have lived up to that trust.

Authors' Note

Language has always been a critical battlefield in the abortion war. In an attempt at fairness, we have followed the generally accepted style of major American newspapers by using the terms *anti-abortion* and *abortion-rights* to identify the opposing camps in the abortion debate. We have used other terms in direct quotations or when their use is important to provide context.

PART I

INCEPTION

BEFORE *ROE*

I t was just after 10 P.M. on a bitter February night in 1985. Supreme Court Justice Harry A. Blackmun and his wife, Dorothy, sat in the living room of their third-floor apartment in suburban Arlington, Virginia, across the Potomac River from Washington, D.C. Moments after Blackmun left the room to go to bed, a loud crack shattered the silence and a bullet pierced the couple's window, showering Dorothy with splinters of glass. The slug from a 9-mm handgun, which blasted a jagged hole in the window the size of a baseball, was later found embedded in a chair.

The FBI immediately suspected the shooting was connected to threatening letters Blackmun had been receiving from abortion opponents. Since writing the landmark 1973 *Roe v. Wade* decision that legalized abortion, the justice had been the target of dozens of death threats and truckloads of hate mail, some of which called him "the Butcher of Dachau," "a murderer," and "Pontius Pilate." Blackmun had received one particularly chilling threat the day of the shooting. The typewritten letter, sent in an envelope with a Buffalo, New York, postmark, read as follows: "Sir, I do not like the way you are doing your job. One day I am going to see you and shoot your brains out. I am going to shoot you dead and I will be coming to your funeral."

The shooting followed hard on the heels of the most sustained eruption of anti-abortion violence since the *Roe* ruling, highlighted by a series of ten abortion-related bombings in the mid-Atlantic states, and punctuated by the Christmas Day, 1984, bombings of three abortion facilities in Pensacola, Florida.

More peaceful forms of protest against Blackmun's *Roe* decision had reached new heights as well. Six weeks before the Blackmun shooting, seventy thousand abortion opponents had gathered on the steps of the Supreme Court on the anniversary of the *Roe* decision for the annual "March for Life." President Ronald Reagan, calling from the White House (a move calculated by Reagan's media-savvy staff to make sure he could be heard by the crowd but not be seen talking to them by the network news cameras and their wider national audience), had encouraged the marchers to "end the national tragedy of abortion." Reagan had just won a landslide election to a second term, and the demonstrators outside the Supreme Court held out fading hopes that he would make good on his promise to rid the Court of abortion-rights advocates like Blackmun.

After the shooting, Blackmun was placed under constant police protection and his mail was screened. It marked the second time in less than six months that his security had to be increased; the cordon around him had been tightened the previous October, after he received a threatening letter from the so-called Army of God.

"Army of God" had been adopted as the favorite nom de guerre for the anti-abortion movement's violent fringe in 1982, when the kidnappers of abortion doctor Hector Zevallos and his wife in Edwardsville, Illinois, first used it in their communications with the FBI. Zevallos and his wife, the first kidnapping victims in America's abortion battle, were released after eight days, and three men—Don Benny Anderson and brothers Matthew and Wayne Moore—were later arrested and convicted in the case. But even with those three in jail, the appearance of the Army of God designation on the Blackmun letter forced the authorities to take the threat seriously.

Eventually, the FBI concluded that the bullet that pierced Blackmun's window was probably not aimed at him, but rather fired randomly from across the Potomac. To this day, however, those who know Blackmun wonder whether it was only a coincidence that the bullet found its way into the justice's home. The incident marked the first time in history that a Supreme Court justice had ever been the subject of a shooting investigation.

Before January 22, 1973, Harry Blackmun could easily have been voted the least likely Supreme Court justice to evoke public passions of any kind. He was the original "stealth candidate," "Old Number Three," the safe, unexciting third choice of a conservative president who was trying to avoid controversy after his first two nominees for the same vacancy had imploded under Senate pressure. He was the "Minnesota Twin," the old friend of a conservative chief justice who was being counted on as a reliable second vote for his mentor. His initial selection by Chief Justice Warren Burger to write the majority opinion in the *Roe* case so angered the Court's most liberal justice, William Douglas, that Douglas threatened to take the unprecedented step of going public with internal Supreme Court politics. By training and temperament, Blackmun was a doctor's lawyer; he approached *Roe* not with an eye toward expanding the rights of American women, but with an eye toward protecting the professional prerogatives of his former clients, America's physicians.

He was transformed on January 22, 1973: from mousy backbencher to icon of feminism, from Nixonian afterthought to liberal bulwark. In the process he became a despicable enemy to America's religious conservatives.

Within days of the *Roe* decision, Blackmun was met by fifty anti-abortion protesters while on a speaking trip in Cedar Rapids, Iowa. "They weren't loud or anything like that," recalls Randall Bezanson, a former law clerk, "but he was taken aback . . . this was Cedar Rapids." It never stopped. By the time Blackmun retired in July 1994, he had received more than sixty thousand pieces of hate mail, an average of eight a day since *Roe*. He would forever be the man who nationalized America's most volatile, most divisive, and most irreconcilable debate since slavery. It was no accident that anti-abortion activists complained that *Roe v. Wade* was the Dred Scott case of the twentieth century or that clinic bombers compared their actions to John Brown's antebellum raid on Harper's Ferry. All that was needed to complete the parallel was a civil war.

The Supreme Court likes to have the last word; on abortion, it instead had the first. Blackmun's ruling settled nothing; it set in motion a soul-searching, endless national argument over life and death, men and women—and God. One of *Roe*'s most lasting legacies is also one that was completely unintended: the mobilization of America's Christian fundamentalists. More than any other single event, the *Roe* decision stirred them from a fifty-year slumber and served as a catalyst for them to drop long-held theological beliefs that had kept them far removed from politics. In the process, fundamentalists found common ground with the Roman Catholic Church, the institution they had held, not long before, to be the font of all apostasy. They created the first conservative, religion-based social protest movement in modern American history, the subject of this book.

With *Roe,* Harry Blackmun tried to cut off debate and skirt the philosophical and religious issues inherent in the abortion argument, but he inadvertently brought together Jerry Falwell and Randall Terry, Pat Robertson and Cardinal John O'Connor. The decision also forced Americans to add a new phrase to their political lexicon: anti-abortion violence.

Roe v. Wade, like *Brown v. Board of Education,* was a true legal landmark of the post–World War II era. It was one of those rare watershed events that compelled America to see this era along clear dividing lines: pre-*Roe* and post-*Roe.* The lives of American women and the direction of American politics and American religion would be transformed forever.

*R*oe may have stamped abortion forever as a national political and social issue, but Harry Blackmun did not invent abortion, and he did not bring it to America. Abortion is as ancient as sex, reproduction, and the triumph of hope over experience; the way each generation of Americans has come to terms with it has offered a prism showing the shifting mores and political attitudes of the nation.

From America's colonial days until the early nineteenth century, abortion early in the pregnancy, or before "quickening"—defined as the time when a woman begins to feel the fetus move inside the womb, usually between the sixteenth and eighteenth weeks of pregnancy—was widely tolerated or at least widely ignored. Among physicians and political and religious leaders at the time, abortion was perceived to be practiced largely by unmarried lower-class women and thus was not seen as a community problem. This American acceptance had its roots in the pragmatic way in which abortion had traditionally been handled in England.

Recent academic research, however, has debunked the widely held view that abortion before "quickening" was not a crime under English common law. In fact, both infanticide and abortion were criminal offenses, but in the Middle Ages they were punished, for practical purposes, by the ecclesiastical, or church, courts rather than by common-law courts. After the Reformation and the British split with the Vatican ended the power of ecclesiastical courts, records show some abortion prosecutions were shifted into the common-law courts. Still, abortion was commonplace in Britain throughout the seventeenth, eighteenth, and early nineteenth centuries, and criminal prosecutions appear to have been rare. British authorities were clearly turning a blind eye to the fact that the law was being routinely ignored.

That approach was transplanted to the United States in the late eighteenth and early nineteenth centuries; American tolerance may also have been enhanced by the liberalization of sexual attitudes that swept the young nation in the wake of the Revolutionary War.

None of the states outlawed abortion until 1821, when the General Assembly of Connecticut passed the first restrictions in the country, modeled in part on a British anti-abortion law enacted by Parliament in 1803. The Connecticut law banned the use of poison to bring on a miscarriage after quickening. Missouri enacted its first law in 1825, followed by Illinois in 1827 and New York in 1828.

Despite the Vatican's ancient opposition to abortion, early American Catholic leaders quietly ignored the nation's common abortion traditions as well. Politically, the American church was still weak; its flock was made up largely of poor Irish immigrants in a country dominated by an Anglo-Protestant elite. The Catholic hierarchy was focused on the education and development of its own members, rather than on a broader national audience; therefore, the first documented public statement by an American Catholic leader did not come until 1841. Francis Kenrick, the bishop of Philadelphia, reiterated the church's long-declared belief that there could be no "therapeutic" grounds for abortion, not even the safety of the pregnant woman.

By that time, only ten states and one federal territory had enacted legislation similar to the Connecticut law, always as minor provisions in broader revisions to state criminal codes. Yet with the passage of those laws, abortion started to emerge as a public issue. Its visibility was raised in part through the notorious trials of those who performed them. One major case involved Luceba Parker in Massachusetts, who was indicted in 1843 on three counts of using instruments to perform abortions on married women. After the case worked its way through the courts for two years, the state's chief justice ruled that, because quickening had not been proved, Parker was not guilty. A second Massachusetts case arose in 1843 when Maria Aldrich, a single Rhode Island woman, was found dead in a boardinghouse in Boston. Aldrich had gone to Boston to get an abortion and died of infection afterward, and both the doctor and the man who had gotten Aldrich pregnant were indicted for murder. A jury acquitted the men, again on the grounds that "unquickened" abortion was not a crime, but five days later a state legislator requested that a House committee look into enacting a law making the procuring of abortion a misdemeanor. Within a week, the committee had drafted the first bill in United States history to deal exclusively with abortion. The bill was passed, but the law was only rarely invoked afterward.

The rise of the modern medical profession finally transformed abortion into a subject of true controversy. With the formation of the American Medical Association (AMA) in 1847, a group of physicians launched an aggressive campaign against abortion on the eve of the Civil War, lobbying hard in state legislatures and courts around the country to enact new restrictions. American doctors had a natural professional stake in their anti-abortion crusade. A proliferation of poorly trained healers and midwives was forcing physicians to compete for clients as well as status, so that highlighting the abuses and dangers associated with abortion helped encourage the standardization and professionalization of medical practice.

The doctors had plenty of evidence; the stunningly dangerous abortion methods of the times were leading to horrific maternal deaths, and advertising by abortionists made the issue increasingly difficult to ignore. In *Mother's Own Book*, "botanic physician" Alfred G. Hall suggested a recipe of bloodroot, black cohosh, and hemlock, taken with gin, honey, and cayenne, combined with laxatives and a series of hot baths. Frederick Hollick's *Diseases of Women* suggested unblocking a "menstrual obstruction" with a device made of two long leads hooked up to a battery; these "electrical treatments" were "nearly certain" to release the "obstruction."

While the doctors were making their case, a deeper dynamic was being played out: an early version of American immigration politics. Non-English immigrants, many of them Catholic, had been flooding into the United States throughout the middle of the nineteenth century, and the white Protestant elite was starting to harbor dark fears that it would soon be outnumbered. As the United States slowly developed a modern industrial society and the role of marriage and family in urban life changed, more and more white Protestant, middle-class married women were limiting the size of their families, through contraception, abstinence, and abortion. Upper-class physicians soon became alarmed that abortion was no longer being practiced only by unmarried women seeking to avoid the social shame and burden of illegitimate children.

Influential social commentators began to sound warnings that birth rates among women born in the United States were declining, whereas birth rates for immigrants, especially Catholics, were soaring. In the late eighteenth century, the average white woman born in the United States bore seven or eight children, but by the mid-nineteenth century, the figure was down to five. Worried Protestant leaders began to envy the strict Roman Catholic prohibitions on abortion; physicians reported that few Catholic women at the time were willing to violate their church's ban. Abortion came to be seen as a demographic calamity for the upper class.

Declining birth rates among white Protestants prompted political leaders to try to "influence fertility through legislation," observed Rutgers University historian James Reed in his history of the American birth control movement. "Between 1840 and 1870, apparent changes in the social status of women seeking relief from pregnancy alarmed many physicians and led them into successful campaigns to outlaw induced abortion at any stage of pregnancy," he added.

By 1860, twenty states had passed laws restricting abortion after quickening, yet those laws were still intended to protect the woman, not the fetus, and failed to deal with the question of when life began.

Victorian-era morals finally spelled the end of legal acceptance. At least forty laws were enacted in the states and territories between 1860 and 1880. Meanwhile, the federal government stepped in for the first time in 1873, when Congress passed the Comstock Act, named for Anthony Comstock, an anti-obscenity activist and head of the New York Society for the Suppression of Vice. The law made it a federal offense to sell or give away any article or medicine that would prevent conception or cause an abortion. After the law passed, Comstock set out to enforce it, becoming a special agent of the government. From 1873 to 1877, he prosecuted abortionists aggressively, using their ads as a tool.

In early 1878, Comstock targeted one of the most notorious abortionists in the country, Madame Restell, who ran a clinic on Fifth Avenue in

New York City. After disguising himself and purchasing abortifacients from Restell, Comstock arrested her. The day before her trial, Restell committed suicide and was found in a bathtub by her maid, her throat slit from ear to ear.

As the nineteenth century drew to a close, lawmakers crafted ever-tighter abortion restrictions, largely eliminating the distinctions between penalties for abortions before and after quickening. With few exceptions, these laws remained on the books throughout the first two-thirds of the twentieth century.

The modern push to reform America's abortion laws finally gained momentum in the late 1950s and early 1960s, driven largely by Planned Parenthood and the postwar population control movement. Planned Parenthood's roots date back to the days of Margaret Sanger, the public health nurse who was celebrated, reviled, and jailed for defying the old Comstock laws on birth control. Sanger launched the American Birth Control League in 1921, and two years later she founded the Birth Control Clinical Research Bureau, which treated patients and compiled detailed statistics concerning contraceptives. In 1939, Sanger's two organizations merged into the Birth Control Federation of America, later renamed the Planned Parenthood Federation of America.

Sanger was not an advocate of abortion reform, yet a new generation of leaders at Planned Parenthood soon began to pave the way for that movement. At the group's annual meeting in 1942, Alan Guttmacher, chief of obstetrics at Sinai Hospital in Baltimore, became one of the first physicians to call for the liberalization of the country's abortion laws. Saying that "the patent hypocrisy and holier-than-thou attitude of the medical profession in regard to this problem is revolting," Guttmacher recommended allowing abortion if a woman's health was at risk.

Momentum built within the population control movement for abortion reform in 1955, when Planned Parenthood sponsored a landmark conference called "Abortion in the United States." Organized by the group's new medical director, Mary Calderone, and dominated by Guttmacher, the conference first sought to gauge the scale of the problem of illegal abortion, but it lacked conclusive data. Largely on the basis of the controversial surveys of American sexual habits conducted by sex researcher Alfred Kinsey, who spoke at the conference, the conferees speculated that there could be between two hundred thousand and 1.2 million abortions performed annually. Despite the lack of hard numbers, the conference offered strong evidence that the nation's abortion laws were being widely ignored and that unsafe, illegal abortions were a major public health hazard. Speakers included a retired abortionist, Dr. G. Lotrell Timanus, who said he had performed more than five thousand illegal abortions over a twenty-year period in Baltimore and had built up a regular referral system from more than three hundred fifty Baltimore-area physicians. "To keep on the books, unchallenged, laws that do not receive public sanction and observance is of questionable service to our society," the conference participants said in a closing statement. "The demonstrated high evidence of terminations of unwanted pregnancies by illegal abortion could be looked upon as a disease." The conference recommended that legal scholars begin studying the possibility of reform and that the American Law Institute (ALI), a professional group charged with keeping the nation's legal codes updated, be asked to draw up model legislation to be used by the states. By 1959, Guttmacher was sitting in on meetings of the American Law Institute, pushing the organization to do just that.

The model legislation that emerged, later known as the "ALI plan," allowed abortion if two doctors agreed it was necessary to preserve the life or health of the woman and in cases of rape, incest, or severe fetal abnormalities. Those on both sides of the issue later agreed that the ALI model legislation provided the critical spark for reform. Just as the ALI model legislation was starting to circulate among legal and medical professionals, an incident in Arizona finally touched off national, even worldwide, debate and put a human face on the abortion dilemma.

In 1962, Sherri Chessen Finkbine, star of the Phoenix version of the TV nursery school show *Romper Room*, took a tranquilizer that her husband had brought home from England the year before. Pregnant with her fifth child, Chessen had experienced chest pains early in her pregnancy and was taking tranquilizers prescribed by her doctor. However, she ran out of those tranquilizers, and over the coming weeks she took about thirty or forty of the pills from England.

A month later, Chessen read an article in the *Arizona Republic* about a drug called thalidomide. The article warned that medical tests indicated that pregnant women who took the drug ran a high risk of giving birth to severely deformed babies. Thousands of deformed "thalidomide" babies had been born in England, Canada, Germany, and Australia; most did not survive more than a few months.

Chessen still remembers the events of July 21, 1962. "I called my doctor, told him about the pills, and he said, 'It probably isn't it, but bring it in.'" To her horror, she found that the capsules she had been taking not only contained thalidomide but were of the strongest dosage allowed. The chances of her giving birth to a deformed baby were high, her doctor told her. "The doctor called my husband and me into his office and said, 'If you really want to have a fifth baby, let's terminate the pregnancy and start again next month under better odds.'" The doctor said Chessen would have to write a letter to a three-person medical board at Phoenix's Good Samaritan Hospital, but he said the letter was merely a formality. He had already talked to the board and had scheduled her an appointment for an abortion the following week.

"I went home, and I thought, God, if we got a hold of this stuff—there had just been a contingent of Arizona National Guard that had been in Germany, where this drug came from—I'd better call the newspaper and warn them about this drug," Chessen continues. That weekend, Chessen called the publisher of the *Arizona Republic,* whose wife told Finkbine that the newspaper's medical reporter was working on an article about thalidomide. Chessen agreed to speak to the reporter if her name was not used. Her name was not in the story, but the next day the story was on the front page with a black border around it and a headline that screamed, "Baby-deforming drug may cost woman her child here."

After the article was published, Chessen's doctor called and nervously told her they could be prosecuted. The Arizona law at the time allowed abortion only to save the life of the pregnant woman, although in extreme cases the rules were known to be bent. "I can remember saying in my own little naive way, 'What does the government and the county attorney have to do with my taking care of my family?'" Chessen says.

Within hours, the hospital had canceled her appointment, saying the Maricopa County attorney had refused to give his consent without a judge's approval.

A few days later, Chessen's attorney requested a court order to allow the abortion, putting the couple's names into the public record and thrusting them instantly into the national spotlight. Thousands of cards, letters, and calls began pouring in. Some were death threats. "We received pictures of me from the paper, and there'd be an ice pick or a dagger with blood spewing. We'd receive manure in the mail. I was called a baby killer and a piranha and a Jezebel and a murderess and all sorts of ugly things. We had to change our phone number dozens of times." One morning, when her husband arrived at his teaching job at Arcadia High School in Scottsdale, a group from the Sisters of St. Agnes blocked him out of his room.

Chessen had originally requested a court order granting an abortion on the grounds that the birth of a severely deformed child would be an undue hardship on a family with four other small children to care for. Within days of her request, an Arizona Supreme Court judge dismissed Chessen's case on the grounds that there was no legal controversy and gave her ten days to build a case around the real reason she wanted an abortion—her unwillingness to have what would most likely be a seriously deformed child. If she requested an abortion on these grounds, the state would likely contest it, because Arizona law did not allow abortion under that circumstance. Thus, although the judge was sympathetic, legally his hands were tied.

Although a handful of states permitted abortions to preserve the woman's health, Chessen and her husband feared that because of the publicity, none would be willing to get involved. They applied for visas to Japan, but the Japanese consulate, fearful of anti-Japanese sentiment in the United States, refused to grant the visas.

The couple finally went to Sweden, where the laws were more liberal. By then the media attention had become so intense that on the way to the airport, Chessen tried to disguise herself by stuffing her shirt with a pillow to make herself look further along in her pregnancy than she was.

Even in Sweden, government officials warned that Chessen would need to prove she was mentally ill in order to get an immediate abortion. Her story had gone out on the international wires, and the press was following every move. She submitted to a psychiatric examination, and three weeks later the Swedish State Medical Board granted her an abortion. The doctor told her that the thirteen-week-old fetus had been so severely deformed that it would never have survived.

When the couple came home a month later, they were greeted by more threatening letters. FBI agents escorted their children to school, and some of Bob Finkbine's students asked to be transferred to other classes. "I never got to do *Romper Room* again," Chessen says. "I was told by the vice president of the NBC affiliate that I was now unfit to handle children." A month after her ordeal was over, a Gallup Poll found that 50 percent of those surveyed believed that Chessen had done the right thing, compared with 32 percent who said it was wrong.

The Chessen case was one episode that sensitized the public to the issue of abortion and set the stage for reform. "My case," Chessen says now, "got people to start talking." A second incident with a similar effect was a rubella epidemic that struck the United States between 1964 and 1966, during which thousands of women who had contracted the disease during pregnancy delivered babies with birth defects.

With the ALI blueprint in hand and the Finkbine case as emotional ammunition, a handful of activists were ready to go to the state legislatures. On April 25, 1967, Colorado became the first state to pass a reform law; it was followed by North Carolina on May 8. The drive got a major boost when the American Baptist Convention voted to back the ALI-style legislation in May 1967.

The most important endorsement came a month later, when the medical profession, which had been largely responsible for the stringent abortion laws enacted a century earlier, endorsed the ALI model legislation. When the AMA's House of Delegates voted to endorse abortion reform, a poll taken by the editors of the magazine *Modern Medicine* showed that 86.9 percent of the forty thousand doctors surveyed were in favor of liberalized abortion laws. The AMA's backing gave the reform campaign power; the following month, California lawmakers passed an ALI-based measure. In one of the great ironies of the abortion debate, the California bill, one of the first major breakthroughs for the reform movement, was signed into law by California governor—and future president and "pro-life hero"—Ronald Reagan. In 1968 and 1969, seven more ALI-style laws were passed, in Arkansas, Delaware, Georgia, Kansas, Maryland, New Mexico, and Oregon.

But abortion-rights activists were not ready to quit. In fact, by the late 1960s the new women's liberation movement began to focus on sexual freedom and reproductive rights, including abortion. Ultimately, the new women's movement changed the nature of the abortion debate from a public health issue into a woman's issue and finally into a feminist political issue. In the process, these activists forced the physicians and population control advocates who had crafted limited reforms like the ALI model to support more fundamental change and, finally, full legalization.

At the second annual convention of the National Organization for Women (NOW) in November 1967, Betty Friedan, author of the best-selling 1963 book *The Feminine Mystique,* succeeded in getting the new feminist organization to endorse abortion reform for the first time. Some members wanted NOW to stick to economic and job discrimination issues, however, and were so angered by Friedan's abortion initiative that they quit the organization. But soon, NOW's feminists were forming a tentative coalition with the public health experts and population control advocates who had helped kick off the reform campaign years earlier. They came together in February 1969 at the first National Conference on Abortion Laws, held at the Drake Hotel in Chicago. On the conference's final day, the group put together a planning committee, chaired by New York author and abortion-rights activist Lawrence Lader, to form the National Association for Repeal of Abortion Laws (NARAL). The group's mission: to focus on the remaining states that had the best chances of passing abortion-repeal laws and ultimately to win more sweeping change.

Guttmacher, appointed in 1968 by governor of New York Nelson Rockefeller to a commission to reform the state's abortion laws, was still a driving force, and now he was ready for more radical action than ever before: "I came to the conclusion in 1969, forty-seven years after abortion first came to my medical attention when I was a third-year medical student . . . that abortion on request was the only way to truly democratize legal abortion."

By 1970, with the AMA pushing and NARAL and NOW prodding, a dozen states had moved to liberalize their laws. In March 1970, Hawaii became the first state to go further, passing a law that virtually repealed abortion restrictions. Next came New York, then Alaska, and then Washington, whose state legislature passed a repeal referendum that voters approved.

In most states, however, strict abortion laws remained in effect, and the states that had reformed their laws became magnets for women seeking abortions. In the fifteen months after New York's repeal law was passed in July 1970, New York City recorded 195,520 abortions, with 68,391 for residents and 127,129 for nonresidents. California became a

West Coast magnet as well; by 1972 California was reporting about one hundred thousand legal abortions a year, up from just five thousand in 1968. As many as 90 percent were being performed for women on so-called psychiatric grounds. Like many other states that passed early reforms, California allowed abortions to protect the mental health of the pregnant woman, and physicians quickly latched onto that as their favorite loophole.

Although there still was no national policy on abortion, the state-level reforms were having a major impact. For educated, middle-class American women, safe and legal abortions were becoming increasingly accessible; the Centers for Disease Control reported that 586,800 abortions were performed nationwide in 1972. And the Catholic Church, along with the most powerful Irish Catholic family in America, began to notice.

As reform swept from one state to another in 1967, it initially met only scattered opposition, mostly from Catholic doctors and lawyers. Even in large states like California, the opposition was relatively weak and disorganized. Soon, however, the Catholic Church started to weigh in, something abortion-reform activists had long feared. "We should recognize," psychiatrist Theodore Lidz said twelve years earlier at the 1955 Planned Parenthood conference, "the fact that almost anything we are going to say here will be opposed by the Catholic Church."

Indeed, the Roman Catholic Church's fierce opposition to abortion dated back to the early Christian era and had undergone only minor modifications over the centuries. The Vatican had never wavered in its belief that abortion was a sin; the only debates within the church over the years had been on the margins, such as whether a therapeutic abortion to save the life of the mother was acceptable or whether the punishment of excommunication should be meted out for early abortions, performed prior to quickening.

Those theological debates had been settled centuries before. In 1679, Pope Innocent XI ruled that abortion to save the life of a mother was prohibited under church teaching; in 1869, Pope Pius IX returned the church to its medieval practice of imposing excommunication for any abortion. Above all, the church's position was driven by a belief that had evolved over the past few centuries, that "ensoulment"—God's granting of a soul—takes place at conception.

The only Catholic theological debate that continued into the twentieth century was over whether the punishment for abortion applied to the woman, the doctor, or both. In 1917, it was ruled that anyone who procured the abortion, including the woman, would be automatically excommunicated. Church doctrine has not wavered since. However, the fact that church law decreed that abortion was a mortal sin did not mean that the American Catholic hierarchy had to do anything to try to stop it. In fact, the Catholic Church hardly played any role at all in the nineteenth-century campaign against abortion.

Vatican II, the cornerstone of Pope John XXIII's early-1960s church reform campaign, first forced American Catholic leaders to confront the issue. Vatican II not only called on church leaders around the world to become more socially and politically active, but also renewed the church's opposition to abortion. A Vatican II statement lumped abortion in with murder, genocide, and euthanasia, calling it a "supreme dishonor to the Creator." American bishops accepted this stance, but they were not stirred to action until a key member of the Kennedy family, Eunice Shriver, sister of John F. Kennedy and Robert F. Kennedy, and head of the family's well-endowed Joseph P. Kennedy Jr. Foundation, arrived on the scene.

The fact that one of her sisters was mentally retarded deeply influenced Eunice Shriver. Under her direction, the Kennedy Foundation had been funding medical research in the area of mental retardation as well as in the emerging field of bioethics. By the mid-1960s, Shriver began to fear that the new abortion reform campaign represented a threat to the mentally retarded. Reformers were making the case that legal abortion, coupled with prenatal testing, could help families avoid having children with serious birth defects. Shriver saw that argument as callous and cold, the mark of a society that believed in disposable human beings, and she saw abortion reform as an early step on a slippery slope toward eugenics and euthanasia.

In September 1967, Shriver arranged for the Kennedy Foundation and the Harvard Divinity School to cosponsor a major conference on abortion in Washington. The Kennedy name ensured a blue-chip crowd; the three-day conference brought together seventy-three top-ranked scholars, theologians, public policy experts, and political leaders—even a pair of Supreme Court justices. The conference was to serve as a watershed for the Catholic anti-abortion movement in much the same way that the 1955 Planned Parenthood conference was for the reform campaign.

The minutes of the conference, published the following year, suggest a sober and high-toned debate, with both sides of the reform issue represented. But co-chairman Herbert Richardson of Harvard Divinity School later acknowledged there was an "unspoken consensus" among the Protestant, Catholic, and Jewish theologians who attended the conference that the fetus had a certain dignity and should be accorded human rights.

In addition, some abortion-rights activists felt excluded; of the dozens of panelists, only a handful were women, and of those, many were abortion opponents. The conference attracted picketing from abortion-rights activists, therefore, who stood outside the Washington Hilton, where the conference was being held, with signs bearing slogans like "End Butchery."

Undeterred, Eunice Shriver had the minutes of the conference published as a book, *The Terrible Choice,* with an anti-abortion forward written by Nobel Prize winner Pearl S. Buck. Eunice and her husband, Sargent Shriver, took the book with them wherever they traveled and often passed it out to Catholic leaders or left copies in Catholic churches.

Although having the Kennedy name attached gave the new anti-abortion cause a certain political cachet among Catholic leaders that it had previously lacked, the Shrivers' involvement in the fledgling anti-abortion movement did not cause them problems within the Democratic Party; the issue of abortion was not yet a litmus test for liberals. In 1972, Sargent Shriver served as George McGovern's vice presidential running mate, and his opposition to abortion was never an issue.

In fact, Eunice Shriver's brother, Senator Edward Kennedy (D-Mass.), issued a statement in 1971 at the behest of the Massachusetts Catholic Conference that strongly suggested he shared his sister's opposition to abortion reform. Kennedy's statement, published by Massachusetts's bishops as part of a package of materials distributed during a local debate on state reform legislation, stated that Kennedy would never "support the hard society wherein a child in the womb could be victimized legally." Kennedy called instead for a "soft society," one that coupled opposition to abortion with government support and compassion for women. Soon after *Roe v. Wade,* Eunice Shriver quietly lobbied her brother, on behalf of the church, to get him to agree to vote in favor of so-called conscience legislation, which prohibited the government from denying federal funds to Catholic hospitals and other health care facilities that refused to perform abortions. The law, which was passed in 1973, also prohibited hospitals that did perform abortions from firing doctors or nurses who refused to participate. Kennedy ultimately voted for the conscience provision.

For years afterward, Kennedy's letter to the Massachusetts bishops was offered up as proof by his anti-abortion critics that Kennedy had altered his position on abortion after *Roe v. Wade* to get into line with the growing pro-choice consensus within the Democratic Party.

S oon, the National Conference of Catholic Bishops (NCCB), the American Catholic Church's main policy-making body, began to mount its own campaign to curb the drive for state-level abortion reform. The NCCB quietly asked local bishops to recruit Catholic volunteers to set up local anti-abortion organizations, and the national group retained a political consultant to support these new "right-to-life" organizations. These state groups later formed the backbone of the mainstream anti-abortion movement when they united under the umbrella of the National Right to Life Committee, founded by the American bishops in 1972.

Time and again, these groups were established soon after reform legislation surfaced in a state. The Virginia Society for Human Life was the first, established in February 1967 in response to a reform drive that gained momentum in 1966 when the Virginia public health director gave a speech in Roanoke calling for liberalization. Geline Williams, a Catholic mother from Richmond, and a few other Catholics began to meet to counter the threat. Soon, Richmond's Catholic bishop, John Russell, began to provide financial support as well as the free use of church buildings for meetings and secretarial help.

"The Diocese of Richmond was very helpful to the formation of the Virginia Society for Human Life," says Williams, now president of the National Right to Life Committee. "This was a lay organization, but we welcomed the church support, because at that time, everyone was so at sea as to what to do and how to do it. We were very grateful for the help given us."

In fact, the Catholic hierarchy was the engine driving virtually all anti-abortion lobbying efforts prior to *Roe v. Wade*. In 1972, the bishops officially established a pro-life activities committee to take over its anti-abortion campaign, and they placed Monsignor James McHugh, a

Catholic priest who had been lobbying against abortion from another staff job, to head the new office. (McHugh is now bishop of Camden, New Jersey.) One of McHugh's first actions was to create the National Right to Life Committee. Formed in 1972, it was initially run out of the NCCB's offices; Michael Taylor, an NCCB staffer, was chosen by McHugh to be its first director. The National Right to Life Committee was spun off into an independent lay organization by the Catholic Church only after the *Roe v. Wade* decision, when church leaders realized abortion had become such a hot national issue that they had to put some distance between the church and direct political lobbying.

The emergence of the state-level anti-abortion lobbying campaigns seemed to slow the reform drive in at least a few states. In New York, Cardinal Terence Cooke helped lead a counterdrive that succeeded in 1972 in getting the state legislature to overturn the state's 1970 reform law. Governor Nelson Rockefeller vetoed the new abortion ban in New York, but Connecticut enacted a more restrictive law that same year.

The Catholic Church's campaign gained virtually no support from other religious denominations; in many cases, the Protestant clergy supported abortion reform. That became clear in 1967, when a group of twenty-one Protestant ministers and Jewish rabbis gained nationwide attention by founding an abortion-referral clearinghouse in New York, the Clergy Consultation Service, to help women obtain safe abortions.

Until then, few pastors had spoken out in support of abortion rights. However, the Reverend Howard Moody, the Baptist minister from New York City who spearheaded the group's efforts, believed ministers had a duty to help women avoid the dangers of back-alley abortions. "Women who had abortions didn't talk about it," Moody says. "Ministers didn't talk about it. It was going on, but you didn't use the word in public."

Moody's group made stunning headlines when it went public, describing the underground service in a front-page story in the *New York Times,* thus making it clear that other denominations were not lining up behind the Catholic anti-abortion campaign. Eventually, the clergy group went national, always finding an enormous demand for the service.

While Catholic Church leaders were pulling the strings behind the scenes for statehouse lobbying, street-level anti-abortion protest was breaking out as well, without any official sanction from the church.

The nation's first anti-abortion sit-in took place in February 1970, when Michael Schwartz, a conservative Catholic student at the University of Dallas, organized a brief occupation of the Planned Parenthood offices just north of downtown Dallas. Although Texas still outlawed abortion at the time, Schwartz wanted to protest the fact that Planned Parenthood's Dallas office was helping women who wanted abortions fly to states where the procedure was legal, primarily California and Colorado. A group of students from the University of Dallas, a small Catholic college, staged a six-hour sit-in that ended quietly, without any arrests, after Planned Parenthood obtained a court order and the demonstrators complied with a police request to leave.

The incident went almost entirely unnoticed, except at *Triumph Magazine,* a tiny right-wing Catholic magazine based in Washington, D.C., and run by Brent Bozell, William F. Buckley's brother-in-law and a former editor at Buckley's *National Review.* Fritz Wilhelm, a professor at the University of Dallas, did freelance writing for *Triumph,* and when he mentioned the demonstration to Bozell, the editor was intrigued. In January 1970, Washington's old abortion law had been struck down by a federal judge, and the city was fast becoming an East Coast magnet for abortions, just as California and Colorado had become in the West. In June, Schwartz and a few other students from Dallas joined Bozell and about two hundred fifty others for a protest rally at George Washington University Hospital in the District, where abortions were already being performed. Bozell and four others split off from the main protest, sneaked into the hospital through a side entrance, and tried to stage a sit-in inside.

The District police were in no mood for tricks, however; the huge May Day protest, one of the biggest antiwar demonstrations of the Vietnam War era, had just been staged a month earlier, and the police were tired of politics. The five who made it into the hospital were man-handled and quickly taken into custody, the first arrests of the anti-abortion movement.

Washington's Cardinal Thomas O'Boyle secretly paid their bail, sending a quiet signal of approval and blessing. However, most mainstream Catholic leaders were horrified by the illegal actions. The Catholic press denounced the sit-in, and the group made no effort to stage follow-up demonstrations. The anti-abortion movement, at the time still dominated by Catholic doctors and suburban housewives, was not ready to take to the streets; the early sit-ins remained isolated incidents and were quickly forgotten.

A debate has raged among activists on both sides ever since that time over whether the state-level reform effort stalled in the early 1970s in the face of the mounting Catholic opposition. That debate quickly became academic, however, thanks to three people who could not have been more different: a lesbian carnival barker, a newly minted lawyer who had never tried a contested case, and the "Minnesota Twin." They took the abortion debate out of the statehouses and put it in the Supreme Court. Together, they forced Americans to start thinking about abortion as a national issue for the first time.

2

THE STRUGGLE FOR *ROE*

Sarah Ragle was the daughter of a Methodist minister, a brilliant student who had skipped the sixth and twelfth grades, graduated from high school at sixteen, and received her law degree from the University of Texas School of Law at twenty-one, while others her age were still undergraduates. While in her third year of law school in 1967, however, she found herself lying on a table in Piedras Negras, Mexico, getting a $400 abortion, only to wake up later in a small motel, a wave of relief washing over her as her boyfriend told her everything had gone all right. She had crossed the border because abortion was illegal in Texas. Sarah Ragle came by her interest in abortion reform the hard way. "I was one of the lucky ones," she later wrote.

When she graduated from law school in 1967, Ragle was frustrated to find that interviews with mainline law firms, who shunned women attorneys, failed to net even one offer. She took a job in Austin helping one of her law school professors research a new canon of professional ethics, while her boyfriend, Ron Weddington, began law school in June 1968. The couple married that August.

It was while Ron was in school and Sarah was working on the ethics code that she was asked by friends to do legal research for an abortion referral project they had set up to help local women. At an Austin garage sale to raise funds for a local feminist group in November 1969, Sarah Weddington and her friends first began to talk about the lawsuit that would eventually become *Roe v. Wade*. The talk focused on the Texas anti-abortion statute and whether those involved in the abortion referral service could be prosecuted for their actions. The women wondered whether their legal liability would be different if they sent women only to states where abortion was legal.

Weddington did not know the answers to the questions, but she told her friends she would be happy to find out. She began to study the history of the Texas law, the history of abortion in the United States, and the status of the issue in legislatures across the country. Eventually, the members of the referral service asked her to take the next step and file a lawsuit to challenge the Texas law, which had remained unchanged since 1854.

It was a daunting prospect. "A lawsuit was an obvious route," Weddington says, but "my total legal experience consisted of a few uncontested divorces for friends, ten or twelve uncomplicated wills for people with little property, one adoption for relatives, and a few miscellaneous matters. I had never been involved in a contested case."

As soon as she decided to go ahead, Weddington realized she needed backup. In December 1969, Weddington asked Linda Coffee, one of the few other women who had been in her law school class, if she would help. Coffee quickly agreed, and the two began searching for a pregnant Texas woman who wanted an abortion and would be willing to be a plaintiff in their lawsuit. They found Norma McCorvey.

McCorvey was hardly a model plaintiff. At twenty-one she was a street-smart high school dropout, a drug user, a lesbian, and the victim of abusive men and neglectful parents. She was pregnant for the third time, had put one child up for adoption, and had watched in horror as her mother took another from her. This time she was pregnant as a result of a casual affair.

McCorvey had been in Florida working as a carnival barker for a traveling carny show when she realized she was pregnant. She barely scraped up the money to make it home to Dallas; broke and dejected, she lived in the Dallas Greyhound station for five days before she found a job in a bar and moved back in with her father. McCorvey knew she did not want another child, but she did not even know what the word *abortion* meant. She called the doctor who had delivered her other children and had the following conversation:

> I said, "I want you to take my baby away." And he said, "I don't understand." And I said, "Well, you know, I don't want it." And he says, "Oh, you want to abort." I asked him what that meant, and he told me to look it up in the dictionary, and then hung up. All I knew is that it was like taking a baby away.
>
> So I looked up the word and found out it meant exactly what I thought. I called the doctor's office the next day and made an appointment. I was so totally dumb, I thought I'd made an appointment for an abortion. I went in, and the doctor told me he didn't do abortions and didn't know anybody who did. He said they were illegal in Texas. He told me I really should have thought of that before I got pregnant again.

Finally, her doctor gave her the number of Henry McCluskey, a Dallas attorney who handled adoptions. McCorvey cried for several days, then tried to self-abort by eating peanuts and drinking castor oil. All it did was make her sick. Still desperate, she called McCluskey. McCorvey insisted that she wanted an abortion rather than an adoption, and after she said she would do anything to get one, McCluskey told her he knew two young lawyers who were looking for someone to help them challenge the state's abortion law. McCorvey said she would think about talking to them.

In the meantime, she went to an illegal abortion clinic she had heard about in Dallas. "Nobody was there. It was an old dentist's office. Then I saw dried blood everywhere and smelled this awful smell." She rushed out, not realizing until later that the clinic had been shut down by the police. The next day, she called McCluskey and told him to give the young attorneys her name. McCluskey, a friend of Coffee's, arranged for a meeting, and in February 1970, the three women sat down together at a corner table at a pizza parlor on Mockingbird Lane in northeast Dallas.

Dressed in jeans, a shirt tied at the waist, and sandals, McCorvey felt out of place. "They were strange," McCorvey says. "They were educated people; they were dressed nice. Everything about them was just the total opposite of what I was. I had a very low self-esteem, no self-confidence at all. I wasn't able to sit down and make conversation. I felt like I was jinxed."

At the meeting, Weddington and Coffee told McCorvey about their idea for a lawsuit, but all McCorvey could think about was getting an abortion. Eventually, they asked McCorvey to tell them about herself. So she told them "the whole miserable story": about the years she spent in reform school for repeatedly running away from home; about her marriage at seventeen to a man who beat her half to death when he learned she was pregnant; about her mother, who took McCorvey's daughter away because she thought she was unfit to raise her; and about the fact that she was a lesbian.

Afraid that she was driving the lawyers away with her troubled past, McCorvey panicked. "You know," she said, "I was raped. That's how I became pregnant with this baby."

It was a lie, but it got Weddington and Coffee's attention. They asked if the rapist had been arrested and whether she'd reported the incident to police. When McCorvey said no, Weddington told her that although it was awful that she'd been raped, it did not matter under Texas abortion law; there were no exceptions for rape. By the end of the meeting, surprised that the women were still willing to take her case, McCorvey, two and a half months' pregnant, agreed to be an anonymous plaintiff in the lawsuit. Her pseudonym: Jane Roe.

Weddington later said that neither she nor Coffee pushed McCorvey on the question of how she had gotten pregnant. "I was not going to allege something in the complaint that I could not back up with proof," she says. "Also, we did not want the Texas law changed only to allow abortion in cases of rape. We wanted a decision that abortion was covered by the right of privacy. Our principles were not based on how conception occurred."

On March 3, 1970, Coffee filed a class-action lawsuit against Henry Wade, the district attorney of Dallas County. The lawsuit challenged the constitutionality of Texas's criminal abortion law, which prohibited procuring or attempting an abortion except to save a woman's life. It also asked for an injunction restraining the district attorney from enforcing the Texas criminal abortion statute.

McCorvey's one-page affidavit said, in part,

Since my pregnancy I have experienced difficulty in securing employment. Each month I am barely able to make ends meet.

Consequently I cannot afford to travel to another jurisdiction in order to secure a legal abortion. I understand that there are competent licensed physicians in Dallas County who do perform apparently illegal abortions, but I have never been able to afford their services. I fear that my very life would be endangered if I submitted to an abortion which I could afford. I believe that the enforcement of the Texas Abortion Laws against licensed physicians has forced me into the dilemma of electing whether to bear an unwanted child or to risk my life submitting to an abortion at the hands of unqualified personnel outside of clinical settings.

On June 17, a three-judge federal court declared the Texas statutes unconstitutional but refused to order the district attorney to stop prosecuting doctors for performing abortions. The day after the ruling, Wade said he would appeal, but he added that once a law had been declared unconstitutional, he did not think he could try people for breaking it. The following day, however, he reversed his statement and said he would continue to try doctors who violated the Texas law.

The ruling came too late for McCorvey. By then, she was nearly ready to give birth. "Right then, I suddenly realized that this lawsuit was not really for me," she says. "It was really for all the women who came along after me." Furious and dejected, McCorvey vented her frustrations on McCluskey, who found her a couple who was eager to adopt her baby.

Weddington and Coffee appealed the case directly to the Supreme Court. On the morning of December 13, 1971, the twenty-six-year-old Weddington found herself in Washington, D.C., arguing the case before seven black-robed justices. Two longtime jurists, Hugo Black and John Harlan, had recently died and had not yet been replaced.

There were no reporters or throngs of protesters waiting outside on the steps. "It was not the scene you get now," recalls Weddington. "None of that."

"Part of that day I remember very well, and part of it's a blur," she says. "I was scared." During her argument, Weddington did not mention McCorvey's story about the rape. She simply contended that the Texas abortion law violated a woman's fundamental right to choose whether to continue or terminate her pregnancy. "I think it's without question that pregnancy to a woman can completely disrupt her life," Weddington told the Court. "It disrupts her body; it disrupts her education; it disrupts her employment; and it often disrupts her entire family life. And we feel that because of the impact on the woman, this certainly, insofar as there are any rights which are fundamental, is a matter which is of such fundamental and basic concern to the woman involved that she should be allowed to make the choice as to whether to continue or to terminate her pregnancy."

Justice Potter Stewart asked Weddington which provisions of the Constitution she was relying on for her argument. Weddington replied the Ninth Amendment, which reserves to the people those rights not specifically given to the government, and the due process clause of the Fourteenth Amendment. Then Justice Byron White asked how far Weddington believed the right to an abortion should go: "Will that take you right up to the time of birth?"

Weddington's response: "It is our position that the freedom involved is that of a woman to determine whether or not to continue a pregnancy. Obviously, I have a much more difficult time saying that the state has no interest in late pregnancy." White asked her why. "I think it's more the emotional response to late pregnancy," Weddington said. "By whom?" White prodded. "I guess by persons considering the issue outside the legal context," Weddington said. "The Constitution, as I see it, gives protection to people after birth."

Once Weddington finished, Jay Floyd, the assistant attorney general of Texas, began to defend his state's abortion law with a stab at humor: "It's an old joke, but when a man argues against two beautiful ladies like this, they're going to have the last word." After an awkward silence, Floyd began his argument: that the case was moot because Jane Roe was no longer pregnant, that the Constitution did not address the abortion issue, and that the issue should be left to the states.

A second abortion case, *Doe v. Bolton,* was argued before the Supreme Court the same day by Georgia attorney Margie Pitts Hames and Dorothy Beasley, a Georgia assistant attorney general. The plaintiff, Mary Doe, was described as a twenty-two-year-old woman from Georgia who was nine weeks' pregnant and already had three children. According to her affidavit, two of those children were in foster homes and the third had been placed for adoption because of her poverty and mental instability. Her husband, arrested several times for trying to abuse children, had recently abandoned her, and she had been forced to move in with her indigent parents and their eight children. Doe, later identified as Sandra Cano Bensing, had been advised by doctors that having another child would threaten her health. She had applied for a therapeutic abortion at an Atlanta hospital, but her application had been denied.

Three days later, the justices gathered for their conference on the cases they had heard that week. Both William Brennan's and William O. Douglas's notes indicated that the tally was 5 to 2 in favor of affirming the Texas three-judge panel's decision—thus declaring the Texas abortion law unconstitutional—with White and Chief Justice Warren Burger in opposition.

Even though he was not in the majority, Burger stirred controversy within the Court by deciding himself who should write the majority opinion in both abortion cases. He gave the job to one of the Court's newest and least-tested justices, his friend Harry Blackmun.

Harry Blackmun was born in Nashville, Illinois, in 1908, more than a decade before women had the right to vote. By 1910, his family had moved to St. Paul, Minnesota, where his father ran a grocery and hardware store, and where Blackmun would spend almost his entire life until he was called to the Supreme Court.

After high school Blackmun went East to Harvard on a scholarship, majoring in math and working as a janitor and a milkman to pay for the chance to join America's elite; he graduated summa cum laude in 1929. He briefly considered becoming a doctor but chose the law—and Harvard Law—instead. When he graduated in 1932, Blackmun seemed on track for a respectable, but hardly glamorous, career as a Midwestern attorney. He returned to St. Paul to become a clerk for U.S. Circuit Court Judge John B. Sanborn, taught briefly at the Mitchell College of Law in St. Paul, and after a year went into private practice. In 1941, he married the strong-willed Dorothy Clark, and together they raised three daughters, forming the backdrop for Blackmun's thinking on a woman's role in society. In 1950, Blackmun entered into what would become the most influential attorney-client relationship of his career, when he became counsel for the renowned Mayo Clinic in Rochester, Minnesota.

There, Blackmun had his first exposure to the legal and medical dilemmas posed by abortion. His job included advising the staff on the legality of abortions performed at the hospital. A. M. Keith, chief justice of the Minnesota Supreme Court, later wrote that "as counsel for the

Mayo Clinic . . . he may have had more influence on the medical profession than if he had been a doctor. He has always had a sympathetic attitude toward the medical profession and for the medical mind."

Blackmun lived a frugal, unadorned life, never squandering money or making much of a splash of any kind. Neighbors recalled that he always mowed his own lawn with a push mower and drove a Volkswagen Beetle. Yet his work for the Mayo Clinic had gained him enough stature in Minnesota that by 1959 he was chosen by President Eisenhower to fill a vacancy on the Eighth U.S. Circuit Court of Appeals.

Finally in 1970, after Blackmun had served eleven years on the appeals court, and after two other nominees were rejected by the Senate, President Richard Nixon appointed the seemingly noncontroversial judge, considered to be a conservative Republican, to sit on the Supreme Court. Blackmun, who soon took to calling himself "Old Number Three," packed up and headed for Washington, bringing his cherished VW with him.

Around the Supreme Court, Blackmun quickly gained a reputation as a quiet workaholic. Allan Gates, a Little Rock, Arkansas, attorney who clerked for Blackmun from 1974 to 1975, recalls that his clerks nicknamed him "The Horse," reflecting their "healthy respect for his prodigious capacity for hard work."

At first, Blackmun was so concerned about controlling his own workload that he refused to let his law clerks help write opinions, allowing them only to proofread or check citations. "But as time went on, he lightened up and realized there was no sin in having law clerks draft sections," Gates says. "He was wound much tighter about things, but as he went along, those rough edges got knocked off."

If anything was predictable about Blackmun, it was his morning routine. "He was extraordinarily punctual," Gates says. "He would get there early, work for about a half hour, then, as the second hand swept up around eleven or twelve, he would come sauntering in to the law clerks' room and say, 'Well, anyone interested in breakfast?' It was right at eight o'clock every morning."

Occasionally, Blackmun would talk about his days at the Mayo Clinic over breakfast, and it soon became clear to his clerks just how influential his role as the clinic's attorney had been in shaping his thinking. "One time, he was talking about the [Mayo Clinic's] Peer Review Committee," Gates recalls. "It's the committee that looks into a death or something that has gone awry. And it was plain that he enjoyed sitting on it. He was very impressed by the medical profession, and he had an enormous amount of respect for it. He was very fond of those days."

Yet when Blackmun arrived at the Supreme Court, the easy, Beltway rap on him was that he was going to be the "Minnesota Twin," a lightweight clone of his old friend Chief Justice Warren Burger. The two were former schoolmates; Blackmun had served as best man at Burger's wedding; and Burger had recommended Blackmun to Nixon. Then in December 1971, Harry Blackmun's old friend assigned him to write the majority opinion for what were known inside the Court as the "abortion cases."

The Blackmun assignment infuriated Douglas, who took the view that Blackmun was too close to Burger and felt that, as the senior member of the majority, he should have been allowed to assign the cases to someone of his choosing. Douglas accused Burger of playing politics because of the upcoming presidential election. In a December 20, 1971, response to Douglas's criticism, Burger insisted that he had not kept track of the justices' preliminary votes on either the *Roe v. Wade* case or its companion, the *Doe v. Bolton* case, and in any event, he did not believe it was clear yet how the Court would vote. He reminded Douglas that he had said the cases "would have to stand or fall on the writing [of the opinion], when it was done."

Blackmun, who was only in his second year on the Court, worked on the opinion through the winter and spring, finally finishing a draft in May. In a May 18, 1972, memorandum to his colleagues, he said he believed the Texas abortion law was unconstitutional because it was so vague that no one could tell what it meant. "I think that this would be all that is necessary for disposition of the case," he said.

Blackmun's first draft of the opinion, dated the same day, was seventeen pages long and did not address the issue of whether a woman had a constitutional right to an abortion. It merely struck down the Texas law because of its vagueness. Blackmun complained that the Texas law was so poorly crafted and worded that it left physicians unfairly vulnerable to prosecution.

Blackmun wrote that the Court did not accept the argument that a pregnant woman had a right to do with her body as she pleased. "The long acceptance of statutes regulating the possession of certain drugs and other harmful substances, and making criminal indecent exposure in public, or an attempt at suicide, clearly indicate the contrary."

Those who read the opinion felt it was unorganized and poorly written and were disappointed that it failed to settle the question of whether a woman had a constitutional right to an abortion. That same day, Brennan sent a memo to Blackmun, saying the opinion needed to be reworked to address the constitutional issue. Douglas agreed and wrote a note to Blackmun the next day, emphatically stating that the majority had called for a broader ruling: "So I think we should meet what Bill Brennan calls the 'core issue.'"

On May 31, however, an uncertain Blackmun moved instead for a reargument of both cases to await President Nixon's two new appointees to fill the vacancies on the nine-member Court. Blackmun was not sure of his own thinking on all the larger issues as he was writing: "Although I have worked on these cases with some concentration, I am not yet certain about all the details."

Douglas was becoming suspicious that this was all part of a Burger strategy to give Nixon time to pack the Court and change the earlier vote on *Roe*. Late that day, Chief Justice Burger also called for a delay and reargument: "I have had a great many problems with these cases from the outset. They are not as simple for me as they appear to be for others. This is as sensitive and difficult an issue as any in this Court in my time and I want to hear more and think more when I am not trying to sort out several dozen other difficult cases."

Burger's memo convinced Douglas that his suspicions were right. Burger was waiting for newly appointed justices Lewis Powell and William Rehnquist to support his views, Douglas believed. Potter Stewart was equally mad. In a note to Douglas, Brennan wrote the following: "I will be God-damned! At lunch today, Potter expressed his outrage at the high handed way things are going. . . . Potter wants to make an issue of these things . . . maybe fur will fly."

Douglas was so enraged that he threatened to oppose the order for reargument and make public the full text of his angry dissent. He sent a June 1, 1972, letter to Burger: "If the vote of the Conference is to reargue, then I will file a statement telling what is happening to us and the tragedy it entails." Douglas lost on the issue, after the new justices, Powell and Rehnquist, supported Burger for reargument. In a scathing dissent, Douglas wrote that "there is a destructive force at work in the Court."

Douglas accused Burger of playing politics: "The Abortion Cases are symptomatic. This is an election year. Both political parties have made abortion an issue. What the political parties say or do is none of our business. . . . We decide questions only on their constitutional merits. To prolong these Abortion Cases into the next election would in the eyes of many be a political gesture unworthy of the Court."

Douglas stormed off for his summer mountain home in Goose Prairie, Washington, without revealing whether he would actually make his stinging denunciation public, thereby airing the Court's dirty linen. He finally dropped the issue, and on June 26, the final day of the term, the Court announced that the cases would be set for reargument, with the simple notation that "Mr. Justice Douglas dissents."

Blackmun worked on the opinion throughout the summer, spending two weeks in the Mayo Clinic's medical library doing research. He traced down the attitudes toward abortion held by the American Medical Association, the American Public Health Association, and the American Bar Association. He also looked into the history of state abortion statutes and studied the origin and acceptance of the Hippocratic Oath, which forbade doctors from performing abortions. Blackmun kept to himself, holed up in a corner of an associate librarian's office, and did not tell anyone at the clinic what he was working on. "The only reason we even knew he was here is that he was paged," recalls Pat Erwin, the head reference librarian at Mayo, who had just started working there the summer Blackmun visited. "He was working in the history of medicine area, which is a restricted area. We didn't see him. When he needed materials, he sent for them."

On October 11, 1972, the Supreme Court heard rearguments in the abortion cases, with Nixon appointees Powell and Rehnquist now joining the other seven justices. Weddington again handled the oral argument, and this time Justice Stewart asked Weddington if it was critical to her case to say that the Fourteenth Amendment did not protect a fetus as a person: "If it were established that an unborn fetus is a person, within the protection of the Fourteenth Amendment, you would have almost an impossible case here, would you not?"

"I would have a very difficult case," Weddington said.

This time, the assistant attorney general of Texas, Robert Flowers, replaced Jay Floyd at the podium. Flowers said the state's position was that life begins at conception; therefore, a fetus was protected under the Constitution: "I think that here is exactly what we're facing in this case: Is the life of this unborn fetus paramount over the woman's right to determine whether or not she shall bear a child? This Court has been diligent in protecting the rights of the minorities, and, Gentlemen, we say that this is a minority, a silent minority, the true silent minority. Who is speaking for these children?"

In her rebuttal, Weddington said that "we are not here to advocate abortion. . . . We are here to advocate that the decision as to whether or not a particular woman will continue to carry or will terminate a pregnancy is a decision that should be made by that individual. That in fact she has a constitutional right to make that decision for herself."

On November 22, Blackmun circulated a new and radically revised draft. Not only had it grown from seventeen to fifty-one pages, but he had dropped the argument that the Texas law was invalid because of its vagueness and had switched to an entirely new concept that incorporated the research he had conducted over the summer: that a woman had, at least to a certain point in her pregnancy, a constitutional right to an abortion.

"It has been an interesting assignment," he said in a memo to the other justices. "As I stated in conference, the decision, however made, will probably result in the Court's being severely criticized."

Blackmun's new draft began with a lengthy history of abortion laws throughout the world and included a discussion of how the American Medical Association had changed its position over the years, from opposing abortion to supporting reform laws. Ever the doctor's lawyer, Blackmun wrote an opinion that placed a premium on the rights of the physician, rather than on the rights of the pregnant woman.

He said his ruling "vindicates the important rights of the physician to administer medical treatment according to his best professional judgment up to the point where important state interests provide a compelling justification for intervention. Up to that point the abortion decision inherently is a medical one, and the responsibility for that decision must rest with the physician."

Blackmun wrote that the Texas abortion law was a violation of the due process clause of the Fourteenth Amendment. Through the first trimester, he said, the abortion decision must be left to the best medical judgment of the pregnant woman's attending physician. After the first trimester, he wrote, the state may restrict abortions to those "reasonable therapeutic categories that are articulated with sufficient clarity so that a physician is able to predict what conditions fall within the stated classification." Blackmun added that an abortion at any state of pregnancy would be legal if done to preserve the life or health of the woman and performed under the direction of a licensed physician. Finally, Douglas was appeased. "You have done an excellent job," he wrote.

There were, however, still questions from other justices about Blackmun's proposal to set the end of the first trimester as the point when states could begin regulating abortion practices. Powell, Brennan, and Marshall suggested that viability, rather than the end of the first trimester, might be a better point at which to allow states to pass regulations.

Blackmun acknowledged that the trimester-viability issue was difficult to resolve. On December 21, Blackmun circulated his final version: A woman's decision to get an abortion in the first trimester was a constitutionally protected right of privacy, and during those first three months, the state could regulate only that the abortion be performed by a licensed physician. In the second trimester, the state could regulate the procedure only to protect the health of the woman.

Blackmun had decided to equate viability with the end of the second trimester; therefore, *Roe* recognized that the state did have a compelling interest in the viable fetus during the third trimester. The decision defined *viability* as the time at which a fetus could potentially live outside the womb and said that states could regulate or even ban abortion during that period unless the procedure was necessary to protect the life or health of the pregnant woman.

Five other justices signed on in support of the *Roe* decision, with Stewart and Douglas writing concurring opinions and Rehnquist and Byron White dissenting.

In mid-January, Burger shocked his colleagues by saying he would join the majority. He still had not signed on, however, leading some justices to accuse him of stalling. Burger was scheduled to swear in President Nixon for his second term on January 20, and it could have been an uncomfortable situation for the man who had just supported one of the Court's most controversial opinions in history to swear in the man who had appointed him.

On January 16, Burger wrote to Blackmun, saying he was working over some concurrences in the case "and will try to have them in your hands and circulated sometime tomorrow. I see no reason why we cannot schedule these cases for Monday." The same day, Blackmun wrote to his colleagues, enclosing a draft of an announcement he planned to distribute to reporters about the decision. Blackmun's press statement suggests that he did not fully comprehend the sweeping change his own ruling was about to bring: "I fear what the headlines may be, but it should be stressed that the Court does not today hold that the Constitution [provides] abortion on demand. It does not today pronounce that a pregnant woman has an absolute right to an abortion."

True enough, yet *Roe* did not *require* states to regulate abortion; it only *allowed* them to do so after viability. Late-term abortions would be legal unless specifically outlawed by the states. Blackmun's statement dramatically underplayed his own ruling.

The announcement came at 10 A.M. on January 22, 1973.

Supreme Court observers were astonished. The ruling was so broad and far reaching that virtually every state was affected. At the time of the decision, only the four repeal states, Alaska, Hawaii, New York, and Washington, had no criminal penalties for abortions performed by doctors early in a pregnancy. Thirty states had laws on the books banning abortions except to save the life of the pregnant woman, and a dozen or so others had laws allowing abortions in cases of rape, incest, or severe fetal abnormalities. "It was," says Lawrence Lader, "probably the fastest social revolution in American history."

News of the *Roe* decision was overshadowed by the death the same day of President Lyndon B. Johnson, as well as ongoing coverage of the peace agreement reached earlier in the month, ending U.S. involvement in Vietnam. But there were hints in the media of the firestorm that was to come. *Time,* reporting on new polling data from Gallup that showed that 46 percent of those surveyed favored leaving the abortion decision to the woman and 45 percent opposed the idea, predicted that "such a close division of sentiment can only ensure that while the matter has been settled legally, it remains a lightning rod for intense national debate." *Newsweek* added that "the end of a war and the death of a president got bigger headlines. But in a quiet way, a third event last week may have as lasting an influence on American life."

The dissents issued by Rehnquist and White also seemed to presage the national debate that would follow. "I have difficulty in concluding, as the Court does, that the right of 'privacy' is involved in this case," Rehnquist wrote. The fact that a majority of states have had restrictions on abortion for at least a century "is a strong indication, it seems to me, that the asserted right to an abortion is not so rooted in the traditions and conscience of our people as to be ranked as fundamental. Even today, when society's views on abortion are changing, the very existence of the debate is evidence that the 'right' to an abortion is not so universally accepted as [*Roe*] would have us believe."

White complained that the ruling was nothing more than an "exercise in raw judicial power." He said that "during the period prior to the time the fetus becomes viable, the Court has ruled that the Constitution of the United States values the convenience, whim or caprice of the putative mother more than the life or potential life of the fetus." The issue, he said, "should be left with the people and to the political processes the people have devised to govern their affairs."

The next day in Dallas, Norma McCorvey sat in her kitchen after a hard day of painting houses and began reading the *Dallas Times-Herald.* In the lower right-hand corner on the front page was an article that said the Supreme Court had legalized abortion. McCorvey was staring into space when her lover, Connie Gonzales, came into the room and asked her what was wrong. "They've legalized abortion," McCorvey said. "That's good," Gonzales replied. McCorvey asked Gonzales if she had seen the part where they mentioned the plaintiff. Sure, Gonzales said. Said McCorvey, "I looked her straight in the eye and said, 'How would you like to meet Jane Roe?'"

Hours after the decision, hospitals around the country began receiving calls from women asking where they could get an abortion. In Detroit, equipment was flown in to a clinic that had been shut down, and twenty abortions were performed by the next day. By the end of the week, three private clinics had opened in the city. In Austin, a doctor whose equipment had arrived the morning the decision came down performed an abortion that afternoon.

By the end of 1973, the Alan Guttmacher Institute, Planned Parenthood's new research center named for the father of the reform movement, reported that 744,600 legal abortions had been performed that year on women between the ages of fifteen and forty-four. The annual total reached 1 million in 1975 and is now estimated to be about 1.4 million.

One of the few abortion-rights advocates who predicted the powerful rise of the opposition was NARAL's Lader: "We had a celebratory meeting the next day," he said. "The champagne flowed and flowed—we were almost delirious. And everybody was ready to disband the networks that had been built. And I said, 'No, you can't do this. This isn't the end. This is just the beginning. There will definitely be a counterattack.'"

Embraced by feminists and liberals, Blackmun's *Roe* was quickly enshrined as the cornerstone of modern reproductive rights in America, and over the years it has become politically incorrect for liberal scholars to attack it. Whether or not Blackmun's opinion was good law, it made for poor philosophy; his refusal to delve into the deepest issues raised by the case, or to provide his opinion with stronger philosophical underpinnings, left the door wide open for abortion opponents to continue their fight. Even Justice Lewis Powell, who voted in favor of *Roe,* later ruefully told his biographer that the ruling was "the worst I ever joined."

In developing a new legal right to abortion, Blackmun had failed to come to terms with the existential issue at the heart of the abortion debate: when life begins. "Texas urges that life begins at conception and is present throughout pregnancy, and that, therefore, the State has a compelling interest in protecting that life from and after conception," Blackmun wrote. "We need not resolve the difficult question of when life begins. When those trained in the respective disciplines of medicine, philosophy, and theology are unable to arrive at any consensus, the judiciary, at this point in the development of man's knowledge, is not in a position to speculate as to the answer. It should be sufficient to note briefly the wide divergence of thinking on this most sensitive and difficult question."

Yet elsewhere in his opinion, Blackmun conceded that if Texas could prove its case that the fetus was a person, then Weddington's "case, of course, collapses, for the fetus' right to life would then be guaranteed specifically by the [Fourteenth] Amendment."

Blackmun's attempt to skirt the issue of life and death thus represented a failure to respond to critics who said their opposition to abortion was based on deeply held religious beliefs. With his *Roe* ruling, Blackmun was trying to cut off the debate with the opponents of abortion reform. The Supreme Court decision left opponents few legal or political options. In the years since *Roe,* a few legal scholars, even some who support abortion rights, have criticized Blackmun's ruling for crudely short-circuiting a national debate that was really still in its earliest stages.

University of Chicago law professor Richard A. Epstein wrote that "the diversity of opinions on all aspects of the abortion question" should have convinced the Court to be "careful not to foreclose debate on the issue by judicial decision, and [to be] more careful not to use constitutional means to resolve the question."

Twenty years after *Roe,* future justice Ruth Bader Ginsburg, a supporter of abortion rights, also argued that Blackmun went too far, too fast, taking a giant leap the country was not prepared to make. "Suppose the court had not gone on, as it did in *Roe,* to fashion a regime blanketing the subject, a set of rules that displaced virtually every state law then in force," Ginsburg said. "Would there have been the twenty-year controversy we have witnessed? . . . A less encompassing *Roe,* one that merely struck down the extreme Texas law and went no further on that day, I believe . . . might have served to reduce rather than to fuel controversy." The *Roe* decision, Ginsburg said, "invited no dialogue with legislators. Instead, it seemed entirely to remove the ball from the legislators' court. . . . No measured motion, the *Roe* decision left virtually no state with laws fully conforming to the Court's delineation of abortion regulation still permissible. Around that extraordinary decision, a well-organized and vocal right-to-life movement rallied."

In other words, *Roe* led almost inevitably to revolution and sent opponents out into the streets.

Mainstream abortion opponents—the Catholic Church and its allies in groups like the National Right to Life Committee—had only two legitimate political avenues left open to them: ratification of a constitutional amendment to overturn *Roe,* or the election of presidents and congressional leaders who could gradually change the composition of the Supreme Court. Both were long shots at best, and both ultimately ended in failure and despair. In the end, the mainstream anti-abortion organizations became content with waging small battles on the margins, such as for federal funding restrictions, parental notification, and restrictions on late-term abortions.

It was frustration and despair that split the anti-abortion movement in two. Those who refused to accept the mainstream, incremental lobbying efforts moved into a "direct-action" movement, following younger, more radical leaders. It was a movement led first by Catholic leftists who drew on their 1960s traditions of social protest but later by newly militant Christian fundamentalists, who co-opted those traditions and transformed civil disobedience into a conservative tool.

A new, religion-based social protest movement was born, one that drew Protestant Evangelicals out of their churches and to the barricades. These activists set out to transform the law, but in the process they transformed themselves, transformed their theological beliefs, and ended generations of isolation. Now, thanks to Harry Blackmun and *Roe,* they are in the political arena to stay.

PART II

QUICKENING

3

THE FATHER OF RESCUE
John O'Keefe

R oy O'Keefe was the second son of a NASA scientist at the dawn of the space age; one of nine children in a devoutly Catholic, affluent Irish-American family in Chevy Chase, Maryland; a well-loved brother and admired mentor; and a patriot. He never knew what hit him.

In early 1968, Sgt. Roy O'Keefe was a medic and platoon leader in one of the U.S. Army's most elite combat organizations, the 28th Mobile Strike Force of the Fifth Special Forces Group. Roy had enlisted after his sophomore year at Catholic University in Washington, D.C., had quickly shown soldierly promise, and was accepted for Special Forces training. He arrived in Vietnam in July 1967, three weeks after his marriage to his college girlfriend. In February 1968, Roy was battling to survive the Tet Offensive.

On February 6, one week after North Vietnamese and Viet Cong forces began an all-out, nationwide offensive, Roy O'Keefe's outpost was assaulted. As his platoon held a defensive position on a hill, O'Keefe moved from man to man, exposing himself to enemy fire in order to tend to the wounded while making sure his men were all dug in along their line. As he was returning to his own position, an enemy mortar round exploded right next to him.

On February 10, his family was told he was missing in action. On February 13, his family was told he was dead. For his actions Roy O'Keefe was awarded the Bronze Star, posthumously. He was buried at Arlington National Cemetery with full military honors.

Roy O'Keefe was twenty-two.

No one took the news harder than John, the O'Keefes' third son. Roy was only four years older, but he was as much a teacher and mentor to the younger boy as was their father. John's goal in life had always been to be like Roy, and of course that meant he would eventually join the Special Forces and fight for his country. Roy's death changed the course of John's life.

John was a senior at St. Anselm's, a small and elite Catholic high school in Washington, when he learned that his brother had been killed. John O'Keefe was a rail-thin, extraordinarily intense and bright young man, already more successful academically than any other O'Keefe, which was saying quite a lot in a family of achievers.

John seemed too good to be true; he had an ethereal quality, a bookish earnestness. He was achingly pale; wore unfashionable clothes and thick glasses; and had a soft, halting manner of speaking. Tall and angular, he had the look of a nineteenth-century schoolteacher, perpetually lost in thought.

John had attended parochial schools all his life. At St. Anselm's, he was at the top of the American Catholic educational pyramid, a school that graduated only two dozen or so students each year but boasted as many National Merit scholars as most factory-sized suburban high schools. In the fall of 1968, he was to enter Harvard College, the institution that had made it possible for his family to rise out of Irish immigrant poverty in Boston nearly a century before. John's father, his grandfather, and his great-grandfather had all been Harvard men before him.

John was schooled in the traditions of the Roman Catholic Church, and the church's mysticism—its reliance on faith in the unseen Trilogy of the Father, Son, and Holy Spirit—attracted him early on. He prized the day of his First Communion. Unlike other teenagers, he took religion seriously and thought about it in sophisticated yet devotional ways. He seemed to have an intuitive sense of the place of the church and of faith in the modern world. His father, John O'Keefe III, was not only a space scientist with a background in geology, but a lector at their parish church, Blessed Sacrament, where he led Bible readings from the altar.

John's earliest memory of his father is of the older man standing before the congregation reading aloud from the first chapter of John in the New Testament: "In the beginning was the Word, and the Word was with God, and the Word was God. He was in the beginning with God; all things were made through him, and without him was not anything made that was made. In him was life, and the life was the light of men. The light shines in the darkness, and the darkness has not overcome it."

The backdrop for John's religious training was America's race for the moon. NASA assigned John's father to investigate John Glenn's strange sightings of "fireflies" outside his Mercury spacecraft during America's first orbital mission; he solved the mystery by proving to Glenn personally that the phenomenon was nothing more than condensation shearing off the capsule's hull. John grew up listening to his father talk about the origins of the earth-moon system; he came to assume that faith and science fit together, and he could not understand when his father told him that others saw a conflict between the two.

Roy's death further deepened John's Catholicism. The devout Catholic boy embraced his family's religion more than ever before and was thankful for its power to provide answers. John had never experienced the death of a close friend or family member before. Even his grandparents were all still alive. Death was an alien concept, but after Roy died he held death up and examined it, as if it were a geometric shape to be analyzed from as many angles as possible.

At Roy's funeral Mass, as his brother was mourned, John heard the story of the life and death of Jesus Christ in a new light. He developed a deeper respect and affection for Jesus Christ, "because a lot of the things that people said about him were things I knew to be true about my brother."

The death of his brother made it possible for him to understand that he could love someone who was dead; he could love Jesus as he did his brother, and that seemed to open a whole new realm of faith. Often, John left his family's home in Washington's Maryland suburbs and crossed town by himself to go to Arlington to sit beside Roy's grave in solitude and prayer.

John began to think about joining the priesthood. He even had a favorite order—the Dominicans, which emphasized community service—the way other young men had favorite football teams. Still, he went through with the plans he had already started to develop for his life. He entered Harvard in the fall of 1968, where he was to major in physics. On Harvard's campus, he quickly ran head-on into the antiwar whirlwind.

Vietnam-era protests and student strikes were at their most frenzied at Harvard during John O'Keefe's freshman year, but O'Keefe was not active in organized antiwar protests. Ultimately, he came to oppose the war, joining in the endless campus debates among friends and even volunteering at a draft counseling center run by the American Friends Service Committee. The committee operated one of the hundreds of storefront clinics set up around college campuses during the 1960s to help young men avoid the draft.

Yet O'Keefe felt that he did not fit in with the campus peace movement. He saw it becoming harsh and radicalized and was soon disillusioned and angry that so many antiwar activists seemed unwilling to separate their hatred for the war from a hatred for those soldiers, like his brother, who were fighting and dying for America. He believed that many of the leading antiwar demonstrators were lazy, inconsistent thinkers, lacking a coherent intellectual framework for their political activity. Finally, he became convinced that many in the peace movement were cowards, people who did not hate war but hated the Vietnam War because they might be called to fight in it. Later, O'Keefe was outraged to see that antiwar demonstrators had erected a mock cemetery at Harvard. It was as if they were taunting him, deriding Roy's death.

When his freshman year ended, O'Keefe continued to assume that he would go into the Army after college; that he would become an officer; and that, despite his misgivings about the war, he might end up with the Special Forces in Vietnam.

Roy had been named for an uncle who was an attorney, and now that Roy was dead the uncle felt bad that he had never spent much time with his namesake. Because he wanted to do something for his surviving nephews, he arranged for John O'Keefe to get a summer job with a law firm in Manhattan following his freshman year at Harvard. For the summer, O'Keefe lived with some cousins in New Jersey and commuted into the city, to an office in Chase Manhattan Plaza.

He hated it. He hated everything about the law firm. He hated the commute and the work and the frenzied chase for money. O'Keefe saw the adult world of work and careers up close for the first time, and he blanched in disgust. After six weeks, he visited a local priest at his cousin's parish church in New Jersey and asked for guidance. He was learning to hate for the first time in his life, O'Keefe told the priest, and he did not know what to do. How should a Catholic deal with hate?

This strangely earnest boy befuddled the priest, who was accustomed to dealing with the predictable confessions of suburban sinners, not the existential angst of obsessive Ivy Leaguers. He breezily suggested that O'Keefe volunteer at the church to teach catechism class (the Catholic version of Sunday school) and then sent O'Keefe on his way. O'Keefe went back to his summer work increasingly depressed.

Later that week, the law firm sent O'Keefe on a flight to Detroit to get signatures on some documents, and delays forced him to stay overnight. He took advantage of the time by driving out to see his sister, Mary, who was then a novice in training to become a nun with the Sisters of the Immaculate Heart of Mary, a convent in Monroe, Michigan.

His sister later decided not to become a nun and got married and had children. But that night she took O'Keefe with her to a unique prayer meeting in Ann Arbor, near the University of Michigan campus, which was then blossoming as a center of Catholic religious ferment as well as of antiwar protest.

Suddenly, O'Keefe found himself drinking in the words and prayers of a band of young religious renegades who were just as intense about their Catholicism as he was. They had the energy and enthusiasm of converts to a new faith, but they were, like O'Keefe, steeped in the ancient ways of the oldest Christian church. They were, they said in their prayers, overcome by an outpouring of the Holy Spirit, the third aspect of the Holy Trinity, the one element of the triune God whose meaning in the world has been, throughout Christian history, most subject to interpretation.

O'Keefe quickly and enthusiastically dove headfirst into their new movement: the Catholic Charismatic Renewal. Founded by a group of students at Duquesne University in Pittsburgh in 1967, the Charismatic Renewal was rapidly spreading in the late 1960s among Catholic students on college campuses around the country, and in Ann Arbor O'Keefe had stumbled on one of the largest of the fledgling Charismatic communities.

The Charismatic Renewal was a Catholic version of the Pentecostal Evangelical movement that had already swept through American Protestant churches earlier in the twentieth century and was about to do so again. At its heart, the Charismatic Renewal was Catholic fundamentalism: a belief in the literal power of baptism in the Spirit, a power that could return believers to the simple faith of the earliest Christians, to a rudimentary church that received wisdom from the mysterious fire of the unseen Spirit. It was a mystical power that was responsible for visible miracles on earth, "charisms" that were direct gifts from God. Unlike other American Catholics, Charismatics believed in faith healing, speaking in tongues, and the ability of the spiritual person to know and speak God's inspired prophecies about the future.

But it was fundamentalism with a twist: a faith, rooted in the Catholic traditions of Augustine and Thomas Aquinas, that taught that devotion to God did not require the religious person to abhor modernism or to withdraw from the secular humanist world. At first, the Charismatic Renewal made no political demands on its adherents. In fact, Catholic leaders felt they had to prod many Charismatics to look beyond their own spiritual needs and get involved in social causes. Yet among the Charismatic Renewal's young adherents in the late 1960s, there was a small cadre of students, nuns, and priests who were veterans of the antiwar and civil rights movements and who had sought out the Charismatic movement as a badly needed source of spiritual energy. The Charismatic Renewal helped them recharge and continue their activist battles.

Some among this small band of activist Charismatics coupled their fiery Pentecostal theology with the socioreligious teachings of Thomas Merton, the Catholic monk, philosopher, and bestselling author who had become a hero among liberals in the early 1960s by writing of the power of contemplative prayer to plumb eternal truths and provide a righteous path to nonviolent protest. Early in his life, Merton had converted to Catholicism and retreated to a Trappist monastery. Like the young John O'Keefe, Merton had found the world too profane.

"Back in the world," Merton wrote in *The Seven Storey Mountain*, his classic autobiography, "I felt like a man that had come down from the rare atmosphere of a very high mountain. How strange it was to see people walking around as if they had something important to do, running after buses, reading the newspapers, lighting cigarettes. How futile all their haste and anxiety seemed. . . . I turned and fled from the alien and lunatic street, and found my way into the nearby cathedral, and knelt, and prayed, and did the Stations of the Cross."

By the 1960s, however, Merton had emerged from his isolation to become the social conscience of the American Catholic Church and

had begun writing fierce, antiwar essays calling on the religious to follow the lead of Martin Luther King Jr. and Mohandas Gandhi in the use
of civil disobedience. Merton argued that such action fit in perfectly
with religious contemplation and prayer; the contemplative man's intervention in the active life of society was his own personal service to God
and man, his way of worship.

"What is the contemplative life if one becomes oblivious to the rights
of men and the truth of God in the world and in His Church?" Merton
asked his friend Daniel Berrigan, a Jesuit priest, in 1963. "To obey Him
is to respond to His will expressed in the need of another person, or at
least to respect the rights of others," Merton wrote. "No man who
ignores the rights and needs of others can hope to walk in the light of
contemplation, because his way has turned aside from truth, from compassion and therefore from God."

Merton believed, paradoxically, that the faithful could move political
mountains if they truly were not concerned about the outcome of their
actions and, instead, worried only about witnessing to God and truth.
Individual redemption through uncompromising and dangerous service
to the truth was the path to Christ, as well as the path to political victory. Merton believed that Gandhi had seen that, had rejected accommodation, and had become a martyr to the truth.

Merton's belief system was tailor-made for the social activism of the
1960s, and soon Merton's liberal Catholic followers began to claim
prominent roles in the antiwar movement. For the first time in the history of the American Catholic Church, which had always prided itself
in its patriotic fervor and full-throated support for U.S. wars, a major
Catholic peace movement had developed. It made for strange bed-
fellows: There was a smattering of college-age Charismatics side by side
with Catholic socialist holdovers from Dorothy Day's Catholic Worker
movement, mixed in with a small group of newly radicalized priests like
Daniel Berrigan. Berrigan and his brother Philip, a priest of the
Josephite order, became national symbols of this new Catholic left
wing; they emerged as antiwar celebrities after they raided the offices of
the draft board in Catonsville, Maryland, in 1968, and burned the
board's files with homemade napalm in front of local television news
cameras. Following his conviction for the raid, Daniel Berrigan disappeared into the antiwar underground, eluding the FBI for four months
until he was arrested and sent to join his brother in federal prison.

Berrigan's courtroom explanation for his actions fit perfectly with the philosophy Merton had articulated, that of the action-oriented contemplative. Berrigan called on the dictates of St. Ignatius, the founder of the Jesuit order: "We [Jesuits] belong . . . in society, in the culture, in the schools, in the ghettos among the poor, as the servants of men . . . it [is] there that we would find God or nowhere." Berrigan's words spoke powerfully to a few young Catholic Pentecostals like O'Keefe, who were soon mixing themselves a heady theological cocktail: one part Merton and one part Charismatic Renewal.

In the process, they were creating something new in modern America: a politically active Christian Evangelical movement. Nearly a decade before Protestant fundamentalists emerged from their spiritual isolation to burst onto the political stage, a handful of Catholic fundamentalists were being drawn to the streets, taking with them their belief in the power of the Holy Spirit and of contemplative prayer to show them the way.

They became the first American fundamentalists to discover abortion as a breakthrough issue.

By the 1980s, Catholic Charismatics tended toward conservative politics, led by their opposition to abortion into gradually joining other religious fundamentalists in a loose and shifting Republican coalition. Yet in the late 1960s, Charismatic politics were still fluid; Merton's philosophy and the antiwar struggle had a natural pull.

Drifting since his brother's death, John O'Keefe had found a spiritual home. He devoured Merton's writings, was captivated by Merton's thoughts on prayer and contemplation, read *The Seven Storey Mountain*, and was moved by Merton's essay on Gandhi. O'Keefe returned to Harvard in the fall, but college life, the path to a conventional career, no longer seemed to hold meaning for him. Throughout October 1969, O'Keefe, intense and careful as ever, sat in his dorm room at Harvard and read one page each day from Merton's *Seeds of Destruction,* a collection of the monk's most radical essays on social issues and nonviolent responses.

He never finished the book, but what he read he took to heart. From *Seeds of Destruction,* O'Keefe drew a simple lesson: Killing is always wrong. O'Keefe reasoned as follows:

> When somebody dies, there are two possibilities—they either go
> to heaven or hell. If you kill somebody and they go to hell, then
> you have made a mistake, because you could have bought them

more time to repent for their sins, and they could have turned their life around. By killing them, you have taken away that chance, and there is nothing on earth to compare with the colossal tragedy of going to hell. If you kill someone and they go to heaven, then you've made a mistake, because you have judged their stewardship of the world's goods lacking in some way, and God didn't. So there are two possibilities, and in either one, you've made a mistake.

He began to think about the Vietnamese soldier who had killed his brother, who had loaded the shell into the mortar and killed Roy by long distance, probably without ever realizing it, and for the first time O'Keefe felt sadness, and sympathy, for the man. That soldier would be marked throughout eternity by Roy's death and would suffer more than Roy. He would probably not be damned for killing in the midst of combat, O'Keefe reasoned, but Roy's death would be with him somehow. The tragedy of killing, O'Keefe figured, is not the physical death of the human body, which is after all just a temporary shell, but the damage done to the soul of the person behind the gun. That pain lasts throughout time. By the end of the month, O'Keefe went home to tell his parents that he was ready to quit school.

"I told them, 'Look, I've made this decision, and I should see what this is like.' I said I wanted to get rid of ingrained habits of arrogance and impatience, and I wanted to go learn humility and patience, and I thought working in a hospital would be a good thing, because I would need to be humble and patient dealing with crap."

Although this choice would cost him his student deferment, he also said he was ready to declare as a conscientious objector (CO) to the draft. O'Keefe had become a pacifist, almost overnight. In November 1969, John O'Keefe left his father's Harvard and applied to his draft board in Bethesda, Maryland, for conscientious objector status.

The local draft board was dominated by Catholics, who did not know what to make of O'Keefe. They had never given CO status to a Catholic, and they were not in the mood to start. The American Catholic Church accepted war and defended killing in a just war. Merton did not speak for the American bishops. Archbishop Francis Spellman of New York had been Catholic military vicar and unofficial chaplain to American forces overseas during World War II, a position he still proudly held as Vietnam unfolded in the 1960s. As Pope John XXIII began to push for the modernization of the Catholic Church and a rethinking of social values at the Second Vatican Council (Vatican II) in Rome, Spellman and his American colleagues held to their traditions, known as "Americanism" within the Vatican hierarchy. Spellman publicly dissented from a statement issued by Vatican II that offered praise for the use of nonviolence and civil disobedience and, indirectly, for Catholics who claimed to be conscientious objectors to participation in their national defense. "If the leaders of a nation decide in good faith and after mature deliberations that military service by their citizens is absolutely necessary for the defense of peace and justice, how can the citizens justly refuse?" Spellman asked during a floor debate at Vatican II.

When he died in 1967, Spellman was perhaps the best-known Catholic prelate in America; as long as bishops following in his footsteps were in charge, leftists like the Berrigans would remain outcasts, stuck in prison. It was difficult to see how a devout Catholic, at least one living in America in the 1960s, could legally claim that his church had led him to object to war.

The draft board's work was complicated, however, by the fact that O'Keefe was the brother of a dead war hero, and there was clearly no appetite for plunging his family into even deeper sorrow, either by sending him to jail for avoiding the draft or by sending him to face combat and possible death in Vietnam. The draft board tried to skirt the philosophical and religious issues entirely by offering O'Keefe a sole-surviving-son deferment, given to sons of families that had already suffered combat deaths. But he was not the sole-surviving son. His oldest brother, George, who had completed a tour of duty in Vietnam just in time to attend Roy's bittersweet wedding, was still alive.

O'Keefe's dilemma spread pain and division throughout his family. His parents, still grieving over Roy, supported the war to which they had sacrificed a son and were confused by John's sudden decision not to fight. Kathy, John's older sister, feared for John and raged against the war and her parents; one after another, two of her brothers had gone to Vietnam, but only one had come back. Now a third was being forced to choose sides. Unable to speak with her father and mother, she cut her family ties and fled, burying herself for the next decade in the backwash of the antiwar counterculture in Canada. While there, she had an abortion, a secret she kept from her family for years.

Finally, George, the oldest, stepped in. He told his father that the war was going badly and that fighting in it did not necessarily make sense.

He could not endorse John's decision to become a conscientious objector, but he also could not fault him for it. Maybe what John was doing was right. Because George was a veteran, his words made all the difference. John's parents finally understood that their third son was not a coward and was not insulting the memory of their second boy.

After months of squabbling, the draft board reluctantly gave in, and O'Keefe received his objector status in the spring of 1970. He was assigned alternative service duty as an aide at Springfield State Hospital, a mental hospital in Sykesville, Maryland.

O'Keefe was quickly fired for insubordination, however, after he allowed a mental patient to put on a tie while getting dressed for a transfer to another hospital. O'Keefe figured the man was not suicidal and had no intention of using the tie to hang himself; he reasoned that it might help the man's self-esteem to put on his own, long-denied suit. The head nurse said O'Keefe was just a kid not fit to make such decisions, and within an hour the hospital's personnel director told him he was terminated.

In the fall of 1970, O'Keefe took another job as an orderly, this time at St. John of God Hospital in Brighton, Massachusetts, where he would complete his alternative service. Despite his firing in Maryland, O'Keefe had come to love the menial work of an orderly. He loved the simplicity of helping people with his hands, and he stayed on at St. John of God until early 1972. He found that he did not miss Harvard.

One night near the end of his time at the hospital, O'Keefe fell into a private conversation with a nurse named Suzanne (her last name is being withheld to protect her privacy). She was a Catholic woman from the blue-collar town of Fall River, Massachusetts, who told O'Keefe matter-of-factly that she had had an abortion the previous year. It was the first extended conversation O'Keefe had ever had with anyone about abortion.

All that O'Keefe knew about abortion was that it was the termination of a pregnancy and that the Catholic Church said it was wrong. He had never paid much attention to it, because it was not a public issue that he had heard much about. Yet just below the radar of national awareness, abortion reform had quietly been gaining momentum at the state level throughout the late 1960s and into the early 1970s. Young women like Suzanne were finding safe, legal abortions increasingly accessible in spite of the total absence of a national abortion policy in the United States.

The nurse discussed her abortion in a straightforward way with O'Keefe and seemed convinced that she had made the right decision. What O'Keefe heard, however, was a woman who wanted to talk about abortion for a full hour, who could not drop the subject, and who seemed to want O'Keefe's understanding and approval of her decision. What bothered O'Keefe was that Suzanne was still keyed up about the abortion a year later. Over the next week, in his intense and methodical way, O'Keefe began to read about abortion in order to understand what Suzanne was going through. Soon, the story of her abortion clicked with O'Keefe's emerging beliefs on death and pacifism. He became convinced that she was a mother, her child was dead, and she had no way to grieve for her child. She never said those things, but O'Keefe believed she was in denial and that she had been talking about the subject with him as a substitute for mourning for her baby. O'Keefe equated her with the Vietnamese soldier who had killed his brother; they were both badly scarred by death and killing.

Finished with his alternative service, O'Keefe left the hospital in the summer of 1972 and retreated to the desert of New Mexico, following a popular countercultural path. Near the town of Abiquiu, along the Sangre de Cristo (Blood of Christ) mountain range, he pitched a tent. He stayed in the desert, in a self-conscious, adolescent effort to emulate events of the Bible, for forty days. He lived alone, just outside Christ in the Desert Monastery, run by a group of Benedictine monks. O'Keefe wanted to explore for himself what was meant by the phrase "God, the Father"; he was curious to see whether he was cut out for a life buried in religious thought; the isolated, contemplative life; the life of Thomas Merton.

He read Scripture and went fishing to fill his time. He avoided projects except for one, and that was to write a letter to Suzanne back in Brighton. He wrote the letter over and over, all summer. It became as much a letter to himself as it was to her, a way for him to explore his own feelings about abortion, an issue that had come to preoccupy him ever since his talk with Suzanne months earlier at the hospital.

He wrote Suzanne that he loved her, that he admired her and trusted her, but that he was convinced that she had made a mistake. After weeks of writing and rewriting, he eventually got up the nerve to send the letter to her. It could have been the source of enormous embarrassment; she could have seen it as a juvenile mash note or, worse, an intrusive insult by a pseudoreligious busybody. But she seemed to take it in the spirit O'Keefe intended, and they remained friends afterward. It was a private letter, yet the process of writing it gradually led O'Keefe to conclude that he had found his mission. Abortion was killing, he told himself, just like the killing being done in Vietnam, like the killing that resulted in Roy's death. O'Keefe reasoned that religious people who believed in the power of prayer and the contemplative life to help bring social justice to the world could not sanction the killing of the unborn.

O'Keefe had considered joining a monastery, following Merton's example, and had been attracted to the Benedictine life in the desert. But he decided to return to Boston, convinced that what he really wanted was a life of social and political activism.

O'Keefe took a new job as an orderly at a nursing home and moved into a group house outside Boston, in the town of Weston, with other young converts to the Charismatic Renewal. By then, Charismatics were becoming increasingly controversial within the Catholic Church; many American bishops feared they represented a breakaway movement chafing under the church's rigid hierarchical system.

Charismatic theology was becoming suspect as well. Charismatics believed in a "renewal" by a baptism in the Holy Spirit and were thus widely seen as "born-again" Catholics. The bishops suspected that the Charismatics believed they had experienced a second baptism, one unauthorized by the official church. Charismatics dismissed such fears and insisted their renewal was simply a traditional effort to come to terms with confirmation, the sacrament designed to allow Catholics to experience the pouring out of the Holy Spirit on Pentecost. It was supposed to be a return to basics. But when Charismatics talked of their "authentic personal conversion to Christ," they sounded to the bishops dangerously like Protestants.

Such concerns hardly touched O'Keefe, who returned from the desert determined to turn his life over to the Charismatic movement and the abortion cause. Yet he found it increasingly difficult to control his passions, either for his religion or for his newfound cause. In Weston, O'Keefe and two roommates prayed for forty hours a week, to prove somehow that worshipping God was their real job. O'Keefe then cut his hair into a monklike tonsure, a bald crown surrounded by a medieval-looking fringe. He was going out of his way to draw stares, to "get a little taste of public embarrassment and humiliation," to understand "a little bit of the embarrassment that unwed pregnant women go through" while deciding whether to have an abortion. The head nurse at the hospital where O'Keefe worked became so worried about his mental state that she wondered aloud whether he needed to be committed.

O'Keefe and his roommates dubbed their home, which was little more than a shed in the back of a Weston mansion, "Guadalupe House," after the visitation by the Virgin Mary in Guadalupe, Mexico, in 1531. The Virgin Mary is supposed to have appeared to a poor Aztec, Juan Diego, leaving an image of herself on his cloak. Over the next seven years, word of the miracle is said to have convinced 8 million Indians to agree to Spanish demands to be baptized and to convert to Christianity, which meant abandoning human sacrifice—and infanticide. In the early 1970s, the Guadalupe visitation was fast becoming a touchstone for Catholics in the new American anti-abortion movement, especially for Charismatics and other fundamentalist Catholics who believed in "charisms" and the healing power of miracles. The idea that the Virgin Mary had returned to earth—to North America—to put an end to the killing of children served to underscore the Catholic belief that God was angry at the use of abortion in the United States.

O'Keefe organized a pilgrimage with his housemates to the Mexican site of the vision to coincide with the December 12 Feast Day, just before Christmas in 1972, and there they camped out in the Mexican streets and prayed for unborn children and their parents. O'Keefe was clearly floundering, spiritually and emotionally. "There was a real hunger there, but I didn't know what I was doing," he recalls, sheepishly.

O'Keefe's new interest in the abortion issue led him to contact the fledgling anti-abortion organizations in the Boston area in January 1973, at the time that the landmark U.S. Supreme Court decision in *Roe v. Wade* legalizing abortion was announced. *Roe* suddenly nationalized the abortion debate, and that caught the handful of anti-abortion activists who were already engaged completely off guard. In Massachusetts, as elsewhere, abortion opponents were prepared to lobby the statehouse, not the policy makers in Washington.

In 1970 Dr. Joseph Stanton, a Brighton physician, had organized Massachusetts's first anti-abortion group, the Value of Life Committee, to fight state reforms, and now he was on the lookout for enthusiastic young Catholic students like O'Keefe to inject some life into a movement dominated by the middle class and the middle aged. *Roe* changed everything, and Stanton knew he could no longer depend solely on the Irish Catholic housewives of suburban Boston to staff his organization.

After meeting with Stanton, however, O'Keefe realized he had no use for the Value of Life Committee, which he quickly saw was little more than Joe Stanton and a telephone. Stanton, in turn, pegged O'Keefe as a "very intellectual boy," which in the anti-abortion movement was not necessarily a good thing.

O'Keefe decided to keep his distance from the storefront right-to-life groups that were proliferating in the wake of *Roe,* just as he had stayed away from organized antiwar activity. He shared little in common with the early right-to-lifers: He was young, they were middle-aged; he approached abortion from the left, they from the right. "I thought they were just a bunch of right-wing nuts."

In addition, their tactics were far too timid for O'Keefe; the commitment was not there. Most seemed to treat anti-abortion activity like a hobby rather than a matter of life and death. They drank coffee, read the few books about abortion that were available, and wrote letters to the editor. Just as the antiwar activists did not respect Roy, these anti-abortion "activists," who had taken to calling themselves "pro-life," did not respect the unborn.

O'Keefe knew that much greater sacrifice was needed. He began to think back to his Harvard days, to the antiwar movement and the way student activists used sit-ins and the raucous occupations of administrative buildings on campus to gain attention. Civil disobedience had helped change the terms of the national debate on the Vietnam War, and O'Keefe began to realize that was exactly what the anti-abortion movement needed. Sit-ins, arrests, building takeovers.

Yet O'Keefe was coming to realize that he was an oddity in the world of protest. He was a pacifist who hated war, an individual who believed in the power of civil disobedience and the need to challenge the system but who found himself drawn to an issue that was dominated by conservative bishops and Catholic suburbanites. Those suburbanites had been horrified by the street theater of the antiwar protests and had no interest in allowing their new movement to use the same tactics. There seemed little room for a frighteningly earnest young man who took to heart—and hoped to act on—their rhetoric, which said that abortion was the killing of an unborn human being.

As O'Keefe moved away from the right-to-life groups, he kept reading Merton, kept reading about Gandhi and King. His favorite book at the time was King's *Strength to Love,* a collection of sermons the Southern minister had written and given from the pulpit, including those from his time in Montgomery, Alabama, when King first rose to prominence as the leader of the Montgomery bus boycott.

"'Do not conform' is difficult advice in a generation when crowd pressures have unconsciously conditioned our minds and feet to move to the rhythmic drumbeat of the status quo," King wrote. "Many voices and forces urge us to choose the path of least resistance, and bid us never to fight for an unpopular cause and never to be found in a pathetic minority of two or three."

King's words resonated with O'Keefe. He had been desperately searching for some way to prove to himself that he was not a coward, that he could do something difficult and painful, that his decision not to follow Roy to Vietnam and possible death did not mean he was weak and irresolute. Civil disobedience in the name of a cause was the answer. Here was pain and suffering, martyrdom that could lead to personal redemption.

O'Keefe had been struck by something that had been said of Martin Luther King Jr.: that the service King had performed for blacks was not nearly as important as the service he had performed for whites. He had worked for blacks to help them gain dignity and economic advancement, but he had worked to free whites from blindness, blindness about what it means to be a human being.

To O'Keefe, his cause would also cure blindness, the blindness of men and women who did not agree with him that abortion was the killing of unborn children. Not only did he have to save the unborn, but he had to make America realize that the fetus was a child. He realized that the anti-abortion movement, above all, was about definitions. If he could control the language of the debate, convince people that abortion was killing, then they would see what he saw.

The suburban anti-abortion groups were not ready for what O'Keefe thought needed to be done. They were blind as well, O'Keefe believed, blind to the fact that they were engaged in a new civil rights campaign, however unpopular and out of step they were with the mainstream of American politics and culture. They were not taking the risks, making the sacrifices, that black leaders in the American South of the 1950s had taken to win civil rights for their people.

As a result, by the mid-1970s, their movement was going nowhere, unable to attract significant numbers of new recruits, confined to the margins of the national debate. Their pickets and marches and leaflettings and letter-writing campaigns and speeches were not changing hearts or minds—and were not changing the law. *Roe* was gaining greater acceptance among Americans.

O'Keefe was not ready to lead, either. He knew what needed to be done, but he did not know how to do it. He saw that the anti-abortion movement did not have true leadership. It did not have Martin Luther King Jr. or anyone even remotely like him.

O'Keefe went back to Harvard, and for the next few years, he largely ignored the anti-abortion movement. That was easy to do. It seemed to consist of little more than desultory picketing and sporadic legislative lobbying campaigns by the Catholic Church and its allies. Victories in Washington for the Catholic Church and its friends at the National Right to Life Committee were on the margins of the abortion debate. In 1973, for example, the National Conference of Catholic Bishops successfully lobbied Congress to pass the "conscience clause" law. The National Right to Life Committee's most notable legislative victory came with the 1976 passage of the Hyde amendment, which cut off Medicaid funding for abortions for poor women. The Hyde amendment survived lengthy court challenges and was finally upheld by the Supreme Court in 1980. It served as the prototype for the kind of limited political action that the Catholic Church and the mainstream anti-abortion organizations were willing to conduct. With the church and its allies focusing increasingly on incremental change, the chances of overturning *Roe* through polite, mainstream political lobbying seemed to fade.

Through the Charismatic Renewal, O'Keefe met Betsy Cavanaugh, who ended any thoughts he had of joining the priesthood. They were married just as O'Keefe finally graduated from Harvard in 1976; he sought to prove his feminist stripes by changing his name to John Cavanaugh-O'Keefe. (For simplicity, he is identified as John O'Keefe throughout this book.) The couple eventually had six children, naming their oldest son John Paul, after the Pope.

O'Keefe was still harboring his ambition of applying the lessons of nonviolence and civil disobedience when he attended a bioethics conference at the University of Massachusetts in 1976. He struck up a conversation about the anti-abortion movement with Burke Balch, a younger but equally intense Catholic and abortion opponent, who was then a student at Williams College.

After telling Balch about his proposed strategy of civil disobedience, O'Keefe was shocked to hear Balch say that he and a tiny band of other liberal Catholic activists, including veterans of the peace movement, had already staged one tiny sit-in at an abortion clinic outside Washington in the summer of 1975. And they wanted to do more. O'Keefe could not believe that there were others who shared his left-leaning vision of nonviolent civil disobedience to protest abortion, and he was angry at himself because someone else had beaten him to it.

Balch's group had been prodded into action through an odd connection to the civil rights movement. In the summer of 1974, Charles (Chuck) Fager, a Quaker peace activist who had just written a book on Martin Luther King Jr.'s famous 1965 march on Selma, Alabama, was invited to give a speech in Boston at a regional conference of the National Youth Pro-Life Coalition. That student group, founded a year earlier just after the *Roe v. Wade* decision, was based in Washington and was affiliated with the National Right to Life Committee, the new national anti-abortion organization that in turn had been founded by the National Conference of Catholic Bishops in 1972. Tom Mooney, a former antiwar activist who headed the student group, had read a provocative article Fager had written for an alternative magazine in Boston chastising other leftists for moving so quickly to cement a new political orthodoxy surrounding their acceptance of abortion.

In his speech to the youth conference, Fager drew on the lessons of the civil rights movement to argue that fundamental social change cannot be accomplished through the use of force but requires the changing of people's minds. Fager observed that the whole point of nonviolent direct action in the civil rights movement was to accept suffering, which allowed King and the movement's other black leaders to draw a sharp and visible contrast with the force used by the white power structure. When blacks marched peacefully across the Edmund Pettus Bridge into Selma, only to be clubbed and beaten by Alabama state troopers on national television, their suffering served as a wake-up call to America.

Fager said that anti-abortion protesters could engage in similar acts of civil disobedience by entering clinics before abortions were under way and peacefully intervening, demanding that the "violence be visited on me, not the unborn." Those actions would create a new political climate, one in which more people would be willing to go to jail to accept suffering for their cause.

Fager warned, however, that such activity had to be conducted in "the context of absolute nonviolence, not just in act but in word as well." Pure nonviolence would not only protect the woman and the fetus but also allow the movement to get its message "through to people who had not accepted the humanity of the unborn child before."

He warned that such action could be devastated by any hint of violence. The civil rights campaign in Birmingham, Alabama, never received the level of public support that King won in Selma, Fager said, because photographs from Birmingham, published around the world, made it appear that both sides were responsible for some violence.

Fager's speech had an immediate impact on the young abortion opponents, and he was asked to give a second speech, along with a workshop on civil disobedience, at the group's national convention in November. Soon, Mooney and his wife, Chris, began planning a sit-in for the summer of 1975. Unsure how to start a sit-in movement from scratch, they asked Balch to do some research on civil disobedience. Balch tackled his research as if it were for a college term paper, spending his days inside the cavernous Library of Congress, poring over old Quaker tracts and academic treatises on the history of direct action. There, Balch came across an old manual on civil disobedience, published in the 1960s by a Quaker group that had developed a training center for the civil rights movement; it was the closest thing he could find to a how-to book on protest. He made copies and passed them around.

Armed with the fruits of Balch's research, the group developed a fairly sophisticated three-page logistical plan, setting a tight, detailed schedule for the morning of the sit-in, while assigning specific duties to those involved. Led by Chris Mooney, the group met for training and "role-playing" sessions during the summer, practicing how to "go limp" by offering passive resistance when confronted with the clinic staff and local police. Ultimately, the group decided that only women should be involved in the sit-in, limiting the men to picketing and supporting roles outside. "You had to get across something that would break the stereotype of misogynistic males who were trying to control women," says Balch. "We were trying to get people to stop and listen, and to rethink."

A pamphlet handed out to activists just before the sit-in offered a more telling rationale, one that spoke volumes about the desperate state of the anti-abortion movement at the time: "The most important thing is to show the media and the public that the movement is not as dead as they think."

Their target was the Sigma Reproductive Health Services clinic in Rockville, Maryland, one of the first abortion providers to open in the Washington area after the *Roe* decision. The clinic was one of two in the area owned and operated by Gail Frances, a nurse-practitioner who had seen the horrors of illegal abortion and had become an early convert to the cause of reproductive rights.

The sit-in, starting at 8 A.M. on August 2, 1975, was peaceful and went off without any major problems. One woman was sent in before the others to ask about an appointment and thus tip off the others that the clinic was open. Others followed her in, then sat down in front of the doors from the waiting area to the procedure rooms. Six women, including Chris Mooney, were arrested. As they waited for the police, they sang songs and prayed; others outside passed out literature and tried to talk to women going into the clinic. John Meiklejohn, a Montgomery County, Maryland, police officer, later testified that before he arrested the women, he and the clinic director pleaded with them for three hours to leave on their own.

In an effort to capture some of the mystique of the antiwar movement, the group dubbed the women arrestees the "Sigma Six." But the press did not bite. The event received virtually no media coverage, and the group's conviction on trespass charges in Montgomery County District Court in September warranted only a brief story in the *Washington Post*. It barely caused a ripple at the clinic. Frances shrugged it off. "At the time, I just thought all the clinics were going through this. I didn't know I was the only one." It turned out to be an isolated event, which made the group even easier to ignore and dismiss. A year passed before they tried again, on the Bicentennial, July 4, 1976.

By the time Balch met O'Keefe, many of those involved in the first sit-ins were drifting away, including the Mooneys. Balch was worried that their fledgling direct-action movement might disappear completely before it ever got off the ground. But as O'Keefe listened to Balch, he heard possibilities, not problems. He knew instantly that this was the cause and the group to which he could devote himself and his pent-up religious zeal. Here were fellow young Catholics like himself, committed to fighting abortion for all the same reasons that had drawn him to the movement. He was no longer alone.

He joined up immediately and was soon working to organize a new round of sit-ins, both in Washington, D.C., and in Connecticut, where he had moved following his wedding and graduation. To pay the bills while he worked nearly full-time on activism, he once again took a job as a hospital orderly, despite his new Harvard degree. "I still thought it was really important to be involved in direct service with my hands. If I wasn't, then the words that I was spewing out about service to mothers and children just wouldn't ring true to me. I loved it."

O'Keefe's first arrest came in January 1977 in Norwich, Connecticut. In what was probably a major tactical mistake, his group ended the original ban on male involvement in the sit-ins. "He always wanted to be a martyr," said his younger sister, Lucy, who joined him in the early sit-ins. But civil disobedience would not have been difficult and painful for John O'Keefe—it would not have served as penance for outliving Roy—if he did not risk arrest.

As others from the 1975 sit-in fell away and O'Keefe began to devote all his energies to the cause, he emerged as the de facto leader and soon was helping to create a series of new ad hoc organizations to sponsor sit-ins against abortion as well as "crossover" demonstrations against nuclear weapons.

O'Keefe was still deeply concerned with attracting veterans of the peace movement to the anti-abortion issue. Along with Juli Loesch, an Erie, Pennsylvania, Catholic leftist and veteran of Cesar Chavez's farm workers movement in California, O'Keefe joined Pro-Lifers for Survival, which was created to prove that opposition to abortion could be part of a "consistent ethic" against killing. Loesch alternated sit-ins at defense plants in the Northeast with acts of civil disobedience at abortion clinics. She liked to confuse people and challenge stereotypes by handing out anti-Pentagon tracts at anti-abortion rallies and anti-abortion tracts at peace rallies.

Like O'Keefe, Loesch had converted to the anti-abortion cause from the hard left, and her personal journey continued to give him hope that he could recruit other leftists. Loesch had returned to Pennsylvania from the California farm fields to help launch a new Catholic peace organization, Pax Christi, with a small group of newly liberated Catholic nuns. The anti-abortion movement made no dent in her thinking until she noticed a group of middle-class Catholic women who kept vigil in front of an abortion clinic in Erie, saying the rosary. She thought she had nothing in common with them. "I didn't like those women. They looked like female impersonators, they had this big hair."

But when she happened to read one of their flyers, she was surprised to see that they used the same biblical quotations used by Pax Christi.

From Deuteronomy 30:15: "I have set before you life and death, blessing and curse; therefore choose life, that you and your descendants may
live."

"It struck me as fascinating that their flyer was so similar to ours. I
watched their film. They asked me to come to their vigil. I said it can't
do any harm," she recalls.

Loesch founded Pro-Lifers for Survival to bridge the cultural and
political divides that she herself had crossed between the anti-abortion
and antinuclear movements. Meanwhile, in 1977 O'Keefe created what
would become his main organization, the Pro-Life Non-Violent Action
Project, which was to sponsor his sit-in campaign against clinics in both
Washington and New England.

With his new group, O'Keefe went out of his way to mimic the civil
rights movement, often to the point of excess. At one of the first sit-ins
he organized on his own in Connecticut in early 1977, he made picket
signs that said simply "Strength to Love," which was the title of King's
book of sermons that O'Keefe had read years earlier. "I don't think anybody besides me understood those signs."

While waiting to be arrested inside clinics, O'Keefe's group would
sing civil rights protest songs—"We Shall Overcome," among others—
updated with new and jarring, homemade anti-abortion lyrics. Their
new lyrics never caught on. "I always thought that one of the problems
with this movement was that we never had any good songs of our own,"
says Balch. "Every good protest movement needs its own music, but we
never had it."

Encouraged by Loesch, O'Keefe tried to draw non-Catholic peace
activists to join his Connecticut sit-ins by participating in their civil disobedience activities first. When Mobilization for Survival, a 1970s antinuclear group, protested at the Electric Boat Company's submarine-
building yards in Groton, Connecticut, O'Keefe and a handful of
Charismatic Catholics climbed the shipyard's fences and staged a brief
sit-in before being arrested.

But the antinuclear activists never returned the favor and in fact soon
began to scorn O'Keefe and his bid for a coalition. In 1978, O'Keefe
attended a conference held by the New England Catholic Peace
Fellowship, a pacifist group, on whether there could ever be such a
right-left alliance among pacifists. Titled "Nuclear Disarmament and
Right to Life: A Day for Dialogue," the conference at the University of
Massachusetts was highlighted by a speech by Daniel Berrigan, who

had completed his prison term for his antiwar protests. But when Berrigan compared abortion to nuclear bombs, a campus feminist group burst into the auditorium to picket, jeer, and disrupt the conference. The demonstration stunned Berrigan and left a deep impression on him, he later recalled; he had been a star of the left and was not used to being the object of its derision.

Berrigan rarely spoke out publicly against abortion after that, and O'Keefe came away from the conference convinced that he would never win over large numbers of leftists to the anti-abortion cause; he thought Loesch was tilting at windmills.

Abandoning hopes for a coalition with antiwar activists—the same people who had so angered him during the Vietnam era—O'Keefe gave up all pretense; he would focus on abortion. By 1983, when Chicago's Cardinal Joseph Bernardin, head of the pro-life office of the National Conference of Catholic Bishops, gave a major address in which he argued that opposition to abortion must be part of a "seamless garment" of support for peace and opposition to war and poverty, O'Keefe dismissed the speech as nothing more than an attempt to curb anti-abortion protest. It was one more sign, O'Keefe believed, that the Catholic hierarchy was not serious about the issue.

O'Keefe decided that his main objective now should be to spread the idea of civil disobedience throughout the anti-abortion subculture and to recruit other young activists with similar roots to form sit-in groups of their own. He began circulating pamphlets that explained his ideas, traveling around the country to give workshops on civil disobedience at conferences held by the National Right to Life Committee and other anti-abortion groups. He was frustrated that his sit-ins in Washington and Connecticut were still so small, never attracting more than about a dozen people, and were still getting brushed off and ignored by the media, police, and the clinics. He saw that only large-scale, coordinated activity around the country could garner enough attention to make a difference.

His recruiting efforts finally began to pay off in early 1978, when O'Keefe published *A Peaceful Presence,* a recruiting pamphlet that laid out what was happening in Washington and why. It circulated widely among right-to-life organizations and soon caught the attention of young Catholics in cities like Cleveland and St. Louis, eager to take their activism to the next level. "I have been involved in pro-life activities for a year now but I became dismayed by the fact that so much energy and effort is being wasted," wrote David Eckard, a Virginia high school student, in a letter to O'Keefe's organization in 1978. "I read the pamphlet *A Peaceful Presence* and agree wholeheartedly with the principles stated in it."

A Peaceful Presence became a landmark within the small community of anti-abortion activists, serving as a kind of ideological road map for activists for years to come. In O'Keefe's words, "Any movement that sets out to change a society has to provide a picture of a world that is an ideal, that is convincing, so you can compare what is going on with what ought to be, and so you can be prepared to struggle for it."

In the pamphlet, O'Keefe once again made the connection to King and the 1960s. "With Reverend Martin Luther King, Jr., we must come to believe that unearned suffering is somehow redemptive," O'Keefe wrote. "A change of heart will not occur without suffering, and we have to ask ourselves whether we are willing to suffer ourselves or only ask others to suffer. . . . It is not enough to change people's minds; we are engaged in a struggle to change people's hearts. We are engaged in a process of metanoia—conversion, repentance."

Above all, O'Keefe believed that sit-ins would show a "solidarity with the child," a vaguely leftist-sounding concept that turned off conservatives in the movement, especially the few Protestants who had slowly begun to get involved in the late 1970s. But that was the point: O'Keefe wanted new blood. *A Peaceful Presence* read like a recruiting appeal to activists tired of the orthodoxy of the left, tired of the groups like Mobilization for Survival that had rejected O'Keefe's appeals for a coalition. If leftist institutions would not support him, O'Keefe was willing to make one last bid to win over their grassroots followers by appealing to their sense of nonconformism.

"The pro-abortionists," the pamphlet said, "are fond of dismissing the pro-lifers as right-wing Catholics who have never before shown any concern for social justice. . . . Many pro-life activists, particularly in New England, have anti-war backgrounds. They say it is utterly inconsistent to oppose killing overseas and then tolerate massive slaughter here in the U.S."

The pamphlet did not succeed in recruiting leftists to the abortion movement, but it was compelling to a few young Catholics who already were involved in anti-abortion activities and who shared O'Keefe's frustrations with the "mainstream" right-to-life movement's caution and failures.

Soon, a handful of Charismatic Catholics and others around the country began to follow O'Keefe's lead. By January 1978, O'Keefe was able to coordinate with other new groups to stage sit-ins in six cities on the East Coast on Epiphany (the twelfth day of Christmas, January 6), with a combined total of thirty-six arrests. Jeanne Miller, a Yale undergraduate and an early member of the Washington sit-in group, began developing the first mailing list and newsletter to form a national activist network.

O'Keefe's pamphlet had its biggest impact in St. Louis. Students at St. Louis University began a sit-in campaign led by a Franciscan seminarian named Vince Peterson and a freshman, Samuel Lee, who was thinking about becoming a priest, both of whom read O'Keefe's pamphlet. They later heard O'Keefe speak at a workshop on civil disobedience at the 1978 National Right to Life Convention, which was held in St. Louis. Eventually, their St. Louis sit-ins led to the longest lasting civil disobedience campaign in the anti-abortion movement prior to the formation of Operation Rescue in 1987. Their group also developed into an early proving ground for many of the more militant and aggressive leaders of the anti-abortion movement of the 1980s. St. Louis provided tactics and ideas for Joseph Scheidler, the founder of the Chicago-based Pro-Life Action League, who twisted many of O'Keefe's original methods for use in more aggressive clinic actions, as well as for Operation Rescue founder Randall Terry.

Slowly, O'Keefe's activism had a broad ripple effect, influencing every major activist in the anti-abortion movement, for good or ill. For example, his Washington sit-ins caught the attention of a small band of demonstrators from Philadelphia led by conservative Catholics Jack O'Brien and Michael McMonagle. This group had done little more than picketing until members came to one of O'Keefe's Washington sit-ins and then took his tactics home to stage clinic sit-ins of their own. McMonagle later became one of Randall Terry's first lieutenants in Operation Rescue and sponsored the group's first major act of civil disobedience, a sit-in outside an abortion clinic in the Philadelphia suburb of Cherry Hill, New Jersey, in November 1987. O'Brien later took up O'Keefe's argument that his group was not engaged in symbolic acts—it was actually saving lives—and used the term *rescue* to describe the Philadelphia sit-ins. It was a small but important semantic shift that caught on almost immediately throughout the country and that later helped attract conservative Protestants who had been reluctant to join in actions that were advertised as reruns of the 1960s. A young Presbyterian minister who joined McMonagle's sit-ins, Joseph Foreman, went on to become second in command of Operation Rescue—and later Randall Terry's greatest enemy.

O'Keefe has long since been forgotten, lost in the shadows of more flamboyant and outrageous figures like Terry and Scheidler, but within the anti-abortion realm he is widely credited as the architect of the largest American social protest movement since the 1960s, a movement that Terry and his band of conservative Protestant Evangelicals later co-opted and claimed as their own.

O'Keefe's original strategies for disciplined nonviolence provided a blueprint for every anti-abortion activist to follow. But there were two great ironies in O'Keefe's life. One was that his efforts to attract left-wing Catholic peace activists to his cause led instead to the creation of the first conservative civil disobedience movement in modern American history, a movement that mobilized Protestant fundamentalists for political action for the first time in more than fifty years.

O'Keefe never gained recognition outside a small circle of anti-abortion activists. He was not a natural leader and lacked the outward strength to control those drawn to his cause. He was not capable of translating his sixties-style protest rhetoric or his Catholic emphasis on suffering into the lurid language of judgment and wrath that would later resonate with Protestant Evangelicals drawn to the cause. Finally, just as his sit-in movement in Washington was finally gaining numbers and attention, it collapsed and faded into obscurity, more than three years before Randall Terry began making national headlines. Many believe that the chances for a peaceful and nonviolent civil disobedience movement in opposition to abortion faded with it. O'Keefe's organization collapsed because of the second great irony of his life. O'Keefe the pacifist, follower of Merton, King, and Gandhi, was the victim of a betrayal of biblical proportions, a betrayal by violence and lies perpetrated by one of his own people. He watched in horror as his organization crumbled, as the clinics he had targeted for "a peaceful presence" began to blow up.

At first, O'Keefe's small group, rarely totaling more than a dozen people, caught both the abortion clinics and legal system completely off guard. Hardy bands of right-to-life picketers had been outside clinics ever since *Roe v. Wade* was announced, but after a few years they had become an accepted, and ignored, part of the urban landscape, deemed harmless and ineffective by everyone. The sit-ins threatened to change that dynamic—and quickly.

By the mid-1970s, small clinics, stand-alone businesses operated by medical professionals or chains run by groups like Planned Parenthood, were becoming the nation's primary abortion providers, as hospitals and other large health care facilities backed away under political pressure. At the time, these independent facilities had small staffs and virtually no security. Volunteer escort and clinic defense groups, which later became as much a part of the abortion issue as the protesters themselves, were still years away from being established by the National Organization for Women and other feminist groups.

At the time, apathy had set in among feminists, who were more concerned with the passage of the Equal Rights Amendment to the Constitution. "People thought the battle was over," recalls former NOW president Eleanor Smeal. "Some groups had even disbanded after *Roe*. The Supreme Court had ruled."

Sarah Weddington, the attorney who argued and won the *Roe* case before the Supreme Court, notes that "our energy and contributions sagged and we seemed only to plod forward. It was hard not to give the impression [to supporters] that we were simply crying wolf. When we talked about the importance of organizing and pro-choice voting, people tended to think, 'Now, really, I'm so busy. And after all, *Roe versus Wade* decided the matter.' We missed the energy of our pre-*Roe* crusade. The opposition was fighting a battle of attrition, keeping the pressure on in so many different arenas, [hoping] that eventually our resources would collapse, and it was working." The clinics were unprepared to deal with sit-ins or invasions, therefore, and they had no idea how to keep O'Keefe and his followers out.

O'Keefe continually emphasized to his fellow activists that his guiding principle was nonviolence and passive resistance; no one should fight back, damage equipment, or resist arrest in any way other than by going limp on the floor or sidewalk. The whole point of the sit-in was "to be defenseless, to put yourself in the same position" as the fetus.

But almost from the beginning, there were small debates within O'Keefe's organization about the kinds of physical resistance that were permissible. Were they really being passive by locking arms? What about grabbing onto furniture or something else to prevent the police from dragging them away? O'Keefe thought all such actions were wrong. He thought going limp meant just that. If confronted by clinic personnel or angry patients or their boyfriends, the only acceptable action was to sit down on the floor, not try to push past them to block a door. Yet he failed to demand purity and never spoke up forcefully as the internal debates raged. O'Keefe saw a slippery slope toward greater physicality developing and came to regret later that he had failed to halt the slide when he had the chance.

Clinic owner Gail Frances claims that the demonstrators sometimes shoved past women and clinic personnel, a charge that O'Keefe and other members of the group still deny. Yet O'Keefe acknowledges that at least one demonstrator, Brent Bozell, the organizer of Washington's first anti-abortion demonstration before *Roe v. Wade,* destroyed equipment at one clinic during a sit-in. Clinic sit-ins separately organized by Juli Loesch of Pro-Lifers for Survival in Pittsburgh also led to the destruction of equipment. Loesch was consciously trying to mimic Berrigan's "Plowshares" antinuclear movement, in which demonstrators damaged missiles and other equipment in defense industry facilities. However, even Frances acknowledges that O'Keefe's early sit-ins in the late 1970s were far more peaceful than those staged later.

"I think O'Keefe was a man of his convictions. I think he was true to his beliefs," she says with grudging respect.

While Frances and her clinic personnel were still trying to figure out what to do about O'Keefe, the police and courts in many local jurisdictions where the sit-ins took place were caught off guard, too. When O'Keefe's tiny band began to target Frances's second clinic in Washington's Northern Virginia suburbs in January 1977, they were stunned to find that Virginia law enforcement officials and the local courts were actually on their side.

In a series of sit-ins throughout 1977, O'Keefe and a half-dozen or so other activists were repeatedly arrested for blocking the doors at the Northern Virginia Women's Medical Center in suburban Fairfax. Robert Horan, Fairfax County's chief prosecutor, was personally opposed to abortion, and in April he dismissed charges against the group for its first Fairfax sit-in that took place in January.

Encouraged, the protestors got arrested at the same clinic again in May. This time they wanted a trial to test the legal waters, and they were brought up on trespassing charges before Judge Lewis Griffith in Fairfax County General District Court. Their attorney, John Brandt, tried to be creative, thinking of ways to use the trespassing case as a vehicle through which to make a political statement. He reread the Supreme Court's *Roe v. Wade* decision and noted that in the majority opinion, Justice Harry Blackmun had written that there was no agreement among medical professionals, philosophers, or ethicists on exactly when life began. That lack of consensus had played a central role in Blackmun's decision making; now Brandt decided that it also offered him a little bit of legal running room.

Brandt asked Judge Griffith to view a graphic anti-abortion film and then put a pathologist who opposed abortion on the stand to testify that life actually began at conception. When the bemused prosecutor decided not to object to the testimony or offer any rebuttal, Brandt argued that the demonstrators should be acquitted on the basis of the "necessity defense." That was an old English common-law concept that held that an individual who breaks a minor law to achieve some greater good should be declared innocent of the lesser charge. A man who breaks into a burning house to save a child, for example, should not be found guilty of trespassing.

Brandt then had all the defendants testify that they entered the clinic because they believed that "each woman going into the clinic was carrying a human being within them." It was a convoluted, long-shot argument, and Brandt had no hopes for success. But to the astonishment of the attorneys on both sides, Judge Griffith agreed with Brandt and acquitted all seven of the demonstrators. He ruled they had a "good faith belief that their actions were necessary" to save lives.

"Did these defendants then, number one, believe that life begins at conception?" Griffith asked while issuing his ruling. "Did they . . . go out of necessity to stop what they considered to be a crime? I think they did. The charges are dismissed."

The case marked the first time since the Supreme Court's *Roe* ruling that the U.S. judicial system had accepted such revolutionary arguments. Later, the necessity defense became tired boilerplate, used again and again by anti-abortion lawyers with virtually no success; state and federal judges simply refused to allow its use. Finally, the necessity argument was badly twisted in the 1990s by extremists seeking to justify murders and bombings. But for that brief moment, Griffith's ruling electrified O'Keefe's group and suddenly injected hope into their movement.

The ruling also prompted Horan, the county prosecutor, to throw in secretly with the defendants. He met privately with Mary Ann Kreitzer, a leading member of the sit-in group, and encouraged her and the others to get arrested again and this time to try to go before a different judge to test the law further.

Arrested for blocking the front door at Frances's Northern Virginia clinic in November 1977 and January 1978, the protestors went on trial in Fairfax General District Court again, this time before Judge J. Mason Grove. To their amazement, Grove not only accepted their necessity defense and dismissed their trespassing charges, but also ruled that Virginia's abortion law, written to comply with the *Roe v. Wade* decision, was unconstitutional under the Virginia state constitution.

Elated, O'Keefe's group went back to the clinic the next day, and Horan, the local prosecutor, made it clear he had no interest in arresting them again in the face of the favorable rulings by the two judges. It was a remarkable turnaround, and suddenly it seemed to O'Keefe that the sit-in movement would gain momentum and break into the national spotlight. Previously, O'Keefe's sit-ins had attracted only marginal media coverage, but the two court victories prompted major stories in the Washington press. A national civil disobedience campaign, backed by the support of the courts—reminiscent of King's civil rights movement—no longer seemed far-fetched.

Steven Merril, who handled the prosecution in the case, told the *Washington Post* the next day that the ruling "really leaves that abortion clinic in a very difficult position as far as receiving some relief from the court in trespass cases." But just as quickly, the window of opportunity closed. Abortion-rights activists, who had previously ignored O'Keefe's actions, finally shook off their apathy and began to pay attention. The clinic quickly called for legal help, and the American Civil Liberties Union (ACLU) stepped in.

Judith Levin and other attorneys from the ACLU's Reproductive Freedom Project quickly did what the ACLU almost always does: federalized the whole affair. On behalf of Frances's clinic, in 1978 the ACLU filed a civil lawsuit in U.S. District Court in Alexandria, Virginia, against both Horan and the demonstrators, while seeking a federal injunction against further sit-ins. The ACLU countered Brandt's necessity defense with civil libertarian arguments of its own, stating that the demonstrators were not acting in the best traditions of civil disobedience but rather as a "private conspiracy" to deny the rights of others, just as the Ku Klux Klan had conspired to deny the rights of blacks in the South's Jim Crow days.

This first major federal test case thus moved almost immediately to the legal and ideological positions that would later become hardened dogma for a generation of attorneys and activists on both sides of the abortion battle. The fight was over before it even began. U.S. District Court Judge Calvitt Clarke refused to allow the necessity defense, leaving Brandt without a legal leg to stand on. To the delight of the ACLU, he imposed the nation's first federal court injunction against anti-abortion sit-ins, prohibiting eleven people named in the injunction from entering the Fairfax clinic. Clarke's injunction served as a model to be followed by federal judges throughout the country over the coming decade as anti-abortion protests spread.

The ruling was like a body blow to O'Keefe's followers. The disappointment was only made worse by the fact that their expectations had been raised so high by the earlier rulings. The Washington sit-in campaign quickly began to evaporate in the face of Clarke's injunction.

O'Keefe and a few others tried to continue. Mary Ann Kreitzer and Dave Gaetano, a St. Anselm's classmate of O'Keefe and a regular protester, tried for months in 1979 to recruit local Catholic priests and Protestant ministers to join in a new round of sit-ins to challenge Clarke's injunction. Gaetano and Kreitzer were finally granted a private audience with Bishop John Welsh, head of the Catholic diocese of Northern Virginia, and pleaded with the bishop to call out his legion of priests. But Gaetano and Kreitzer made Welsh nervous; they were asking him to put his diocese on the line to defy a federal judge.

According to Gaetano, "He said, 'Won't they put us in jail?' I said, 'Not if there are too many of us.' He said, 'Don't be too sure.'" Welsh agreed to urge his priests to join, but only if Gaetano could also gain support from local Protestant leaders. It was a cop-out and Gaetano knew it. After meeting dozens of priests and Protestant ministers, only four agreed to see him a second time. Finally, Welsh agreed to lead a march, but he refused to violate Clarke's injunction. He would not go near the clinic.

Years later, Gaetano's concept—recruiting ministers to lead their flocks out to mass arrests—proved stunningly successful for Randall Terry. Operation Rescue attracted large numbers of Christian fundamentalist demonstrators only after Terry spent months recruiting their pastors. But in 1979, Gaetano's left-leaning rhetoric of Catholic street activism fell flat with Protestants.

O'Keefe kept going, staging small sit-ins throughout the late 1970s and into the early 1980s, but he could never attract more than ten to fifteen people; by 1980 and 1981 his sit-ins were no larger than they had been in 1977. He grew frustrated with his inability to stage a breakthrough campaign of civil disobedience that could gain widespread public support and attention, and he was angry that the movement was turning toward other, more aggressive leaders like Joseph Scheidler, a conservative Catholic and former public relations man who did not share O'Keefe's compunctions about nonviolence. Scheidler had already turned so-called sidewalk counseling into a sophisticated protest device, and with his trademark bullhorn, he was trying to transform Chicago into his own personal laboratory to experiment with new, more militant forms of civil disobedience.

O'Keefe was privately horrified that the movement was being taken over by men like Scheidler, and he remained convinced that pure nonviolence was the only way to change hearts. Yet setbacks sowed seeds of doubt. There were unborn children dying, and he was not stopping it.

O'Keefe had always told volunteers that, unlike those used in the civil rights movement, anti-abortion sit-ins were not symbolic; by blocking clinic doors, they could actually save lives. When a woman went home rather than run the protest gauntlet, O'Keefe felt victorious. That woman might ultimately keep the child. "A sit-in is a great deal more than a protest: it is an attempt to save lives right there, that day," O'Keefe wrote in A Peaceful Presence.

Yet if the intention was to prevent a murder, how could O'Keefe be so certain that pacifism was the only answer? The old debates about the limits of physical intervention still haunted him. O'Keefe secretly began to sympathize with those engaged in violence to stop abortion. They were not the ones tied up in intellectual knots. They had found the kind of relief for which O'Keefe had always yearned, the relief that comes with clarity of purpose.

In the late 1970s, anti-abortion violence was limited to sporadic and amateurish fires that did little damage. The first documented act of violence took place in March 1976 at a Planned Parenthood clinic in Eugene, Oregon, where a man named Joseph Stockett set fire to the building and was sentenced to five years in prison. The following February, a Planned Parenthood clinic in St. Paul, Minnesota, was set on fire, causing two hundred fifty thousand dollars worth of damage.

Clinic arsons and bombings became more common—and more serious—by the early 1980s. The violence escalated to a new level in 1982,
when three men who called themselves the Army of God were arrested
and convicted on charges of kidnapping abortion doctor Hector Zevallos
and his wife in Edwardsville, Illinois. The three suspects—Don Benny
Anderson (a father of seven) and brothers Matthew and Wayne Moore—
were also convicted of bombing and burning one clinic in Virginia and
two in Florida before the kidnapping.

Army of God leader Anderson represented everything that O'Keefe
abhorred, yet O'Keefe was strangely drawn to him. Despite his misgivings, O'Keefe realized that Anderson's violence had been successful,
however briefly; Zevallos had not been able to perform abortions while
he was being held. O'Keefe quietly contacted Anderson in prison and
tried to decide whether he had accomplished more with one act of terror than O'Keefe had with all of his acts of nonviolence. Then he wrote
a tortured, secret letter to Scheidler, whom O'Keefe had previously criticized for refusing publicly to condemn clinic bombings. The letter so
surprised Scheidler that he still keeps it stored away in his office more
than a decade later. In the letter, which has never before been revealed,
O'Keefe bared his soul, and his growing doubts and ambivalence about
violence came flooding out:

> I have been in touch with Don Anderson (though not as much
> as I should have been). I had two arguments with what I heard
> about the Army of God. The first argument is one I have with
> almost everybody in the pro-life movement: I think that non-
> violence is an urgent necessity. But to be sure, I am not going to
> hold it against anybody that they disagree with me about that. So
> while it was a criticism I had of Anderson's work, it was not the
> most important one.
>
> The second problem [I had] was that the Army of God let
> Zevallos go. I considered that inexcusable, and in my thinking it
> destroyed the credibility of their effort altogether. In the just war
> theory—which I reject, but respect—it is of course legitimate to
> take somebody by force and hold them by force if that will pro-
> tect lives. In fact, such kidnapping can be consistent with—
> even mandated by—some theories of nonviolence.
>
> Life is a higher value than freedom. Further, the loving
> response to a sinner who refuses to cease a destructive activity is

to restrain him forcibly until he has a chance to think quietly, to consider the possibility and advisability of repentance. But the Army of God let Zevallos go; it looked like a straightforward publicity stunt.

But the fact is that . . . [Anderson's] response was courageous, and in a bloody war courage is a higher value than ideological purity.

In the letter, O'Keefe also vowed that he would no longer criticize Scheidler for his refusal to condemn violence publicly: "I have made only one New Year's resolution, without compromising my vision of the pro-life movement, I intend to cease and desist from criticizing yours. We agree too much. I guess I could have made that decision without telling you, but if I put it in writing I am less likely to backslide. If I tell you about it, you can hold me to it."

Clearly worried about how such thoughts would affect his reputation and credibility, O'Keefe added: "Joe, for God's sake, be discreet about quoting any of this."

O'Keefe's philosophy of nonviolence was unraveling. He had lost sight of the most important thing Merton had said of Gandhi: "Gandhi is chiefly concerned with truth and with service, rather than with the possible success of his tactics upon other people" and that "paradoxically it was his religious conviction that made Gandhi a great politician rather than a mere tactician or operator."

Once O'Keefe decided that his actions were not symbolic but actual attempts to protect unborn children, perhaps it was inevitable that his own belief system would be sorely tested and that even he, the most disciplined pacifist in the movement, would begin to think about ends that might justify other means.

O'Keefe managed to keep the Washington sit-in movement alive, but just barely. By 1984, he was determined to mount fewer, but larger, demonstrations. He set a goal of recruiting one thousand people who would pledge to get arrested in what he hoped would be the largest act of civil disobedience ever staged in the anti-abortion movement, one targeted against a brand-new clinic in the Washington suburb of Gaithersburg, Maryland.

To get the numbers of arrests he wanted, O'Keefe knew he would have to go beyond the usual prospects among the young Catholics who were by now hardened veterans of sit-ins. For the first time, he began to recruit in the rapidly growing ranks of Protestant fundamentalists, who had just begun to show an interest in the abortion issue.

O'Keefe was so eager for fresh shock troops, so determined to prove the effectiveness of people power, that he did little to screen his new recruits. When an eager young Lutheran lay minister from Bowie, Maryland, named Michael Bray joined the ranks, O'Keefe never questioned him about his commitment to nonviolence.

4

THE FATHER OF VIOLENCE
Michael Bray

If O'Keefe was the "father of rescue," then Bray was to become the "father of violence." Certainly he was one of the first anti-abortion leaders to engage in it himself.

O'Keefe and Bray were photographic negatives of each other, intensely religious baby boomers who had read the same Bible, prayed to the same God, been drawn to the same cause, but found themselves in a war with each other for the heart and soul of their movement.

If John O'Keefe could, despite his doubts, yearn for a Martin Luther King Jr. to lead the movement, then Michael Bray could yearn for a Malcolm X. If O'Keefe could envision a merciful, suffering Christ, the Christ of the Sermon on the Mount, Bray could see an angry Christ, a wrathful Son of God who could overturn the money-changing tables in the Temple of Jerusalem.

In May 1984, when Bray first joined O'Keefe's sit-in campaign in Gaithersburg, Maryland, his involvement in anti-abortion violence, or his belief in the just use of force to end abortion, was still a carefully guarded secret. When Bray's secret was finally unraveled by persistent agents of the Federal Bureau of Alcohol, Tobacco and Firearms (ATF),

O'Keefe's movement, as well as his faith in the power of nonviolence, was shattered.

"WAR!"', Edwin Starr's hip, Vietnam-era, anti-war protest song, served as Michael Bray's unofficial anthem during his first and only year as a midshipman at the United States Naval Academy in 1971. Bray and his roommate subversively chanted Starr's song as they marched and drilled across the Annapolis campus.

The son of a career naval officer—Annapolis class of 1951—Bray had the classic, square-jawed good looks and broad, easy smile of the all-American boy. An Eagle Scout, football player, and Maryland state wrestling champion at Bowie High in the blue-collar Washington suburb of Bowie, Maryland, he briefly dated the equally attractive Kathie Epstein, later known as talk-show host Kathie Lee Gifford.

In high school, everything went right for Bray, and his prestigious appointment to the Naval Academy seemed the inevitable capstone. But privately, he was restless, emotionally unprepared for a lifetime commitment to order and discipline. He needed to breathe, to get away for a while from being the Eagle Scout on the track to success. By the time he arrived at the Naval Academy, he saw the chance to follow in his father's footsteps not as an opportunity but as a trap. Marching to Edwin Starr's lyrics was just one small act of rebellion, a symptom of his worsening claustrophobia.

Bray's repeated violations of academy disciplinary rules meant that he was the only plebe, or freshman, confined to campus over Christmas break. By the end of his plebe year, Bray's poor grades ranked him just fifteenth from the bottom of his class and thus subject to a review board's decision on whether he could stay in the school. His poor attitude during a meeting with the review board ensured that the academy would not give him a second chance.

Getting kicked out of the Naval Academy actually came as a relief to Bray. It meant he did not have to make the decision to leave school himself. For the first time in his life, Bray felt free, and soon he was hitch-hiking across the country with an old friend, experiencing life on the road, briefly working on a ranch in Oklahoma or catching sharks while fishing in the Florida Keys. In Orlando, he attended a Baptist tent revival and, still piecing together a new direction, began to think seriously about the role religion should play in his life.

He went to live with his parents in Germany, where his father was stationed in a staff job, and there began to explore new religious strains. Bray considered joining the Mormons and began meeting with a group in Germany, only to be turned off by what he saw as their "cultlike" traits. He traveled to Switzerland and stayed briefly at the L'Abri Fellowship, an international Christian retreat founded by Francis Schaeffer, an American expatriate and conservative Presbyterian minister who by then had become an influential Protestant fundamentalist writer.

Bray returned to Bowie and spent a year at the University of Maryland before finally deciding to join his sister at Rockmont College, a small Bible school in Denver. Bray began to find himself in Denver. Rockmont's conservative emphasis on biblical teachings suited both Bray's temperament and his evolving religious beliefs. He found that theological studies excited him as had no other scholastic work, and he decided to go on to the nearby Denver Theological Seminary for graduate work.

At Rockmont, Bray met Jayne Green, a pretty, blond Rockmont freshman, while they both were acting in a hokey floor show at a large Mexican restaurant to pay their tuition bills. In the show, Mike sometimes played an Acapulco cliff diver and would dive into a pool; other times he was Tarzan to Jayne's Jane, saving her from the clutches of a gorilla. The role of entertainer did not suit Bray, however, and at one point he threatened to quit because the floor show included phony palm reading; Bray proclaimed it was immoral to fool the audience.

Jayne shared Michael's growing religious intensity, and they married in 1976. She later wrote that they formed a close partnership in which Michael "dreamed the dreams and I helped him live them out."

At the Denver Theological Seminary, Bray became immersed in the Evangelical theology of the school's founders, the Conservative Baptist Association (CBA). The CBA was a breakaway denomination formed in 1947 in the wake of a deep and bitter rift between modernists and early fundamentalists among Northern Baptists. Bray was taught the pietistic views that had held sway among Protestant Evangelicals for generations: that religion, the following of Christ, is very much a personal issue, confined to thoughts of salvation.

But Bray was uncomfortable with the limits of traditional Baptist teaching, and he soon began reading the works of Francis Schaeffer and other Protestant writers who were also searching for ways to combine their fundamentalist theology with a more activist approach to life. In hopes of leading fundamentalists like Bray to become more politically active, Schaeffer urged readers to return to the teachings of Reformation theologians John Calvin and John Knox.

In the late 1970s, Bray and other young fundamentalists began to follow Schaeffer into Calvinism; together, they embarked on a bracing return to the early roots of Reformation theology. That meant a return to concepts that had been out of fashion in mainline American Protestant churches for generations: a return to the Puritans, to predestination and Godly election, and finally, to "Dominion" teaching. Ultimately, it led fundamentalists back to the Augustinian view that God intends his followers to build a City on a Hill: a Christian city.

This was a strain of fundamentalism free of the so-called premillennial dispensationalist theology that until the late 1970s and early 1980s still held a chokehold on most Evangelicals. At the heart of premillennial dispensationalism was a mystical eschatology, also known as "rapture theology": the belief that the Second Coming of Christ was close at hand—the End Times—so that there was no point in worrying about events on earth. Indeed, some premillenarians believed that before Christ could return, the Antichrist would appear, bringing darkness before the final light. Christians thus should not stand in the way of chaos, because it was a necessary precursor to Christ's return.

Rapture theology has roots that date as far back as the mystical millenarian sects of the Middle Ages, and over the centuries it has often been backed by self-proclaimed prophets who named specific dates for the world's end and the Second Coming. In the United States, such thinking has served to keep generations of Protestant fundamentalists out of politics. Throughout most of the 1970s, it kept Protestant fundamentalists out of the anti-abortion movement. It did not help that Protestant fundamentalists viewed abortion as a Catholic issue; they also believed the Roman Catholic Church to be the source of apostasy.

Through his writings and lectures, Schaeffer was working hard to break fundamentalists free from the premillennial trap, and by the late 1970s he was having an impact on young fundamentalists like Bray. Bray came to see the rapture as a distraction, and he was anxious to find an alternative vision of Evangelicalism. With Schaeffer's help, he found it in the Reformation theologians, in Geneva's Calvin and Scotland's Knox.

Calvin, like Martin Luther, the Reformation's first leader, taught that

God chooses those who will be saved long before they are ever born, through a process called "predestination." No matter what people do during their life, they cannot save themselves; "good works" on earth will not open the doors to redemption and heaven. Faith alone leads to salvation. Yet Calvin argued that those who are "elected" are still obligated to do God's work, to create a godly kingdom on earth. Such a faithful mission transcends all other worldly authority. "If God is for us," Calvin asked, "who can be against us?"

According to Ronald Bainton, in his landmark book *The Reformation of the Sixteenth Century*, Calvin, like Luther, "had an overwhelming sense of the majesty of God, but whereas for Luther this served to point up the miracle of forgiveness, for Calvin it gave rather the assurance of the impregnability of God's purpose." Calvin believed that "this God who is able to perform that which he has promised has a plan for mankind to be achieved within the historical process." In other words, Calvin and his followers believed that God wanted them to run things on earth. Calvin provided Protestant fundamentalists with a "resolute summons to action within the sphere of society," Bainton observed.

But it was Knox, one of Calvin's leading protégés and apologists, who pushed further, who could convince impressionable readers like Michael Bray to fight with everything at their disposal—tools of politics as well as weapons of war—and that it was appropriate for the godly man to take the law into his own hands, because his hands were the tools of the Lord. Calvin had made it clear in his writings that he believed that only the "magistrates"—faithful public leaders—had the right to resort to force to punish wrongdoing. Knox, on the other hand, believed that any members of the "elect"—anyone saved by God through faith—had the right to "rebellion against idolatrous and tyrannical sovereigns." Later, Michael Bray came to believe that John Knox was speaking to him across the centuries, telling him that it was his duty as a Christian to fight abortion by any means necessary.

Bray graduated from the Denver Theological Seminary in 1979 with a master's degree in religious studies, rather than in divinity, which meant that he did not have the appropriate degree for ordination as a minister. Bray weighed two job offers: one from a conservative Denver church that wanted him to create an anticult program, and another to become lay pastor for youth activities at Grace Lutheran Church in Bowie, Maryland.

Grace Lutheran was the mainline church in which Bray had been raised, and its pastor, the Reverend Al Ericksen, was the same man who had confirmed Bray as a boy. Although he now had deep theological disagreements with mainstream Lutherans, Bray was drawn by the chance to return home. He joined Grace Lutheran in 1980. His hiring turned out to be a horrible mistake for Bray, for Ericksen, and for Grace Lutheran.

In Denver, Bray had focused his political activity on picketing and leafleting religious groups he considered to be cults, including the Mormons, a church he had once considered joining. But by the time he was settling into Bowie, the election of President Ronald Reagan and the conservative flood tide in Washington put abortion back into the headlines. Abortion soon became Bray's main focus.

When the head of Bowie's local right-to-life organization came to the church to ask Bray to volunteer, Bray was receptive, and after reading her literature and viewing some anti-abortion films, he was hooked. But like O'Keefe, it took an encounter with a woman who had experienced abortion to motivate Bray fully. During one of his Sunday school classes for adults, a woman in the class came forward to tell Bray that she felt deep remorse over the four abortions she had had before *Roe v. Wade*. Her story brought clarity for Bray: Abortion was murder, a sin against God; she was a sinner seeking salvation; and now it was up to the faithful, the elect, to stamp out this evil. If the church failed to act, then the church would be guilty of sin as well.

"What motivated me was her story," Bray recalls. After listening to her, Bray later wrote to a federal judge, "it became impossible for me to continue to permit the tragedy to continue without direct intervention."

At first, intervention meant political involvement. In 1981, Bray spoke at a rally in Bowie in support of Larry Hogan, the county executive of Prince George's County, Maryland, who had proposed a ban on abortions at county-run hospitals. At the rally, Bray met another young abortion opponent named Thomas Spinks, a small-time home improvement contractor. Spinks, like Bray, was a fundamentalist, a member of Cornerstone Assembly of God, a new Evangelical church in Bowie. At the Hogan rally, Spinks carried a sign that said "Save the Whales, Save the Snail Darters, Kill the Babies."

"I went up to him and complimented him on his sign, and he said, 'I'm glad somebody likes it. I've been getting a lot of grief over it,'" Bray recalls.

Hogan's proposal failed, but Bray struck up a friendship with Spinks, and they soon discovered they both were frustrated that the anti-abortion movement was engaging only in half-measures to protect the unborn.

Bray began to dive headfirst into the anti-abortion cause and soon prodded his church to help the Bowie Right to Life Committee to establish a local "crisis pregnancy center." Since the first such anti-abortion counseling centers for women were opened in Cincinnati in 1971 by Dr. Jack Willke, a Catholic physician and early leader of the mainstream anti-abortion movement, some three thousand have been set up around the country. Many have been criticized and investigated for using misleading advertising to attract women who believe the centers provide abortion services, only to find that the crisis pregnancy staffers are there to talk them out of abortions.

Church funding for the Bowie crisis pregnancy center was a controversial move at Grace Lutheran, where many church members were advocates of abortion rights; Bray was soon the target of criticism from some in the congregation for failing to follow proper budgetary procedures in funding the center. But that issue turned out to be merely the opening skirmish in a feud within the church between Reverend Ericksen and Bray, a battle that finally led to Bray's ouster and left Grace Lutheran scarred for years to come.

Although Bray was not a minister, he still chafed under the liberal Lutheran theology preached at Grace Lutheran. He believed that the Lutheran denomination to which Grace Lutheran belonged indulged in excessive modernism and, worse, adhered to a revisionist interpretation of the Holy Scriptures, heresy to a fundamentalist. He believed that Ericksen agreed with him but that he was too soft, too comfortable in his position, to rock the boat with the Lutheran hierarchy.

Bray liked to say that he held to a "high" view of Scriptures—that the Bible is truly the inerrant word of God—but that the Lutheran bishops to whom Ericksen and Grace Lutheran were beholden held a "low" view. By 1983, Bray began to push for a church fight with the Lutheran hierarchy, perhaps even a split from the denomination. Ericksen refused to go along.

Bray and Ericksen now put different spins on how their theological differences turned into a bitter war for control of Grace Lutheran. Bray says he confronted Ericksen and told him he was in "sin" for going along with the hierarchy. "You are not doing your job, protecting your sheep, your flock, from false teachings coming down from the top. . . . He [Ericksen] then said to me, 'You are charging me with sin.' And I said, 'Yes.'" Bray's Reformation beliefs had made him a theological fish out of water at Grace Lutheran. Now, Knox and Calvin were leading him to rebellion, a very different kind of rebellion than the one he had engaged in at the Naval Academy, but a rebellion nonetheless.

Ericksen, meanwhile, recalls that he returned home from a vacation in Israel to find that Bray was busy making major church decisions without his permission, in effect mounting a coup. "He had already started changing things; he was taking control of things that weren't in his assignment," says Ericksen. "It was a very disturbing thing to have happen. I asked for his resignation." Bray refused, and then he demanded that a five-member panel of church members judge the two men to determine who was responsible for the rift.

The panel called for reconciliation, but Ericksen no longer trusted Bray. He was convinced Bray wanted his church; Ericksen believed that Bray was using a Friday-night prayer group that he had established as a personal power base from which to manipulate the church's larger congregation. Finally, in the fall of 1983, Ericksen eliminated Bray's salary from the church budget, and Bray responded by calling on his supporters in the church to back him in a showdown with Ericksen. A congregation-wide vote on the church budget turned into a bitter referendum on Bray versus Ericksen.

Ericksen's wife claims that, prior to the meeting, members of Bray's prayer group began a feverish lobbying campaign. She says one member of Bray's group came to see her to ask her to stop sleeping with her husband—"to deny him conjugal rights"—until he agreed to let Bray stay. Bray says, in contrast, that infrequent churchgoers, "Easter-Christmas" Lutherans, were rounded up by Ericksen to pack the meeting and to cast votes in opposition to Bray and his hard theology. "These people despised me for what I was saying."

Ericksen clearly did pull out all the stops; he even brought the local bishop and other Lutheran officials to the budget meeting in November 1983, where they presented a united front, announcing that they firmly backed Ericksen and believed that Bray should be fired.

"The bishop said I had a real Calvinist view of Scriptures and that I should go. They held a vote and I was out of a job," Bray says. Bray left Grace Lutheran in December yet retained a core of support from members of his prayer group. Eight families agreed to follow him to found a new, more conservative church that would hew to the "reformed" teachings of Calvin and Knox. In 1984, they formed the tiny Reformation Lutheran Church of Bowie, meeting in school basements and rented halls, and "ordained" Bray their pastor.

While he was trying to start the new church, however, Bray needed a job. He turned to his friend and fellow abortion foe Thomas Spinks, who took him on at his home improvement business as a roofer and day laborer. At work, Bray and Spinks once again found common ground on abortion, and once again they began talking about what should be done about it.

Ostracized by his church, pushed into religious militancy by his feud with Ericksen and the Lutheran hierarchy, Bray finally felt free to act on his belief in the sublime power of God's unyielding justice. Before long, Bray and Spinks were planning clinic bombings.

"Before God, we both felt committed that we had to do all we could to save as many of these children as we could, short of destroying the human lives who took human lives," Spinks said later, when he testified against Bray in federal court as part of his own plea agreement. "In other words, it would be okay to destroy buildings . . . we viewed them as death camps. So we came to the agreement that it was okay to destroy these places as long as it was carefully carried out so that no human life would be lost in the process."

Their first target was the Reproductive Care Center, a clinic in Dover, Delaware, which Bray had scouted out while visiting nearby relatives. Early on the morning of January 14, 1984, just two months after Bray had been ousted from Grace Lutheran, he and Spinks drove through a brutal winter ice storm in Bray's yellow Honda from Maryland to Delaware. Things went bad right away: They had an accident on the ice-slicked Chesapeake Bay Bridge when Bray slid into the back of a van that had stopped to avoid a jackknifed tractor-trailer. Bray exchanged insurance information with the driver of the van and filed a $1,400 damage claim, which later provided police with critical evidence of his whereabouts. After debating whether to turn around, he and Spinks drove on through the darkness to Dover. This first arson was crude—they used nothing more sophisticated than homemade Molotov cocktails—yet it was still devastatingly effective. Spinks later provided a vivid word picture:

We drove past the clinic and went up maybe a quarter of a mile past the clinic. We pulled off on a side street, and I took a knife and poked holes in the top of the cans that were filled with gas. We opened up bottles that were capped and put rags in them. Then Mike drove back to the clinic and backed the car up to the front. We had a cinder block and a log for breaking through the glass, and the containers with gas and everything were inside a couple of cardboard boxes. So Mike opened the hatchback, and I grabbed a log and threw it through the door. Mike was to the right of me, and he threw a cinder block through the window, the big plate of glass. We began to throw the cans and things of gas inside. Mike got back in the car and closed the lid while I was lighting the Molotov cocktails, and I threw them through the window. As soon as I was sure everything was on fire, I began to move toward the car. I slipped and fell on the ice, and I half crawled and half pulled myself back into the car, and we drove away.

Remarkably, Bray and Spinks got away undetected. The Dover clinic was completely destroyed in the fire, and the two men vowed to repeat their act. Bray quickly sold the Honda.

Clearly the brains of the outfit, Bray picked the next target as well, the Hillcrest Clinic in Norfolk, Virginia. Bray believed that it made a perfect target, because its owner had just filed a lawsuit against local picketers. Bray had even visited the clinic to determine its layout and the best way to blow it up.

On February 17, Bray and Spinks, who had begun reading up on more sophisticated weapons, wired together seven pipe bombs and planted them against the outer wall of the clinic. Bray also left a small sign outside that read "AOG"— for Army of God—the same name used earlier by Don Benny Anderson during the Zevallos kidnapping.

Only one of the pipe bombs exploded, however, limiting the damage to the Norfolk clinic and providing agents from the Bureau of Alcohol, Tobacco and Firearms with their first break. After Norfolk, Bray started getting nervous and decided not to go with Spinks on any more bombing runs. He told Spinks he needed to protect his fledgling church, to get it up and running, and he did not think he could do that from behind bars. Instead, Bray would direct Spinks from a distance, suggesting targets and providing inside information on the clinics.

Bray found a perfect way to gather intelligence that spring, when he was asked to join John O'Keefe's Pro-Life Non-Violent Action Project (PNAP).

O'Keefe had spent years rebuilding his sit-in movement after the legal setbacks and injunctions of the late 1970s. Now, in the spring of 1984, after months of intensive recruiting in churches and right-to-life organizations, he was planning what he hoped would be the biggest act of civil disobedience in the history of the anti-abortion movement: a clinic sit-in by 1,000 people. O'Keefe printed up pledge cards for volunteers to sign, in which each promised that if 999 others agreed to participate in the sit-in, he or she would become the thousandth person to be arrested.

O'Keefe had turned over day-to-day organization of the Pro-Life Non-Violent Action Project to his young protégé, Harry Hand, a soft-spoken Catholic volunteer from Long Island who lived with O'Keefe and his family. While O'Keefe used his contacts around the country to attract other leading activists, Hand focused on recruiting priests and Protestant ministers in the Washington area.

Dave Gaetano had tried and failed five years earlier to recruit members of the clergy, but Hand had better luck. A large group of Dominican priests and monks, the order O'Keefe had once hoped to join, agreed to risk arrest, along with a handful of young and aggressive Protestant fundamentalists who were willing to put aside their distaste for Catholics to join O'Keefe and Hand. Michael Bray was among them.

Hand saw Bray as an important recruit, an enthusiastic member of the Protestant clergy in the process of founding a new church, an activist who had established a crisis pregnancy center, and someone who was ready to take the next step into civil disobedience. Bray and his wife, Jayne, signed up as soon as Hand came to see them. Says Bray, without a hint of irony, "They were talking about getting arrested. I thought, 'Getting arrested. That sounds like something we should do.'"

Before long, Bray became impatient, and he began to prod O'Keefe to quit recruiting and go ahead and launch his campaign. Despite his months of organizing, O'Keefe was far short of the 1,000 pledges he had hoped to receive. "'How many do you have?' I asked him," Bray recalls.

"He said maybe three hundred. I said, 'Let's just go. Let's do it.'"

O'Keefe finally agreed and scheduled the start of Pro-Life Non-Violent Action Project's renewed campaign for May 19 at a brand-new clinic in Gaithersburg, Maryland. Of the approximately three hundred who had signed cards, only about one hundred forty people showed up, yet that was still by far the biggest crowd O'Keefe had ever generated. With advance warning of O'Keefe's plans, the clinic shut down for the day, handing him an easy victory.

Only one activist was arrested: Joan Andrews, a young Catholic from Tennessee who insisted on going into the building to make sure that no abortions were being performed. Andrews and Tom Herlihy, a New Yorker who later became engaged to Andrews while she was in prison, were both irked that O'Keefe seemed so willing to declare victory without truly confronting the system. Andrews's extremist views would be put to the test two years later, when she was jailed for two years for breaking and entering and damaging equipment in a clinic in Pensacola, Florida. Her total refusal to cooperate with the Florida prison authorities ultimately transformed her into a martyr and rallying point for anti-abortion activists across the nation.

If Andrews and Herlihy were upset, however, O'Keefe barely noticed. He was ecstatic. Finally, this was it. He could feel his movement taking off. Throughout that summer, he staged more sit-ins and prayer vigils at the Gaithersburg clinic, all building toward one massive blockade, an event that would put him back on the map. It was scheduled for November 17, 1984.

"Rescue those being dragged to slaughter," his recruitment flyers said, in "the largest pro-life sit-in in the country."

Michael Bray would be there.

Thomas Spinks stayed away from the sit-ins, and Bray made certain that Spinks never attacked the Gaithersburg clinic, for fear of injuring protesters or perhaps drawing police suspicion directly on O'Keefe's movement. Yet federal prosecutors alleged that Bray took full advantage of his new ties to O'Keefe's group to aid Spinks in his bombings, through both intelligence gathering and the recruitment of potential accomplices.

"He would give me information about the clinics," Spinks said. "He would support and encourage me in what I did. He would pray for me. I needed it. He was involved actively in the pro-life movement and the picketing. As he was picketing, he would kind of go through the ranks of the pro-life people and search for any people in the movement who might be what we considered radical enough that they might be interested in being involved in what I was doing."

While Bray served as his mentor and father-confessor, Spinks was becoming a more sophisticated—and effective—bomber. The morning after Spinks's first solo job left a clinic in College Park, Maryland, in ruins, Bray and Spinks met for breakfast at a Roy Rogers fast-food restaurant a block away, with smoke still billowing out of the charred rubble. Bray was impressed: "Good job."

Bray directed Spinks toward ever more ambitious and brazen targets, and Spinks began working on ever-bigger bombs, with the help of another friend and abortion foe, Kenneth Shields. Shields was a Virginia accountant who owned a small business on the side that reclaimed silver from X-ray film, a process that required bulk chemical purchases.

Bray handed Spinks a brochure from the National Abortion Federation, headquartered in downtown Washington; Spinks blew it up on the Fourth of July 1984. Three days later, Spinks blew up the Planned Parenthood clinic in Annapolis, Maryland; he had upgraded to a deadlier bomb, a large CO_2 canister of the type used for fire extinguishers, filled with a mixture of sugar and potassium nitrate. Spinks drilled a hole in the canister for a fuse. The results were spectacular. "It was awesome," said Spinks, and he stuck mostly to the bulky canister bombs from then on. Because he needed someplace to keep them, Jayne Bray rented a storage locker, which she later testified that she believed contained only painting and construction supplies for her husband and Spinks and that Mike Bray and Spinks used it to hide the canisters and chemicals.

By late November, Spinks was anxious to go after the Gaithersburg clinic, but again Bray warned him off: O'Keefe was planning a major sit-in there. Instead, Spinks targeted Gail Frances's Metro Medical and Women's Center in Wheaton. Frances had hired twenty-four-hour guards to patrol the facility and deter bombers, but Spinks had been studying them and knew their secret: They were really there only twenty-one hours a day. That gave him plenty of time to get in and out.

O'Keefe's protests against the new Gaithersburg clinic had been so successful that as soon as the staff heard he was coming back in November, the owners arranged to close again. O'Keefe was again willing to accept that as a triumph, but he knew he had to find a way to satisfy his militant supporters, who yearned to get arrested. Therefore, two or three days before the Gaithersburg sit-in, O'Keefe and a handful of his organizers, including Harry Hand, secretly decided that on the morning of the event they would announce they were switching targets—to the Metro Medical and Women's Center clinic in Wheaton.

The sit-in on Saturday, November 17, was everything O'Keefe had hoped; forty-six people, including seventeen Catholic and Protestant members of the clergy, were arrested, which at the time was the largest number of arrests for any one anti-abortion event. More than one hundred demonstrators were blocking the clinic's doors while the arrests were being made, and the local media, led by the *Washington Post,* were out in full force to record the incident.

What the *Post* recorded was one of the first acts of 1980s-style anti-abortion street theater, a scene that would be repeated hundreds of times over the coming decade. The larger numbers outside the clinic entrance—this time a mix of both anti-abortion activists and the new volunteer abortion-rights escorts—changed the social dynamics of the scene, transforming it into an event unlike any of the tiny, half-forgotten sit-ins O'Keefe had staged in the 1970s.

O'Keefe had the crowd he had longed for, but with it came a raucous, barely controlled chaos that would become the movement's most enduring media image. The *Post* story the next day documented what would soon become familiar on the American cultural landscape: "Don't you care that they're killing babies by the minute?" ChristyAnne Collins of Falls Church asked a Montgomery County police officer as she sat cross-legged in front of the door to the clinic. "I'm not leaving," said Collins, who was then handcuffed and dragged to a police van. Members of a Baltimore pro-choice group, wearing white armbands and placards reading "Peacekeeper," escorted patients into the clinic as protesters yelled "Please don't go in there" and "Don't murder your baby." Inside the clinic's crowded waiting room, head nurse Lisa Ammerman told patients that they would not be disturbed. "Everyone has been arrested that's blocking the doorway, so you can rest assured that they won't get inside," Ammerman said.

Outside the Wheaton clinic, Michael Bray sat down with his young son in his arms, waiting quietly for the police to take him away. He offered a perfect image of nonviolent civil disobedience, one that was quickly captured by local television cameras and broadcast on that evening's newscasts.

At 8 A.M. on Monday, November 19, 1984, Harry Hand was jolted awake by the telephone. Still groggy, he soon recognized that the voice on the other end belonged to a Montgomery County, Maryland, police detective who had been tracking the sit-ins. "Harry," the detective asked casually, "what have you been doing this morning?"

"Nothing, you just woke me up. Why?"

"The clinic you were at this weekend just blew up."

"Oh, shit."

Thomas Spinks had been annoyed by O'Keefe's last-minute change from Gaithersburg to Wheaton, but he did not let that get in the way of his plans. He had already cased the place, and he did not want that effort to go to waste.

"All the pro-life people made a snap decision, I suppose, and went to this place in Wheaton," an impatient Spinks later said in federal court. "I had already determined that I was going to do it, so after they picketed there, then I blew it up immediately after they picketed. . . . It didn't look too good for the pro-life people."

Did Bray know beforehand that Spinks was going to violate their standing rule not to bomb clinics that were also targets of major acts of civil disobedience? Bray still refuses to comment directly. He says only, "It was a shocker. . . . It was well done."

By the time the police detective woke Harry Hand, Spinks had been hard at work for hours. He had been so busy that he did not have time for neatness or sophistication. In the predawn darkness, he took a canister bomb out of his car and simply tossed it through the window of the Wheaton clinic, which was located in a town house complex of medical and professional offices. He then drove a mile to a second clinic in nearby Rockville, Maryland, and left two bombs on the building's back sidewalk. The bombs at both facilities went off just after 6 A.M., eleven minutes apart; the Wheaton clinic was totally destroyed. The force of the blast sent the front door flying an estimated seventy-five feet, landing in a nearby residential neighborhood, and only luck prevented any deaths or injuries on the street.

The Wheaton blast finally made anti-abortion bombings national news. No one could miss the apparent connection between the sit-ins and the bombing two days later. The next day, White House spokesman Marlin Fitzwater was asked uncomfortable questions about President Reagan's position on the bombings, and a few days later, FBI director William Webster was grilled by reporters on how federal law enforcement officials were handling anti-abortion violence. When Webster insisted that the bombings did not constitute domestic terrorism, that investigating the bombings was not a job for the FBI but rather the ATF, his comments served only to stoke the controversy further. The FBI, still recovering from the damage done to its reputation by its involvement in infiltrating and spying during the antiwar and civil rights movements in the 1960s, through secret intelligence programs like its infamous COINTELPRO operations, was wary of getting drawn into yet another politically tinged investigation of protest groups. As a result, the FBI made a pointed determination that the bombings were not the work of terrorists and that the crimes were not serious enough to trigger an antiterrorist investigation by the FBI.

With the FBI taking a hands-off approach, there was suddenly enormous political pressure on the ATF to solve the bombings. That pressure soon trickled down directly on John O'Keefe and the Pro-Life Non-Violent Action Project.

O'Keefe was shattered by the Wheaton bombing; he could see his dream of a large-scale sit-in movement evaporating almost overnight. Troubling questions—from the press, from the clinics, from the churches, even from supporters—poured in. O'Keefe's ambition of winning widespread public support for civil disobedience disappeared as ATF agents and local police sifted through photographs taken at his protests in their search for suspects. O'Keefe himself had to submit to a polygraph test for the ATF.

"It was a shot in the heart for the work we had done," remembers Hand. "We had worked so hard. . . . Here we had a rescue, and we're moving along, and then somebody goes and blows up the same clinic and you say, 'My God.' You know, it just didn't make sense."

O'Keefe had no idea who had committed the bombings and in fact harbored suspicions that abortion-rights extremists might have set off the Wheaton blast to destroy his movement. When the reporters crowded in, demanding a statement on whether the Pro-Life Non-Violent Action Project was truly nonviolent, O'Keefe seemed paralyzed; he found it impossible to take a firm public stand against the violence. When he spoke out, he seemed to go public with the doubts he had expressed in his letter to Scheidler about Don Benny Anderson a year earlier.

"Yes, it [the bombing] is just," O'Keefe told the *Washington Post* hours after the bombing. "Is it prudent? No. [But] it is just to respond to violence against people by destroying property. Human life is far more valuable than property. Pro-lifers are going to act. . . . The question is what shape will the action take."

O'Keefe's statement served only to tar his movement, to make it impossible for clergy members or other community leaders to continue to have any ties to him or his supporters. ChristyAnne Collins, who had been quoted in the *Post* at the Wheaton sit-in, was eventually ostracized from her church for her refusal to swear off the movement.

Worse, O'Keefe failed to control who was allowed to act as a spokesperson for his group in the wake of the bombing. Almost immediately, Jayne Bray, who had joined the Pro-Life Non-Violent Action Project with Mike, stepped in to fill the vacuum.

"I am personally opposed to the destruction of property, but I respect the right of people who do it where babies are being slaughtered," Jayne Bray told the *Post* the day of the bombing, in a story that identified her as a member of O'Keefe's group. "I don't know who they [the bombers] are. . . . I know no babies will be killed today. I'm not sad that clinic is not in operation today. I would be just as happy if it was struck by lightning."

Harry Hand, unlike O'Keefe and Jayne Bray, offered a quick and unqualified denunciation. "I was really angry about it happening," he told the *Post*. "The work we're doing, it totally shoots it down. There are a lot of minds and hearts to win over. Blowing up clinics only hardens hearts."

Hand's statement was too little, too late. A month later, early on Christmas morning, three massive bombs rocked two clinics and a doctor's office in Pensacola, Florida, sites that had also been frequent targets of protest. It was becoming harder for the public and the media to tell the difference between leaders like O'Keefe—leaders who could not bring themselves clearly and simply to denounce the violence—and the bombers themselves. O'Keefe had devoted his life to nonviolent civil disobedience, but now, at the moment when his movement most needed brave and disciplined leadership, he hesitated and ultimately failed to provide it.

In his rush to bomb as many clinics as possible, Spinks was getting sloppy. He bought his CO_2 canisters in bulk from a wholesaler and then made large purchases of chemicals from retailers and chemical distributors, using the same false name, Lou Burns. According to James Moore's book *Very Special Agents*, which includes details of the ATF's role in the case, the ATF now launched an intensive and wide-ranging investigation, involving forensics work on the materials used in the bombings and the tedious culling of receipts at chemical suppliers, metal fabricators, and other contractors in the mid-Atlantic region. The "AOG" sign that Bray had left outside the Norfolk clinic prompted the ATF to interview friends and associates of Don Benny Anderson. The federal agents went down one dead end after another and made little progress for months. Finally, ATF agents found a serial number from a fragment of one of the exploded tanks, traced it back to the F&M Fire Protection Company in Hyattsville, Maryland, and found that the tank with that serial number had been purchased by Lou Burns. Soon, the ATF found invoices for Lou Burns's bulk purchases of chemicals from local chemical suppliers; at one supplier, Lou Burns had claimed to work for Shields Industries, Ken Shields's silver-extraction company.

Confronted, Shields confessed, just as other evidence, including a fingerprint, linked Spinks. After Shields and Spinks were arrested, ATF agents opened the Spinks-Bray storage locker and saw it all: chemicals, canisters, hardware. The ATF also found Bray's name in Spinks's notebook, and Spinks's wife told investigators she had seen Bray go into Spinks's workshop with her husband. Oddly, Bray was already under suspicion by the ATF, initially because of an erroneous tip from an anonymous caller to a local television station. The caller said he had been out jogging early on the morning of the bombing and claimed that the man shown on the news coverage of O'Keefe's protests holding his infant son while awaiting arrest had also been outside the Wheaton clinic just before the blast. Bray had been interviewed by the ATF and put under surveillance; he gave a hair sample to investigators that matched hair found with one bomb.

On January 18, 1985, just as anti-abortion demonstrators from across the country were arriving in Washington for their annual march on the twelfth anniversary of the Supreme Court's *Roe* decision, the ATF arrested Michael Bray. "This was the biggest anti-abortion bombing case the federal government had ever had, and what made it bigger was the fact that you had someone who had been a leading activist in the movement," observes Robert Mathias, a former assistant U.S. attorney in Baltimore who prosecuted Bray.

However, the government had much better physical evidence against Shields and Spinks than it did against Bray, who, with the backing of his small church congregation, loudly proclaimed his innocence. Shields was not talking, which meant that the government would have to turn up the heat on Thomas Spinks.

O'Keefe and Hand both shuddered when they heard Bray's name announced on the local television news; they knew instinctively what it meant to their movement, so they refused to believe what they heard. Hand went to see Daniel Bray to ask if the charges against his brother were true. Hand returned to O'Keefe to report that "Dan says Mike is innocent."

"Yes, innocent," said O'Keefe's skeptical sister, knowing the possible double meaning of that answer. "But did he do it?"

Hand trudged back to see Dan again and this time got a more specific denial. "Dan says he didn't do it." Finally convinced, O'Keefe and Hand began a campaign to free Mike Bray, a man they now saw as their movement's first political prisoner. They found Bray high-priced Washington lawyers, Robert Muse and Gerald Mitchell, and then launched a legal defense fund to pay their fees. Along with Daniel Bray, they circulated pamphlets explaining Bray's plight, asking for donations, and using Bray's arrest as a rallying point for further protests.

"As most of you are already aware, Michael Bray, a member of PNAP, was falsely arrested and accused in connection with the Washington D.C.–area abortion clinic bombings," wrote Hand in a newsletter published in early 1985. "He is innocent. Keep the Brays in your prayers and in mind when you're deciding whether to sit-in or not."

The Bray legal defense fund was quite successful, raising nearly thirty-five thousand dollars. On the Friday before Bray's trial began, however, Harry Hand got a curious call from the lawyers he and

O'Keefe had hired for Bray. "They asked me to come downtown for lunch," recalls Hand. "I went down and saw Mitchell and Muse, and basically . . . I was told to back off" from further fund-raising for Bray's legal defense. "They said it wasn't so clear that he was innocent. The picture wasn't as clear as I thought."

The situation was actually much worse than the attorneys were letting on. Thomas Spinks had just cut a deal to become the government's star witness against Michael Bray.

S pinks's decision to cooperate with federal prosecutors proved to be devastating to Bray's case, and Bray's lawyers and his family knew it. In fact, during Bray's trial, federal prosecutors strongly implied that Jayne Bray mounted a campaign of intimidation, couched in the language of Christian fundamentalism, to try to make sure that Thomas Spinks would keep his mouth shut. She admitted during her testimony in the case that she sent seventeen anonymous letters to Spinks while he was in jail, before Bray's trial, to try to "bolster his spirits."

"I'm sure there are great temptations by the evil one to give in and say, what's the use," she wrote in one unsigned letter to Spinks. "But the eyes of many Christians are on you and we are so encouraged by your suffering."

Although Jayne Bray was never charged in the bombings, federal prosecutors repeatedly hinted at her involvement during her husband's trial. Those hints were never thoroughly explored by the government, however, and she denied any knowledge of the bombings. Yet she confirmed in court that she had blurted out a damaging statement when ATF agents came to arrest her husband.

"The night of your husband's arrest, you asked one of the ATF agents how the ATF had found you and your husband, didn't you?" Mathias asked Jayne Bray on the stand.

"Yes I did."

"You asked them who told the ATF about you and your husband, didn't you?

"Yes I did."

In addition, Jayne Bray's testimony in her husband's trial was highlighted by a provocative and telling statement, one that certainly did not do much for her husband's defense: "I am tickled pink with the results [of the bombings]. I am happy that that suction machine is not there to

destroy that baby. . . . I am happy that that abortion clinic is not in operation."

As he sat in the courtroom listening to the trial, O'Keefe, now convinced that Bray was guilty, slowly came to believe that Jayne Bray had
played a complex and largely hidden role in prodding her husband into
his extremism. Mike Bray was an intense and complicated man,
O'Keefe now knew, but perhaps not as intense and complicated as his
wife.

"I think Jayne Bray is a woman of enormous sexual energy, and
because she is a Christian, she has focused all that energy on one man,"
O'Keefe later said. "I think that she knew how to get him to do what she
wanted."

In fact, Jayne Bray later emerged as a major activist and leader in her
own right while her husband was in jail, becoming for a time a key
member of the inner circle of Operation Rescue and lead plaintiff in a
major Supreme Court case—*Bray v. Alexandria Health Services*—challenging the constitutionality of court injunctions against clinic sit-ins.

Despite Jayne Bray's anonymous letters, Spinks talked and gave up
Michael Bray in exchange for a lighter sentence. His betrayal of
Bray in turn uncovered Bray's betrayal of O'Keefe and Hand. It was a
story of faith and fallen men worthy of the Old Testament, and it
spelled the end of the Pro-Life Non-Violent Action Project.

"I felt betrayed, very much betrayed," says Hand, still bitter more
than a decade later. "You get burned and hurt."

O'Keefe and Hand had been fooled by Bray in part because, after his
arrest and throughout his trial, Bray had avoided talking directly to
either man about his guilt or innocence and, instead, had left it up to
his uninformed brother Daniel to answer their questions. With little
else to go on, O'Keefe and Hand had assumed Bray was innocent; they
took at face value the statements he made in an interview with the
Washington Post immediately after his arrest, when he insisted he had
been framed and that he was not guilty of the charges brought against
him. At the time, that statement was technically accurate; the initial
arrest warrant was narrowly drawn, charging him only with having been
a direct participant in one of the bombings that Spinks had committed

alone. After the charges were redrawn and his brother Daniel was under pressure from Hand and others to state his innocence, Bray refused to answer. Daniel Bray drew from his brother's silence his own inaccurate conclusions.

When Bray saw that the fund-raising letters written on his behalf stated unequivocally that he was innocent, he finally told Daniel that he had "trouble with the wording" but refused to explain himself. Finally, his father told him to leave the fund-raising to his brother and to the PNAP leadership.

To this day, Bray has never publicly talked about the facts surrounding his case, but he recently came closer to admitting guilt than ever before by acknowledging that he regrets that he "acquiesced" in the distribution of a fund-raising appeal that he knew inaccurately depicted him as an innocent man.

"I do have regrets about the fact that they came to my aid on the assumption that I had not done it and that there was no involvement," Bray says now. "I think Harry [Hand] in particular felt used. He thought I was some doctrinaire pacifist and that I wouldn't do these things. And then things came out at the trial."

Thanks to Spinks's testimony, Bray was convicted in May 1985 of two counts of conspiracy and one count of possessing unregistered explosive devices, but he was acquitted on two other counts of possession. After he was sentenced to ten years in prison, his conviction was reversed in 1986 on a technicality related to jury selection. Instead of a retrial, in 1987 Bray entered an "Alford plea," under which he did not admit guilt but conceded there was enough evidence to convict him. He received a six-year sentence and was released from prison in 1989. He spent nearly four years in prison and was one of the first major "prisoners of conscience" of the militant wing of the anti-abortion movement. Both Spinks and Shields pleaded guilty on bombing-related charges and also spent time in federal prison.

O'Keefe tried to stage more sit-ins, but his Washington civil disobedience campaign never recovered from its association with Bray, and it soon faded away. In 1988, John O'Keefe participated in his last small sit-in, in southern California, just before Operation Rescue came onto the scene.

In a plaintive letter to U.S. District Judge Alexander Harvey in June

1985, seeking a light sentence after his conviction, Bray promised that he would "not engage in or encourage others to engage in the bombing, burning or destruction of abortion-related facilities in the future." Yet he emerged from prison in 1989 to become one of the nation's leading advocates of clinic bombings and later of the murder of abortion providers. He and Jayne eventually had nine children, naming one Beseda, in honor of Curt Beseda, a convicted clinic bomber from the Pacific Northwest.

"My legacy?" Bray asks. "Upholding truth. And clarifying what it is."

Yet Bray's continued caution about how much he is willing to say about his own case, despite the fact that he has already served his time, raises more questions. In part, his reluctance stems from his fear that he is still a target of federal investigators searching for clues that a conspiracy lies behind ongoing anti-abortion violence. But in an interview, he suggests other, far more intriguing reasons for maintaining silence on the details of the bombings:

"I've kept silent about the facts of the case," he says. "I still maintain my silence with Daniel [his brother]. Some of the reasons for doing so probably aren't there anymore. But I haven't evaluated enough whether I should speak about it.

"There are other matters, though, that I have to reevaluate. I believe it was right. But let me give you an example. Suppose there were other people involved [who were never arrested], and for good reasons they wish not to be known?"

5

THE NEW MILITANTS
Joseph Scheidler, Francis Schaeffer, and Jerry Falwell

John O'Keefe fathered "rescue"; Michael Bray provided the theological justification for clinic violence; but it was Joseph Scheidler of Chicago who founded the militant wing of the anti-abortion movement. In the late 1970s and early 1980s, Scheidler, a twice-failed candidate for Catholic religious orders, played a critical role in melding the disparate strands—O'Keefe's style of quiet civil disobedience and Bray's hot brand of extremism—into something new. An inveterate social and political networker, Scheidler bridged the gap between the advocates of "a peaceful presence" and the advocates of biblical retribution; by uniquely combining the two he created the loud, volatile, and slightly dangerous activism that became the hallmark of the anti-abortion movement in the 1980s.

Scheidler made his name barnstorming the countryside championing acts of anti-abortion protest and harassment while generating national headlines by voicing support for extremists who bombed clinics. He was a big bear of a man, a hulking six feet four inches tall, weighing between 230 and 250 pounds, and he was quite capable of dominating a picket line or shouting down his smaller foes, who were usually women. His trademark beard, deep baritone voice (amplified by his ever-present bullhorn), and ill-fitting black and white three-piece suits together lent him a sinister air. A tradition-bound Catholic and the father of seven children, Scheidler was, until Operation Rescue founder Randall Terry came on the scene, the anti-abortion leader who feminists most loved to hate. "He was just damned scary," shudders Ann Baker, a leading abortion-rights activist and researcher.

Scheidler was the first of a new breed of purposefully outrageous and judgmental anti-abortion activists to become a national figure and the first to challenge the authority and influence of the American Catholic bishops over the anti-abortion movement. He was also the first to make an open break with the right-to-life mainstream, which he dismissed as weak and irresolute. After serving for three years as the first director of the Right to Life Committee in his home state of Illinois, Scheidler was fired for his radical tactics; however, it was more of a divorce by mutual consent. Scheidler believed that the mainstream right-to-life movement was so tied to America's political and financial establishment that its leaders would never treat abortion as actual murder even though they believed it was, would never challenge the Supreme Court's authority to establish laws, and could never countenance violence.

Nevertheless, Scheidler used his uneasy connections to the mainstream whenever it suited him, twice joining right-to-life leaders in their private White House meetings with President Ronald Reagan. During his second, and last, Reagan meeting, Scheidler stunned White House staffers and the mainstream anti-abortion leaders in attendance by asking Reagan to meet personally with the family of Don Benny Anderson, the man convicted of bombing clinics and kidnapping an abortion doctor. "A cold chill came over the room," Scheidler remembers. He was never invited back.

Defending his rift with the mainstream right-to-life movement, Scheidler once wrote that "I am not in the pro-life movement to make other pro-life leaders comfortable. I am in the pro-life movement to save the lives of unborn children. Some pro-life directors have spoken about winning brownie points by condemning violence. I am not interested in brownie points. . . . We are at war with a grave moral and social evil."

Still, Scheidler thought of himself as a pragmatist, willing to try anything that worked. When abortion clinic administrators charged that his use of a bullhorn outside their windows led to stress and a higher incidence of complications among patients, Scheidler took that as a compliment; he was having an impact. After hearing that an eleven-year-old Chicago girl was scheduled for an abortion, Scheidler and his followers formed a picket line at the hospital specifically to put pressure on the girl and her mother. He later shrugged off criticism that he was heartless: "Everybody had this image of this skinny little girl. She was a big girl. It wasn't like it was going to kill her to have a baby." When activists in his group covertly obtained dead fetuses from a Chicago pathology laboratory used by a large number of abortion clinics, Scheidler casually stored them in his children's playhouse in his backyard, waiting until he could use them for their shock value in protests, one more element in his campaign to win hearts and minds.

Many of his tricks and gimmicks failed, but some worked. In 1978, when he heard about some of the first sit-ins at abortion clinics, he invited the leader of a small St. Louis sit-in group to come to Chicago to explain the tactic to his organization. Scheidler soon was leading sit-ins of his own in Chicago and talking up the idea around the country.

Above all, he was an indefatigable recruiter, always traveling, always on the lookout for the young and the frustrated who would be willing to follow his lead into militant action. After he began to proselytize among young right-to-lifers in the late 1970s, Scheidler led a whole generation away from stuffing envelopes and licking stamps to take the battle out into the streets.

Scheidler "played very heavily into a lot of people's involvement," recalls Andrew Burnett, a Portland, Oregon, activist and former Operation Rescue leader who eventually moved to the extremist fringe. To Burnett and others, Scheidler's early vision of nationwide, coordinated protest was a revelation: "I remember listening to him talk. . . . It was like, wow, we can actually accomplish something here if we all get together and work and organize."

Scheidler's influence and his national reach came largely from his unique ability to manipulate the media, to leverage his protests into big news so that he—and the movement—could not be ignored. A former newspaperman, journalism professor, and public relations man, Scheidler knew exactly what reporters wanted, and he gave it to them on a platter.

"He was great at coming up with good sound bites," observes Don Treshman, an early Scheidler follower and later a militant leader in his own right. "Most pro-lifers at the time didn't know how to do that."

Scheidler understood far better than his rivals in the mainstream that by controlling the spin, by offering outrageous and combative sound bites, he could transform himself into a national spokesman for the movement, eclipsing staid establishment leaders who had never learned that the media hate the predictable. In his 1985 book *Closed: 99 Ways to Stop Abortion,* which was to become the how-to manual of the militant wing of the anti-abortion movement, Scheidler shrewdly observed that "conflict is always newsworthy. If there is a chance of confrontation, the press is more likely to cover the event." One chapter in the book is entitled "Use Inflammatory Rhetoric."

"The whole point of Joe," says friend and former colleague Tom Roeser, is "make it memorable. Be outrageous."

Scheidler's press-baiting skills were instinctive. He proved that one rainy Mother's Day in Chicago, while leading a demonstration that seemed to everyone else a total bust. The weather kept the turnout down to a handful of the faithful, and the press contingent was limited to one lonely cameraman from a local TV station. When Scheidler saw the disappointed cameraman packing up to leave, he improvised. Scheidler ran to an empty playground, found a swing set, and began to push the empty swings through the air. He cried out to the cameraman that the swings symbolized the "lives of the children who will not be born" because of abortion. That night Scheidler's protest, highlighted by the vision of the empty swings silently heaving back and forth through their arc, was all over the local news.

"Who in the world," marvels Roeser, "would've thought of doing that?"

For years, Scheidler was the only activist who could generate significant press coverage and public attention, and in a protest movement that ability translates into power and influence. At a time when sit-ins by small, isolated groups like O'Keefe's Washington organization were being ignored, Scheidler was already the man the press turned to for radical quotes when a clinic was bombed or the Supreme Court issued a new abortion ruling.

Much to the chagrin of mainstream leaders, Scheidler used his notoriety and celebrity to cajole and prod the movement toward militancy and away from the political compromise, accommodation, and marginal victories that the National Right to Life Committee and the Catholic Church had come to accept by the late 1970s.

When a clinic blew up, Scheidler told reporters that he would "shed no tears over bricks and mortar." If extremists were arrested for violence, Scheidler rushed to their defense, flying around the country to visit them in jail, picketing their trials, and issuing public statements in support of them. "Your editorial refers to the bombers as 'the fringe,'" Scheidler wrote to a Catholic newspaper in 1986. "Have you ever bothered to go talk with these 'fringe' people? . . . I have. I know them all." All the while he was generating public debate about extremism in the name of fighting abortion, but more important, he was increasing the visibility of Joseph Scheidler.

His tactics worked; Scheidler's infamy spread rapidly. Making a prison visit to convicted clinic bomber Curtis Beseda, Scheidler was taken aback by the extraordinarily close supervision ordered by prison officials. Other convicts were enjoying more relaxed visits with friends and relatives. He soon found that the extra security was not prompted by concerns about Beseda. "It's you they're keeping an eye on," Beseda told Scheidler.

Press attention brought speaking invitations from anti-abortion groups around the country, and Scheidler turned each engagement into a recruiting trip, encouraging local leaders who seemed willing to follow his militant example. He began to build a formidable contact network as a result. He made it his business to get to know every key anti-abortion figure in the United States, and before long he was serving as a central clearinghouse for gossip and information among those who shared his frustration over the paralysis of the mainstream movement. Ultimately, Scheidler's contacts formed the basis for a new activist network that by the mid-1980s was setting the agenda for the movement, leaving National Right to Life in its shadow.

The contacts and personal relationships that led to the formation of Operation Rescue, and nearly every other militant anti-abortion organization in the late 1980s and early 1990s, were almost all first made through Joseph Scheidler. Thanks to Scheidler, there were, in effect, two anti-abortion movements: one mainstream and polite, focused on the corridors of Congress, and one radical and impolite, focused on the doorways of American abortion clinics.

Scheidler was successful in drawing others to his new militancy because his timing was so right. By the late 1970s, the failure of the right-to-life cause was becoming painfully obvious, not just to Scheidler but to hundreds of others within the movement, and their frustrations were building to a boiling point.

To the dismay of the small but steady stream of young activists like John O'Keefe who were being drawn to the cause, the years after *Roe v. Wade* had seen a dramatic rise in the acceptance of abortion in the United States. By 1980, the number of abortions performed annually in the country had soared to more than 1.5 million, double the 1973 figure. The United States soon had the highest abortion rate in the industrialized world. (Abortions leveled off at the 1980 rate, finally declining in the 1990s owing to changing demographics.)

By 1982, there were nearly three thousand clinics, hospitals, and other medical facilities providing abortion services throughout the nation, with freestanding clinics performing the majority. When *Roe* was issued in 1973, many obstetricians thought abortions would have to be performed in hospitals by specialists, but it soon became clear that the procedure could be done safely, and more cheaply, on an outpatient basis, leading to the development of the abortion clinic industry. (Many obstetrician-gynecologists also felt that it was too emotionally wrenching to place women recovering from abortions in the same maternity wards with women who had just given birth, recalls Jeannie Rosoff, president of the Alan Guttmacher Institute, the research affiliate of Planned Parenthood.) Abortion thus lead the way for expanded outpatient care for other medical procedures when hospital costs and medical insurance premiums began to soar.

By 1983, the Supreme Court recognized the new status of freestanding clinics in a series of related decisions led by the *City of Akron v. Akron Center for Reproductive Health*, ruling that it was unconstitutional for cities or states to require that all abortions after the first trimester of pregnancy be performed in full-service hospitals. Consolidation and economies of scale soon led to the development of regional and nationwide chains; abortion clinics became part of the accepted urban and suburban landscape. Abortions became so easily accessible that between 1976 and 1981 the real cost of an abortion fell 28 percent, and the time that elapsed between a woman's first contact with a clinic and the scheduling of an abortion declined significantly as well.

A profession and an industry had grown up, giving newfound institutional stature and power to providers who had faced the threat of criminal prosecution and community ostracism little more than a decade earlier. Even more significant is the fact that the anti-abortion consensus that had existed in the United States in the pre-*Roe* 1960s had all but vanished. When the Gallup Organization conducted its first poll on American attitudes concerning abortion in 1962, it found that only 10 percent of those surveyed believed abortion should be made available to women "on demand." A 1980 survey found that 25 percent of Americans supported abortion "on demand," which was a loaded phrase that by then had come to signify intense political support for abortion. An additional 53 percent believed abortion should be available in a wide range of circumstances; 78 percent thus accepted the idea that women had the right to choose. It had taken Americans just seven years to come to terms with *Roe*.

Politicians, even Catholic public officials, read the poll numbers and came down on the abortion-rights side. Many were still unwilling to say so forthrightly, however, leading to a barrage of contorted public statements and increasing cynicism on the part of the press and the public.

New York governor Mario Cuomo, a rising star in the Democratic Party, set the tone in a speech at the University of Notre Dame in 1984. Cuomo and Geraldine Ferraro, a fellow New York Catholic and Walter Mondale's vice presidential running mate, both had been engaged in an ongoing feud with Archbishop John J. O'Connor of New York over their refusal to abide the church's teachings on abortion. Cuomo had accepted the Notre Dame speaking engagement to respond to the Catholic hierarchy. He said that although he personally opposed abortion, most voters supported a woman's right to choose, and so he would give the people what they wanted. "I accept the church's teaching on abortion," Cuomo said. "Must I insist you do? By law? By denying you Medicaid funding? By a constitutional amendment? If so, which one?"

There was nothing wrong with Cuomo's pragmatic political choice, except he sought to depict it as an act of moral and philosophical courage. Cuomo warned other Catholic politicians against imposing their religious and moral values on the nation, because other groups might "someday force theirs on us." Despite his philosophical inconsistencies, Cuomo's speech was widely praised in the press, and it gave other politicians the cover they needed to follow his lead. Further political protection came in the polls at the end of the 1984 presidential race. Although Ronald Reagan won reelection in a landslide, only 4 percent of the voters surveyed by pollsters for the *New York Times* and CBS News said they would cast their ballots on the basis of the abortion issue. Jack Willke, president of National Right to Life, tried to claim credit for Reagan's landslide, insisting that "the abortion issue clearly was a significant part of the Reagan-Bush sweep." But Nanette Falkenberg, executive director of the National Abortion Rights Action League, just as strenuously disagreed, saying that while abortion "was highly visible through the campaign season," most voters "were uninfluenced by the debate" and "remained strongly pro-choice."

A deep sense of malaise among anti-abortion activists was setting in as a result of the political stalemate, especially among young Catholics. For all those looking for someone to lead them to a new way of protest, there was Joseph Scheidler.

The day the *Roe* decision was issued in 1973, Joe Scheidler was home sick in bed from his public relations job in Chicago. "I got up and started reading about it and hearing about it; I went into a deep, deep depression."

Scheidler read the *Roe* decision over and over. He wrote letters to the Supreme Court justices, wrote letters to newspapers, and read books and articles about abortion; when he returned to work, he tried to discuss the issue with his colleagues. Nobody seemed to care.

His new obsession began to take over his life. "I couldn't concentrate on my work. It seemed so banal to be writing copy for Marlite paneling, Richardson Ink, Shakespeare fishing tackle. My whole personality seemed to change. I had a cause."

"He wasn't the same person," remembers his brother, Jim Scheidler.

Scheidler's boss soon became impatient. He politely told Scheidler that he should go to work on the abortion issue full-time and agreed to keep him on the payroll for a few months while he tried to form an anti-abortion organization. By June 1973, Scheidler was on his own. Unable to start his own organization from scratch, Scheidler convinced the Illinois Right to Life Committee to hire him as its director in January 1974.

Illinois Right to Life had been formed in 1969 by a group of affluent and well-connected Catholic doctors, lawyers, and businesspeople. The job offered Scheidler just $12,000 a year, a big cut from the $20,000 he had been earning in his public relations job, but he took to it with a newfound zeal. Within two years, he had expanded the group's membership from five thousand to twenty thousand.

It was not long, however, before Scheidler began to feel stifled by the limitations the leadership of Illinois Right to Life placed on the group's actions. Abortion could not be stopped by handbills, speeches to the Rotary Club, and letters to Congress. Scheidler took his first big step toward militancy in June 1977, when he heard that Senator Birch Bayh, an Indiana Democrat and an abortion-rights advocate, was scheduled to give the commencement address at St. Joseph's College, a Catholic school in Rensselaer, Indiana, not far from Chicago.

Scheidler was outraged; his rich uncle had given millions to the school. Already frustrated that the Catholic hierarchy was doing so little to protest abortion, Scheidler could not believe they were actually condoning abortion rights by inviting Bayh to a Catholic college. "Unless he is disinvited, or unless you let me speak from the same platform to express my grievance, I'm coming down," Scheidler threatened in a phone conversation with college officials.

"What are you going to do?"

"I don't know. I'll think of that on the way."

Scheidler arrived just as the graduation ceremony was beginning in the gymnasium. Wearing a white hat, white suit, and white shoes and carrying a bullhorn, he made his way to the top of the bleachers. When Bayh began to speak, Scheidler stood, punched the button on the bullhorn, and bellowed, "Birch Bayh, the pro-abortion senator of Indiana, is bringing scandal to this college, dedicated to St. Joseph, patron of the Catholic Church, and it's an insult to you students."

That was all Scheidler could say before the booing began. Moments later, he was escorted out by police.

An irate faculty member confronted him. "We can't believe you'd do this."

"You know," Scheidler quickly replied, "I always thought this was a Catholic college."

Scheidler made his name with the Bayh incident, which gave him his first taste of press attention; he began to understand the power of militant actions to generate headlines in a way that quiet lobbying and letter-writing campaigns could not. But Scheidler's colleagues at Illinois Right to Life were getting more and more uneasy about his tactics, especially as he began to pull more stunts designed to create controversy. He caused a scene when he took seventy protesters into an abortion clinic's public open house. He put up posters of aborted fetuses around the Loop. He passed out anti-abortion flyers in rush-hour traffic downtown. And he waged a graffiti war, spray-painting construction sites and sidewalks outside abortion clinics with anti-abortion slogans.

In 1978, Scheidler heard that a small group of student activists had just staged a sit-in at an abortion clinic in St. Louis, and he was intrigued; Scheidler had picketed, but sit-ins sounded more effective. He invited Sam Lee, the leader of the St. Louis group, to Chicago to learn more about the concept.

Lee "laid out the whole thing," Scheidler recalls. "You case the clinic, you send somebody in as a patient to find out the layout as best they can and make a sketch. We had a great big storage room upstairs, and so we chalked off the layout of the whole clinic. The rooms, the chairs, the waiting room. We planned the whole thing; every move."

After a training session, they were ready for their first sit-in. Their target: Concord Medical Center on West Grand in Chicago. On March 11, 1978, about three dozen protesters jammed up against the clinic door. Some went inside, locking arms and blocking the hallway, chanting, "All we are saying / is give life a chance." Outside, dozens of others carried signs with slogans like "Adoption, Not Abortion" and "Life Ends Here." The demonstrators adopted the same name then in use in St. Louis, PEACE (People Expressing a Concern for Everyone).

Scheidler did not participate in the sit-in and did not risk arrest. He was too busy making sure the protest got enough press coverage. "The police allowed us a lot of time to give interviews and explain what was happening," he wrote excitedly to supporters at the time. "We had all three major stations, several radio stations, and the two remaining daily newspapers. Radio reports began almost at once and continued all day."

Scheidler considered the sit-in a major success, but he also knew that it might be the final straw for his association with Illinois Right to Life. After the sit-in, he hurriedly wrote to a supporter that he was preparing to set up a new office "in the event that the ax falls when my beloved board convenes to fire me."

He was right. Shortly after the sit-in, the board of directors asked Scheidler to leave. Tom Roeser, a former vice president at Quaker Oats, was one of only two board members who voted to retain him. "He had a vision of activism, and the Illinois Right to Life group was determined to just simply pass out leaflets and write letters," says Roeser. "They were terribly worried about tax status, almost unduly so. And Joe was trying to push them into activism."

Scheidler landed on his feet, establishing a group called Friends for Life in April 1978, along with Roeser and the Reverend Charles Fiore, a Dominican priest. Scheidler was named executive director. The new group mounted sit-ins about every six weeks, prompting arrests for his followers but not for Scheidler himself. (His first arrest did not come until 1983.)

It was not long before Scheidler's new Friends for Life group was developing a nationwide reputation for being one of the most militant, hard-core anti-abortion organizations of its day. Columnist Pat Buchanan called Friends for Life the Green Berets of the right-to-life movement. Scheidler was never arrested while he led Friends for Life, but he was so pleased with the Green Beret label that he included it in his résumé.

Soon, however, Scheidler faced a rerun of his experience at Illinois Right to Life, when the board of Friends for Life became wary of Scheidler's illegal tactics. "He was difficult—impossible—to manage," recalls Roeser. When asked by Roeser at least to keep him informed of his plans for protests, Scheidler refused, saying, "These ideas hit me at midnight."

At one Friends for Life meeting, chronicled by a *Chicago Sun-Times* reporter pretending to be a new recruit, Scheidler outlined his next project: defacing placards belonging to the Chicago Transit Authority (CTA). He handed out cans of spray paint and maps of CTA routes. "If you're caught, you're on your own," members were told. "If anyone asks, tell them you're an irate citizen or something . . . do not implicate anyone else or say you got this stuff from Friends for Life."

By 1980, Scheidler was ousted after a bitter internal battle that divided Scheidler and his old friend Roeser. Before the dust had settled, Scheidler formed another group, the Pro-Life Action League; he was his own boss now. He had learned his lesson, and this time he set up a tame board, naming himself, his wife, and one close friend as the only directors.

Scheidler immediately began serious fund-raising, using old Right to Life and Friends for Life mailing lists while developing new ones. He found his maudlin charms and marketing skills often worked on older supporters, who then named his group in their wills. One woman left the Pro-Life Action League 25 percent of her Federal Employees Group Life Insurance benefit; another left the organization $25,000.

With his own organization, Scheidler began to experiment with a wide-ranging menu of militant tactics to see what worked. He thought a single-minded focus on sit-ins was too narrow and constricting. He attended conventions of the National Abortion Federation to learn more about the cause he was fighting, and he was one of the first activists to focus on doctors as the "weak link" of the abortion industry. He soon began trying to convert as many of them as possible to the anti-abortion movement.

Scheidler joined forces with some doctors who quit performing abortions and arranged press conferences and speaking engagements for them to speak out against abortion. He ultimately produced a "Meet the Abortion Providers" video, which he sold for $19.95. Doctors who refused to quit were subjected to personal and professional harassment. "If you can't convert them, then get them to quit," he wrote later. "Not violently, but any other way. Make it unpleasant to be an abortionist. Call their wives . . . get their landlord to kick them out. . . . Find out where he lives, and pick a time when his neighbors will be home. . . . Carry signs that mention the name of the abortionist in conjunction with the word abortion. Leaflet the entire neighborhood around his home just prior to the picket."

Scheidler eventually decided that his most effective tactic was "sidewalk counseling," or trying to discourage women from having abortions when on their way into a clinic. Scheidler believed sidewalk counseling had a direct impact on women, and the tactic had the added advantage of being legal and not leading to arrest. However, the "Chicago method" of sidewalk counseling still cut a few ethical corners.

"Give the pregnant woman and her escort factual information about the specific abortuary they are about to enter. Repeat this information until it produces the desired effect of disturbing them," Scheidler wrote in a pamphlet laying out his sidewalk counseling guidelines. In addition, he wrote the following:

> When the potential abortion client is sufficiently and justifiably disturbed by negative factual information about the abortion clinic, give her literature about an alternative center where she can go immediately for a free pregnancy test and counseling help. The pregnancy help agencies used in conjunction with this method will ideally have a neutral-sounding name like "Women's Aid Center." If the woman asks whether the alternative center performs abortions, do your best to change the subject by telling her how to get to the alternative center. . . . Let them find out for themselves that the pregnancy help center is in the business of saving lives and not destroying them.

Scheidler's tactical experimentation made him the leading expert in the movement on what kinds of militancy worked best. His 1985 book *Closed: 99 Ways to Stop Abortion* detailed many of his favorites, and the book soon became must reading among emerging young activists.

By the mid-1980s, Scheidler had transformed the Pro-Life Action League into a national bullhorn, shouting out his fiery brand of aggressive tactics at speaking engagements and protests all around the country. As his infamy soared, Scheidler parlayed the contacts he made on his travels and speaking engagements to build a loose-knit network of anti-abortion activists. Scheidler's network soon became the basis for the first national anti-abortion activist organization, the Pro-Life Action Network (PLAN). Through PLAN, the movement's most militant leaders were able for the first time to gather and coordinate their efforts, at times right under the noses of the more mainstream National Right to Life leaders.

Scheidler first began to develop PLAN during late-night bull sessions with frustrated activists at the National Right to Life Committee's convention in Orlando in 1983. Meeting with them in his hotel room, Scheidler convinced a small group of sympathizers that they needed to form their own group, one not bound by National Right to Life's limits on aggressive action.

The first PLAN convention, with six hundred in attendance, was held in Fort Lauderdale in May 1984, but despite the strong turnout, Scheidler considered the convention a bust. Too many mainstream right-to-lifers had come and not enough true militants. It was too much like a National Right to Life convention.

At Scheidler's urging, some of the more seasoned activists once again broke away for private late-night meetings to coordinate their activities. This time, they agreed that PLAN should have regional directors to carry out its national agenda, and more significantly, they endorsed the use of civil disobedience to try to shut down clinics. Now Scheidler felt they were finally making progress.

"I think it was a very good thing for us to get together in Ft. Lauderdale and organize this kind of pro-life mafia to work in concert on important activist programs," Scheidler wrote to another activist later. "I think we are obliged to give strong leadership to all the new people who want to get active. I even believe we are beholden to these people to grab them away from the moderates who will only hold them in inaction until they lose their zeal."

Finally, in April 1985, in Appleton, Wisconsin, Scheidler staged the first PLAN convention to be attended only by like-minded militants, who eagerly met to compare notes on protest tactics and plans for future demonstrations. Scheidler had found a way to bring together his growing legion of young pupils.

Randall Terry soon became Scheidler's most important protégé. Scheidler came to protest alongside Terry in Terry's hometown of Binghamton, New York, in January 1986, and Terry joined him at the PLAN convention in St. Louis the following summer, marking the first time Terry had joined a major national activist event. By the next year, as he was beginning to put together the organization that would evolve into Operation Rescue, Terry was named one of five regional directors of PLAN at the group's convention in Atlanta.

Scheidler's networking success made PLAN the organization that abortion-rights advocates reviled—and feared—the most. It was Scheidler and PLAN that finally triggered a nationwide counterattack against anti-abortion activism by abortion-rights forces in the mid-1980s. Before Scheidler and PLAN, the abortion-rights supporters' response to anti-abortion activism was uncoordinated and localized, varying widely from city to city and heavily dependent on relations between local abortion clinic owners and local feminist groups. But in Scheidler, the abortion-rights movement found its first major villain.

What made PLAN seem so sinister to feminists and abortion-rights advocates was that it emerged right in the midst of a cresting wave of anti-abortion violence. And Joseph Scheidler, PLAN's founder, was openly applauding it all. With 319 acts of violence committed against 238 clinics between January 1983 and March 1985, the period when Scheidler was forging his new national network was by far the most violent ever recorded in the abortion industry, either before or since. Whereas National Right to Life condemned the violence, Scheidler reveled in it. He usually tried to be careful with his words, but his message was unmistakable: "I don't condone, I don't advocate, but I don't condemn."

In private, he was even less cautious. The night before he appeared at a congressional hearing on clinic violence in March 1985, he stayed at Michael Bray's home outside Washington; it was soon after Bray had been arrested for his bombing spree. Bray helped Scheidler prepare his unapologetic testimony. Scheidler also kept in close contact with convicted clinic bomber John Brockhoeft and with Don Benny Anderson, the convicted kidnapper he had mentioned to President Reagan at the White House. In a 1986 letter to Bray's brother, Scheidler wrote that "the list of good results that has come from the violence is clear. I hardly think it is violence, since it is against brick and glass and not people." Those who commit violent acts, he added, are "my heroes. They represent total conviction and total commitment."

Feminists and abortion-rights advocates soon became convinced that there was a direct link between the new, Scheidler-sponsored militancy and increasing clinic violence, and they began to press federal officials to take action. Meeting privately with FBI Director William Webster in January 1985, Faye Wattleton, the president of Planned Parenthood, and Barbara Radford, executive director of the National Abortion Federation, complained about Scheidler and the rise of clinic violence and personally pressed Webster to launch an aggressive investigation into whether Scheidler was behind the wave of bombings. But the FBI had little interest.

Webster was "unconvinced that Scheidler's war cries met the guidelines set for the FBI's intervention," Wattleton recalled in her 1996 autobiography, *Life on the Line*. Webster also had doubts about whether "gatherings to discuss putting clinics out of business through violent tactics fell under terrorist or national conspiracy definitions."

Despite the dark allegations by abortion-rights advocates, there is no evidence that Scheidler ever engaged in violence himself or that he conspired with others to do so. It does not appear that he tried to direct clinic violence from a distance. Instead, what Scheidler did was use his role as a national spokesman to encourage and condone violent acts. Extremists could read between the lines.

By taking on the role of extremism's public champion, Scheidler was inevitably suspected of having direct links to violence. He appeared to the public to be like the Sinn Fein leaders in Ireland who serve as a political front for the terror squads of the Irish Republican Army. "There's no question in my mind that Scheidler wanted people to go out and light matches, and there's no question in my mind that he inspired and incited and knew about people doing it," charges Fay Clayton, an attorney for the National Organization for Women. "And even if he wasn't responsible for arsons, he used the threat to try to force clinics to close."

By 1986, Eleanor Smeal, president of the National Organization for Women (NOW), was fed up and ready to take on Joe Scheidler. Smeal had just returned to the presidency the year before, in a bitter election campaign in which the issue of clinic violence had played a pivotal role. During her campaign, Smeal had pledged to mount NOW's first, centralized response to the new anti-abortion militants and, after she was in office, quickly decided to make Scheidler her prime target. "We knew he had set up a national group, had written a book, and that he was traveling to encourage this kind of behavior," recalls Smeal.

On June 9, 1986, NOW filed a class-action antitrust lawsuit against Scheidler and other militant leaders, and it immediately served its primary function of nationalizing the abortion-rights response to the new activism. Observes Ann Baker, a freelance abortion-rights researcher, "Clinics had been obtaining [local] court injunctions against demonstrators throughout the early 1980s, but there hadn't been anything that resonated nationally until we went after Scheidler."

NOW's case, filed on behalf of almost every clinic in the United States, was eventually modified to charge Scheidler and other leaders with racketeering and conspiracy. The suit marked a novel use of the Racketeer Influenced and Corrupt Organizations (RICO) Act; it was delayed for years until the Supreme Court ruled on whether RICO could be used in a case in which the prime motivation of those charged with racketeering was not financial but political gain.

Scheidler has steadfastly denied the conspiracy and racketeering accusations. Still, he calls the RICO suit "one of the greatest diamonds in my crown. . . . To me, it's a testimony that we're doing something effective."

Defending himself against NOW's lawsuit cost Scheidler plenty of money but never forced him to give up his leadership role in the activist movement. Only Joe Scheidler's own inner demons could do that.

Joseph Scheidler sank back on the psychiatrist's couch as his mind and body gave in to the sodium Pentothal. It was 1958; Scheidler was thirty and at a transformative moment. In a few days, he was to become Brother Gregory, O.S.B., Benedictine monk. But on the brink of ordination, he had stepped back in terror. "I was afraid." Scheidler laid bare his fears to his brother-confessor at his Indiana monastery, who sent him to see a sympathetic psychiatrist in Michigan City, Indiana. Both Scheidler and the members of his order needed to know if he was cut out for the spare life of monastic sacrifice. Once the truth serum began coursing through Scheidler's veins, the psychiatrist asked the most awful, the most penetrating, question:

"If your mother were dead, would you become a monk?"

"No!"

Scheidler's reflexive, revealing response ended the debate. He left the monastery. Later, he tried to commit himself again, this time as a diocesan, or regular parish priest. Just as he was preparing for ordination, he froze once more; finally, he gave up and went home to face his Freudian moment with a mother who yearned for a priest in the family. "I thought my mother was going to have a heart attack."

Seven years after leaving the seminary, Scheidler proposed to his girl-friend, yet he was so openly fearful of going through with the marriage that his own family had a priest stay with him the night before the wedding. Finally, in middle age, his fears of commitment returned, and his paralysis changed the course of the American anti-abortion movement.

Joseph Scheidler's dark secret was that he was fearful of doing what he asked others to do. He could not back up his fiery words with brave deeds. In private letters to convicted clinic bombers, he often admitted that he lacked their nerve.

He was deeply afraid of getting arrested, and that meant that he would often pull his punches. Over a span of more than twenty years on the front lines of the abortion battlefield, Scheidler was arrested fewer than ten times, and he never spent more than a few hours in a police lockup; by contrast, other anti-abortion activist leaders endured hundreds of arrests and spent months or years in prison. Scheidler's arrests were sometimes accidental, coming only when he failed to get out of the way fast enough. Scheidler was so claustrophobic that he once promised God he would attend Mass every day of his life if he could stay out of jail following one particularly close call. God came through: Scheidler stayed out of jail, and he rarely missed a Mass afterward. "I cannot stand to be handcuffed," he said. Scheidler once privately confessed that "I lack the courage to face possible arrest, conviction, and a long prison term. I am the first to admit that I am something of a consummate coward."

For years he was able to use his talent for bluster and loud rhetoric to hide his fears. He did such a marvelous job of masking his true nature that abortion-rights advocates completely bought into the Scheidler-manufactured myth of Scheidler as the tough-as-nails intimidator. But as the young radicals he had cultivated rose to power and began to push

Scheidler's concepts and tactics to their logical extremes, Scheidler found he could no longer hide his cowardice. He was finally cornered in 1988 by his protégé, Randall Terry.

Terry was then launching Operation Rescue, the first major nationally coordinated activist campaign, to coincide with the 1988 presidential race. Terry had planned Operation Rescue with Scheidler in mind. Operation Rescue was to launch in the spring of 1988 with protests in both New York and Chicago; Terry would handle New York, and Scheidler would run the Chicago operation.

In the final weeks of intense preparation for the kickoff of Operation Rescue's first major event in New York City, when it was time to make a commitment, Scheidler began to get cold feet. In their planning meetings, Scheidler saw that Terry and his new band of supporters were intent on civil disobedience on a massive scale, forcing the police to make hundreds, perhaps thousands, of arrests. Terry's entire focus was on "rescue," or sit-ins, whereas Scheidler preferred a more diverse mix of tactics. But all he kept hearing from Terry was "arrest, arrest, arrest."

In late March 1988, Terry, Scheidler, and other activists met in a run-down hotel in New York's Times Square to finalize their plans for a New York sit-in campaign scheduled to begin in May. On the last day of the planning session—and in front of dozens of Terry's new acolytes—Scheidler spoke up: "What's this arrest thing? Is that going to separate us into two groups: the heroes and the cowards?"

Mass arrests would bring down the full weight of the government, Scheidler warned Terry. Activists would burn out, especially because Terry was not adequately preparing the rank-and-file demonstrators who were traveling cross-country to join in the protest for the arrests that would come. They can only go to court so many times; they can only hire so many lawyers.

"You're taking people's lives in your hands. You're not being honest about the risks with them. You're telling them to come out here, join a great big rescue. . . . It's not fair. . . . You have to tell people what they are in for."

Terry responded that he would inform his followers of the risks they faced after they arrived in New York. He chided Scheidler that his confrontational strategy would succeed where half-measures had failed before. That was, after all, the message that Scheidler had been preaching for years.

"We're going to break the system," Terry said.

"The system was here a long time before you," Scheidler anxiously replied. "They can always get extra people, go on to double time. You'll never break the system."

With that, Scheidler stalked out of the meeting, leaving stunned activists in his wake. Until that moment, Scheidler had always managed to finesse his reluctance to get arrested. But this time his claustrophobia had taken over, and Scheidler had panicked.

Terry was furious. "I had a roomful of leaders from all over the country, and Joe stood up and threw a frag bomb. And I'm thinking, What do you think this is? What are you here for?"

As Scheidler tried to hail a cab, Terry ran out of the hotel and followed him into the street.

"Joe, Joe, maybe you'd better not come," Terry told his erstwhile mentor. "Maybe you'd better just forget it; just don't come to the rescue. I'd rather you didn't come."

Says Terry, "I know what it means to lead people, and I know what it means for people to hear a discouraging voice that would put fear in their heart. And so I said to Joe, 'If you don't want to be involved, that's fine, but don't come back and sow that kind of discord.'"

Scheidler did go back, but the damage had been done. Operation Rescue never came to Chicago. "I never wanted to be close to Randy after he told me to get out." His rift with Terry ensured that Scheidler would never become a leader in Operation Rescue or any of its spin-offs in the late 1980s and early 1990s. As Operation Rescue came to dominate anti-abortion activism, Terry supplanted Scheidler as the movement's most prominent leader.

It was probably inevitable that Scheidler would eventually be forced to cede his leadership position to a Protestant fundamentalist like Randall Terry. Scheidler's emergence as an early force in anti-abortion activism in the late 1970s and early 1980s had, in fact, coincided with the political reawakening of Protestant Evangelical America.

The political mobilization of fundamentalists in the late 1970s and early 1980s was a natural outgrowth of a massive surge in Evangelical church membership throughout the previous decade; with hindsight many church historians mark that period as the start of America's Fourth Great Awakening. Pollster George Gallup Jr. dubbed 1976 the "Year of the Evangelical" after his survey found that 50 million

Americans reported having a "born-again" experience, including the newly elected president, Jimmy Carter. In a huge generational shift, hundreds of thousands, perhaps millions, of young people were attracted to Evangelical Christianity in the late 1970s. Middle-class suburban teenagers and young adults like Michael Bray found Jesus and were "born again," deserting the Catholic Church and the mainline Protestant denominations of their parents. Between 1970 and 1977, Methodist church membership dropped by 886,000, membership in the United Presbyterians by 526,000. The Baptist Bible Fellowship, meanwhile, which had only two hundred ministers in 1950, had more than three thousand churches by 1977.

Those in the new generation quickly came to dominate the tiny Charismatic churches they found on their personal journeys of religious discovery. As the born-again teenagers of the 1970s came into their own, married, and started families, they created their own new and bigger churches, and they discovered politics.

Soon, Evangelicals were focusing much of their newfound political energy on abortion. Fundamentalists had ignored the *Roe v. Wade* decision in 1973. Some Evangelical denominations, including the Southern Baptist Convention, had even supported a woman's right to an abortion in the early 1970s. But by the close of the decade, the anti-abortion cause had become one of the priorities on the new Christian political agenda, largely because of two men: Evangelical author and agent provocateur Francis Schaeffer, and a Southern Baptist preacher-turned-politician named Jerry Falwell.

Ultimately, fundamentalists would come to dominate anti-abortion activism, transforming it into a key point of contact between Evangelical America and the New Right. (The most widely quoted sociological study of the right-to-life movement, Kristin Luker's *Abortion and the Politics of Motherhood*, published in 1984, missed the young and angry activist wing that Scheidler and the fundamentalists were helping to build. In her work she insisted that the vast majority of anti-abortion activists were Catholic housewives, which was only true for the mainstream right-to-life committees and only in the movement's earliest stages; it was never true for the radical activist wing.)

The new activism washed in with the Reagan flood tide; the 1980 presidential election not only put a "pro-lifer" in the White House but gave instant legitimacy to anti-abortion militancy. After Reagan's inauguration, reversing *Roe v. Wade* no longer seemed far-fetched, and that prospect briefly reenergized the entire movement. As the Reagan era began, there was a half-hidden sense that a new kind of drama was straining to be played out; frustrated Catholics, newly politicized Protestant fundamentalists, and Reagan ideologues were all converging on the abortion issue.

Francis Schaeffer, Jerry Falwell, and Joseph Scheidler, in different ways, all played critical roles in quickening the movement's pace, paving the way for a new kind of anti-abortion militancy. They set the stage for the street theater to come.

Francis Schaeffer was the unlikeliest fundamentalist. His flowing gray hair, goatee, deeply creased face, and Bohemian style of dress all gave Schaeffer the air of a wayward college professor or counterculture icon gone to seed. A "Reformed Presbyterian" Evangelical minister, he lived most of his adult life isolated in the Swiss Alps at a retreat that he dubbed L'Abri, French for "the shelter." It was as far from the fundamentalist culture of suburban America as he could get. Yet by the late 1970s and early 1980s, he had clearly emerged as the intellectual driving force behind the political mobilization of Evangelicals across the country. Barely recognized outside fundamentalist circles, Schaeffer was nonetheless the man who first made fundamentalists care about politics—by making them care about abortion.

As an author, lecturer, and religious mentor to thousands of Evangelicals, Schaeffer provided the theological and intellectual arguments that finally convinced fundamentalists to discard premillennial dispensationalism, the pseudotheology that had undergirded their separatist and isolationist beliefs for more than two generations. Schaeffer angrily scolded them to return to their Puritan and Reformation roots and to start to fight to reclaim the American culture for themselves and for their Bible. Through his books, essays, and documentaries, Schaeffer prodded Protestant Evangelicals to emerge from spiritual isolation to fight to gain control of American culture, which, he lamented, was sinking into the abyss of secular humanism.

Schaeffer believed there was no more powerful—or more disastrous—symbol of the triumph of the central evil in the world, secular humanism, than *Roe v. Wade* and legalized abortion. Therefore, in the fall of 1979 he and his old friend C. Everett Koop, a born-again pediatric surgeon from Philadelphia who had cared for Schaeffer's children, launched a twenty-city film and lecture tour based on their new book about the evils of abortion, *Whatever Happened to the Human Race?*

Schaeffer and Koop, who later became U.S. surgeon general under President Ronald Reagan, were trying to shove Evangelicals out of their churches and into action, and in fact their lecture tour became the event that finally got fundamentalists engaged on an issue that had previously been seen as an exclusively Catholic concern. By 1981, in his landmark book *A Christian Manifesto,* Schaeffer followed up *Whatever Happened to the Human Race?* by calling all born-again Christians to engage in civil disobedience to fight abortion.

Michael Bray—and every other young born-again Christian who joined the anti-abortion movement in the early 1980s—was first mobilized by reading the works of Francis Schaeffer. By 1981, *Time* magazine had dubbed Schaeffer the "Guru of the Evangelicals," and indeed, his influence among American fundamentalists in the late 1970s and early 1980s is hard to overstate. Fundamentalists do not believe in icons or religious statues, observes Randal Stewart, a former minister who is now a staffer with Elim Fellowship, an association of Evangelical churches. "But if I was going to have a statue, it would be of Francis Schaeffer."

Before Francis Schaeffer could mobilize fundamentalists, however, he had a lot of history to overcome.

Elements of "rapture theology" could be traced all the way back to the millenarian sects of the Middle Ages, but in the United States in the twentieth century, such mysticism had served to keep generations of Protestant fundamentalists out of politics. Like a child's security blanket, escapist theology had been embraced by American fundamentalists to deal with the bitter humiliation they suffered in the wake of the Scopes "monkey" trial of 1925. Immortalized in the play *Inherit the Wind* by Jerome Lawrence and Robert E. Lee, the Scopes trial left fundamentalists feeling scorned by America's elites, shamed into a cultural corner, for their opposition to the teaching of evolution in public schools.

"The Scopes Monkey Trial was a great public relations disaster for us," observes Randall Terry. Fundamentalists retreated to their churches for fifty years. They became outcasts, believing that the world was evil, while privately reveling in the self-assurance that the Second Coming was imminent and they were the only ones who would be saved. "We became so heavenly minded," notes Flip Benham, a colorful Dallas preacher and Operation Rescue leader, "that we were no earthly good."

Fundamentalists were also horribly balkanized, obsessed by obscure theological disagreements and divided by petty feuds between denominations and leading ministers. It was a subculture that remained invisible to the larger American society. Francis Schaeffer was the product of that balkanization, and he worked most of his life to reverse it. Born in Philadelphia in 1912, Schaeffer became a convert to Evangelical Christianity at the age of seventeen and was soon a follower of J. Gresham Machen, a leading dispensationalist in the Presbyterian church. In the 1930s Machen helped lead fundamentalists out of mainline Presbyterianism to establish their own denomination, the Orthodox Presbyterian Church.

After studying at a Machen-sponsored seminary in Philadelphia, Schaeffer became a protégé of extremist Carl McIntire, who eventually broke with Machen. By 1938, Schaeffer was the first pastor ordained by McIntire's new fundamentalist Presbyterian splinter group. In the spring of 1947, Schaeffer was assigned to spend three months in Europe to study the conditions of European churches in the aftermath of World War II. Soon afterward he returned to Europe as a missionary, this time for good. In 1951, Schaeffer experienced what he later described as a deeply personal religious crisis that changed the direction of his life, and by 1955 he had founded L'Abri in Switzerland. Soon he began his personal evolution from missionary to author and, finally, to the political conscience of the Evangelical community.

By 1976, Schaeffer was already a bestselling Evangelical author when he published a book that exploded into the fundamentalist consciousness. It was entitled *How Should We Then Live?* and it traced the decline of Western culture back to Thomas Aquinas and the rise of secular humanism in the Renaissance.

Schaeffer's conclusions were wildly simplistic; his writing revealed a spectacular ignorance about the history of Western civilization. At the heart of *How Should We Then Live?*, Schaeffer set up a false conflict between the secular Renaissance (bad) and the Protestant Reformation (good). He baldly stated that the history of Western civilization ever since has been a continuation of the struggle between the humanist impulses let loose first by Aquinas and later by the Renaissance and the purifying Bible-based impulses of the Reformation.

Schaeffer concluded that the West's troubles—from Robespierre to Hitler—have occurred to the extent that the West has failed to look to the Scriptures to guide worldly affairs. Schaeffer thus charged that Christians had a duty to God and to the Holy Bible to work in the world, not remain apart from it. His guidance for believers of premillennial theology was that "even if I knew the world was going to end tomorrow, I would still plant a tree today."

Despite his misreading of Aquinas and his oversimplified version of Western history, Schaeffer's jeremiad against secular humanism resonated with the anxiety-ridden suburbanites who were embracing fundamentalism in the 1970s. And his attacks against escapist theology motivated them to act.

With his landmark 1979 book *Whatever Happened to the Human Race?*, Schaeffer narrowed his focus, turning his broadside against secular humanism into a targeted attack against abortion. Coauthored by Koop and accompanied by a five-episode film documentary produced by Schaeffer's son, Franky, *Whatever Happened to the Human Race?* was a detailed indictment against the dominant culture of the United States for its decision to accept abortion. Schaeffer and Koop believed *Roe v. Wade* marked the triumph of an "evil as great as any in human history" and was the first giant step down a slippery slope leading to infanticide and euthanasia. After *Roe*, Schaeffer and Koop warned, America stands "on the edge of a great abyss."

"Will a society which has assumed the right to kill infants in the womb—because they are unwanted, imperfect, or merely inconvenient—have difficulty in assuming the right to kill other human beings, especially older adults who are judged unwanted, deemed imperfect physically or mentally, or considered a public nuisance?"

This evil had to be stopped, and stopped by Bible-believing Christians. The only way that could happen would be if Christians discarded their old beliefs and became political activists. "We implore those of you who are Christians to exert all your influence to fight against the increasing loss of humanness—through legislation, social action and other means at your disposal, both privately and publicly, individually and collectively, in all areas of your lives."

In 1979, Schaeffer and Koop took *Whatever Happened to the Human Race?* on the road for a four-month, twenty-city tour of the United

States, holding seminars based on their book and the accompanying film series. The tour was targeted at Evangelical audiences and was designed to wake fundamentalists from their long slumber.

Getting Evangelical leaders to listen was not so easy, however. Some church leaders were convinced that Schaeffer was a heretic who was trying to revive the discredited "social gospel" movement, an earlier attempt to bring Evangelicals back into the world. Others could not understand his focus on an issue already decided by the Supreme Court.

Ministers turned their backs on Schaeffer and Koop as a result. When the two took their tour to Jackson, Mississippi, a city known as a Christian stronghold, major Baptist and Episcopal churches arranged mandatory religious services to prevent members from attending the lectures. In Chicago, administrators at nearby Wheaton College, a well-known Evangelical school, scheduled a mandatory chapel service at the same time so the students would not be lured away.

Schaeffer later complained that the treatment their tour received underscored how ministers had abandoned their responsibility to provide moral leadership. "Many in the Evangelical leadership either were totally silent about abortion or qualified what they did say about abortion to such an extent that they really said nothing."

But nothing could stop the Schaeffer-Koop message. The lectures and films, presented over three days in each city, were mobbed like rock concerts. "In big-city auditoriums, we would get 2,500 to 3,000 people," Koop recalls. *Whatever Happened to the Human Race?* quickly became a cultural phenomenon among Evangelicals, and it was instrumental in motivating the new generation that included Randall Terry and Michael Bray.

Says Koop, "I think it was the first time that most Christians even knew what the issue was."

Schaeffer asked Christians to take the final step—radical political activism against abortion—in *A Christian Manifesto*. Published three years before Schaeffer's death, *A Christian Manifesto* was a summing up of his indictment against secular humanism, modern liberalism, and abortion, but above all it was a call to arms for Christians. By the time he wrote *A Christian Manifesto*, observes Pat Robertson, founder of the Christian Broadcasting Network (CBN) and former Republican presidential candidate, "Schaeffer had come to believe that civil disobedience might be the answer."

"It is time for Christians and others who do not accept the narrow and bigoted humanist views rightfully to use the appropriate forms of protest," Schaeffer wrote in outrage. "There does come a time when force, even physical force, is appropriate. . . . When all avenues to flight and protest have closed, force in the defensive posture is appropriate." He continued as follows:

> It is time we consciously realize that when any office commands what is contrary to God's Law, it abrogates its authority. And our loyalty to the God who gave this law then requires that we make the appropriate response in that situation to such a tyrannical usurping of power. . . . This brings us to a current issue that is crucial for the future of the church in the United States—the issue of abortion. What is involved is the whole issue of the value of human life. . . . State officials must know that we are serious about stopping abortion, which is a matter of clear principle concerning the babies themselves, and concerning a high view of human life. This may include doing such things as sit-ins in legislatures and courts, including the Supreme Court, when other constitutional means fail. We must make people aware that this is not a political game, but totally crucial and serious. And we must also demonstrate to people that there is indeed a proper bottom line. To repeat: The bottom line is that at a certain point there is not only the right, but the duty, to disobey the state.

A *Christian Manifesto* was to have a profound effect on virtually every Protestant fundamentalist who joined the anti-abortion movement in the 1980s. Many activists later said they never would have become involved if they had not read Schaeffer's work. Randall Terry simply followed Schaeffer's directions.

"What Schaeffer did," observes Terry, "was to build the off-ramp." It was a new direction for Christians, a new life in worldly activism.

If Francis Schaeffer armed Evangelicals for political battle, it was Jerry Falwell who first tried to lead them into combat. The fact that he ultimately failed to create a lasting political movement does not diminish the significance of his early effort.

Falwell, who himself was deeply influenced by Schaeffer, was among the first of a new group of Evangelical leaders to give their followers an outlet for their newfound political yearnings. With Moral Majority, he laid the groundwork, first for fundamentalist civil disobedience through Operation Rescue in the 1980s, and later for more mainstream Religious Right political activism through Ralph Reed's Christian Coalition in the 1990s. He was at the forefront of a new breed of media-savvy, political-religious figures to emerge from Evangelical America and cross over into mainstream politics and activism. Along with rivals like Pat Robertson, Falwell harnessed televangelism in the name of a political cause, opening up broad new possibilities for religion-based activism.

It was through Falwell and Moral Majority that Francis Schaeffer's call for Christian political action to stop abortion was popularized and disseminated to a mass audience, one far larger than Schaeffer could ever reach directly through his books or documentaries. It was Falwell's emphasis on the politics of abortion as one of the nonnegotiable center-pieces of Moral Majority's agenda that helped cement a new alliance between fundamentalists and Catholic anti-abortion activists.

Ultimately, Falwell also became the most prominent Evangelical leader to give his blessing to anti-abortion civil disobedience. By 1988, Falwell was the first major national figure to jump on the bandwagon for Operation Rescue, personally delivering a $10,000 check to Randall Terry in front of an Atlanta abortion clinic. Later, Falwell broke with Terry and Operation Rescue, after he and New York's Cardinal John O'Connor met privately to decide whether they should both risk arrest and agreed not to join Operation Rescue's protesters in Atlanta's jails. For years, nevertheless, Jerry Falwell was the embodiment of funda-mentalist opposition to abortion.

Jerry Falwell had to work his way up to religion and God, joining a Baptist church in his hometown of Lynchburg, Virginia, at the age of twelve. Seven years later, he had a conversion experience and chose Jesus over the St. Louis Cardinals, who had invited the high school baseball star to a tryout. He went to Bible college, graduated in 1956, and quickly became pastor to a small splinter group that had broken away from one of Lynchburg's established Baptist churches. Before long, Falwell was also preaching on a local radio station and, three months later, on television. Broadcasting made Falwell a nationally known televangelist long before he entered politics; at his peak in 1980, his *Old Time Gospel Hour* was broadcast on 280 radio stations daily and more than three hundred television stations weekly.

Falwell made little effort to engage in the ongoing abortion debate until the 1970s, when he began to read Francis Schaeffer's writings, and Schaeffer's ideas clicked with his own experiences ministering to women who had undergone abortions. Before long, Falwell was preaching regularly against abortion, on the air and at his fifteen-thousand-member Thomas Road Baptist Church, decrying "America's national sin" while picking up Schaeffer's call for an all-out Christian mobilization.

Falwell was already a national figure among Evangelicals when, in May 1979, he met with a group of conservative religious and political leaders—including New Right ideologues Paul Weyrich and Richard Viguerie—who wanted to recruit him to establish a religion-based political organization that could take on the conservative social cause and have an impact on the 1980 presidential campaign. They wanted to form a new group that would put pressure on the Republican Party to accept a more conservative agenda, and they wanted Falwell to be its leader. Weyrich made the case for a focus on abortion, arguing that it would split the Catholic vote within the Democratic Party while alienating few Republicans.

At a lunch break, Falwell recalls, Weyrich said that "there is in America a moral majority that agrees about the basic issues. But they aren't organized. They don't have a platform. The media ignore them. Somebody's got to get that moral majority together." A bell went off. Weyrich was thinking lower case *m*. Falwell capitalized it.

Francis Schaeffer was also helping his friend develop the vision for Moral Majority. Schaeffer had been trying to persuade Falwell to use his national recognition to help push Evangelicals into the political arena. But Falwell did not know how to work with religious leaders from other denominations.

"Since becoming a Christian I had lived a rather separatist life," he said. "I believed that being yoked with unbelievers for any cause was off limits. I didn't even get along very well with other kinds of Baptists, let alone with Methodists, Presbyterians, or Catholics."

Schaeffer pushed Falwell to accept what he called "co-belligerency," the idea that church groups that do not share theology should still work together toward common political goals. "Co-belligerency" sounds like common sense, but among long-divided Evangelicals it was an alien concept to work with each other, let alone Pope-loving Catholics or Jews. Prodded by Schaeffer, however, Falwell made the leap of faith and made co-belligerency the foundation for his new group. It was one of Falwell's most enduring contributions to the growth of a powerful Religious Right.

In June 1979, Falwell and his colleagues organized Moral Majority, with the platform of "pro-life, pro-family, pro-moral, and pro-American."

"America was born in her churches, and she must be reborn there as well," Falwell cried. "The time has come for pastors and church leaders to clearly and boldly proclaim the Gospel of regeneration in Christ Jesus."

Before long, Moral Majority was taking on the trappings and functions of a modern political lobby: registering voters, working for candidates who supported "pro-family" issues, publishing lists of candidates' voting records, holding rallies and parades, and assembling computerized mailing lists.

By September 1979, the Moral Majority claimed to have been in touch with seventy-two thousand preachers to teach them how to get involved in the political process. Falwell told them that fundamentalists should use the Scriptures as their guide to evaluate candidates on the issues of lower taxes, a balanced budget, tax-exempt status for private schools, restoration of the death penalty, prayer in schools—and banning abortion. The group compiled a guide for preachers to accomplish the goal, detailing how to get fundamentalists over their distaste for politics. The Moral Majority, Falwell said, was getting people "out of the pew and into the precinct."

Moral Majority served to bring Evangelicals into conservative Republican politics just in time to play a critical role in the 1980 presidential election of Ronald Reagan. In the process, Falwell helped create the political-religious nexus that came to be known as the Religious Right. By August 1980, Falwell presided over what Ralph Reed later described as the "wedding ceremony" between Evangelicals and the Republican Party, when Ronald Reagan addressed twenty thousand Evangelicals at a meeting of a group called the Religious Roundtable. When Reagan told the crowd that "I know that you cannot endorse me, but I endorse you and everything you do," Evangelicals were hooked on Reagan and Republicanism. In the November election,

6 million Evangelicals switched from the Democratic to the Republican Party. Observes Pat Robertson, with only mild exaggeration, "It was the greatest mass exodus of voters probably in the history of America."

Reagan easily seduced Falwell and other Evangelical leaders who were still naive about politics and the limits of their power and influence. As Reagan entered office in 1981, Evangelicals and other abortion activists were convinced they now had a man in the White House who would lead the fight against *Roe v. Wade* and abortion.

The Reagan administration soon crushed the anti-abortion movement's high expectations. Once the Reagan White House found how easy it was to take Evangelicals and anti-abortion activists for granted—they were never going over to the Democrats—administration officials realized they could get away with offering them table scraps. The Reagan White House mastered the art of policy symbolism, the use of marginal steps that could placate activists without antagonizing mainstream voters.

Reagan gave the anti-abortion movement a few prominent appointments; among the most controversial was naming C. Everett Koop surgeon general in 1981. A handful of other Reagan appointees tried to use their positions to chip away at abortion, but their acts were little more than symbolic, such as stripping abortion coverage from federal employee health insurance and demoting bureaucrats who continued openly to support abortion rights.

These marginal battles generated headlines, but the Reagan administration early on decided that it would not stake the presidency on an all-out assault on *Roe v. Wade*. And any hope that Congress might take the lead was crushed in 1983, when a constitutional amendment that would have returned the abortion issue to the states was defeated in the Senate. In hindsight, it is now clear that the defeat of the amendment, sponsored by Senator Orrin Hatch, a Utah Republican, marked the last time that Washington seriously considered outlawing abortion. The defeat gave the Reagan White House a handy excuse for not pushing to end abortion: Congress would not go for it.

When activists began to grow restless with White House inaction, Reagan aides launched a targeted marketing campaign to shore up conservative support before the 1984 election, highlighted by the publication of "Abortion and the Conscience of the Nation," an impassioned anti-abortion essay issued under Ronald Reagan's name.

However, it was Reagan's Supreme Court appointments that angered activists the most. The movement had counted on Reagan to change the balance of power on the Court enough to overturn *Roe,* but his first appointment, Sandra Day O'Connor in 1981, infuriated anti-abortion leaders. They not only were deeply suspicious of her position but also saw the appointment as a sign that Reagan was not going to make overturning *Roe* his top priority in judicial appointments.

By 1987, after the nomination of conservative Robert Bork failed and moderate Anthony Kennedy was named in his place, Reagan's final chance to overturn *Roe* through judicial appointments was gone. Kennedy went on to become a key swing vote in favor of retaining abortion rights in the landmark decisions of the late 1980s and early 1990s. (By the time Reagan left office in 1989, on the eve of the Supreme Court's landmark *Webster v. Reproductive Health Services* decision, the Court had made only slight inroads into the abortion rights set forth in *Roe.* In *Poelker v. Doe* and *Maher v. Roe,* in 1977, the Court said cities or states could refuse to provide publicly financed hospital services for elective abortions and could restrict state Medicaid funding to medically necessary abortions; in *Harris v. McRae,* in 1980, the Court upheld the Hyde amendment, which banned federal Medicaid funds for abortion except when necessary to save the woman's life; in *Planned Parenthood of Kansas City, Mo. v. Ashcroft* in 1983, a state law requiring parental consent for minors seeking abortions was upheld but only because the law allowed minors to get a judge's approval to have an abortion without parental notification.)

Reagan's failure to remake the Court spawned a deep sense of alienation from mainstream politics among anti-abortion activists as the 1980s wore on.

"The pro-life movement is not winning, we are losing!" cried Randall Terry. "The pro-life movement has been too nice. We've wanted to be respectable. We have failed to produce the necessary social tension that effects political change."

If winning the presidency did not lead to changing the law, then what could committed foes of abortion do? They could turn to militancy—and men like Joseph Scheidler. Francis Schaeffer and Jerry Falwell had stirred a generation. Scheidler hoped to lead as many as he could to activism's jagged edge. But first, the movement had to develop strong grass roots. Those roots grew deepest in St. Louis.

6

THE BATTLE OF ST. LOUIS

Until Operation Rescue exploded on the scene, St. Louis was home to the largest and most significant campaign of anti-abortion civil disobedience in the United States. For nearly a decade, St. Louis was at the vortex of sit-in activity, picking up where John O'Keefe's Washington campaign left off, thanks in part to sympathetic police, prosecutors, and local judges. In St. Louis, mainstream right-to-life leaders, who had previously eschewed the use of civil disobedience by the militant wing of the anti-abortion movement, brought their conservative, middle-class troops out to get arrested for the first time anywhere in the country.

In fact, the anti-abortion protest movement in the United States has never enjoyed, either before or since, the kind of broad public and political backing it had during a few brief months in late 1979 and early 1980 in St. Louis. St. Louis briefly offered a glimpse of the success that the activist movement might enjoy if it were backed by broad community opposition to abortion. By the late 1970s and early 1980s, Americans were gradually shifting their views on abortion, and the outlines of a new national consensus in support of *Roe v. Wade* and a woman's right to choose were beginning to emerge. St. Louis, home to a large and conservative Catholic population, was several years behind and had not yet completed that transition.

In St. Louis, Protestant fundamentalists also began to emerge as a significant force in what had been a predominantly Catholic movement. The city served as the proving grounds for a new generation of aggressive and increasingly militant Protestant fundamentalist leaders from across the country, including Operation Rescue founder Randall Terry.

Years before Michael Bray poisoned his work in Washington, John O'Keefe's concept of a "peaceful presence" found fertile ground in St. Louis. Over Thanksgiving weekend in 1977, Jeanne Miller, Burke Balch, and a few others from O'Keefe's group in Washington went to the National Youth Pro-Life Coalition (NYPLC) convention in Milwaukee. Two months earlier, at a meeting on Long Island, the Washington activists had agreed to take to the road to sell their ideas of nonviolent civil disobedience in an attempt to counter the growing impression that anti-abortion protest was all about violence. The timing seemed particularly apt: Joseph Scheidler had just been quoted in newspapers as saying that he "would not shed any tears" over the burning of an abortion clinic in New Jersey.

"We got together on Long Island because we wanted to respond to what Joe Scheidler was saying," recalls O'Keefe. "We figured that our job was to explain to others what we were doing, to offer leadership, to spread nonviolence as an answer to violence." Burke Balch, who had worked with the NYPLC when its leaders helped organize the first anti-abortion sit-in back in 1975, served as the natural connection between O'Keefe and the youth group.

The coalition's Milwaukee conference was the first opportunity for the Washington group to search for new recruits and to convince activists in other cities to start local sit-in organizations of their own. As college students from around the country floated in and out of the convention, Jeanne Miller met Helen Ann Egan, the head of the student anti-abortion organization at St. Louis University, a Jesuit-run college, and quickly started telling her about the sit-ins in Washington.

"The basic theme I used," recalls Miller, "was that we in the movement aren't sacrificing ourselves."

Once Miller began to detail her group's tactics and strategies, Egan was hooked and became determined to take O'Keefe's tactics back to

St. Louis. When she got home, she quickly went to see Vince Petersen, a Franciscan seminarian at St. Louis University who was a member of her student anti-abortion group, to tell him about what was happening in Washington. Petersen jumped at the sit-in idea, quickly taking the lead. He formed a tiny group that was modeled after O'Keefe's Pro-Life Non-Violent Action Project in Washington.

Petersen was a leftist who had cut his teeth on protest as an antiwar activist at the University of Minnesota in the early 1970s, before he was "born again" and immersed himself in the Catholic Charismatic Renewal. After his conversion experience and his decision to join the priesthood, Petersen transferred to St. Louis University and enrolled at the Franciscan seminary, intending to put politics, activism, and marches on the Pentagon behind him.

Before long, however, his growing opposition to abortion reawakened his activist spirit. Oddly, Petersen first became aware of the anti-abortion movement at a rock concert in Minnesota in 1971, when he ran into students who were organizing to fight a state-level abortion reform initiative.

Like John O'Keefe, Petersen saw the anti-abortion cause as related to his opposition to war, the defense industry, and the death penalty, and he grew angry that other antiwar activists were unwilling to join him in what he believed was a consistent stance against all killing. While he was getting involved in the anti-abortion campaign in St. Louis, he was also participating in protests against St. Louis–based defense contractor McDonnell-Douglas, picketing outside the company's headquarters as part of a support group for activists staging a sit-in inside, once during a meeting of the McDonnell-Douglas board of directors. Petersen's group wanted McDonnell-Douglas, one of St. Louis's largest employers, to convert more of its assembly lines from fighter jet to commercial aircraft production. It was not easy to tell where Petersen placed the greater emphasis: war or abortion. "Not only is the United States the number one manufacturer and distributor of war materials," Petersen wrote at the time, "but it also leads the world in child killing."

Egan's story about the Washington sit-in movement had so captivated Petersen that he sent away for copies of O'Keefe's pamphlet, *A Peaceful Presence,* as soon as it was published in January 1978. Dave Gaetano, Jeanne Miller's boyfriend and a leading activist in O'Keefe's group, quickly followed up by sending Petersen copies of a manual he had written on how to establish a sit-in organization, complete with sample press releases, anti-abortion songs written and sung in Washington, and even detailed recommendations on the correct aperture settings for taking photographs in the midst of a clinic protest.

The Washington veterans, acutely aware of the male-dominated image of the anti-abortion movement, also advised that women play highly visible roles, both by getting arrested during the sit-ins and by handling press relations afterward. Hard experience prompted a further cautionary note for women: To avoid injury, they should not "wear open-toed shoes or earrings" when faced with arrest.

But Gaetano's memo also included more troubling tactics, including some that crossed the border between protest and harassment. He recommended planting "covert counselors": women posing as patients who would loudly question abortion before storming out of the clinic waiting room, as if experiencing a sudden change of heart, in an attempt to plant seeds of doubt in patients' minds. It also was recommended that a few women go through counseling sessions, in part to determine whether the clinic staff properly explained the facts of abortion, but also to learn "the physical layout of the clinic." However, the manual included a sample pledge of nonviolence: "I pledge myself to a policy of loving non-violence in this action. . . . I shall do my best to maintain an attitude of compassion and love toward those who may confront us, as well as toward those whom we may have to approach or confront. . . . I will not shout at clinic personnel or call them murderers."

The St. Louis group was conscious of trying to follow in O'Keefe's footsteps, and it adopted the name PEACE (for People Expressing a Concern for Everyone) that had been in use briefly in Washington as well as in Cleveland.

In late January 1978, just days after O'Keefe's first attempt at coordinated activity, which involved sit-ins in six cities on January 6, six St. Louis University students sat down in front of the doors of Women's Health Center of West County, an abortion clinic run by Dr. Bolivar Escobedo in the Regency Park professional office complex in suburban Manchester, Missouri. Two women students acting as sidewalk counselors and a dozen picketers supported them outside.

Petersen and Egan chose Escobedo's suburban clinic because it was an easier target than St. Louis's main abortion provider, Reproductive Health Services (RHS). The RHS clinic was located in a high-rise professional office building downtown and was a formidable and nearly inaccessible facility for activists bent on shutting it down.

The RHS clinic was run by Judith Widdicombe, who was a difficult target as well; she was a prominent, early pioneer in the nation's abortion battle and was unlikely to give in easily to pressure. One of the founders of the National Abortion Federation, the Washington-based group that lobbies for abortion providers, Widdicombe had first become aware of abortion at age sixteen. Working as a hospital aide, she had watched numbly as a woman who had endured an illegal coat-hanger abortion bled to death while hospital staffers coldly talked of the woman's mistakes and who was to blame for her actions. In 1967, after working at a suicide prevention hot line and listening on the phone to the bleak stories of unwed pregnant women who were considering ending their lives, Widdicombe left to help set up the Missouri branch of the Clergy Consultation Service, the New York–based abortion referral service founded by the Reverend Howard Moody, a liberal Baptist minister in Manhattan. She opened Reproductive Health Services soon after *Roe v. Wade,* and by the late 1970s it had become one of the largest abortion providers in the Midwest.

By contrast, Escobedo, a Peruvian immigrant, had quickly developed a reputation as a bad doctor, even among other abortion providers. "He was worse than the anti-abortion people said he was," remembers Widdicombe. "He was a real schlock—that was the first thing I agreed with the other side about. He was the kind of doctor that the anti-abortion people think all abortion providers are. He gave everyone a bad name."

Escobedo was so incompetent that he could not obtain physician's privileges at any hospital in the state; years later, abortion-rights forces in Missouri, anxious to be rid of Escobedo, picked up on his lack of hospital privileges as a way to force him out of business. In the mid-1980s, they inserted a provision in the state's new abortion law requiring providers to have hospital privileges; the law ultimately forced Escobedo to close his clinic. When the constitutionality of that law was attacked by Widdicombe's clinic in what became known at the Supreme Court as *Webster v. Reproductive Health Services,* the provision requiring hospital privileges was not challenged. In short, Vince Petersen had good reason to believe that Escobedo was vulnerable.

Confounded by the first sit-in, the St. Louis County Police decided not to arrest the students, and in fact they inadvertently aided them by refusing to allow women patients into the clinic while the sit-in was under way. To complicate matters further, the owner of the office building was on vacation and could not be reached; without a complaint from the property owner, the police did not feel they could charge the students with trespassing. About a dozen officers stood around most of the day, simply watching. "The police," recalls Samuel Lee, one of the six protesters, "didn't know what to do with us. It was so brand-new."

Escobedo was confused as well, and after waiting around for a few hours, he decided to close for the day and go home. The students continued to sit and block the doors, all the while praying and singing Jesuit folk music. Finally, after making sure that Escobedo was gone and the clinic was definitely closed, the six students got up and left, untouched by the police.

The sit-in had been a remarkable success, but it went unnoticed; it was not covered at all by the local media. The protesters quickly decided to go back to Regency Park as soon as possible to try to draw attention to their cause.

On March 11, six students, including Lee and Egan, were arrested and quickly released the same day. The group attracted modest press coverage for the first time. A photograph of Egan looking somber and downcast as she sat amid potted ferns in the office building's atrium in front of the clinic door, with a pair of St. Louis County police officers looming over her, was published in the *St. Louis Globe-Democrat,* announcing the group's presence.

This was heady stuff for Samuel Lee, who had enrolled at St. Louis University in January and had stumbled across the group just before the first sit-in. Lee, elated by the group's initial success, soon emerged as PEACE's de facto leader; Petersen had pulled back from intense involvement, and Egan dropped out of school and moved back home to Washington, D.C. Petersen's superiors, fearful that his role in leading the sit-ins could damage the seminary's reputation, were pressuring him to drop out of the group and concentrate on his studies for the priesthood. Ultimately, Petersen was grateful that Sam Lee was so enthusiastic about taking over. "I was afraid I was risking my new life, my vocation to be a priest, that I was slipping back into a life that I had renounced when I had left the secular world of protest."

With long hair, thick beard, and dark, deep-set eyes, Lee seemed to have stepped out of central casting's image of a radical from the sixties. Perpetually garbed in jeans, open-necked shirt, and rumpled sports coat, he did not fit the image of the anti-abortion movement any better than did John O'Keefe.

Like O'Keefe, Lee was a pacifist with a background in the Catholic Charismatic Renewal; he was an intensely religious young intellectual who had come to St. Louis University to prepare for what he hoped would be a vocation as a priest.

It was at age fifteen, while he was at Our Lady of Providence Catholic High School in Clarksville, Indiana, that Lee had a "conversion experience," which he later described, in words often used by Protestant fundamentalists, as the most intense and important moment of his life. But when Lee was "born again," he did not leave his Catholic faith; instead, he immersed himself in the Charismatic Renewal and began spending most of his free time at Mount St. Francis, a nearby retreat and Charismatic center run by the Franciscan order. After graduating from high school in 1975, Lee left home and moved into Mount St. Francis, where he lived among the Franciscan priests and friars intermittently for the next three years.

Lee had never applied himself to his studies in high school, but now at Mount St. Francis he had free run of the center's library. He began poring through classic works of faith and activism: the Bible, of course, but also the works of Thoreau, Gandhi, and King. He was seven years younger than O'Keefe, too late for the antiwar or civil rights movements of the 1960s, yet sitting in the quiet of the Franciscan center, reading of the bitter battles for human rights fought by Southern blacks and Indian peasants, the teenager was drawn powerfully to the images of protest and religion-based activism.

After a period of drifting, Lee eventually found himself at the Abbey of Gethsemani, the Trappist Monastery in Kentucky that had once been home to Thomas Merton, the monk and philosopher who had served as the social conscience of the American Catholic Church in the 1960s. Lee went to Gethsemani for a personal retreat, and while there he quietly decided to become a priest.

Lee knew that if he was to be ordained, he first needed an education, and so in 1977 he applied to St. Louis University. Soon after arriving in January 1978, Lee was touring the friary of the Franciscan seminary on campus for the first time when someone stopped him and asked if he would like to come to an anti-abortion meeting down the hall.

Lee was opposed to abortion and had even attended one anti-abortion meeting back home in Indiana, but he had not given the issue much more thought. He decided to stop in and listened as Vince Petersen described plans for the first sit-in at Regency Park. By the end of the meeting, Lee was enthralled; Petersen recalls that Lee asked question after question throughout the night. Here was what Lee had read about back at Mount St. Francis; here were "people trying to apply those concepts of the civil rights movement to the issue of abortion."

Lee was told the group planned to have another meeting the following week, and he was invited to come back and join. For the next week, Lee thought about almost nothing else. He was "consumed," and he read everything he could find about abortion. It was not the graphic pictures so often used by the anti-abortion movement that made a connection with Lee, but reading thoughtful works on the beginnings of human life and thinking about the roles that faith and political and social responsibility held in his own life.

By the end of the week, Lee felt that he was a "changed person." He had undergone a political transformation nearly as intense as his earlier religious conversion. Lee threw himself into the sit-in movement, and before long he dropped out of college, never to become a priest.

After the arrests at the March sit-in, David Danis, an attorney who had agreed to represent the group on a pro bono basis, advised Lee and the others not to stage more sit-ins before their trial. In June 1978, during this enforced inactivity, the National Right to Life Committee held its national convention in St. Louis; for the first time this group gave permission for O'Keefe and other members of his Washington sit-in organization to conduct a workshop on civil disobedience at the convention. Behind the scenes, National Right to Life was in the midst of a bitter internal power struggle, and its leaders were too distracted to give much thought to whether it should sponsor activists who advocated breaking the law and going to jail.

O'Keefe began the workshop by talking about his belief in the power of nonviolence; he watched as, one by one, the local television news crews clicked off their cameras, turned off their lights, and packed up their gear. Reporters had come hoping for sound bites of fiery rhetoric endorsing violence, not O'Keefe's intellectual meanderings about a "peaceful presence." But sitting out in the audience, Sam Lee was spellbound; O'Keefe had put into words everything that Lee felt and believed. Lee sought out O'Keefe after the workshop, and the two quickly struck up a friendship.

At the heart of O'Keefe's philosophy was something that would stick with Lee ever after: Anti-abortion protesters had to share the vulnerability of the unborn, show solidarity with the unborn by sharing their helplessness. Tactically, that meant pure nonviolent protest, but to Sam Lee it meant something more: It was another way of saying that being pro-life should mean being a loving Christian, that "pro-life" was not a political position but a way of life.

Within months, Lee was called on to spread the philosophy to the man whose rhetoric had so offended O'Keefe back in 1977: Joe Scheidler. Scheidler had heard about the St. Louis sit-ins and asked Lee to come to Chicago to talk to his organization. Members of Scheidler's Chicago anti-abortion group had never been arrested before, but after Lee came and explained what PEACE was doing, Scheidler sent his followers out to get arrested in sit-ins of their own. Scheidler quickly dispensed with O'Keefe's philosophical underpinnings; he saw the sit-in as one more weapon in the battle to shut down the clinics, not as a way to "share the vulnerability of the unborn."

One of the most important things O'Keefe told Lee was about the Washington group's successful use of the necessity defense in its early trials in Virginia. O'Keefe gave Lee materials from the trials to take back to PEACE's lawyers in St. Louis. In the first trial in November 1978, the necessity defense did not work. The six from the March sit-in were quickly convicted by a jury on misdemeanor trespass charges in St. Louis County Magistrate Court and were fined $10 apiece. Undaunted, the protesters staged another sit-in in December and started an appeal of their earlier conviction. Eventually, they won a new jury trial in St. Louis County Circuit Court and used the necessity defense again. This time, they followed a carbon copy of the legal strategy that had proved successful for O'Keefe's group in Virginia.

The court allowed expert medical testimony from Dr. Paul Byrne, director of the neonatal intensive care unit at Cardinal Glennon Memorial Hospital for Children, as well as from two other physicians, who argued that life begins at conception. Linda Brooks, a woman who said she had decided not to have an abortion after a clinic sit-in in Washington, also testified for the defense.

Finally, the defendants testified that at the time they staged their sit-in, they had believed that life begins at conception and so had trespassed in order to save lives. Their attorneys, Danis and Jerry Murphy, argued that because *Roe v. Wade* had not determined when life begins, their clients were legally free to determine the onset of life for themselves.

Lee and the other defendants were stunned when the tactic worked. They were acquitted, one juror said, because the jury "accepted the students' argument that they believed trespassing was necessary to save the lives of unborn human beings."

Although in Washington the successful use of the necessity defense had done little to boost O'Keefe's sit-in campaign, in St. Louis a similar acquittal had an electrifying effect on the city's much larger anti-abortion community. From the Catholic hierarchy to the mainstream activists at Missouri Citizens for Life—the state chapter of National Right to Life—local leaders who had never considered joining the sit-ins when they had appeared dangerous and criminal suddenly began to climb on the bandwagon.

"I thanked one of those students on behalf of all of us," Midge Ratchford, a board member of the St. Louis Catholic Archdiocese's anti-abortion committee, told the *St. Louis Post-Dispatch* immediately after the verdict came in. "You can talk and talk, but sooner or later if you really believe what you are saying you must take action."

Now, as Lee began planning more sit-ins, mainstream right-to-lifers and Ratchford's Catholic clergy came in droves to join up. The tiny group of St. Louis University students was suddenly dwarfed by larger numbers of priests and older, middle-class Catholics, who until then had been afraid to go beyond legal picketing yet were frustrated by the ineffectiveness of their modest actions.

By November 1979, as many as seventy people at a time were protesting alongside Lee and the students, and fifteen to twenty of them were getting arrested, including Loretto Wagner, vice president of Missouri Citizens for Life. "I read John O'Keefe's *A Peaceful Presence*, and it drew me in," recalls Wagner. "Here was this romantic notion, to be like the civil rights campaign. We had been stuffing envelopes and writing letters, but now, this was exciting."

Soon she was joined at the sit-ins by Ann O'Donnell, the matriarch of the St. Louis anti-abortion community, who was not only a leader of the Missouri state organization but also vice president of National Right to Life. As the leaders of Missouri Citizens for Life began streaming out to join Sam Lee's sit-ins, National Right to Life became increasingly concerned about its potential legal liability; clinic owners might sue the national organization for allowing one of its top officers and most of its Missouri chapter to attempt to shut the clinics down. But National Right to Life was too weak to try to stop the radicalization of Missouri Citizens for Life. Before she joined Wagner at the sit-ins and got arrested for the first time, O'Donnell filed an undated letter of resignation with National Right to Life. The organization never took her up on the offer.

In the local press, Wagner was soon being identified as a spokeswoman for PEACE; planning sessions for the sit-ins were being held at O'Donnell's house. The line separating the sit-in movement from the mainstream right-to-life movement had completely disappeared in St. Louis. Soon, Sam Lee was recruiting for his sit-ins right in the middle of meetings of Missouri Citizens for Life; older Catholics like Dorothy Schonhorst were laying down their picket signs in order to block clinic doors, and middle-aged men like Orville Burkemper were piling into police paddy wagons wearing suitcoats, ties, and fedoras.

By the spring of 1980, the sit-ins were attracting huge crowds; Lee had to organize regular training exercises for the new recruits and appointed "marshals" to direct the bulging ranks of his followers. Recalls Wagner, "The sit-ins would be announced at churches, the priests would say, 'Come out and give your support.' It became the thing to do on a Saturday morning."

The protests also began to attract a group that had never been heard from before in St. Louis: fundamentalist Protestants. As many as twenty Presbyterian students from the Covenant Theological Seminary, with the blessings of its president, William Barker, began to join the protests by late 1979 and were soon getting arrested, marking the first time that large numbers of Protestants had participated in the Catholic demonstrations.

The Covenant Seminary taught a deeply conservative strain of Presbyterian theology, one that was strongly influenced by Francis Schaeffer and his new brand of "activist" fundamentalism. In late 1979, when Schaeffer's film series of *Whatever Happened to the Human Race?* was shown to students at Covenant Theological Seminary, Sam Lee was invited to attend. Soon after, the seminarians came out in force to join Lee's sit-ins. Barker told reporters that he wanted "to express my own personal support of these men. They have acted on their conscience, believing, as it says in Acts 5:29, that it is better to obey God than man." The Covenant students brought a new style to Lee's sit-ins, loudly singing Protestant fundamentalist songs for the first time outside an abortion clinic: "A Mighty Fortress Is Our God" and "Crown Him with Many Crowns." In Schaeffer's next major book, *A Christian Manifesto,* he praised the seminarians in St. Louis and specifically called on fundamentalists nationwide to conduct civil disobedience to end abortion. That 1981 work was to have a profound effect on virtually every Protestant fundamentalist who joined Operation Rescue in the 1980s.

As mainstream right-to-lifers, older Catholics, and fundamentalist Protestants flooded into the St. Louis sit-in campaign, the protests generated remarkable community support. The entire legal system seemed to be on Sam Lee's side. Suburban St. Louis County was far more conservative than the city of St. Louis; County Executive Gene McNary, the county's top public official, proudly sported a small embroidered rose on his lapel, a popular anti-abortion symbol at the time. McNary, Missouri governor Joseph Teasdale, and U.S. Senator Thomas Eagleton (D-Mo.) were all honored guests when sixty thousand anti-abortion demonstrators staged a march through the streets of St. Louis in 1980. Democratic politicians in St. Louis often wore buttons proclaiming "I'm a Democrat for Life." Representative Richard Gephardt (D-Mo.), a St. Louis native and a future Democratic leader in the U.S. House of Representatives, was an ardent supporter of the anti-abortion cause at the time; he ended his support for the movement only when he decided to run for president and realized that opposition to abortion would torpedo his chances of winning the Democratic nomination in 1988.

The attitudes of the suburban police and judiciary reflected the anti-abortion mood of St. Louis County. In April 1980, James Kohnen and other St. Louis County police officers, including several who had been ordered to arrest anti-abortion activists, pooled their money to hire an airplane to fly over Escobedo's clinic during a demonstration, trailing a banner that read "Pro-Life." Kohnen was so opposed to arresting the activists that he began to schedule himself to be off duty on days when he knew sit-ins were planned. St. Louis County police captain Gerald Mizell, who supervised police operations at many of the sit-ins, said that Kohnen was never disciplined for his actions.

Soon, clinic staffers began to complain that the suburban police were reluctant to respond to requests for assistance when demonstrations were under way. "St. Louis County Police would not even come unless [the demonstrators] were already staging a sit-in," recalls Vivian Diener, now clinic administrator at Reproductive Health Services, which for a few years operated a second clinic in the same Regency Park office complex that housed Escobedo's clinic. "If you just told them there was a demonstration outside, and you asked them to come and keep an eye on it, they wouldn't do it." Mizell disputes those charges but concedes that many of his officers were opposed to abortion.

While the police were dragging their feet, judges and juries continued to acquit Lee and the others on the basis of the necessity defense; in some cases the charges were simply dropped or dismissed. St. Louis was full of conservative Catholic lawyers who were eager to represent the activists for free; ten to twenty attorneys from a local group called Lawyers for Life often were crowded together at the defense table during cases related to sit-ins. Their success in the courts kept the activists coming back for more. Sam Lee was arrested fifty times before he was ever convicted. He never spent a night in jail until 1983, five years after his first sit-in.

"We would just be in jail for a few hours," recalls Dorothy Schonhorst, who was a forty-five-year-old mother when she first joined the sit-ins. She was eventually arrested thirty-eight times. "I never spent any significant time in jail. It was never more than four or five hours. We were never required to pay a fine. I was never convicted. The charges were dismissed in most cases. I only testified in court one time that I recall. It was scary at first, but it turned out okay."

Emboldened, Lee's group fanned out to target other clinics in the St. Louis area: The Ladies Center in suburban University City, Missouri, which was the local affiliate of a national chain of abortion clinics; the RHS office downtown; and the Bridgeton, Missouri, clinic operated by Drs. Martin Roitman and Allen S. Palmer.

When the sit-ins began at RHS downtown in 1979, Judith Widdicombe felt betrayed; she and Vince Petersen had gone to lunch to

try to talk things out, and now PEACE was closing off their back channel of communications. Before staging sit-ins there, Sam Lee and Jean
Klocker, another student activist, went to RHS pretending to be a couple interested in an abortion. Clinic personnel quickly determined that
Klocker was not pregnant and instead discovered and warned her of an
ovarian cyst. The timely diagnosis did not deter the two from coming
back to block the doors.

However, Lee rarely went after RHS; the police and courts in the city
of St. Louis continued to be less accommodating to the anti-abortion
movement than were those in the suburbs. In fact, as the sit-ins spread
throughout the suburbs, judges in some smaller municipal jurisdictions
were openly supportive of the demonstrators. In Bridgeton, a small,
blue-collar suburb near the St. Louis airport, the demonstrators quickly
realized that the deck was stacked in their favor.

The Bridgeton clinic became an even more inviting target when the
activists discovered that both Roitman and Palmer had been convicted
of income tax evasion for failing to report hundreds of thousands of dollars in cash payments for abortions to the Internal Revenue Service.
Both doctors were sentenced to prison, but they were allowed to serve
at different times so that they could keep their clinic operating; this
fact, coupled with Escobedo's troubles, provided Lee with fresh ammunition in the public relations war with the city's clinics.

As the sit-in campaign began to focus on the Roitman-Palmer clinic,
the arrests began to pile up in the Bridgeton Municipal Court of Judge
Harold Johnson. Johnson, an attorney who had been elected to the part-
time post of municipal judge in 1973, had been born a Baptist. In 1978,
however, not long before the first sit-in cases began to reach his bench,
he converted to Catholicism as his mother lay dying of cancer in a
Catholic hospital. "I made a promise to God, to help my mother out by
becoming a Catholic," recalls Johnson.

Johnson had never thought much about abortion before, but his newfound faith helped shape his response to the activists as they began to
line up before him in court. "Sitting on the bench, hearing these cases,
made me rethink how I felt about abortion," he says. He soon became a
convert to the cause. Meanwhile, Bridgeton's city prosecutor, Thomas
Howe, was an avowed supporter of the anti-abortion movement, and he
made no secret of the fact that he did not want to prosecute the
activists.

Between the two of them, Johnson and Howe arranged throughout

1979 and 1980 repeatedly to delay or reschedule court dates for the cases so that they never came up on the Bridgeton court calendar. Finally, just before Christmas of 1980, Johnson bundled fifty arrests against fourteen protesters that had built up over the previous year and dismissed all of the charges.

U nlike John O'Keefe, who had failed to screen out Michael Bray from his organization in Washington, Sam Lee worked hard at first to drill his troops to remain nonviolent. He required everyone participating in a sit-in to first attend three training sessions, which covered the philosophy, tactics, and legal implications of nonviolent civil disobedience. Lee lectured them on the city ordinances and laws they would be violating and warned them repeatedly that they might face stiff fines and jail time. Those unwilling to do serious jail time, he said, should not get involved. He explained the necessity defense and said it was important for them to understand the facts of abortion so that they could honestly testify in court that they believed they were trespassing to save a life.

Lee placed his greatest emphasis on the philosophical underpinnings of protest and on the meaning of true nonviolence: "How do we conduct ourselves, what do we think about abortion, what do we think about the police, the clinic personnel? I wanted to emphasize that we couldn't say the doctor or the clinic staffers are bad people, that a woman is not a bad person because she has had an abortion." The last thing Lee wanted was to allow his protests to turn into shouting matches.

A lthough those blocking the doors were quiet, the picketers and side-walk counselors supporting them out on the street were not. They rapidly became loud and belligerent, quickly destroying the image of the "peaceful presence" that O'Keefe and Lee had sought to project.

The sit-ins were not intended only for symbolic effect; they were intended to block the doors long enough to prevent specific abortions from happening at that clinic that day. Those blocking the doors were trying to buy time for the sidewalk counselors, who were supposed to try to persuade women to go home or to nearby anti-abortion "crisis pregnancy centers." But the excitable picketers and sidewalk counselors had little or no supervision from sit-in leaders, who were in the process of getting arrested at the clinic doors. They often vented their frustrations over their inability to convince women not to go through with their appointments by shouting at patients and clinic staffers. Recalls Widdicombe, "There was a lot of screaming at patients, an invasion into the space of women who the demonstrators thought might be coming into the clinic. I would be taunted and screamed at and called vile names."

Often, the sidewalk counselors stalked women as they drove into the clinic parking lot, hovered over them while they walked into the building, and tried to hand them graphic pamphlets while feverishly explaining the consequences of abortion. Inevitably, that tactic led to pushing and shoving, as patients and their boyfriends or husbands tried to work their way through the crowded parking lot.

A 1980 article in the *St. Louis Post-Dispatch* provided a sense that although physical harassment had not yet begun outside the clinics, the rhetoric was heating up. In a story headlined "Unpleasantry, No Violence at Abortion Protest," the paper reported the following:

> One protester broke down as police removed her from the clinic door, sobbing "we're trying to save babies, we're trying to save babies." Other protesters pressed pictures of fetuses to the clinic windows to try to sway the clients inside. Emotional exchanges began when Ingrid Smith, the clinic director, came out and talked with protesters. Some referred to her German heritage and compared the work of the clinic to Nazi Germany. A bystander said she was for freedom of choice and took several minutes to talk with some of the protesters. As she turned to depart, a protester shouted, "Go back to your killers." She responded, "shame on you name-callers."

Years later, of course, the scene became much worse. But in 1979 and the first few months of 1980, it was still possible for Lee and others to argue that they were conducting a campaign of civil disobedience that was nonviolent, a campaign that was frustrating to abortion providers because it was gaining mainstream adherents, popular support, and momentum. That became clear to Sam Lee when Dr. Bolivar Escobedo, responding to a note Lee left on Escobedo's car suggesting that they meet, asked Lee to come in off the picket line to talk. In a rambling conversation, Escobedo talked about his Catholic upbringing and privately expressed concern for Lee—for the fact that he was risking imprisonment.

Lee came away from his meeting with Escobedo with the clear impression that the sit-ins were getting to him, that he might be rethinking things. By the early spring of 1980, as many as one hundred thirty demonstrators were attending Lee's protests and nearly twenty-five were getting arrested at least once a week, including a handful of Catholic priests.

Just as the city's sit-in fever was reaching its height in March 1980, Archbishop John May was installed as the new religious leader of St. Louis's five hundred thousand Catholics. May had just transferred from the smaller diocese of Mobile, Alabama, and was completely unaware of the surging tide of anti-abortion civil disobedience under way in St. Louis. When his staff told him what was going on, and explained that priests under his supervision were getting arrested and were regularly featured on the local news being led away in handcuffs, May was horrified.

May had arrived in town just in time for Easter, but his preparations for the holiest of Catholic holy days were interrupted on Good Friday by a call from a worried manager at the Red Cross of St. Louis. Samuel Lee's organization had been calling the Red Cross, asking if the organization would support their sit-ins by bringing the Red Cross disaster-relief trucks out to clinics to dramatize how the sit-ins were designed to "rescue" the unborn from disaster.

The Red Cross staff immediately rebuffed the activists but on second thought grew worried that the decision might hurt relations with the Catholic Church. Therefore, the Red Cross manager was calling May to find out if the archdiocese was going to end its cooperation with Red Cross blood drives because of the refusal to get enmeshed in the anti-abortion fight. After quickly reassuring the Red Cross, May realized that his church was now directly linked in the public's mind with the St. Louis civil disobedience campaign. His priests were getting arrested in demonstrations that had the potential to turn violent.

In addition, after tolerating the sit-ins for months, the clinic owners and their landlords were now starting to seek court injunctions and were pursuing civil lawsuits seeking damages. Alfred Fleischer, who owned the Regency Park office complex, had just filed a $1.1 million suit against the demonstrators, charging that they were hurting all the businesses in the building. It seemed to May and his staff just a matter of time before the archdiocese itself might become the target of a major lawsuit.

It did not help that one of the priests who had become a regular at the sit-ins, Father Jim Danis, was a hulking, overweight man who was straining the patience of the St. Louis County police officers, who had to carry him to the paddy wagon whenever he went limp during an arrest. The brother of PEACE's attorney, Father Danis became a major liability when one police officer charged that he had badly wrenched his back while trying to haul him away. Ultimately, the officer sued both Danis and the archdiocese, seeking damages for his bad back, making Archbishop May's legal fears come true.

Privately, May upbraided his priests. At a closed-door meeting of the council of priests in the archdiocese, May announced that he would no longer tolerate their involvement in the sit-ins. They could pray or picket outside, but they could not engage in any illegal activity. May's new rule for his priests did not remain secret for long, however, and when May went to Regency Park to see the sit-ins for himself in April, he was bombarded with questions from reporters. May responded that he thought the sit-ins were "ill-advised and counterproductive." His statement was splashed across the top of the front page of the next day's *St. Louis Post-Dispatch*. Local television news showed May standing in front of Escobedo's clinic, in clerical garb, calling on the activists from PEACE to end their campaign. The image could hardly have been more powerful—or more devastating—to Sam Lee and Loretto Wagner.

Wagner and Lee both tried to argue with May. In the parking lot outside Escobedo's clinic, Wagner confronted May and demanded an explanation for his statement. May told Wagner that it was wrong for the protesters to block clinic doors, that abortion was legal, and that the Supreme Court had given the right to women. He simply said that it was wrong to break the law. Wagner's heated argument with May was caught on local television, reinforcing a new public image that the sit-ins were being led by dangerous renegades.

May followed up with a formal statement denouncing the sit-ins and then went even further in his column in the *St. Louis Review*, the local Catholic newspaper. "I yield to no one in my abhorrence of abortion on demand as unleashed on this nation by the tragic 1973 Supreme Court decision," May wrote. "At the same time, I do not believe that incurring arrest by violating the just laws of a municipality is the best strategy for influencing the thinking of our fellow Americans toward our pro-life position."

He added that although the necessity defense had worked in the local courts to provide legal backing for the sit-in movement, he was convinced that such arguments would never stand up in higher courts. The strategy being followed by Lee's group, he wrote, "is doomed to failure. The defendants here may win a battle but I am afraid they will lose the war. . . . I just do not think that the sit-in approach is good for the overall pro-life movement in this country and I believe it is harmful to the image and work of the Catholic Church here in St. Louis."

Lee tried to meet with May privately to discuss the sit-ins, but after his public debate with Wagner, May refused. May wrote a letter to Lee saying, "I have listened to representatives of your group and there is not anything further for me to review."

May's statements had an immediate chilling effect on the sit-in movement in St. Louis. The mainstream Catholics who had followed Loretto Wagner and Ann O'Donnell out of the meetings of Missouri Citizens for Life and into the streets quickly pulled out, as did Father Danis and the other priests. The first sit-in after May's announcement drew only half as many people as the one the week before, and the protests continued to shrink in subsequent weeks. "A lot of Catholics believed that if they disobeyed the archbishop, they would be in sin," recalls Wagner. "That cut the crowd down to almost nothing."

May's attack seemed to mark a sharp turn in public opinion against the sit-ins, a sign that St. Louis was finally running out of patience.

Mary's opposition to the sit-in movement reflected the deep ambivalence that secretly pervaded the American Catholic Church's hierarchy over how aggressively to combat abortion. By the late 1970s and early 1980s, many American bishops had quietly come to believe that the church was wrong to make abortion the central focus of its national political agenda. All the bishops still personally opposed abortion and believed with the church that it was a mortal sin, yet many had privately concluded that the country was moving toward a consensus in favor of abortion rights and that it was wasteful to put the church's political and social standing on the line in pursuit of a lost cause.

Increasingly, many Catholic bishops were doing the minimum required to oppose abortion, paying lip service to the issue when they came to Washington for national meetings while quietly letting their anti-abortion campaigns back home atrophy. Their apathy led to bitter frustration within the National Conference of Catholic Bishops (NCCB), where senior staffers watched in dismay as their ambitious plans for political action repeatedly failed to be implemented. Former senior staffers, who have previously remained silent about the NCCB's internal politics, now describe a group of bishops who secretly came to fear that an all-out battle against abortion would threaten one of their most cherished assets: the American Catholic Church's tax-exempt status. Political action would generate lawsuits, and the Catholic Church was a rich and inviting target for lawyers.

The Roman Catholic Church had worked hard for generations to gain political acceptance and financial independence in the United States, and its leaders were not about to throw that all away in the name of fighting abortion. The high visibility of a few abortion foes in the church hierarchy, most notably Cardinal John O'Connor of New York, obscured the fact that so many others were doing so little and that what they were doing was so ineffective.

"To be fair, you've got to remember that the bishops had never been confronted with anything like this before," observes Bishop James McHugh, now bishop of Camden, New Jersey, who as a young monsignor directed anti-abortion activities for the National Conference of Catholic Bishops in the late 1960s and early 1970s. McHugh is critical of the bishops' failures, but as a bishop now himself, he is sympathetic:

> Up until *Roe v. Wade,* the church's primary political interest had been on schools and school funding. The lobbying that the church did was usually very personal; the Cardinal would talk to the senator about some problem the church needed dealt with. And the senator would take care of our problem.
>
> But suddenly with abortion, that kind of politics didn't work anymore. So this was a learning experience for the American hierarchy. After *Roe,* the bishops were writing a statement at every meeting they had in Washington. But when they went back home, they didn't know what to do.

Ultimately, the bishops' inaction and failure to provide leadership allowed the anti-abortion movement to drift into increasingly militant and radical action. After helping to launch the movement, the American bishops had a responsibility to harness and guide it, but they did not do that.

Initially, of course, the American bishops were stunned by the Supreme Court's *Roe* decision. They had been so shocked, in fact, that they briefly encouraged Catholics to take to the streets. In a meeting on February 13, 1973, less than a month after the *Roe* ruling, the National Conference of Catholic Bishops drafted a public statement that for the first time made the case for civil disobedience by Catholics, which was a revolutionary step for the American Catholic leadership.

After an internal debate, the bishops released a rousing statement saying that "there can be no moral acceptance of the recent U.S. Supreme Court decision which professes to legalize abortion." The bishops rejected the ruling as "erroneous, unjust, and immoral," adding that "Catholics must oppose abortion as an immoral act. No one is obliged to obey any civil law that may require abortion."

The statement was in part an attempt to reassure Catholic physicians and other medical personnel who initially feared they might be compelled to participate in abortions; the bishops wanted to convince them that they had their church's backing if they chose to ignore any such rules. But the statement could also be read more broadly, as a call to all Catholics to break the law and fight the state in the name of God.

Yet the bishops never publicly followed up on that theme; they never again suggested that American Catholics should engage in civil disobedience to fight abortion. The National Conference of Catholic Bishops soon began to tone down its rhetoric, on the advice of its attorneys. The bishops pulled back.

To be sure, the Catholic Church remained highly visible on the issue of abortion, and it won a few modest victories. In 1973, Congress passed the so-called conscience clause law. In March 1974, the Catholic leadership also caused a stir when four cardinals testified jointly before the Senate Judiciary Committee in support of a constitutional amendment to ban abortion.

Again in November 1975, the National Conference of Catholic Bishops moved directly into the political arena when it issued its first "Pastoral Plan for Pro-life Activities," designed as a blueprint for Catholic anti-abortion activity. In its own way, that plan was a watershed document for the American Catholic Church; it called for a public relations campaign against abortion and grassroots political mobilization down to the parish church level. The plan was highlighted by a proposal for "tightly knit, well-organized pro-life units" in each congressional district to provide shock troops for protests and to influence lawmakers in Washington directly.

The church's most notable legislative victory came with the Hyde amendment, which Congress passed in 1976 to cut off Medicaid funding for abortions for poor women. In 1976, Henry Hyde, a freshman representative from Illinois, proposed a measure that would ban the use of public funds for abortions. The proposal came as an amendment to Title XIX of the Social Security Act, which provided for federal funding of medical treatment for indigent persons.

Since the *Roe* decision, Medicaid had been funding more than three hundred thousand abortions a year. Although some states had banned the practice, Hyde wanted to implement the ban on a national level. According to his thinking, public funding of abortions was encouraging women to get them. Furthermore, he said, taxpayers who opposed abortion should not be required to pay for them. Abortion-rights groups argued that it was common for taxpayers to pay for programs they did not support. They also said that the measure would be discriminatory, cutting poor women's access to abortions. The proposal, they charged, was nothing more than anti-abortion politics.

The Hyde amendment passed with an exception for cases in which the woman's life was in jeopardy. The measure was immediately challenged by a young pregnant woman from Brooklyn named Cora McRae, who filed a class-action lawsuit against Secretary of Health and Human Services Patricia Harris. McRae alleged that by refusing to fund medically necessary abortions while funding maternity care, the Hyde amendment discriminated against poor women and denied them their constitutional right to an abortion as established by *Roe v. Wade*. A federal court ruled in McRae's favor, setting the stage for the 1980 Supreme Court case known as *Harris v. McRae*.

In that decision, a divided Supreme Court upheld the Hyde amendment, saying that the amendment, by "encouraging childbirth except in the most urgent circumstances, is rationally related to the legitimate governmental objective of protecting potential life." Whereas the government may not place obstacles in the path of a woman's exercise of her freedom of choice, the Court said, "it need not remove those not of its own creation, and indigency falls within the latter category." NCCB lobbyists worked closely with Hyde's staff to push the Hyde amendment through Congress. The law survived lengthy court challenges, was finally upheld by the Supreme Court in 1980, and served as the prototype for the kind of limited political action that the Catholic Church was willing to conduct. The church would go at abortion on the margins, engaging in quiet, polite lobbying, playing the Washington game.

Despite their rhetoric, the church leaders clearly were not willing to put their credibility on the line for an all-out social and political assault on *Roe*. Church officials now acknowledge, for example, that the pastoral plan of 1975 was never put into effect nationwide. Many bishops ignored it altogether.

"The plan was excellent, the organization could have implemented it, but there wasn't the support from the bishops," concedes Father Edward Bryce, who succeeded McHugh as director of the Office of Pro-Life Activities for the National Conference of Catholic Bishops in the late 1970s and early 1980s. "They [the bishops] were all good guys, they were well intentioned, but they paid lip service to this. These were people who could build cathedrals, and they knew that you don't do something like this halfheartedly. The skills were there. But some of them made a determination early on that this battle was lost, and decided they would not devote extraordinary resources to it."

Ultimately, the plan to organize along congressional district lines was dropped, and grassroots mobilization only occurred in a few scattered archdioceses. "Some of the bishops were fearful of it [the plan]," adds McHugh. "Some of the bishops were overcautious because they thought this plan would put their tax-exempt status at risk. And Washington [NCCB headquarters] always had that fear, too."

The bishops had good reason to fear a legal backlash. In 1980, Abortion Rights Mobilization, an ad hoc group headed by Lawrence Lader, a longtime abortion-rights activist, filed suit in federal court seeking to revoke the tax-exempt status of any Roman Catholic church that engaged in political activity on behalf of anti-abortion political candidates. "They alleged electioneering by the church, which we found ironic, since we were so overly conservative on avoiding doing anything that might violate the tax law," observes Richard Doerflinger, now director of the pro-life office at the NCCB. The case dragged on for ten years and went to the Supreme Court three times. The church finally won when the case was thrown out in 1990, but the court battle convinced the bishops to be even more cautious and instilled an even deeper fear of political activity.

"The fear of losing the tax-exempt status induced a chilling effect," says McHugh. "The opposition among the bishops to any kind of political activity was always there because of the tax-exempt status, and that boiled down to constant pressure on us [the NCCB staff] to ease up."

If Sam Lee and other young activists were going to act, therefore, they would have to do so without the life raft of the Catholic Church: the church that had urged them out into the streets, the church that taught them that abortion was an immoral act, the church that said it was a mortal sin punishable by excommunication.

"The American Catholic hierarchy," John O'Keefe later wrote in despair, "exercised prudence without fortitude."

Just as Archbishop May issued his statement denouncing the sit-ins, court injunctions were beginning to take effect at most of the clinics in the St. Louis area, upping the legal ante. Protesters would no longer face trespass charges and fines of ten dollars; instead, violating the injunctions would mean contempt of court charges and the potential for lengthy jail time. David Danis and other attorneys advised Lee to stay one step ahead of the courts by moving the protests to clinics that had not yet won injunctions, but that tactic only convinced abortion providers and local judges and prosecutors that the injunctions were effective. Soon, almost all of the local clinics obtained them.

The combined force of May's announcement and the injunctions led to the rapid collapse of Sam Lee's movement. PEACE all but disappeared. By the time the Missouri Court of Appeals ruled that the necessity defense could no longer be used in state courts in anti-abortion protest cases, ruling that abortion is a "constitutionally protected activity and therefore legal and its occurrence cannot be a public or private injury," PEACE, which had sought the appeals court ruling in an effort to set a lasting precedent, was long gone.

Soon the St. Louis media, the clinic personnel, and the courts assumed that they had heard the last of anti-abortion sit-ins. But they had only begun to hear from one young local activist named John Ryan, and they did not realize that he was about to make St. Louis once again the center of anti-abortion activism in the United States.

7

JOHN RYAN'S OBSESSION

When everyone else in St. Louis abandoned sit-ins because of court injunctions and Archbishop May's denunciation, local activist John Ryan kept going alone, blocking clinic doors by himself—and getting arrested—at least once a week for nearly two years. He eventually lost track of exactly how many times he was taken into custody; his police record included well over four hundred arrests, by far the most of any individual in the history of the American anti-abortion movement.

His solitary actions went almost completely unnoticed by the St. Louis press. He had no impact on stopping abortions. He did not try to convince any other activists to join his sit-ins. No one on either side of the abortion battle could comprehend why he kept doing it. At times, he could not understand it himself. His wife grew depressed, unable to decide whether she had married a saint or a madman, or maybe a touch of both. Local police officers threatened to take him to a mental hospital, and staffers at the abortion clinic abused him. Yet in the end, he built a movement out of his personal obsession.

John Ryan was no philosopher. He was happy that John O'Keefe had written *A Peaceful Presence* and that Sam Lee had come to the sit-ins after a long spiritual journey. That meant he did not have to. He could just join up.

Ryan was no Charismatic, either. He considered himself a devout yet traditional Irish Catholic, and he had not undergone the blinding flash of religious conversion. He called himself a "pragmatist," a simple Midwesterner attracted to the movement for simple reasons: Abortion was clearly killing, and sit-ins were clearly the most effective means to stop it. "To me it just makes sense," he says. "There are so many different levels at which it works; philosophically, ethically, morally, it was the thing to do."

Yet Ryan was a far more complex character than he ever let on to anyone around him, maybe even to himself. In some ways he was the most complex figure in the entire movement, the most difficult for both friends and foes to decipher. His uncertain grammar, pleasant if unremarkable looks, and laid-back manner masked the fact that he was extraordinarily bright, remarkably intense, and clearly driven; he earned a master's degree in social work even while he was spending time in jail every week and while holding down a full-time job and getting married. John Ryan was like a bottle of energy, strongly corked.

John Ryan's father, George, was a World War II veteran of the Italian campaign, a Joliet, Illinois, native who had earned a master's degree in social work and had carved out a career as a social services administrator. He moved the family to St. Louis when he was named the director of the Missouri Hills Home for Boys, an old-style, city-run home for St. Louis's wayward youth. He and his wife and their six children lived in a house reserved for the director on the campus of the boys' home, on the bluffs overlooking the Missouri River about ten miles from St. Louis. It was there that John Ryan grew up, among the boys confined to the home. He walked freely among them on campus, and they walked freely past his home, but John and his siblings were expressly forbidden by their parents from ever talking to any of them. And so in a sea of youth, John Ryan was almost always alone.

John went to school in the town of Spanish Lake, Missouri, but his isolation at the boys' home made it difficult to develop close friendships. His home was intimidating to local children; Spanish Lake parents made a habit of driving their miscreant sons to Missouri Hills to warn them of their fate if they did not shape up. The last thing any of them wanted to do was to come play at John Ryan's house; it was like going to jail. So John would climb down the bluffs to play along the Missouri River, by himself.

George Ryan often had to leave home in the middle of the night to help track down runaway boys, and he seemed to his son, who would lie awake in bed worrying about his father until he heard his car pulling up to the house, to devote far more time and energy to dealing with the problems of the young boys in his care than to his own family. But what his father did pass on to John was an old-fashioned sense of justice and idealism—and a hatred of prejudice. About half of the boys in Missouri Hills were black, and George Ryan made it clear to John that he believed blacks had been victims of prejudice for far too long. So when other boys in school chided John for being a "nigger lover," John would take it personally; even though he really did not know the boys at the home, he would defensively respond, "Yeah, I do love them."

John was sixteen when the Ryans finally moved out of Missouri Hills and into a regular suburban neighborhood in unincorporated north St. Louis County; his father had changed jobs to become director of Father Dunne's Home for Boys, a juvenile home run by the Catholic Church. At Rosary Catholic High School, John played the drums in the school band and worked on the stage crew for school theater productions, but he was plagued by a lack of self-confidence, and he never quite fit in. After he graduated from high school, he briefly attended a local junior college but soon dropped out. Living at home, he was shiftless for the next few years, working at gas stations and a series of other dead-end jobs.

Meanwhile, his father suffered a heart attack and was forced to retire; on disability, he began to devote his time to volunteer work, especially for Missouri Citizens for Life's North County chapter, which was headed up by Dorothy Schonhorst. John began to tag along to the meetings.

By the age of twenty-one, he was a regular volunteer, working the election polls for anti-abortion candidates, handing out flyers and literature, and wearing his "give-life-a-chance" pins. Ryan's life finally began to click into gear when he took a job as a supervisor at a sheltered workshop for the handicapped. He found he enjoyed working with people, switched to a job as a teacher's aide in a special school, began dating an attractive young teacher named Karen Cutsoukos, and finally became motivated to go back to college to get a degree. He got scholarships to St. Louis University for a bachelor's degree and then a master's degree in social work.

As a commuter student at St. Louis University, Ryan was haunted by a controversial book written by William Brennan, a St. Louis University professor, called *Abortion Holocaust,* which marked one of the first attempts by the anti-abortion movement to link abortion with the genocide of Nazi Germany. The book was graphic and distasteful, yet Ryan was somehow moved by the Holocaust comparison. "I would think to myself, what am I going to tell my children? What did I do to try to stop it? That personalized it for me."

Still, the anti-abortion cause never grabbed him until 1980, when Dorothy Schonhorst told him about the new student sit-in movement that she and others from Missouri Citizens for Life were joining. After a few visits to watch the protests at Regency Park, Ryan became convinced that Sam Lee had found the answer. He had never done any picketing with Missouri Citizens for Life, but the idea of civil disobedience now struck a chord. As he stood watching Lee and the others get arrested, he thought back to seeing the civil rights battles of the 1960s on television, feeling helpless as black activists endured firehoses and beatings and police dogs.

His father had taught him to hate prejudice; now Ryan came to believe that abortion was a new kind of prejudice and that what Sam Lee was doing was a new kind of civil rights campaign. Ryan worried about how his involvement in civil disobedience might affect his scholarship and college education, which was finally on track, but on Easter weekend, 1980, he took the plunge, joined a sit-in, and was arrested for the first time in his life. "The night before, I sat up all night thinking. . . . I decided this is as good a time as any. But I tell you, I was shaking like a friggin' leaf."

Not long after, Ryan was sick and sitting at home when Dorothy Schonhorst called to tell him to turn on his television, quick. There, on the local news, was Archbishop May, standing in front of Dr. Escobedo's clinic at Regency Park. For a moment, Ryan was elated, thinking that May had come out to support the protests. He was stunned when he turned up the volume and heard what May was actually saying.

Unlike so many other Catholics who had been flocking to Sam Lee,

Ryan refused to quit because of May. He came out to get arrested the next Saturday and every Saturday thereafter. When most of the clinics obtained injunctions and killed Sam Lee's movement, Ryan kept going to the one facility that did not have an injunction: the Bridgeton offices of Drs. Roitman and Palmer. Soon, Sam Lee was gone; he turned to lobbying and legitimate political action. Loretto Wagner went back to Missouri Citizens for Life. Everyone was gone, but John Ryan inexplicably kept coming.

Bridgeton's sympathetic municipal judge, Harold Johnson, refused to hear the cases that were piling up against Ryan, and so the Bridgeton police would hold him for a few hours and then let him go. He was being arrested constantly but not paying any fines or doing any jail time. Even after Johnson disqualified himself from hearing further abortion cases at the end of 1980, Ryan still avoided fines and imprisonment. Bridgeton, and the Roitman-Palmer clinic, did not want to take him seriously. "When it got down to one person, they figured, we'll just wait him out," says Ryan. "I mean, what's one person?"

Complicating matters, the clinic was located in an office condominium, and Drs. Roitman and Palmer needed the approval of all other physicians in the building to bar protesters; Sam Lee had earlier found some doctors there who were sympathetic to the cause, and they had long refused to give their consent to a ban on demonstrations.

Within a few months, Ryan had it down to a routine: Go to work, go to school, get arrested. Get bailed out by a friend from the movement, and start all over again. He got a job at Catholic Charities, an arm of the archdiocese, and arranged to have Fridays off so he could take the bus to the clinic.

He would walk up to the clinic and simply stand in front of the door, refusing to let anyone pass. Because he was alone, he acted as his own sidewalk counselor, trying to hand out literature and talk to women even as he was blocking the doorway. Clinic staffers, boyfriends, and even many of the women patients themselves considered him an unstable gadfly, and they would just push him aside; when they realized no one was watching, some clinic staffers began to harass him further. When the police arrived, Ryan would sit down and go limp, awaiting arrest.

Soon, most of Bridgeton's police force knew him by name, and they were getting pretty sick and tired of John Ryan. Especially since they had to cart him away, only to watch in frustration as the local courts let him go unpunished. But Ryan had become obsessed, either with arrest, with martyrdom, or both. Soon, he became numb, dulled to the trauma; he felt guilty whenever he considered abandoning his protest activity. "I was getting really depressed," he said. Ryan was spent, mentally and emotionally. He was one of the first of many in the anti-abortion movement to be consumed by obsessive behavior. "I don't think I was crazy," Ryan says now, after having undergone therapy. "But certainly I wasn't healthy."

Loretto Wagner was one of the few people who kept track of Ryan. "I didn't think what he was doing was quite normal," she recalls. "This had become a magnificent obsession. It was an addiction, really. I knew what that was like, because I had begun to feel that way myself, this sense that if you weren't there, babies would be dying, and so you couldn't leave for a day, even an hour. . . . But he wouldn't be reasoned with. I was really worried, because he was getting pretty banged up, boyfriends would just haul off and hit him."

In the midst of his obsession, Ryan got engaged and then married to Karen Cutsoukos, whom he had been dating for five years, a woman who was completely uninvolved in the anti-abortion movement. But Ryan's marriage did not stop him from going to the clinic, and that drove a sharp wedge down the middle of his life. Karen soon started pushing John to start a family, hoping that if he had children of his own he would give up his obsession with other people's unborn.

To her dismay, Karen found she was infertile and began her own obsessive quest to get pregnant; she thought it was the only way to force John to end his lonely anti-abortion fight and the only way to save their new marriage. She began difficult fertility treatments, and marital sex for John quickly became not a labor of love but a mechanical labor, drained of passion, something that had to be done in between sit-ins and arrests. The focus of Ryan's life now narrowed to trying to stop other women from terminating their pregnancies during the day and trying to initiate a pregnancy for his own wife at night. Her failure to conceive only made Karen more desperate and John more distant.

"I was getting [frustrated] because I wanted a family, I wanted children," Karen said in an interview. "It was just that I wanted him to balance himself. I feared that something would happen to him if he continued to live so out of balance. It was his whole life." John Ryan, the son, had become George Ryan, the father—the man who let the concerns of others crowd out his own.

Karen poured out her grief to Loretto Wagner. "She told me she didn't know what to do; she was caught up in this thing that was not really a marriage. She didn't know if she was married to a saint or a crazy person. She felt helpless. She felt that if she protested, she might be keeping him from doing God's work. But she still felt that it wasn't right, that she deserved a husband. She felt guilty."

Catholic Charities eventually tired of Ryan's actions as well, and Ryan lost his job, forcing the couple to rely on Karen's paycheck as a teacher and, later, donations from anti-abortion supporters. Still, he refused to quit. He and Karen now had nothing to talk about. "We didn't have much of a relationship," he recalled in an interview. "There was this intense dedication over here, but at home I was just sort of reliving my parents' marriage. Our relationship was pathetic."

J ust when Ryan was on the verge of collapse, a local newspaper reporter, intrigued by his solitary and quixotic campaign, came out to do a feature story on him. The media had ignored his actions until then, but the first time he went back to the clinic after the story appeared, he was surprised to see a small cluster of women saying the rosary, waiting for him. Ryan was euphoric; he was no longer alone. With witnesses, the police and clinic staff became more circumspect, and Ryan's own psyche seemed to stabilize. It was as if he had been running blind through a dark, mental tunnel, and now he was emerging on the other side.

Soon, Sam Lee called, eager to renew his sit-in campaign. Since the collapse of PEACE, Lee had been making ends meet selling pharmaceutical books, but he told Ryan he was recruiting people willing to test the court injunctions that protected the other clinics in town.

Ryan eagerly joined up, and along with Lee and two other hard-core veterans of Lee's earlier campaign, Ann O'Brien and Joan Andrews, began sit-ins at The Ladies Center clinic in University City. Beginning in September 1982, the four conducted six sit-ins before they were finally found in contempt of court.

Now, for the first time, they faced a no-nonsense judge who was not willing to let them escape without paying a price. In December 1982, St. Louis County circuit judge Richard Provaznik found all four in contempt of court and sentenced them to jail terms ranging from 225 to 314 days; after their appeals failed, the four began serving sentences in June 1983. It marked the first time anyone in the St. Louis campaign had to spend more than a few hours in jail. Sit-ins were no longer free.

In jail, Lee began to catch up on his reading; he read *Concerning Dissent and Civil Disobedience* by former Supreme Court justice Abe Fortas. Slowly, he was recognizing the same thing that had dawned on John O'Keefe, that the only way to make civil disobedience work was with large numbers. Far more people had to be willing to risk arrest than had yet done so in either St. Louis or Washington. Swamping the legal system and the prisons might force change. "With all the problems of crowding in jails, there is no way we would have gone to jail for seven and a half months if there had been forty or four hundred of us," Lee told reporters at the time.

Lee, O'Brien, and Ryan were placed on work release, and that gave Lee an opportunity to proselytize during the day for larger sit-ins. In July 1983, he flouted the courts while on work release by holding a lunchtime press conference with Ryan and O'Brien at St. Louis University to announce that he was trying to recruit two hundred fifty people to stage another sit-in at The Ladies Center. Ryan talked in support of Lee's plan at the press conference as well; it was the first time he had spoken in public in his life, and he was surprised to find that he was not so bad at it.

After his release, however, Lee found that he was far short of his goal. Only fifty to sixty people had signed up for a new round of sit-ins, and Lee did not think that was enough. Lee's life had also changed by the end of his sentence. He was now married, and his wife, Gloria, the former director of an anti-abortion home for women, was soon pregnant with their first child. It did not take much prodding from his wife for Sam Lee to realize that he had responsibilities at home that had to come first. After five years of skirting the edges of the legal system, he had finally paid a price for his arrests; he had spent an extended period of time in jail, and he did not like it.

He got a new job as a legal researcher, putting his experience working with David Danis and PEACE's other attorneys to work. Once he saw how few people were still willing to risk arrest with him, Lee concluded that he should focus his energy on working in the political mainstream. Lee was still willing to join sit-ins occasionally, but he did not want to let activism run his life anymore. He set his sights on becoming an anti-abortion lobbyist in Jefferson City, the state capital.

John Ryan, on the other hand, thought fifty or sixty people was plenty. "Hey, I figured even if we had two people, that was double what I had been doing." Ryan also saw that Lee was losing interest and that if sit-ins were going to continue, he had to take the lead. He asked Sam Lee if he could have the mailing list Lee had compiled of those who had pledged to go to jail with him, and Lee turned it over. With it, Lee turned over control of what little was left of the movement.

Sam Lee may have changed, but so had John Ryan. Whereas Lee had begun to despair over the failures of direct action and civil disobedience, Ryan's years of lonely protests and his time in prison had only made him harder, even more intense. Now he was a battle-wise veteran; he had put up with more than his share of humiliation and abuse and was no longer afraid to do what was necessary.

Unlike Lee, Ryan had never devoted much time to thinking through the philosophical justifications for civil disobedience, and now his thoughtlessness began to show. He wanted to take what he called a "pragmatic" approach to protest: doing what worked to close clinics. Symbolism and the public perception of his actions had little meaning.

"John changed after he got out of jail," says Loretto Wagner. "When he first came out to our sit-ins, John couldn't have been sweeter, more polite. But the intensity of this whole thing got to him. And when he took charge, the whole tone changed."

As Lee faded out of leadership in early 1984, the focus he had placed on a disciplined approach to nonviolent civil disobedience, inspired by John O'Keefe's *A Peaceful Presence,* faded with him. The leadership transfer broke the fragile connection between the leftist actions of the 1960s and the anti-abortion movement that O'Keefe had tried so hard to foster. Lee had been O'Keefe's most significant recruit anywhere in the nation, and now he was gone. That spelled the end of the early leadership provided by Charismatic Catholics, who had been driven to anti-abortion activism by a quiet, prayerful spirituality.

Ultimately, those leaders were replaced by fundamentalist Protestants like Randall Terry, who came to their activism steeped in a church tradition of vocal, militant prayer and judgmental sermonizing, which did not translate well when it exploded into public view in the political arena.

Before all that happened, however—and years before anyone outside Binghamton, New York, had heard of Randall Terry—John Ryan, along with Joseph Scheidler, a fellow "pragmatist," emerged to play leading roles in transforming anti-abortion activism in the United States into something harsh and militant, something that was barely recognizable to pacifists like John O'Keefe.

Ryan began to phone everyone on Lee's mailing list, asking all of them to go back to Bridgeton with him, back to the offices of Drs. Roitman and Palmer, where he had staged his one-man protests. More than thirty people showed up at a planning meeting, veterans of Sam Lee's sit-ins as well as newcomers, and when they started asking Ryan probing questions about jail time and fines, he knew they were serious.

"I guarantee you," he told them, "if this group sits in, all thirty of you, there will be no abortions there that day." Among those asking Ryan the tough questions was an attractive brunette in her thirties, a mother of three named Linda Kimball. Ryan had never met her before, but she seemed eager to try her first sit-in.

On February 18, 1984, they gathered in a parking lot across the street from the clinic, and Ryan was elated; thirty-four people were there to get arrested, more than had ever been arrested at any one time in Sam Lee's sit-ins; dozens more were there to picket in support.

Ryan waited until just before noon, knowing that the doctors saw pregnant women who were going to have babies in the morning and performed abortions only in the afternoon. The clinic staffers, accustomed to seeing Ryan alone, were stunned when he walked into the building's atrium with a crowd behind him.

First, the thirty-four willing to risk arrest sat down in front of the door; to Ryan's surprise, many of those who had planned only to picket outside were emboldened to pile in as well, and the building's atrium was soon packed. One of the clinic employees made the mistake of opening the office door, and Ryan told the demonstrators nearest the door to plunge past the staffer to occupy the clinic's waiting room.

When the police came, they did a double take. John Ryan was back, but this time with a small army. Ryan and a handful of others were arrested, but the police, despairing of hauling off the entire crowd, finally convinced the doctors and staff to come out and close up for the day. After waiting to make sure that the clinic was really closed, the protesters went home. For the first time, Ryan saw how the calculus of protest changed with numbers; a sense of elation, power, and vindication surged through him. Single-handedly, Ryan had sparked a second wave of activism in St. Louis; he quickly began attracting new followers to his sit-in campaign.

Word spread quickly throughout the anti-abortion subculture nationwide that something new was happening in St. Louis, and Ryan became a hot commodity. By June, he was invited to address the National Right to Life Committee's annual convention in Kansas City, the biggest forum the movement had to offer. Despite National Right to Life's growing concerns about its connections to civil disobedience, this convention was being hosted by Missouri Citizens for Life, whose leaders had regularly gotten arrested with Sam Lee. They had also invited Franky Schaeffer, the son of Evangelical Protestant minister and author Francis Schaeffer, who had recently died, to speak about the theological justification for civil disobedience. Now, they wanted to hear from Ryan, the man who seemed to be picking up where Sam Lee had left off.

Ryan found fire inside himself for this speech. He won the audience with tales of his arrests and then brought his listeners to their feet with his call for a massive campaign of civil disobedience. "If it's radical for us to enter an abortion clinic and place ourselves physically between a murderer and his victim, then I want to be a radical." He was greeted by loud cheers and a standing ovation from hundreds in the audience. His rousing reception seemed to embolden other speakers; even Catholic clergy who privately opposed civil disobedience seemed caught up in the enthusiasm. Cardinal Joseph Bernardin of Chicago told the convention that "simply because a law is in place does not mean that it should be followed."

Kansas City marked a turning point in Ryan's life: his emergence onto the national stage as an activist leader. At the convention, Ryan was excited to meet John O'Keefe and the handful of others active in the civil disobedience movement. Ryan also met Joe Scheidler, who by then was styling himself the "godfather" of the direct-action movement. Scheidler hated getting arrested, but he was happy to encourage others—from a distance—to go to jail. Scheidler, who was a traditional Catholic like Ryan, immediately saw Ryan's potential as a protégé and took the younger man under his wing. Together they quickly planned a sit-in at the closest abortion clinic they could find, but the clinics, after hearing of their plans, all closed for the day. Exhilarated over their first attempt at joint action, the small band of activists agreed to what they called the "Kansas City Resolve," a pledge to stage sit-ins whenever they got together at any sort of national conference. Ryan and Scheidler pushed the idea of the "Kansas City Resolve" a step further and began putting the pieces together to form their own national activist organization, which Scheidler dubbed the Pro-Life Action Network, or PLAN.

A month earlier, Scheidler had staged the first meeting of a group he also called PLAN in Fort Lauderdale, Florida, but it had not been the same crowd; the conference had drawn mainstream leaders, not those committed to activist protest. Now, Scheidler and Ryan wanted to reorganize PLAN into a central clearinghouse for the activist wing, to help coordinate sit-ins and clinic blockades from coast to coast. They scheduled the newly reconstituted PLAN's first convention for April of 1985 in Appleton, Wisconsin, and they planned to make sure that every anti-abortion activist in the United States was there. The Appleton convention would be the first official PLAN gathering for activists in the movement.

About eighty activists from thirty states attended the convention. Those arriving were greeted by a marquee that said "Welcome Pro-life Activists. Have a Blast!" Inside, some of the activists had attached firecrackers to their name tags; Scheidler now acknowledges those actions were in "bad taste," considering how many clinic arsons and bombings were occurring across the country at the time.

Those attending announced that they were willing to go to jail and confront police in their attempt to shut down clinics and run abortion doctors out of business. Ryan said the purpose of the mass arrests across the country was to clog up the court system. He said activists would be trained in nonviolent demonstrations, but he added that future sit-ins would "probably be more violent" in terms of clashes with police. Scheidler told followers, "The old movement is dead. There's a new movement of action and prayer." Leaders have called on God, he said, to bless their efforts. "We are going to protect those children. We are going to make this a year—twelve months—of pain and unpleasantness for those who are destroying our posterity."

Activists from across the country attended, including Monica Migliorino of Milwaukee and Andrew Burnett of Advocates for Life Ministries in Portland, Oregon. They all took ideas back to their local groups.

Among the most important concepts to emerge from Appleton was a critical change in the semantics of anti-abortion activism. Joe Wall, who had helped launch a sit-in campaign in Philadelphia after participating in John O'Keefe's sit-ins in the Washington area, announced in Appleton that his local group now called its actions "rescues." The phrase "sit-in," so reminiscent of the sixties, turned off the conservatives that he wanted to recruit in Philadelphia, Wall said. The term *rescue* also conveyed the message that their actions were not symbolic, as were the sit-ins of the civil rights movement, but were designed to impede clinic access and thus stop individual abortions—to "rescue" the unborn. The term had immediate appeal to other activists at Appleton, and *rescue* came into broad usage almost overnight. Ryan quickly adopted the word for use in St. Louis, and the term *sit-in* quickly disappeared from the movement's lexicon.

"It was amazing," Ryan says. "To see all these people who each represented a group of people who had this commitment was just a shot in the arm. It encouraged us. It was important to have this awareness that there were supporters all across the country." The outcome of the Appleton convention, Ryan adds, was that activists agreed to get the abortion issue "in front of the world."

Ryan also realized that he needed a new local structure in St. Louis; Sam Lee's PEACE had never been a "real" organization. On the advice of his attorneys, who feared lawsuits, Lee had never incorporated or taken any other steps to give PEACE legal standing. When Lee dropped out, PEACE ceased to exist.

Ryan had lost his job at Catholic Charities, and he wanted to make activism his full-time occupation. He saw that he could use the people on Sam Lee's mailing list, coupled with the people who had come to his sit-in in February, to launch a new group, one headed by a full-time director: John Ryan. He asked Scheidler if he could borrow the name of Scheidler's Chicago organization: Pro-Life Action League. Scheidler was flattered and quickly gave his approval.

Ryan mischievously liked the idea that abortion-rights activists would now think of him as "Joe Scheidler South," and he enjoyed planting the idea that there was more of a national organization behind anti-abortion activism than there really was. Ultimately, he modified his organization's name slightly to the Pro-Life Direct Action League, just to throw the other side off even more.

By the end of the summer, Ryan had begun a determined campaign against Drs. Roitman and Palmer, hitting the Bridgeton clinic again and again with his new cadre; he finally forced the doctors to take him seriously and obtain a court injunction. Unlike Lee's group in 1980, Ryan's new organization ignored the court order. As a result, he and Ann O'Brien, who had emerged as his most loyal supporter, along with eleven others, spent up to three months in jail for contempt of court.

Ryan shrugged it off and kept going. He led seventy-five supporters in an action to picket Dr. Escobedo's home. "He's going to be labeled an abortionist no matter where he goes," Ryan said. Ryan rummaged through clinic refuse to retrieve fetal remains and staged a mock funeral, complete with a sympathetic Catholic priest.

In August 1985, activists from around the country who had attended the Appleton convention came to St. Louis to participate in a sit-in led by Ryan; sixty-one people were arrested. Both the earlier Appleton conference and the subsequent St. Louis protest were captured on tape by a crew filming an abortion-rights documentary, entitled *Holy Terror,* that focused heavily on Ryan. It was later shown on the abortion-rights fund-raising circuit, and although it painted the anti-abortion movement in a dark and sinister light, anti-abortion activists got a perverse pleasure out of it; at least somebody was paying attention. The film inadvertently served to give Ryan even greater prominence.

Ryan was developing a rapidly expanding mailing list that provided a steady stream of financial support, and he could now count on a tightly knit band of activists who felt an enormous sense of personal loyalty to him. Joan Andrews, a Catholic woman brought up on a farm in Tennessee who had helped Sam Lee test the injunctions in 1982 and had since become something of an itinerant protester, returned to St. Louis to get arrested with Ryan. She had been bouncing between O'Keefe's dwindling sit-in movement in Washington and a new group of Catholic activists in Philadelphia led by Michael McMonagle, a Naval Academy classmate of Michael Bray's who had begun his own Philadelphia campaign in 1984 after joining in O'Keefe's Washington-area sit-ins. Andrews's return to St. Louis, and her new involvement with Ryan's protests, was a sure sign to Ryan's other followers that they were on the national activist map.

Soon Ryan began to feel that he could lead his followers to do almost anything, and he started challenging the judicial system by launching as many sit-ins as possible. His tactics of constant protest eventually thinned his ranks, but he was supported by a hard-core group of militants willing to get arrested whenever Ryan called for it. Eventually, it was said that as much as one-third of the backlog on the court docket in St. Louis County's courts was due to John Ryan and his sit-in campaign.

With Joan Andrews prodding him, Ryan also began to test the limits of nonviolent civil disobedience that Sam Lee had sought to impose; he then went beyond those limits. Ryan imposed his own ad hoc guidelines: Do not do anything that has the potential to harm another person. That meant he opposed any sort of physical harassment of clinic staffers and more serious forms of violence such as acid attacks on clinics, arson, bombings, or shootings. In theory, Ryan also opposed verbal abuse of staffers or doctors, as well as shouting at women patients who ran the protest gauntlet.

In practice, however, Ryan often shouted himself—"Please don't kill your baby!"—and he failed to tone down others who screamed at staffers or shadowed patients all the way to the clinic door. He allowed the rhetorical level on the picket line to escalate. To the clinic staffers who monitored the protests, it seemed that Ryan entered a "trance" during the sit-ins, and in fact, a videotape of the August 1985 sit-in shows Ryan, glassy-eyed, shrilly and repeatedly demanding that a police officer reading aloud from a court injunction call the abortion clinic an "abortion mill."

In response to Ryan, the clinics in St. Louis began recruiting volunteer "escorts" to help patients make it past Ryan's protests. They were thus among the first clinics anywhere in the country to counter anti-abortion demonstrations with what later became known as "clinic defenders." Confrontations—pushing, shoving, and shouting by both sides—inevitably followed. Eventually, a local clinic administrator was convicted of assault for attacking Ryan, although Ryan's actions were almost designed to incite a response.

Instead of instructing his group to go limp when facing arrest, Ryan began to urge activists to grab on to doors, railings, or furniture to resist arrest and slow down police efforts to remove them. He had few qualms about pushing past clinic staffers to bolt through an open office door. Eventually, Ryan and a few other hard-core activists in his new group began to bring steel cable and padlocks with them to chain themselves to tables and furniture inside the clinics, and they sometimes struggled with police when officers attempted to prevent them from getting chained in. A few, like Joan Andrews, squirmed and resisted so force-fully that it took several police officers to wrestle them into waiting paddy wagons.

Andrews always seemed to be at the center of things when aggressive actions were taking place in St. Louis. In one protest at the Reproductive Health Services satellite clinic in Regency Park, Andrews stormed into the waiting room, kicked out a small receptionist window, and then climbed over a staffer and through to the back office in an effort to get into the clinic's procedure rooms.

Ryan also did not mind damaging clinic equipment when he or his followers were able to get inside clinic procedure rooms. That became increasingly difficult as the St. Louis clinics began to tighten their secu-rity in response to his protests; however, occasionally new targets pre-sented themselves. In February 1985, Ryan caught the police off guard by targeting Barnes Hospital, a St. Louis hospital that performed abor-tions but had never before experienced sit-ins. With Joan Andrews by his side, Ryan raced into a procedure room with a pair of wire-cutting pliers in his pocket intending to disable the suction machine used in abortions. But Andrews eagerly beat him to it; she began pulling wires out by hand. Fearful of being caught with pliers in hand, Ryan threw them out the window. He heard them bounce off a lower edge of the building's roof just as he was being hauled away by the police.

Andrews was an admirer of the "Plowshares" protests of Daniel Berrigan and his fellow peace activists of the 1970s, who had been arrested for damaging missiles and equipment at defense installations, and she believed damaging clinic equipment was part of the same protest tradition. But Ryan did not care about parallels to antinuclear demonstrations: "Joanie and Sam Lee knew about Berrigan and the Plowshares. But I couldn't understand passing all these abortion mills where they are killing people left and right in order to go to a missile silo that has never killed anyone, where there is just the potential for killing. I had the greatest respect for people who were consistent in their oppo-sition to killing, like Sam or John O'Keefe. But I think Father Berrigan needed to spend more time in his hometown worrying about victims there."

There had not been any serious injuries or costly damage done in any of Ryan's sit-ins, and except for a few instances, the members of the Pro-Life Direct Action League were still avoiding significant jail time. However, Sam Lee and Loretto Wagner, watching from a distance, were becoming more and more concerned by Ryan's actions. He had transformed their St. Louis campaign into something far more militant, far more controversial, and far less popular. "I know that some of the clinic personnel were scared of Ryan," says Lee. "The women working at the clinics despised him." The police were clearly becoming more frustrated and angry with Ryan as well. After one sit-in, Ryan provided the media with strong evidence that he had been clubbed in the head and torso by a St. Louis County officer.

Sam Lee was so concerned about Ryan's actions that he briefly tried to make a comeback, quitting his job as a legal researcher in a bid to regain control of the St. Louis campaign and get it back on course. But he quickly found that Ryan was entrenched as the leader, and he decided against trying to oust him. Like John O'Keefe, Lee was a thinker, planner, and organizer, but not a natural leader. He could not compete with Ryan's appeal. "John had more charisma than I did; he could appeal to people's emotions," he said.

Later, Lee came to regret his failure to curb Ryan's militancy and faulted himself for failing to lead the movement back toward true nonviolence. Lee still occasionally joined Ryan's sit-ins and sometimes subtly questioned Ryan about tactics. But Ryan dismissed criticism from Lee and others in the anti-abortion movement with a ready conversation stopper: If a child was being killed in an office across the street, would it be enough to sit down in front of the door? Do we really believe what we say? Are we really trying to protect children?

Like O'Keefe, Lee was paralyzed, unable to counter Ryan's harsh arguments. Lee let the issue drop and never made a serious effort to upbraid Ryan. He could not bring himself to force Ryan to listen to his mounting concerns about his successor's tactics. The only person who made a real effort to get Ryan to change his tactics was Loretto Wagner, who had handled press relations for PEACE as well as Missouri Citizens for Life and had been more concerned than either Sam Lee or John Ryan about the public image of the sit-in movement.

Wagner was not a regular in any of Ryan's sit-ins; from the beginning she had been opposed to Ryan's focus on the Roitman-Palmer facility because the two doctors also treated pregnant women who were planning to give birth. She was fearful that the furor surrounding the sit-ins and picket lines would pose a threat to pregnant women going into the offices for routine prenatal visits. Early on, Ryan had dismissed her concerns by saying that those women should know better than to go to an abortion doctor, that they should see different physicians. Wagner was flabbergasted by Ryan's arrogance and refused any further personal involvement with Ryan's campaign.

From the outside, she saw that the press coverage of Ryan's protests was becoming critical, and the televised images of Ryan and his followers convinced her he deserved the kind of coverage he was receiving. She tried to lecture Ryan to tone things down, like "a mother to a son," but he was not listening. When she told him he was hurting the image of the movement, he would deride her: "Image! Image! Image! Don't you know there are babies dying?"

Wagner pleaded with John O'Keefe to intercede with Ryan, to try to guide him back to a more genuine approach to nonviolent civil disobedience. But O'Keefe, mentally burned and paralyzed by his battles with Michael Bray, wanted nothing to do with a similar battle in St. Louis.

Disgusted by the mainstream anti-abortion activists' refusal to accept his more assertive approach to protest, Ryan went out of his way to make it difficult for people like Wagner to deal with him. "It seems to me," he said in one dismissive speech, "the status quo in the pro-life movement continues to be, as it has since 1973, that we attend conventions, emphasize education, work in the political arena and provide alternatives to abortion. . . . The problem is that status quo has brought us a society even more entrenched in the abortion ethic."

His dismissive words were backed up by dismissive deeds. In May 1985, Missouri Citizens for Life and the Catholic archdiocese jointly planned a prayer vigil to be held by children outside the Reproductive Health Services clinic in downtown St. Louis. To recruit children to join the vigil, the two organizations had promised parents that there would be no sit-ins or other acts of civil disobedience that might put their children in harm's way.

After acrimonious negotiations, Ryan promised not to crash the event with his activists. Just before the prayer vigil was to be held, however, Catholic Church leaders were enraged to discover that he was planning to stage a sit-in piggybacked on the children's prayer vigil. The St. Louis Catholic Archdiocese soon broke its last, thin connection to Ryan when it ordered him to be stripped of his unpaid post as the "pro-life activities" representative for his local parish church. Loretto Wagner had seen enough, and in 1986 she began pushing for the board of Missouri Citizens for Life to pass a resolution forbidding officers of the organization from engaging in acts of civil disobedience.

Wagner's resolution drew an emotional response from Sam Lee, who by then was working as the Jefferson City lobbyist for Missouri Citizens for Life; he agreed with Wagner about Ryan, but he was not ready to end completely his own involvement in sit-ins. In addition, he thought a complete divorce between the mainstream and activist wings of the movement would lead to disaster. He believed that isolating Ryan would only make him more militant.

Terry Wycoff, who was the president of Missouri Citizens for Life, strongly opposed Wagner's resolution as well; she was deeply involved in Ryan's Pro-Life Direct Action League and didn't want to give up on sit-ins, either. But in June 1986, the Reproductive Health Services satellite office in Regency Park was hit by arson—the first clinic fire-bombing in the St. Louis area, and one that remains unsolved—and the violence helped tip the scales in favor of Wagner's proposal. (Judith Widdicombe says she was told by law enforcement officials that they believed they knew who was responsible for the arson—and that it was someone in the anti-abortion movement—but they refused to identify the person because they did not have enough evidence to make an arrest.)

The Missouri split marked the end for the only significant alliance between activists and mainstream right-to-lifers anywhere in the nation. The Kansas City convention turned out to be the last occasion at which the National Right to Life Committee allowed militants like Ryan to speak at one of its major forums.

When the ban on civil disobedience was approved by the state board, Sam Lee reluctantly decided to cut his last ties to the sit-in movement in order to stay with Missouri Citizens for Life. Lee was enjoying extreme success as a lobbyist, playing a central role in developing a restrictive new abortion law for Missouri. Ultimately, his lobbying work led to the enactment of a watershed state law, the anti-abortion law whose consti-tutionality was tested by Judith Widdicombe's clinic in what became the *Webster v. Reproductive Health Services* Supreme Court case. Sam Lee was not willing to give up a promising life in politics.

However, an unrepentant Terry Wycoff, loyal to John Ryan to the end, was ousted from the presidency of Missouri Citizens for Life immediately after the passage of Wagner's resolution. Wycoff then led her entire local chapter in St. Charles, Missouri, out of Missouri Citizens for Life to form a new, independent group that continued to encourage members to join Ryan's sit-ins.

The break with the mainstream movement made little difference to Ryan. By 1986, he had emerged as the hottest star in the rapidly expanding activist subculture of the anti-abortion movement. The Pro-Life Direct Action League had a mailing list of some five thousand supporters, and Ryan was earning a salary of $30,000 a year, making him one of the few leaders in the country who had been able to turn anti-abortion activism into a full-time job. Eleanor Smeal, president of the National Organization for Women, inadvertently helped increase Ryan's national standing by branding him a "domestic terrorist" and making him a key target of NOW's antitrust lawsuit (later changed to a RICO case) against activist leaders.

Ryan finally achieved full recognition from the activist movement in April 1986, when he hosted PLAN's second annual convention in St. Louis; John O'Keefe, Joan Andrews, Joe Scheidler, and virtually every other activist leader in the nation came to St. Louis to see Ryan. O'Keefe gave a long, meandering speech at the convention entitled "Why has Pro-Life Activism Failed?" He was followed by Andrews, who called on activists to join her in a campaign of total noncooperation with the legal system. She had just returned to St. Louis from Pensacola, where she faced felony charges for damaging equipment in a clinic there, and she was due to return to Florida, and the likelihood of a lengthy prison sentence, the day after the PLAN convention.

Ryan led the entire PLAN convention, supplemented by rank-and-file St. Louis activists, including a quiet Sam Lee, in the largest anti-abortion sit-in that had yet been staged anywhere in the United States. A videotape of the sit-in shows that it remained largely nonviolent; while awaiting arrest, those blocking the doors sang old-time gospel songs, like "He's Got the Whole World in His Hands," with the lyrics changed to unrhythmic anti-abortion ones. The demonstration was marred, nonetheless, by the raucous efforts of Joan Andrews, Tom Herlihy, and a few other militants to wrestle with and resist police who were attempting to place them in paddy wagons; a few broke free of police custody and tried to run back to the clinic doors, resulting in minor melees in which officers and activists were knocked to the ground.

St. Louis County Police arrested 107 activists outside Dr. Escobedo's clinic in Regency Park that day, including an unknown young Protestant Evangelical from upstate New York named Randall Terry.

Terry was attending his first PLAN convention and was participating in his first sit-in other than those in his hometown of Binghamton. He was accompanied by Gary Leber, the first person to work with him at Project Life, the small protest organization Terry had founded in Binghamton. Terry's main function during the PLAN meetings was to provide the entertainment; a talented pianist, he played a few anti-abortion songs that he had written, including "When the Battle Raged" and "I'm Crying for You, Baby." In a videotape of the event, shot by Leber, Terry can be seen in the background, listening intently to Ryan's directions to the crowd just before the sit-in. During the blockade, he took his place in the back row, up against the clinic door, singing and chanting along with Ryan's other followers; he offered no resistance when he was arrested and carted off by police.

Terry was excited to be with Ryan and Joe Scheidler and the other big names of the activist movement; he eagerly told all who would listen about his dream of a nationwide campaign of civil disobedience built around church congregations. The veterans of the movement, who had dreamed the same dream for years, smiled.

Ryan had reached the peak of his influence. However unpopular and controversial he was, he had become a powerful force in St. Louis. PLAN, meanwhile, finally seemed to offer the promise of coordinated national action, led by John Ryan. Behind closed doors, however, John Ryan's private life was falling apart. Karen Ryan now saw only glimpses of her husband. When he came home from a protest or from jail, he spent most of the evening on the phone, "cooling off" by talking with other activists about their experiences during the day. He then sat by himself in front of the television, hour after hour, watching videos of his protests. He found it harder and harder to sleep.

"It was his whole life," Karen recalls. "It was the phone that never stopped ringing, people that wrote and called and asked questions, reporters wanting to know what was going on. Everyone that we socialized with, every place that we went, every vacation that we took, was with people from pro-life who had invited us. When we traveled it was so John could give a speech. It took over everything."

Karen had hoped that Sam Lee's marriage and fatherhood—and his subsequent withdrawal from leadership—might convince John to give it all up as well. But to Karen's despair, Ryan was unaffected by Lee's departure.

Ryan had a social worker's ability to listen and empathize, and he found that talent was a remarkably useful leadership skill in an all-volunteer social protest movement. The people drawn to his brand of anti-abortion activism were frequently trying to work out other, more personal problems in their own lives, and many—women, in particular—were soon pouring out their hearts and souls to Ryan. It gave Ryan a special power and leverage, and it drew his supporters ever closer, into his orbit. It also fed Ryan's obsession with activism, helping him to block out further any personal thoughts not tied to the movement.

Ann O'Brien, Ryan's loyal lieutenant, became concerned that some in the movement had come to see Ryan as a "spiritual leader," which smacked of a personality cult. "I would say to them, John is not your spiritual leader!" O'Brien says. "John didn't want that, and he would be shocked to even hear it. But they would all tell John their troubles, and there were people who were putting him on a pedestal."

In jail, O'Brien watched, troubled, as Betsy McDonald, a divorced mother, handed the telephone to Ryan so that he could say goodnight to her children. Another activist, Faith Dixon, went through a wrenching divorce and "would talk to John for hours." The only woman John Ryan could not talk to was Karen Ryan.

Soon, one woman came to dominate Ryan's time and attention: Linda Kimball. The mother of three, Kimball had become a regular volunteer at the Pro-Life Direct Action League, and by early 1987 she was spending long hours telling Ryan all about her troubled marriage to Kenneth Kimball, her high school sweetheart. They had grown up together, but now Kenneth Kimball could not understand her zealous activism or her strange loyalty to John Ryan.

Exasperated, Kenneth Kimball came to believe his wife was a "fanatic" enthralled by a cult led by Ryan. "I would come home from work and the police would be there taking her off in handcuffs," Kimball remembers. "One year, she spent the week from Christmas through New Year's Day in jail. One time *Cagney and Lacey* did a pro-choice show, and she banned our kids from ever watching CBS. It was ridiculous. It reminded me of a cult. I thought Ryan had some kind of control over them."

Karen Ryan began to worry about her husband's relationship with Linda Kimball after John and Linda started holding long bull sessions right in front of her. They would sit in Linda's car outside Ryan's house, talking for hours while Karen sat waiting for John to come inside for the night. Other activists slowly began to notice a subtle change in Ryan's relationship with Linda Kimball. "I thought everything was okay, until one day I was sitting in the back of Linda's station wagon and I saw her and John looking at each other, and I thought, 'Something is not right,'" remembers Mary Ann Sheridan. "I prayed, and then I watched some more, and then I knew."

In August 1986, Karen finally become pregnant; those activists who knew how long the Ryans had been trying for a child loudly offered congratulations. Yet John found to his surprise that instead of experiencing happiness, all he felt was a deep emptiness and great depression. As the birth of his first child neared, Ryan began to spend even more time with Linda Kimball, escaping from Karen. Just before his daughter, Katie, was born in May 1987, Ryan finally realized that his relationship with Linda was becoming serious.

Secretly, John and Linda went together to see a family counselor, just when Karen was about to give birth in mid-May, to see if they could sort things out. "Nothing physical had happened, but we were both having feelings for each other," Ryan said. "So we wanted her [the counselor] to figure out what to do about it." The counselor gave them common-sense advice: If they were worried about it, they should stop spending so much time together. When that did not work, they went back to the counselor a second time, and she said they should "part company."

But Ryan could not break it off. Just after Katie was born, he and Linda touched in an affectionate way for the first time. He insisted (in a later deposition for his divorce) that he and Linda had not, by that time, engaged in sexual intercourse, but he was becoming frightened by the power of his emotional attachment to her. That night, he called Father Ed Schramm, a Catholic priest who had supported his sit-ins, and bared his soul.

Father Schramm said he needed to get away. It had finally dawned on Ryan that he was mentally and emotionally crippled, that he was crying for an escape from the pressures he had placed on himself. "I hadn't been getting out of bed much. . . . I had lost my will to live. I couldn't go on living the way I was."

When Father Schramm told him to get out, to leave town, Ryan jumped at the chance. Along with another priest, Father Schramm owned a retreat cottage, which he now offered to Ryan as a place of refuge. Just after his daughter was born, Ryan told Karen he was leaving, packed up a few things, and moved out to Schramm's cottage. He left in July, stayed there nearly three months, and never returned home.

Karen, alone with her new baby, was at first confused and then shattered when John finally confessed that he had fallen in love with Linda Kimball. While he was living at Schramm's retreat house, Ryan saw Linda at least three times; they still were not sleeping together, he insisted in his deposition, but they were engaged in what Ryan described as "heavy petting and necking" whenever they could hold a rendezvous. Whenever they were not together, John and Linda would talk endlessly on the phone, sometimes for four hours at a time, and Ryan began to bill hundreds of dollars in long-distance calls to the credit card of the Pro-Life Direct Action League.

John had little interest in seeing Karen; he said in his deposition that he never invited her to the retreat home and that he was together with his wife and newborn daughter only when they met jointly with a psychologist who began treating John. Karen tried to fight back, tried to keep John. In desperation, she went to see Kenneth Kimball, Linda's husband, who until Karen's visit was unaware of Linda's romance with John. Kimball stood numbly as Karen Ryan told him what was going on.

Kimball is convinced that Ryan and his wife had a sexual affair much earlier than Ryan admits and adds, with a rage that has hardly been diminished by time, "I confronted Linda, and I said, 'You are a goddamned hypocrite.' She didn't say anything. He had written to her, had written that he was making love to my wife with the blessing of Jesus Christ. He wrote her about the 'afterglow' of orgasm. He wrote, 'Thinking of my love for you, of your presence in us before the Blessed Sacrament.' He was a sick son of a bitch. Our marriage was on the rocks, but to go about in the name of Jesus, and the church, and to commit adultery in the name of the church. It just soured me on the church."

John and Karen Ryan separated on July 15, 1987, less than two months after Katie was born, and filed for divorce in August 1987; Kenneth and Linda Kimball followed soon after. Both John Ryan and Linda Kimball eventually obtained annulments of their previous marriages from the Catholic Church, so that in the future they could be married in the church. Before that, however, John Ryan found that Karen was not finished with him. She fought the divorce for three years, delaying John and Linda's marriage plans as long as possible. She still was hoping for a reconciliation.

Barring reconciliation, Karen was hoping for revenge. The splintering and collapse of the St. Louis anti-abortion campaign followed closely the splintering and collapse of John Ryan's personal life. When Ryan was ostracized by the movement in St. Louis that had consumed his life, his absence created a power vacuum at the national level as well. It was a vacuum eagerly filled by Randall Terry, who made sure to quash Ryan for good so that he could never return to a position of power from which to challenge Terry's authority. In the end, Ryan was a broken shell, in therapy for clinical depression and working as a charter bus driver; in fact, he was hired to drive St. Louis activists to Randall Terry's siege of Atlanta.

Karen Ryan did not have many friends in her husband's organization, but when John told her he wanted out of their marriage, she immediately knew the best way to get back at him. She began to call everyone she could think of in the Pro-Life Direct Action League to spread the word that John had deserted her and their new baby after engaging in a secret affair with Linda Kimball. She made a special point of calling the women who had been close to Ryan, and it appears that she put the worst possible spin on her husband's actions.

Just weeks earlier, many of the women members of the league had happily attended the baptism of John Ryan's daughter, unaware of any trouble. Now, they were flabbergasted that Ryan had deserted his family. The women who had turned to Ryan for advice and counsel took it the hardest.

Betsy McDonald had gone to visit Ryan while he was at Father Schramm's retreat house, but now she turned on Ryan. McDonald was a divorced mother who had watched as her husband left her for a younger woman; now her mentor was doing the same thing. To Ann O'Brien, however, there was something more; she detected at least a hint of jealousy in McDonald's reaction to Ryan's involvement with Linda Kimball.

McDonald immediately began calling for Ryan's ouster as the leader of the Pro-Life Direct Action League. Other women members followed McDonald's lead, and by the end of August 1987, Ryan was summarily drummed out of his own organization.

"We just pretty much told him that we couldn't accept his leadership anymore," McDonald says. "The consensus was that we weren't going to continue to work in an organization that had him at the head. I think very poorly of men who leave their wives and children."

Adds Laura Dunn, "It wasn't just because he got divorced; it was because he was involved with another rescuer. . . . Linda was a close friend, and I tried to talk her out of it. She did talk to me [early on] about how they were interested in each other, and I said, 'You can't do this, he's married.' But I think it was really hard for John and Linda to understand why we felt the way we did."

Joe Scheidler got word early of Ryan's crisis; despairing for his protégé, he quickly tried to intervene in St. Louis to help. He attempted to broker a reconciliation between John and Karen, inviting both to Chicago to spend time getting to know each other all over again. Scheidler had a plan to send them off to a secluded hotel while others watched the baby, but on the day of their scheduled arrival, Scheidler waited in vain at a Chicago restaurant for the Ryans to show up. John was not interested. Soon, Ryan's personal scandal was the talk of the entire anti-abortion subculture. And his hopes of becoming a national leader were quickly dashed.

Randall Terry had been an unknown at the 1986 PLAN convention in St. Louis, but by the summer of 1987 he had astonished other activists by successfully attracting significant numbers of Protestant fundamentalists to join his proposed national campaign of civil disobedience. As a result, Terry had quickly become an influential figure within the activist community; he was now trying to put together the infrastructure for what he was calling Operation Rescue, and he wanted to piggyback on PLAN to do it. At the April 1987 PLAN convention in Atlanta, Scheidler and Ryan had called for the election of regional directors for PLAN to provide greater organizational structure, and they had scheduled the first meeting of the regional directors for August in Washington. Terry saw the gathering as a golden opportunity to get the entire leadership of the activist movement behind him, and so he scheduled his own meeting for the same time to plan Operation Rescue's first major event, a clinic blockade in Philadelphia in November.

Not long before the Washington conference, however, Terry heard about Ryan's romance with Linda Kimball, and he quickly called the Pro-Life Direct Action League in St. Louis. Ryan had been elected

PLAN regional director from St. Louis, but Terry now demanded that other activists in St. Louis stop Ryan from coming to the Washington meeting. He wanted Ryan thrown out of PLAN, and he did not want him to have any part of Operation Rescue. St. Louis, Terry demanded, would have to choose a different regional director for PLAN.

By that time, Ann O'Brien was John Ryan's only remaining supporter in the Pro-Life Direct Action League; everyone else was happy to go along with Terry's demand. Betsy McDonald went to the Washington meeting in Ryan's place.

Meanwhile, the local leadership void at the Pro-Life Direct Action League was eagerly filled by Tim Dreste, an ambitious young Protestant fundamentalist who had joined Ryan's sit-in movement just two years earlier. Soon after Ryan's marital problems became known, Dreste, with backing from Betsy McDonald and other Protestants, succeeded in gaining control of the organization. In the months that followed, Dreste was drawn into Randall Terry's orbit as Operation Rescue began to take off. By the summer of 1988, under Dreste, the Pro-Life Direct Action League had become the St. Louis chapter of Operation Rescue.

By 1988, Ryan had hit bottom. When he returned from Father Schramm's retreat house in September 1987, he had no place to live and no job; he and Linda were both embroiled in messy, prolonged divorces; and he was in therapy for depression. He alternated between living with his mother and with his sisters, and he finally got a job as a bus driver for a company owned by an anti-abortion sympathizer.

Ryan was now completely divorced from the Pro-Life Direct Action League, and he had ended all involvement with anti-abortion protests. But that did not stop Betsy McDonald from bashing Ryan one last time.

The St. Louis media had missed the story of Ryan's personal scandal and his ouster, and it was not until the end of February 1988, six months after the fact, that a reporter for the *St. Louis Post-Dispatch* heard that Ryan was no longer involved. When the reporter called Betsy McDonald to find out what was going on, she alleged that Ryan had misused the league's funds by charging on the organization's telephone credit card $600 in long-distance calls, made from Father Schramm's retreat house to his lover, Linda Kimball.

Ann O'Brien, still loyal to Ryan, was furious with McDonald for making the allegations; Ryan had already agreed to reimburse the league for the bills. Also, O'Brien fumed, the league owed everything to Ryan; it could never repay him for all his work. Ryan had even donated all of his own furniture to furnish the league's office.

When the story finally broke, the reporter, who had been sympathetic to Ryan in the past, agreed not to name Linda Kimball and did not report on Ryan's affair with her, the heart of the controversy. Instead, the story said simply that Ryan had been forced to resign both because of his pending divorce and his telephone charges, leaving the impression that Ryan had been pushed out of the league largely because of financial irregularities.

In August 1988, Ann O'Brien promised Don Treshman, a Houston activist who sometimes worked with Scheidler, that members of the Pro-Life Direct Action League would participate in a rally he was organizing in Tallahassee, Florida, to protest Florida's refusal to release Joan Andrews from prison. Andrews had been in prison in Florida since the day she left the 1986 PLAN convention in St. Louis to face charges in Pensacola.

In Pensacola, Andrews had knocked over equipment in a procedure room—nothing she had not done in St. Louis—but the Florida courts were not as sympathetic. Her decision to engage in total noncooperation with the prison system as a protest—and Florida's refusal to reduce her five-year sentence—had transformed Andrews into the central martyr figure for the entire movement. Now Andrews's old comrades from St. Louis were coming to support her at a rally in Tallahassee.

O'Brien had to go to jail herself in St. Louis to serve a sentence on an old case, so she could not make the trip. Tim Dreste would lead the way instead. But first, the St. Louis activists needed transportation to Florida. Dreste chartered John Ryan's bus to get them there. It was the ultimate insult for Ryan, but he went through with the job, mainly because he wanted to show his support for his old comrade in arms, Joan Andrews.

At the rally in Tallahassee, Joan Andrews's sister Miriam saw Ryan in the crowd and immediately urged him to come up to the podium to speak. Ryan felt uncomfortable, but he clambered up onto the stage, took a seat behind the speaker, and nervously began to think about what he should say about Joan.

Just as he was about to get up to address the bulging crowd of several hundred enthusiastic protesters, he felt someone tapping him on his shoulder: A messenger had been sent up to the podium by the rally's organizers. Don't speak, Ryan was told, and get off the stage. You are not welcome here. Numbly, he stood up and quietly walked off, hundreds of people watching him, humiliated beyond words.

At a loss, Ryan got back on the bus and drove the St. Louis activists on to Atlanta, where Dreste was anxious to join Randall Terry's much larger protests. In Atlanta, John Ryan watched from the sidelines as Operation Rescue laid siege to the city; he said hello to Randall Terry, but otherwise he kept to himself, waiting to drive Dreste's group home. Randall Terry was angry that Ryan was there. Ryan was like an unwelcome ghost from the movement's past.

Soon Dreste was in jail, and he found himself briefly sharing a cell with Randall Terry. In the privacy of their jail cell, Terry chastised Dreste for allowing Ryan to come to Atlanta. Ryan, Terry said, was "a brother in sin," and Dreste must separate himself and his movement from Ryan and Ryan's remaining supporters, namely Ann O'Brien.

When he returned to St. Louis, Dreste followed Terry's orders, breaking with Ann O'Brien and the remnants of the Pro-Life Direct Action League, and launched his own new activist group, Whole Life Ministries. But first, O'Brien alleges, Dreste copied computer disks containing the mailing list of the Pro-Life Direct Action League, the group's most valuable asset, and he later sent mailings from his new organization to people listed on Ryan's old membership rolls.

Dreste's new group, like Operation Rescue, was dominated by Protestant fundamentalists, and it served as Operation Rescue's new St. Louis affiliate; Terry was being inundated with mail and phone calls from potential recruits, and he now made certain to refer volunteers from St. Louis to Whole Life Ministries, rather than to the older, Catholic-dominated Pro-Life Direct Action League. Whole Life Ministries soon became the paramount anti-abortion activist group in St. Louis. When Operation Rescue collapsed in the early 1990s, so did Whole Life Ministries, and Dreste eventually moved on to the right-wing militia movement, becoming "chaplain" of the First Missouri Volunteers militia as well as a local Republican Party committeeman.

After Tallahassee and Atlanta, Ryan disappeared from the movement, this time for good, and eventually got his life back on track. His therapy seemed to help his mental state, and after his divorce came through in 1990, he and Linda finally married and had two children together. Oddly, Ryan became a counselor himself, although his anti-abortion background did raise concerns among his supervisors, especially when he made a point of asking women clients seeking help whether they had been traumatized by an abortion.

But there was one last bit of activist business for John Ryan, a bit of business that was unfinished for years after he left the movement. Not long after he returned to St. Louis from his humiliating experience in Tallahassee, he received a letter from Joan Andrews in prison. Ryan could not open it, afraid that Joan Andrews, the martyred woman who had shared his vision of a militant anti-abortion war, might now have joined his accusers. He put the letter away. The letter sat in his home, year after year, unopened, unread, as John Ryan slowly rebuilt his spirit—and his life.

8

PENSACOLA
From Saint Joan to Randall Terry

By 1988, when a broken John Ryan came to Tallahassee to support her, Joan Andrews had transcended St. Louis. She was now the movement's first martyr—"Saint Joan"—the star subject of countless radio and television appeals nationwide by Evangelicals like Pat Robertson, D. James Kennedy, and James Dobson. Andrews had become the movement's "prisoner of conscience," the focus of a furious protest campaign by a strange new alliance of Catholic anti-abortion activists and Christian fundamentalist leaders seeking to win her release from some of the harshest prison conditions ever faced by an anti-abortion activist.

Convicted of third-degree burglary for entering The Ladies Center clinic in Pensacola, Florida, in March 1986 and damaging abortion equipment there, Andrews was sentenced to five years in a Florida state prison. She protested her sentence by refusing to cooperate with the system; she sat down in the courtroom at her sentencing, and from that moment on, guards had to carry her everywhere.

Her vow of total noncooperation earned her twenty months in solitary confinement on the punishment block of the Broward Correctional Institute for Women. In solitary, she spent her days pacing—three steps across, two steps to the side, three steps back—around the perimeter of her cell. Her window was painted out, her cell closed off by a solid metal door with one slot for food and one for eyes. She had a toilet and a cot, and except for brief exercise periods, she stayed in her cell twenty-four hours a day.

While in solitary confinement, she was denied church services, denied almost all visitors, and forced to endure, on at least one occasion, a full-body search by a male and a female guard working together. Claustrophobia and hyperventilation closed in.

Worn by a life of protest, Andrews was still attractive in a rough-hewn, mid-American sort of way. She was a slight wisp of a woman, with a quiet, plaintive voice and a remarkable sense of modesty about her plight. She repeatedly insisted that she did not think of herself as a martyr, and she urged supporters to "focus on the babies." But her willingness to endure such treatment, her show of self-abnegation, and her wholesome appearance combined to increase her standing as a martyr figure. The anti-abortion movement began to unite behind a "Free Joan Andrews" campaign, and ultimately, her case did more than all of O'Keefe's pamphlets and Ryan's rescues to shine a national spotlight on the new wave of anti-abortion activism that was building in the mid-1980s.

Her case never crossed over to become a major national story in the mainstream media, but that almost did not matter. Instead, the Andrews story brought the growing power of Christian Evangelical broadcasting to bear in support of the rescue movement for the first time; in the process, it offered a telling example of how an insular but rapidly growing religious community was finding its own voice, its own culture, its own heroes and villains, and its own causes.

Once they heard her story on Christian television shows like the *700 Club* and the *Coral Ridge Hour,* fundamentalists assumed that the fact that the major television networks ignored her case was simply confirmation that the secular media were biased and out to get them.

Until Joan Andrews, most fundamentalist Protestants did not even know that anti-abortion sit-ins, or rescues, were under way; sit-ins in St. Louis, Washington, and a handful of other cities had received only sporadic, local press coverage. Before Joan Andrews, the only anti-abortion incidents that generated big headlines were clinic bombings. John O'Keefe, Sam Lee, and John Ryan were never big news, even in the Christian media. Theirs had been small, Catholic-dominated protests that did not resonate within the fundamentalist community. But the Joan Andrews story did click. Hers was the best possible face that the anti-abortion activist movement could present to the outside world— and to fundamentalists in particular.

Outraged by what they heard in the Christian media about her plight, fundamentalists came out in unprecedented numbers to support Joan Andrews. She received at least thirty thousand letters of support, many from fundamentalists who wept when they heard her story on Christian television. Another fifteen thousand letters demanding her release fell on the desk of Florida governor Bob Martinez. Martinez, a Republican and conservative Roman Catholic who strongly opposed abortion, tore his hair out in a desperate effort to avoid playing the role of the anti-abortion movement's Pontius Pilate.

It was one of the great ironies of the anti-abortion cause that fundamentalist Protestants, who until then had steered clear of anti-abortion activism in part because of their antipathy toward all things Catholic, were finally mobilized by the plight of a woman who was feverishly Catholic: a woman who gripped her rosary beads at each moment of crisis, who felt the greatest punishment she could endure in prison was to be denied attendance at Catholic Mass and participation in the sacrament of Holy Communion, and who once described her prison walls as having been painted "Blessed Mother blue." She was so closely identified with Catholicism in the minds of Protestant leaders that Pat Robertson later mistakenly referred to her as "that nun in Florida."

Her story ignited fundamentalists at just the right moment, when Randall Terry was searching for a message that would break through to Evangelicals who had little personal experience with militant civil disobedience. To fundamentalists, her Catholicism became a human flaw that could be overcome or overlooked, because Joan Andrews was their new poster girl, a woman doing battle with the secular culture from which Evangelicals felt alienated.

Joan Andrews grew up in rural Tennessee, steeped in a Catholicism that was totally out of place not only in the Southern Bible Belt, but also within her own family. She was the product of a wartime marriage between a devout Irish Catholic woman from Detroit and a laconic, irreligious Methodist from Nashville, a marriage greeted with thinly disguised rage by her father's anti-Catholic mother and sister.

William and Elizabeth Andrews met and fell in love while both were stationed at an Army hospital in Arkansas during World War II. After they married and left the Army, they moved back to Nashville, where Elizabeth found herself surrounded by strange and hostile relatives, pressuring her to renounce her church; in defense, she pressured William to convert to Catholicism. Caught in the middle, William resented his wife's attempts to convert him and was confounded by the fact that religion had become such a weight on his marriage; their relationship began to founder. Nonetheless, they began to have children in quick succession, which created new tensions when it came time to baptize them as Catholics.

As the children grew, their aunt Sara bitterly took to lecturing the children that their mother had forced their father to have such a large family—they eventually had six children—because of her Catholic beliefs. On the verge of a nervous breakdown, Elizabeth Andrews decided she had to break free to save herself. In 1951, she piled her four young children into a car and headed north, leaving William and his family far behind. She settled in a small lakeside village in Canada, and there she raised her children by herself for nearly three years, until her estranged husband pleaded with her to come back.

William had fixed up an old Tennessee farm to serve as his family's new home, far from the turmoil with his relatives. When he told Elizabeth that religion would never again come between them, she agreed to return, and the two fell in love for a second time. On the farm, Elizabeth Andrews was finally free to bring devout Catholicism into their family life, and her husband no longer challenged her on it. Elizabeth would sit and read Bible stories and say a fervent rosary with her children each night.

Joan soon began to fight similar battles over religion at school, where the Andrews children were the only Catholics. William Andrews was now their school principal, but that did not provide enough protection from the rural Protestant children who taunted Joan and her siblings because of their Catholicism. That only led Joan into an early defense of the church, similar to her mother's reaction to attack, and into repeated schoolyard fights. Her mother's miscarriage of a seventh child—and the way her mother involved her children to help her deal with the personal loss—had a profound impact on Andrews's attitudes toward abortion.

Joan was twelve in 1960 when her mother, at home on the farm, miscarried what would have been another son. When Joan and the other children came home from school on the day of her miscarriage, Elizabeth Andrews allowed each of her small children to see and even hold the three- or four-month-old fetus as it lay in the holy water in which it had just been blessed and baptized by a local priest. Together, the family named him John Mary Joel Andrews.

The next day, the family placed the fetus in a can, along with a lock of hair from each Andrews child, and then, following a funeral, buried the unborn child on a farmland plot blessed by the priest.

Joan's religious fervor soon began to match her mother's; it became so palpable that her sister Susan predicted that she would become a nun. But Joan knew a secret about herself: that her love for the church was not matched by a willingness to accept a vow of obedience to it. Behind a quiet facade, Joan had a rebellious heart. "I just knew, even then, at fourteen or fifteen, I couldn't take that vow."

Instead of joining a convent, Andrews headed to St. Louis University after high school, in 1966. She participated in a few antiwar demonstrations but quickly dropped out and returned home to be with her parents when her brother was drafted, an event that sparked in Andrews a personal turmoil about the war and a world that would allow it to happen.

For the next few years, she lived a naive and isolated life on her parents' farm until her life was transformed overnight by the Supreme Court's *Roe v. Wade* decision. Except for Vietnam and the threat to her brother, the outside world had never really intruded, but *Roe* felt like a personal violation. Certainly memories of handling the fetus of her unborn brother after her mother's miscarriage must have come flooding back.

"I just prayed a lot, and right away I knew I had to dedicate my life to protecting the children. But I didn't know how. I didn't know how to go out in the world and do anything. I was overwhelmed with depression."

Her sister Susan reacted just as strongly to *Roe v. Wade* as did Joan; the trauma of legalized abortion convinced her to join a Carmelite convent and escape the world. Joan came to a very different solution: "I knew right away I had to go and bust up the equipment."

In 1973, soon after *Roe*, Andrews decided to find an abortion clinic she could break into. She felt she could not be at peace unless she did as much damage as possible in an effort to stop abortion. Because

Andrews fully expected to get arrested, to avoid embarrassing her family she decided to leave Tennessee before taking action.

She aimlessly hopped a bus for Chicago, which she selected because no one knew her there. In Chicago's main bus terminal, she began poring over the Yellow Pages for names and addresses of the city's new abortion clinics. Her naiveté quickly betrayed her when a man tried to pick her up and a young police officer hauled her into the police substation in the bus terminal on suspicion of prostitution.

She sheepishly returned to the farm, now more frustrated than ever over the issue of abortion, but her anguish found an outlet when she read about the new anti-abortion movement. She contacted Respect Life, the first mainstream Catholic group to be formed in the Nashville area. Jobless and living at home, she immersed herself, and eventually her sisters, in anti-abortion volunteer work, first for Respect Life and later for Tennessee Volunteers for Life, the state affiliate of the new National Right to Life Committee.

In 1974, Joan and her sister Susan, who had left the convent, followed one of their brothers and moved to Delaware. In Delaware, Susan was raped and became pregnant; she planned to give birth until she suffered a miscarriage. Traumatized by her rape, she abandoned any further thoughts of becoming a nun and devoted her efforts to working with Joan in the anti-abortion movement.

Committed to their cause, the two sisters spent their days praying outside abortion clinics, handing out leaflets, and offering shelter in their own apartment for pregnant teens. Unemployed and completely consumed by the cause, Joan relied on Susan to earn enough money for them to get by. Yet Joan remained anxious; she knew she was still drifting and that her anti-abortion efforts were still ineffectual.

Finally, in 1979, her younger sister Miriam, then a student at St. Louis University, called Joan in Delaware to tell her about Sam Lee's first sit-ins. Joan and Susan, realizing this was just the sort of protest action they had been hungering for, rushed to St. Louis to join up, but they arrived during a lull in the action. They went back to Delaware to try to stage a sit-in of their own in December but failed miserably. Andrews decided to move to St. Louis to live with Miriam and wait for the sit-in campaign to start up once again. She did not have long to wait.

When Lee's St. Louis sit-in campaign caught fire in early 1980, Joan Andrews was there, and she was always in the middle of the action. She never led, but she could be counted on to show up whenever shock troops were needed. She was still unemployed, and the protests with PEACE became her life. In the spring of 1980, she was diagnosed with eye cancer and was forced to have one eye removed; she stunned other activists by joining a sit-in at Dr. Escobedo's clinic in Regency Park just days after her surgery. When the sit-in campaign in St. Louis collapsed after Archbishop May's denunciation, Andrews continued the actions and was one of the last to leave John Ryan's group.

She moved on to join O'Keefe's sit-ins in Washington and began to spread the word that she was available to protest anywhere and that she was willing to help start new sit-in campaigns whenever possible. Single and unattached, permanently unemployed, and with no money and almost no need for any except to pay for food and bus fare, she was free to become the movement's first full-time itinerant protester. As new protest campaigns sprung up, she became a crucial link tying together local activists around the country.

With Andrews's participation, however, came her militant tactics and her dismissive attitude toward those who believed in a disciplined approach to nonviolent civil disobedience. When early leaders such as O'Keefe and Lee began to fade away, so did their theories about "a peaceful presence." Instead, it was the street-level aggressiveness of Joan Andrews, combined with the harsh rhetoric of Joseph Scheidler, that began to spread throughout the American anti-abortion subculture.

Andrews also began a more secretive pattern of clinic vandalism, which she has never before revealed. Andrews and Jean Klocker, one of the original members of the St. Louis sit-in group, were sitting alone one night in 1980 when Klocker brought out a can of spray paint, looked at Andrews, and asked, "Do you know what we can do with this?" They quickly took off on a secret midnight tour of St. Louis's abortion clinics, spray-painting anti-abortion graffiti on clinic windows and walls. Seven years after her aimless bus ride to Chicago, Andrews had finally taken a first, modest step toward satisfying her need to damage abortion clinics. Klocker has since died, and Andrews will not name the others still living who joined her later as she escalated her acts of vandalism in St. Louis, Philadelphia, and other cities.

Emboldened by the success of her graffiti spree, Andrews hit harder. She began to go to The Ladies Center in University City and other St. Louis–area clinics late at night to inject superglue, a remarkably tough adherent, into door locks to seal them shut. The tactic was so effective that clinic staffers often had to call locksmiths to open their doors. Andrews occasionally glued clinic locks the night before a sit-in, providing an additional obstacle to abortion on the day of a protest.

Andrews says she glued clinic doors shut at least five or six times over the years, but eventually she began spreading noxious liquids throughout clinics. She used repellents purchased at hunting stores; while posing as a patient, she would walk briskly through the facility and pour the liquid on the clinic floor, leaving a liberal dose in the radiator. By the time she was out the door, the scent would be taking over the building, forcing its temporary closure. When Andrews took to the road as a traveling activist, joining new civil disobedience campaigns as they sprouted, she took her secret tactics of vandalism with her.

When Philadelphia began to heat up as a new center of anti-abortion activism in 1984 and 1985, it became a focus of Joan Andrews's attention; she was soon getting arrested throughout Pennsylvania. Like their counterparts in St. Louis, local police and state courts in the Philadelphia area were reluctant to fill the jails with anti-abortion protesters; leniency helped swell the ranks. Before long, local leader Michael McMonagle could call out hundreds of protesters at a time, and he staged some of the biggest sit-ins anywhere in the nation.

These protests became even more raucous and militant than those staged by John Ryan in St. Louis, spiraling down into angry pushing and shoving confrontations with the new abortion-rights volunteer "escorts" who were beginning to appear at clinics around the country. To add to the tension, McMonagle's group invaded clinics and damaged equipment whenever possible and made a practice of picketing the homes of doctors, clinic owners, and clinic staffers. McMonagle's main target, the Northeast Women's Center of Philadelphia, was operated by Humedco Enterprises, which in turn was co-owned by Malcolm Polis, a Philadelphia-area businessman who had pleaded guilty to tax evasion and was sentenced to three months in federal prison in 1983 for failing to report income generated by his abortion clinics.

Fed up with McMonagle's tactics, the Northeast Women's Center filed a lawsuit in 1985 charging twenty-seven activists in McMonagle's group with violating the federal racketeering laws by conspiring to put the clinic out of business. It marked the first time that RICO was used in the abortion war, and it was also the first major salvo by abortion providers in their new counterstrategy to use the courts to clamp down on the current wave of activism. The Philadelphia RICO case, won by the clinic in a jury trial and later upheld on appeal, served as the model for a broader lawsuit later brought by the National Organization for Women against Scheidler and other activists, alleging a nationwide conspiracy to shut down clinics.

Joan Andrews had no problem with the tactics used in Philadelphia; she reveled in them. She kept her acts so secret that they never damaged her growing reputation among other activists as the heart and soul of the "rescue movement." Activist leaders around the country began to rely on her as a key networker and recruiter, a woman who saw it as her mission single-handedly to spread rescue throughout the country. Her self-designed mission finally brought her to Pensacola—and to a former member of the Ku Klux Klan named John Burt.

While passing through Washington in January 1986, Andrews went to the Capitol Hill offices of Senator Jesse Helms to visit Earl Appleby, a New Right true believer and Helms aide who had quietly become a strong supporter of the emerging activism. Appleby moved in Scheidler's circles; he attended the 1985 PLAN convention in Appleton, Wisconsin, and later served as one of three "judges" at a mock anti-abortion trial staged by Scheidler's organization in Nuremberg, Pennsylvania, in October 1985. He was also tied to the Defenders of the Defenders of Life, a controversial support group for clinic bombers and their families. In an interview at the time, Appleby refused to condemn Curtis Beseda, a convicted clinic bomber in the Pacific Northwest: "I certainly could not judge Mr. Beseda for acting in the defense of innocent human life."

When Andrews arrived in Helms's office, Appleby was talking on the phone with John Burt, an anti-abortion activist leader in Pensacola and another member of Scheidler's growing network of contacts. Burt and Appleby were planning what Burt hoped would be Pensacola's first "rescue" when Andrews got on the phone and begged Burt to let her join in.

In her association with John Burt and Pensacola, Joan Andrews—the obsessed Catholic virginal "farm girl" and newly radicalized activist—was asking for trouble.

John Burt could have come straight from the pages of a John Grisham novel; he was a walking collision of Southern clichés, a Jim Crow character trying to find his way along the margins of the politically correct New South. He was a bearded cracker with the voice of a cement mixer—a former Marine, former Klansman, former alcoholic, former speed abuser, and divorced father, as well as a born-again Christian who found his personal redemption in the saving of girls lost to the evils of drugs and prostitution.

In his home for wayward girls, called Our Father's House, Burt won government approval to use corporal punishment and the right to force his charges to attend church on Sundays. He could not have been more different from Joan Andrews; she was offended when she first visited him and saw anti-Catholic literature in his home. Abortion-rights advocates could not have asked for a better enemy, one who so neatly fit their stereotypes of the anti-abortion movement.

Burt never thought about abortion until 1983, when he saw a newspaper headline that blared the local abortion rate for Pensacola. In 1982, the headline said, Pensacola had seven abortions for every ten live births. The figures were skewed because the city had the only abortion clinics in the region, but the subtleties were lost on Burt. He had to do something.

In early 1983, he marshaled his girls from Our Father's House and a handful of other friends and supporters and began picketing The Ladies Center of Pensacola, part of a Miami-based chain and the city's most visible freestanding clinic. In March 1983, fourteen picketers were arrested for trespassing at The Ladies Center, marking the first abortion-related arrests in Pensacola.

A handful of Catholics had been holding quiet prayer vigils outside the clinic for years, but Burt quickly transformed the clinic's property line into the front lines in his own private crusade. Like Scheidler in Chicago and McMonagle in Philadelphia, he launched into aggressive tactics almost immediately, personalizing his protests against doctors and clinic staffers. Although he still was not staging clinic sit-ins or blockades and was only rarely arrested, Burt had made himself into a constant presence in the local news. Before long, a handful of local Evangelical ministers began to search for ways to join the fight. One of the first was Reverend David Shofner, then pastor of West Pensacola Baptist Church.

In early 1984, John Burt arranged for Penny Lea, a sometime country and gospel music singer, to come to his church, Brownsville Assembly of God, to speak out about abortion. Lea had turned herself into a circuit-riding anti-abortion speaker within the Evangelical community, and when Shofner heard she was coming to town, he invited her to speak at West Pensacola Baptist as well.

Using rhetoric that touched her fundamentalist audience, Lea explained the evils of abortion in detail to Shofner's congregation. For Shofner the message was clear: Christians had been silent for too long. Shofner was burning inside, and as he looked around, he saw tears and pained emotion throughout his congregation. He stood beside Penny Lea when she finished and said, "You've broken our hearts. Penny, what can we do?"

John Burt, who had come to listen, quickly seized the opening. He told Shofner and the congregation they should picket with him. The next Saturday, Shofner and a few others from his church joined Burt outside the offices of a local abortion doctor, Dr. Bo Bagenholm. But Shofner was immediately turned off by Burt's "gross" picket signs and his harsh tactics. "I didn't want to be associated with that ugliness," Shofner recalls.

To distinguish themselves from Burt's group, Shofner and members of his church made their own signs and switched their protests to a different clinic, one operated by Dr. William Permenter. Frustrated that so few other fundamentalist Protestants were joining, Shofner went on a local Christian radio station to criticize local pastors who "preach about abortion in church but don't do anything outside the pulpit." Listening to Shofner's radio interview was Steve Zepp, an associate pastor at Pace Assembly of God Church, who felt a rush of guilt. He quickly arranged for members of Pace Assembly's choir and others in the church to join Shofner.

Shofner was dumbfounded the following Saturday when two buses carrying one hundred Pace church members pulled up to picket outside The Ladies Center, where Shofner was now holding his protests. "Brother Shofner," Zepp explained to him, "I heard you, and it shot me through the heart."

Soon, pastors and congregations from other Assemblies of God were joining as well. The Assemblies of God—Charismatic churches independent of a denominational structure and thus free of any pressures from a church hierarchy—soon formed the backbone of the protests in

Pensacola. They kept coming every Saturday. "Christians are waking up," Reverend Glyn Lowery, pastor of Pace Assembly of God, told a reporter at the time.

"Everybody was just sort of joining in," recalls Zepp. "We would have an announcement at church that there would be a march at The Ladies Center, and we would get anywhere from thirty to one hundred people to come out. It was like that in all the churches, word of mouth from individual pastors and people getting involved and encouraging others."

By local happenstance—and with little encouragement from activist leaders elsewhere—Pensacola had developed one of the first large-scale anti-abortion protest campaigns anywhere in the South, and one of the first anywhere in the nation to be organized and dominated by fundamentalist Protestants rather than Catholics.

Soon Burt and the churches began to coordinate their picketing and "sidewalk counseling" activities under the umbrella of the Pensacola Pro-Life Coalition; Shofner served as the coalition's president. Yet Shofner and the other pastors always tried to keep Burt at arm's length, with mixed results.

It was hard for the casual observer to distinguish between the groups along the picket line; Burt remained the most visible spokesperson for the anti-abortion movement in Pensacola. However, it was not until the Christmas bombings of 1984, when all three abortion facilities in Pensacola were bombed on the same night, that Burt and the Pensacola protests first gained nationwide attention.

Burt had no involvement in the bombings, but he knew a public relations windfall when he saw it. Like Joe Scheidler, he was shrewd enough to realize that even negative press is better than no press at all. He quickly and enthusiastically made the subsequent bombing trial a cause célèbre and, in the process, made it difficult for the public to tell the difference between Pensacola's bombers and Pensacola's protesters.

The Christmas bombing spree put Pensacola on the abortion map. The three bombings, which occurred within minutes of each other between 3 and 4 A.M. on Christmas morning, 1984, were by far the most spectacular acts of anti-abortion violence yet staged. Isolated acts of arson and vandalism had been occurring for years at clinics, but they had never generated this sort of sustained, national press attention.

Coupled with the Washington-area bombing campaign then underway by Michael Bray and Thomas Spinks, who had yet to be caught, the Pensacola bombings left the strong impression with the public that anti-abortion activism had taken a sudden turn to extremism. President Reagan was forced to issue a statement denouncing the bombings.

Unlike Michael Bray, who had been directly involved in O'Keefe's sit-in campaign, the Pensacola bombers were not active members of the anti-abortion movement and in fact had no ties to any of Pensacola's activist leaders. What they shared with the more visible activists was religious fundamentalism and a belief in the literal power of the Scriptures to tell them that abortion was an unholy stain on America.

Matthew Goldsby and James Simmons were both twenty-one and both Evangelicals who attended the First Assembly of God, one of Pensacola's rapidly growing fundamentalist churches that were sending its members streaming out to the picket line at The Ladies Center. Their story, exhaustively reported by the *Pensacola News-Journal* and detailed in a subsequent book, *Religious Violence and Abortion* by Dallas A. Blanchard and Terry J. Prewitt, began in the early spring of 1984.

Many of the Evangelicals in Pensacola were inspired to protest after their churches arranged showings of a new crop of graphic, anti-abortion documentaries that were beginning to circulate around the country. The most powerful, *The Silent Scream,* produced by former abortion doctor turned anti-abortion activist Bernard Nathanson, was highlighted by traumatic footage of an ultrasound examination conducted during an abortion. During the mid-1980s, *The Silent Scream* became the anti-abortion movement's single most successful piece of propaganda and one of its most effective recruiting tools. Both Goldsby and Simmons were badly shaken after seeing *The Silent Scream* and another anti-abortion documentary, *Assignment: Life,* at First Assembly. They felt called by God to act.

Goldsby and Simmons never followed other members of their congregation out to picket at The Ladies Center; they made a conscious decision to keep their growing opposition to abortion under wraps. Instead, in isolation, they moved straight to violence, and in June 1984, they bombed The Ladies Center for the first time. The damage was so extensive that the clinic was forced to move to a new location.

Convinced that God had allowed them to escape detection as a sign of His sanction, Goldsby and Simmons decided to plan a far more ambitious attack. They would strike all three of Pensacola's abortion facilities at once: the two-story, frame building that served as the new location of The Ladies Center, as well as the offices of two local doctors who performed abortions, Bo Bagenholm and William Permenter. Goldsby and Simmons scheduled their attacks for early Christmas morning as a "gift to Jesus."

Simmons was newly married to another member of First Assembly of God, eighteen-year-old Kathren Simmons, and Goldsby was engaged to Kaye Wiggins, also eighteen and a member of Amazing Grace Tabernacle Church. Both young women were drawn in as coconspirators.

Perhaps because they had gotten away with their June attack, Goldsby and Simmons were remarkably brazen in planning the Christmas bombings, ensuring their rapid capture afterward. Goldsby worked for a construction company owned by David Del Gallo, a leading member of First Assembly of God, and he stole timers from one of the company's construction projects; he then purchased steel pipes and end caps from one of the company's suppliers and charged the purchases to Del Gallo's account. He and Simmons also asked Kathren Simmons and Kaye Wiggins to drive around Pensacola to local hunting stores to buy gunpowder for their pipe bombs.

Goldsby and Simmons might as well have taken out an advertisement. It took agents from the Bureau of Alcohol, Tobacco and Firearms (ATF) less than a week to crack the case, and by December 31, Goldsby had confessed to an ATF agent and was being arraigned in federal court. On New Year's Day, Simmons confessed, and he was arraigned the following day. Kathren Simmons and Kaye Wiggins were arrested in quick succession. By the end of the first week of January, the newly famous bombers were holding press conferences to explain themselves; Kaye Wiggins flew to Atlanta to appear on CNN with Joe Scheidler.

Their convictions in April were a foregone conclusion; both Goldsby and Simmons were eventually sentenced to ten years in prison, whereas Kaye Wiggins and Kathren Simmons avoided jail, each receiving five years' probation.

There was no question of their guilt, but John Burt did not care; he did his best to exploit the case for publicity out on the street. Burt picketed the courthouse throughout the trial, parading while carrying a jar containing a dead fetus that he nicknamed "Baby Charlie," provoking disgust, outrage—and attention—throughout the city.

He convinced Scheidler to come to Pensacola to join his protest outside the courthouse during the trial, and before long, every major media outlet in America was beating a path to John Burt's door to ask him his thoughts on abortion, religion, and violence. Following Scheidler's example, Burt had developed a savvy, as-long-as-they-spell-my-name-right approach to dealing with the media.

The bombings and the subsequent trial of four of their own did little to dampen the new enthusiasm for the anti-abortion fight among fundamentalists in Pensacola. Within days of the bombings, Shofner was leading pickets outside Bagenholm's house. In March 1985, just before the bombing trial was scheduled to begin, Penny Lea organized a march on The Ladies Center that attracted two thousand protesters, by far the largest anti-abortion demonstration Pensacola had ever seen.

The bombings had a devastating impact on two abortion providers. Permenter had been planning to drop his abortion practice, and now he did so; he eventually retired to manage his investments. Bagenholm was unable to obtain insurance on a new abortion facility and was hit by a court order filed by other members of his medical condominium building barring him from performing abortions at his new office. He shifted his focus to other gynecological practices as a result.

By 1986, when Joan Andrews arrived in Pensacola, The Ladies Center was the only freestanding clinic in town, ground zero for protesters in what was rapidly becoming the hottest of America's anti-abortion hot spots.

Despite his harsh rhetoric and tactics, Burt and his followers had not yet conducted sit-ins in Pensacola; Burt was intrigued by what he had heard of the new "rescue" movement in St. Louis and other cities. Joan Andrews was eager to teach him all about it. Unconcerned by Pensacola's growing reputation for anti-abortion violence, Andrews put out the word for other Northern activists to join in as well. Soon, both Joe Scheidler and John Ryan were on their way.

The events that followed—Joan Andrews's actions at The Ladies Center clinic in Pensacola on March 26, 1986, and her subsequent treatment in state prison—have been fodder for emotion-drenched partisan debate ever since. Like so much of the abortion debate in America, it comes down to a matter of semantics and definition.

Joan Andrews was frustrated when she arrived at The Ladies Center for the "rescue" that she and Burt had planned; the police and abortion-rights counterdemonstrators, who were relatively new in Pensacola, had beaten them there. Andrews and Burt immediately realized they could not attempt a sit-in, but they were not willing simply to give up. If they could just get into the clinic, they could occupy the procedure rooms and damage the equipment; that would be just as good, maybe even better, than blocking the clinic entrance. Andrews walked away from the protest rally in front of the clinic to the building's side door; the police and abortion-rights activists did not seem to recognize her and made no move to stop her.

When she knocked on the door, clinic administrator Linda Taggart and the president of the local NOW chapter, Georgia Wilde, happened to be walking out. They opened the door, and Andrews breezed past them. As she bounded up the stairs, she heard a voice calling after her, "You're not allowed up there!" She was followed by John Burt and two girls who had planned to join the sit-in: Burt's eighteen-year-old adopted daughter, Sarah Burt, and twenty-one-year-old Karisa Epperley, who had lived at Burt's home for girls.

Taggart and Wilde both later testified that they were shoved and knocked down as the protesters pushed past them into the clinic. Taggart says that John Burt used his forearm to slam her into the wall as he went up the clinic's stairs in his bid to get to the abortion procedure rooms; she adds that she still suffers neck pain as a result. Wilde testified that Burt ran into her, elbowed her in the rib cage, and slammed her into a doorjamb. "I was smashed full force by John Burt," she said. Both Taggart and Wilde were taken to a local hospital where they were examined and released. Abortion-rights advocates who were at the clinic supported the charges by Taggart and Wilde, but Burt and Andrews deny anyone touched either woman.

Burt was stopped by police before he could get all the way to the second-floor procedure rooms, but Andrews got into one room and in a frenzy tried to pull the wires out of an abortion suction machine. Meanwhile, Sarah Burt and Karisa Epperley entered another procedure room, blockaded the door, and began, as John Burt says, to "trash" the room.

While Andrews was yanking on the wires, two police officers arrived and grabbed her; she refused to let go of the machine, presenting a remarkable tableau: She was pulling on the suction machine wires, and the police officers were pulling on her. Finally, subdued and handcuffed, Andrews was marched out to the hallway, and the police left to try to extricate the two younger women from the second room. When

Pensacola police forced open the door and arrested Sarah Burt and Karisa Epperley, they found the room "in total disarray."

But it was a mistake to leave Andrews alone; handcuffed, she went back into the procedure room she had just left and, with her hands behind her back, pushed the suction machine off its table. The sound of machinery crashing to the floor brought back the police; furious, they shoved her out into the hallway and made a human pile of her, John Burt, and the two other women so they could not move. Television news cameras showed Andrews, limp, being dragged by two police officers down the clinic's entrance ramp and to jail.

Outside, Scheidler made the mistake of publicly cheering the action: "We wanted to get more people in, but the front door was locked. The fact we got in at all was quite a coup." After realizing that Scheidler had gone onto clinic property and had been egging on Andrews and Burt, the Pensacola police issued an arrest warrant, which they later served on a shocked Scheidler while he was in Denver attending a National Right to Life convention.

Earl Appleby had also come to Pensacola for the protest, which had, after all, been planned in his corner of Jesse Helms's office in Washington. To the Pensacola media, he did not identify himself as Helms's aide, however; he was, instead, the "national coordinator for Americans for Catholic Values." The *Pensacola News-Journal* also described him as the man leading the chanting outside the clinic as Andrews and the three others stormed inside. Appleby, who now works at the Justice Department and insisted in an interview that he never had anything to do with "rescues," especially while he worked for Senator Helms, said the following to reporters outside The Ladies Center that day: "There is a crime going on, the murder of babies, and I hope the police are here for the proper purpose, to close the clinic down. This is a war. We're at the battlefield. We're soldiers for Christ."

Coming in the wake of the Christmas bombings, the Burt-Andrews action received almost no support in Pensacola, even from other local anti-abortion protesters. Vicky Conroy, a member of Brownsville Assembly of God who had become a leading activist and sidewalk counselor outside The Ladies Center, disavowed it all. "What was the point? They didn't stop any abortions. All they did was get the community upset and give the movement a bad image." Many longtime local demonstrators were so turned off by the action staged by Burt and Andrews that they began to pull back from any picketing activity.

The local police and courts came down hard—at least harder than Andrews had become accustomed to in St. Louis and other cities where she had used similar tactics. She was charged with burglary, criminal mischief, and resisting arrest, whereas Burt faced the more serious charge of burglary with an assault; both activists thus were confronted with felony charges that held the threat of long prison sentences.

Convicted in a jury trial, Burt quickly accepted an offer of probation, which included a requirement that he stay away from The Ladies Center for four years. Both Sarah Burt and Karisa Epperley received probation as well. But Joan Andrews did not want a deal; she saw an opportunity in Pensacola to challenge the system.

Her nomadic activism had given her a better sense than almost anyone else in the movement of the tactics and strategies that were being tried around the country, and in Philadelphia she had watched as a small band of hard-core anti-abortion protesters had experimented with the old Quaker peace activist tactic of total noncooperation with the courts and jails. She saw that local municipal courts and city jails in the Philadelphia area wanted nothing to do with that kind of administrative headache. She became convinced that noncooperation would bring the system to its knees and generate a new spark for a movement that was drifting badly.

Released on bond, Andrews thumbed her nose at the courts by going back to protest at The Ladies Center again; she had her bond revoked as a result. She then had to stay in jail for months while awaiting trial. But just before she went back to jail, Andrews flew to St. Louis to speak at John Ryan's PLAN convention, where she explained her radical new strategy of confronting the entire governmental system at every turn.

Andrews argued that the sin of abortion could occur only with the complicity of all aspects of society and that state officials carrying out arrests and imposing prison terms against protesters were just as guilty as the doctors performing abortions. "Rescuers" had to become a burden on society, or society would not change.

Her St. Louis speech, greeted with wild applause and cheers from activists who shared her beliefs but never her will or nerve, made it clear that almost everything that happened to Andrews over the next two and a half years happened according to her own design, her own timetable. She said the following at the PLAN conference:

What I've been thinking about and praying about is that maybe the way you can keep out of jail is by totally not cooperating. I would recommend that, while you are at the death chamber, to hold on, to try to prevent, nonviolently, your removal. Once you're in the paddy wagon, or once you are in the jail, don't cooperate. Be silent, go limp, don't give your name. . . . We should put the burden on the opposition, those that are trying to prevent us from rescuing children. . . . I do recommend fasting two or three times a week in jail and praying constantly—but total noncooperation. Going limp where you have to be carried to your cell—total disobedience. Now, let me ask you, what jail would want you? You will create such a disturbance in the minds and hearts of all the people you come in contact with that they are going to say, wow, they really mean it. If they won't keep you in jail, you can come back week after week.

In a letter to other activists from jail in Pensacola not long after her St. Louis speech, she wrote, "There will be a time when the courts will begin hitting us hard. We must be prepared."

Convicted in a nonjury trial in July 1986, Andrews was offered the same probation deal given to Burt: If she simply agreed to stay away from The Ladies Center, she could walk away. Andrews refused the offer. Irked, Escambia County circuit court judge William Anderson came down hard on the unrepentant Andrews and gave her five years in prison, double the sentencing guidelines.

"It's a shame Miss Andrews has chosen to waste her life in prison instead of accomplishing something," Anderson said at the sentencing. Andrews remained defiant: "I want to thank you for not insulting me by giving me probation. The only way I can protest for unborn children now is by noncooperation in jail." The Florida Department of Corrections had just been handed a giant headache.

Andrews was not very surprised by the length of her sentence, but her supporters were shocked. Nothing like this had happened in the "rescue" movement before. Joan Andrews had been given the kind of sentence previously reserved for clinic bombers.

News of the stiff sentence handed down by Judge Anderson spread across the anti-abortion grapevine. Andrews had protested alongside virtually every activist leader in the country, and now they were angry and determined to rally to her cause. Working with her sister Susan, Joe Scheidler, John Ryan, Tom Herlihy, Joe Wall, and others started to organize a protest campaign to pressure Florida to free her.

The Andrews case brought together the entire activist wing of the movement in its first truly coordinated national action. None of the PLAN conventions held by Scheidler and Ryan had generated the level of energy and purpose—and the genuinely united front—the movement now displayed as it closed ranks behind Andrews.

Over Thanksgiving weekend, 1986, just two months after Andrews's sentencing, hundreds of activists from all over the nation descended on Pensacola, a city that was gaining a national reputation as the central focus of anti-abortion activism. Hundreds staged protests outside the clinic, where seven people were arrested for blocking the driveway, and then picketed Judge Anderson's house, where another eight were arrested after a confrontation with police. Alongside their harsh, anti-abortion picket signs, "Free Joan Andrews" signs were beginning to proliferate at rallies and protests.

Randall Terry, then director of Project Life of Binghamton, New York, told reporters, "I'm sure we'll be back to do whatever is necessary to secure Joan's release."

Randall Terry had come to Pensacola with more than the freedom of Joan Andrews on his mind. Six months earlier, he had attended the St. Louis PLAN convention and had been roundly dismissed when he detailed his proposal to lead a massive, nationwide "rescue" campaign. He had not given up, and now, with almost every activist leader gathered in one place to support Joan Andrews, Terry saw that he had a second chance to sell his ideas—and himself.

After arriving in Pensacola, Terry asked a few acquaintances to put out the word at a Joan Andrews rally that he wanted to speak to everyone gathered in the city, and then he reserved a room at a nearby Western Sizzlin' steak house for a dinner meeting. Nearly every activist leader came.

That night, in a packed private room at the Western Sizzlin', Terry held nothing back. He used his innate oratorical skills—his easy command of biblical rhetoric—and won over his rapt audience. Activist leaders from around the nation, who had ignored or dismissed Terry before, began to sign up for his new crusade on the spot.

Terry told them their movement was badly stalled, that six years of Republican rule had not led to any significant gains in the fight against abortion. Looking ahead, he warned that the Democrats might take back the White House in 1988, pushing the anti-abortion movement back to square one, and he proposed a national protest campaign that would coincide with the 1988 presidential race. Terry told them he wanted to stage protests in three major cities during the election year, starting with New York; he did not yet envision Operation Rescue as an ongoing national organization that would continue after the election year.

Terry detailed his plan for a national campaign that would, for the first time, draw its strength from the nation's booming Evangelical churches, rather than the Catholic Church. The Catholic Church had never nurtured activism, and even sympathetic priests were beholden to bishops and cardinals. But Terry knew that fundamentalist ministers were free agents; if he could convince pastors to join him, they had the independence—and the religious power—to bring their congregations with them. Without fundamentalist pastors, Terry told his listeners, their activism would only attract "the remnant of the church." But with pastors would come big numbers. And power.

Terry spoke up just as fundamentalists across the nation were despairing of the failure of President Reagan to follow through on his vow to commit his administration to end abortion. Terry's message also came when leading activists in his audience were growing restive with PLAN's failure to live up to its promise of a coordinated national civil disobedience campaign. Scheidler's fear of personal commitment and lack of revolutionary ardor had ultimately left PLAN weak and rudderless.

The movement had been drifting as a result, but now Terry was offering direction, a way for activists to channel their fervor and the new sense of solidarity that Joan Andrews's plight had helped generate. Randall Terry's loyal followers would forever mark the meeting at the Western Sizzlin' as the birth of Operation Rescue. "The whole weekend was focused on Joan Andrews," recalls Boston activist Bill Cotter. But Terry "took advantage of the forum to present his vision. He felt the pro-life movement really wasn't going anywhere. It wasn't growing. He had a vision of how to make it grow—not just bringing out a couple dozen people, but hundreds and thousands of people. He was charismatic. He put together an apologetic on why rescue was scripturally justified."

Left unspoken, but obvious, was the fact that Terry was proposing to replace PLAN with his own structure for national activism. It must have been awkward, therefore, for everyone who noticed that one of the few activist leaders who was not there to hear Terry's speech was Scheidler. His absence was purposeful: Scheidler had been shaken by the fallout from the Andrews-Burt incident at The Ladies Center and his own later arrest, and privately he was having qualms about getting more deeply involved in radical tactics. Scheidler did not realize it yet, but he was rapidly maneuvering himself—and PLAN—out of the picture.

Before Terry left Pensacola to begin plotting his new campaign, he managed to throw a scare into the entire movement by publicly calling for just the sort of radical—and highly illegal—actions that Scheidler feared most. At a rally for Joan Andrews in downtown Pensacola the day after his successful dinner meeting, Terry started to detail exactly what kind of street-level tactics he was planning to employ: He wanted to borrow a few pages from the radical fringe of the antiwar movement.

In a speech in Pensacola's Seville Square, Terry called on his fellow activists to storm abortion clinics; solder shut elevators and blockade doors so that police could not reach them; and completely trash clinic offices, throwing furniture and abortion equipment out clinic windows and down into the street. His speech nearly cost him the support of those he had won over the night before. Others in the movement were aghast.

Terry had also written a detailed plan outlining his radical vision and passed it out to a handful of other activists in Pensacola. A copy soon found its way to the Washington offices of the staid National Right to Life Committee, where alarm bells went off. National Right to Life leaders immediately saw that if Terry carried out his radical tactics on a nationwide scale, he would bring the full weight of the government down on the activists and perhaps do as much to cloud the reputation of the entire anti-abortion movement as had earlier clinic bombings and arsons. Not long after Terry's Pensacola speech, therefore, Scheidler's attorney friend, Tom Marzen, was contacted by a senior official of the National Right to Life Committee, who asked Marzen to send a message to Scheidler: Put a leash on Terry.

Marzen called Scheidler, and warned him that what Randall Terry had written was "felony stuff, dangerous stuff." He told Scheidler not to "get mixed up with this," and he asked Scheidler to call Terry and get him to drop his plans. Scheidler agreed. He knew that a few militants like Joan Andrews would be willing to join in the kind of actions that Terry proposed, but that he could never generate a mass movement on that basis.

Scheidler called Terry to caution him to tone down his plans for illegal actions. "I think everybody was saying the same thing to him," Scheidler adds. Faced with such stern warnings, Terry quickly backed off his most radical ideas. Later that winter, when Terry started holding organizational meetings for Operation Rescue with other activists in Binghamton, he had dropped any mention of building takeovers or property destruction. He even went further, abandoning the clinic invasion tactics previously used by John Ryan and Joan Andrews, and he prohibited Operation Rescue demonstrators from going inside clinics. They would stage their sit-ins outside clinic doors instead.

In a final bit of personal revisionism, Terry tried to make sure that his original speech and written proposal, which had caused so much trouble in Pensacola, never again saw the light of day. Most of the activist leaders who had gathered in Pensacola were willing to forget about Terry's last-minute histrionics in Seville Square because they were so eager to work with a man who seemed to have what Scheidler lacked: the nerve and the determination to pull off a national campaign.

Although Terry had successfully exploited the Thanksgiving rallies and protests for his own purposes, the actions had failed to achieve the stated goal of winning freedom for Joan Andrews. As her supporters left town, Andrews settled in for her own personal duel with the Florida correctional system. To the dismay of the prison system, she seemed to have more patience than they did.

As her term passed, prison officials grew increasingly frustrated with her refusal to cooperate, especially with the added burden she imposed by forcing guards to carry her whenever she was removed from her cell. Florida briefly got rid of her, transferring her to a prison in Delaware, where she could be near her sister; Delaware quickly tired of her noncompliance as well and sent her back.

Once again in Florida, Andrews took her noncompliance and self-denial to their limits. Given a replacement for her glass eye by prison medical officials, she purposefully damaged it. She stopped accepting blankets and sheets from the prison and stopped sleeping on her cot, lying on the bare floor instead. She would eat only the minimum needed to stay alive, one meal a day, perhaps every other day. She refused showers. She stopped accepting any time outdoors in the exercise yard. She refused to accept her mail, even while thousands of letters began piling up for her at the prison. Outraged that a male guard participated in a strip search of her, Andrews tried to shock the guards by taking her glass eye out and throwing it across the room. Guards brought her eye back to her in her cell later that night.

Few in the anti-abortion movement could understand her anymore. Scheidler, who hated jail himself, begged Andrews to cooperate so she could win a quick release. The hierarchy of the Catholic Church could not understand, either. Florida's bishops repeatedly rebuffed requests by Andrews's family to publicly endorse her and call for her release. In a memo to "all Florida bishops" issued in December 1986, Catholic Conference executive director Tom Horkan wrote that "it appears to me that the actions of the court and the prison system are appropriate and in fact compelled by the actions of Miss Andrews. She has the key to her maximum security cell."

That stance became harder for the Catholic Church to maintain as support for Andrews mounted. Letters about Andrews began to pile up at churches, diocesan offices, and Catholic newspapers across the state. Florida's refusal to allow Andrews to attend Mass in prison only made things worse for the Catholic hierarchy. Finally, Florida agreed to let a priest to visit her cell to give her Communion but still refused to let her join other inmates at Mass.

Andrews had only one night of doubt: a few hours of panic alone in her cell in the dark, when she began to fear that her noncooperation was a show of pride rather than an act of obedience to God. "What if God doesn't want me to do this, and I'm being willful? I had never questioned it before."

But the next day, Curt Young of the Christian Action Council, a Protestant anti-abortion group founded by Reverend Billy Graham, and Dr. Bernard Nathanson of *Silent Scream* fame came to visit and to tell her that her "witness" in prison had persuaded them that anti-abortion activism was right and just. They were beginning to understand "rescue" thanks to Andrews's stand in prison.

"I thought, 'Dear God, the one night I came to the dark night of my soul, you gave me confirmation that what I was doing was right.'"

What she did not fully realize was that, hidden away in prison, she was becoming a legend in the anti-abortion movement, even among those who did not agree with her methods and could not understand her obdurate noncooperation. Whether she was engaged in an act of devotion or one of obsession almost did not matter; she was forcing others to reevaluate their own limits.

Shame, guilt, and outrage are powerful motivating forces, especially among fundamentalist Protestants whose views are shaped by biblical stories of good and evil. All three emotions washed over Evangelical America as the news of Joan Andrews's plight spread. Joan's sister Susan Brindle made sure the news got around. Desperate to pressure Florida through publicity, Brindle began to circulate handmade flyers about Andrews's case at anti-abortion marches and conferences. She and other members of the Andrews family wrote constantly to everyone they could think of: senators, bishops, televangelists.

The story did not break through as big news in the fundamentalist subculture until Peter Lennox, an Atlanta businessman who had dipped into the anti-abortion cause, heard about Andrews and was stunned into action. With connections in the fundamentalist community, he began to contact key Christian broadcasting outlets to get them to take up Andrews's cause.

Finally, D. James Kennedy, an influential televangelist whose hour-long *Coral Ridge Hour* was seen on hundreds of television stations nationwide, broadcast a prison interview with Andrews. Kennedy, a fundamentalist Presbyterian minister who heads Coral Ridge Ministries in Fort Lauderdale, Florida, used Andrews's story to introduce his audience for the first time to the "rescue" movement, and he closed the piece by calling for a letter-writing campaign to convince Florida governor Bob Martinez to set Andrews free. "For nine months, she's been in solitary confinement," Kennedy said in wonder. "It seems it's a worse crime today to save a life than it is to take a life."

An important part of the segment was an interview with Curt Young, the head of the Christian Action Council, who had earlier visited Andrews in jail. Young explained Andrews's case by using the rhetoric that fundamentalists, who had a long history of distrusting all things Catholic, could understand. He also sought to reassure fundamentalist viewers that Andrews was not trying to win her place in heaven through her acts of self-denial. To fundamentalists brought up to believe that salvation comes to the predestined and elected, the idea that "good works" bring salvation is heresy.

"She has a very close walk with Christ," stressed Young in the interview. "I asked her, 'Do you think somehow you are earning merit with God through what you are doing?' And she said to me, 'No, I could never do that. Christ has already accomplished my salvation for me. All I can do is accept it. I'm just giving my all for his infinite goodness.'"

Tom Bush, a Florida attorney who had represented Andrews, was also interviewed. "I wonder if she doesn't challenge all of us," he said. "Maybe we all need to realize that abortion is not going to end by picketing abortion clinics and by jawboning. It's going to end when people are willing to give up their liberty for it."

The appearance on the *Coral Ridge Hour* marked a decisive turning point in Andrews's long-running battle with Florida; Joan Andrews was now one of the hottest stories in the fundamentalist and New Right media. A book of her prison letters was rushed out, and there was even a special edition published for fundamentalist Protestants, a kind of cultural crossover to explain once again her very Catholic approach to the abortion issue.

Ultimately, the Andrews case resonated with fundamentalists because it seemed to confirm their darkest fears: that any Christian who fought the secular culture would be hounded and persecuted. When abortion-rights activists in Florida and around the nation tried to pressure Florida officials to keep Andrews in jail, that only served to highlight her plight and make her seem even more of a martyr to Evangelicals. Legions of fundamentalists were soon flocking to her cause. They jammed phone lines to radio talk shows and launched nationwide letter-writing campaigns to state prison officials and Governor Bob Martinez.

By the summer of 1988, thousands of pro–Joan Andrews letters were pouring into Martinez's office in Tallahassee. Mother Teresa kissed a religious medal and mailed it to Andrews. Pax Christi, the Catholic peace group, named Andrews "Christian of the Year" for 1988. The

Vatican began to ask questions. Liberals felt guilt; former California governor and Democratic presidential candidate Jerry Brown wrote to the governor of Florida to ask for clemency.

Meanwhile, Operation Rescue was suddenly taking off as a national phenomenon. Florida's Catholic bishops, who were also being inundated with calls and letters, were quietly signaling to Martinez that it was time to do something. Florida began to buckle.

Another big Joan Andrews rally was scheduled for August in Tallahassee, and Martinez was desperate to make the problem disappear. He had been elected as one of the most ardent anti-abortion governors in the nation, yet he was also a law-and-order Republican who could not begin to grant clemency to convicted criminals. His maddening dilemma was compounded by the fact that under Florida law, clemency could only be granted with the approval of his cabinet.

It was left to a woman named Carol Griffin to try to find a way out for both sides. Griffin, a longtime volunteer lobbyist in Tallahassee for anti-abortion groups and causes, was a pragmatic activist with good contacts in Martinez's conservative administration. She first heard about the Andrews case when Houston activist Don Treshman, then working with Scheidler in PLAN, asked her to help organize the August rally in Tallahassee. After serving as negotiator with local and state authorities on the rally's logistics, Griffin became convinced that Andrews did not deserve her fate, and she opened quiet, back-channel negotiations with her contacts in the Martinez administration.

It turned out that, privately, Martinez was willing to agree to almost any deal, and Griffin took advantage of his desperation. She secretly proposed a creative plan: Release Joan Andrews to Mother Teresa. Andrews's service in Mother Teresa's campaign for the world's poor could count as community service to work off the remainder of her Florida sentence. Everyone could come out looking and feeling good.

Martinez and his staff agreed. Mother Teresa also agreed to take Andrews. It seemed like a perfect ending, except for one thing: Joan Andrews turned the whole deal down. She did not want to let Florida off the hook.

Finally, Joan Andrews's attorney, John Broderick, saw a way out. Andrews had an outstanding conviction in Pittsburgh; Florida could turn her over to Pennsylvania and be done with her. That was fine with Martinez, and so in October 1988, as Operation Rescue was making

John O'Keefe, the "father" of the rescue movement, is hauled away by police after staging a sit-in at a Planned Parenthood clinic in Norwich, Connecticut, on October 31, 1977. Courtesy of Dave Gaetano

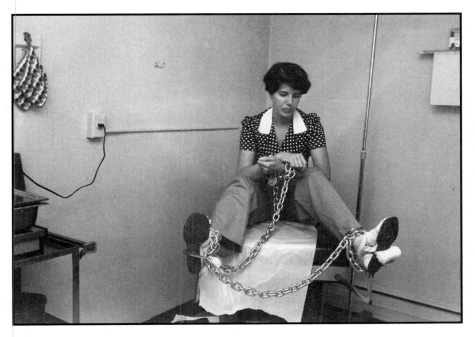

Abortion protester Mary Ann Kreitzer sits chained to an operating table after entering an abortion clinic in Washington, D.C., on August 20, 1977.
Courtesy of Dave Gaetano

Francis Schaeffer, the fundamentalist Christian theologian who was a key architect in spurring Evangelicals into action on the abortion issue. Courtesy of L'Abri Fellowship Foundation

Anti-abortion activists gather around a billboard at the Pro-Life Action Network (PLAN) convention in Appleton, Wisconsin, in April 1985. The convention was the first PLAN gathering for activists and took place during a period when clinic bombings were on the rise. Included in the photo are Joseph Scheidler (*at the left edge of the billboard*) and John Ryan (*second from right*). Howard Hugh Deever, all

John Ryan *(left)*, Tom Herlihy *(center)*, and Joan Andrews *(grabbing onto tree)*, participate in a sit-in outside a St. Louis abortion clinic during PLAN's convention in April 1986. Police arrested 107 protesters that day—the largest sit-in until that time.

Prior to founding Operation Rescue, Randall Terry performs at the keyboard at the PLAN convention in St. Louis in April 1986.

Randall Terry and Joseph Scheidler pose in a gag photo mocking abortion-rights groups' RICO charges, 1986.

Joseph Scheidler leads a protest against Democratic presidential candidate Michael Dukakis in Wisconsin in July 1988. PHOTO BY ANDREW SCHOLBERG, COURTESY OF THE PRO-LIFE ACTION LEAGUE

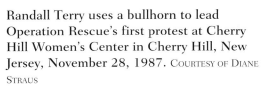

Randall Terry uses a bullhorn to lead Operation Rescue's first protest at Cherry Hill Women's Center in Cherry Hill, New Jersey, November 28, 1987. COURTESY OF DIANE STRAUS

Protesters block the entrance to Cherry Hill Women's Center at Operation Rescue's first protest in Cherry Hill, New Jersey, November 28, 1987. COURTESY OF DIANE STRAUS

Joseph Foreman *(holding bullhorn)* leads Operation Rescue protests in New York City, May 5, 1988. COURTESY OF MONICA MIGLIORINO MILLER, CITIZENS FOR A PRO-LIFE SOCIETY

Randall Terry shouts instructions to demonstrators at Operation Rescue's protests in New York City, May 1988. PHOTO BY ANDREW SCHOLBERG, COURTESY OF THE PRO-LIFE ACTION LEAGUE

Randall Terry displays a box containing an aborted fetus outside Northeast Women's Center during Operation Rescue's Philadelphia campaign, July 6, 1988. COURTESY OF DIANE STRAUS

Randall and Cindy Terry and their children, 1988. COURTESY OF BOB JEWITT

Operation Rescue leader Keith Tucci cries as officers arrest him in Atlanta during the group's protests, August 4, 1988. COURTESY OF LYNNE RANDALL

Protesters crawl toward the gates of the Atlanta Surgi-Center as police warn them to stay back during Operation Rescue's demonstrations, October 1988. COURTESY OF BOB JEWITT

Randall Terry shouts "Hallelujah!" after being handed a check for $10,000 by the Rev. Jerry Falwell. Watching are Moral Majority president Jerry Sims and Joseph Foreman. The check was passed at a demonstration outside the Feminist Women's Health Center during Operation Rescue's protests, August 10, 1988. AP/WIDE WORLD PHOTOS

Police use pain compliance on a protester outside the Atlanta Surgi-Center during Operation Rescue's siege of Atlanta in October 1988. COURTESY OF ANN BAKER, NATIONAL CENTER FOR THE PRO-CHOICE MAJORITY

Atlanta police arrest a protester outside the Surgi-Center during Operation Rescue's second wave of protests in the city in October 1988. COURTESY OF BOB JEWITT

Demonstrators crawl past police barricades outside the Feminist Women's Health Center in Atlanta during Operation Rescue's second wave of protests, October 4, 1988. COURTESY OF LYNNE RANDALL

Operation Rescue leader Joseph Foreman is carried away by Los Angeles police during the second Holy Week campaign in April 1990. PHOTO BY DENNIS PAUL GAUCI, COURTESY OF OPERATION RESCUE CALIFORNIA

Protesters crawl toward an abortion clinic as police try to keep them back during Operation Rescue's second Holy Week event in Orange County, California, April 1990. COURTESY OF OPERATION RESCUE CALIFORNIA

Randall Terry confronts abortion doctor George Tiller
as Tiller tries to enter the gates of his Wichita, Kansas,
clinic during Operation Rescue's "Summer of Mercy"
protests in 1991. Tiller, wearing a bulletproof vest,
tries to ignore Terry. COURTESY OF THE *WICHITA EAGLE*

A group of children ranging in age from eight to sixteen
lie in the street outside George Tiller's abortion clinic in
Wichita, Kansas, during Operation Rescue's "Summer of
Mercy" protests in August 1991. In the background, a
Wichita police captain tells the children they are
violating a federal court order. COURTESY OF THE *WICHITA EAGLE*

Protesters kneel and pray at barricades across from George Tiller's abortion clinic in Wichita, Kansas, as U.S. Marshal's deputies guard the clinic gate, during Operation Rescue's "Summer of Mercy" protests, July 1991. COURTESY OF THE *WICHITA EAGLE*

Randall Terry prays with Operation Rescue leaders Keith Tucci, Joe Slovenec, and Pat Mahoney outside George Tiller's clinic in Wichita, Kansas, during the "Summer of Mercy protests," August 1991. COURTESY OF THE *WICHITA EAGLE*

U.S. Marshal's deputies pull protesters from underneath a car attempting to enter George Tiller's clinic in Wichita, Kansas, during Operation Rescue's "Summer of Mercy" in August 1991. COURTESY OF THE *WICHITA EAGLE*

Children stretch out in the street in front of George Tiller's abortion clinic in Wichita, Kansas, in an attempt to block cars from entering during Operation Rescue's "Summer of Mercy" protests, August 1991. In the foreground, Wichita police are standing on pieces of a federal court injunction banning clinic blockades. The protesters tore up copies of the injunction when police served them. COURTESY OF THE *WICHITA EAGLE*

Firefighters battle a fire at the Catalina Medical Center in Ashland, Oregon, on April 11, 1992. Shelley Shannon later pleaded guilty to setting the fire, which caused $379,000 in damages and closed the clinic for good. COURTESY OF THE ASHLAND DEPARTMENT OF PUBLIC SAFETY

Operation Rescue leaders conduct training sessions in preparation for their protests in Baton Rouge, Louisiana, in July 1992. PHOTO BY JED WHITE, COURTESY OF OPERATION RESCUE CALIFORNIA

Michael Griffin sits at the Okaloosa Correctional Institution in Florida, where he is serving a life sentence for the March 10, 1993, killing of abortion doctor David Gunn. PHOTO BY JUDY L. THOMAS

Paul Hill and John Burt (*wearing cap*) protest outside The Ladies Center in Pensacola, Florida, on November 19, 1993. COURTESY OF THE FEMINIST MAJORITY FOUNDATION

Paul Hill holds up his infamous sign outside The Ladies Center in Pensacola, Florida, November 19, 1993.
COURTESY OF THE FEMINIST MAJORITY FOUNDATION

Kansas City activist Regina Dinwiddie pickets outside a clinic defense training seminar in Pensacola, Florida, on March 12, 1994—a year after Michael Griffin killed physician David Gunn outside the Pensacola Women's Medical Services clinic. COURTESY OF THE FEMINIST MAJORITY FOUNDATION

Randall Terry tapes a "Randall Terry Live" program at his radio station in Windsor, New York—the site of his former car lot, August 1996. PHOTO BY JUDY L. THOMAS

un WANTED

John Bayard Britton

HOME ADDRESS - 2120 Beech St. Fernandina Beach Fla. 32034
OFFICE ADDRESS - 34 N 14th St. Fernandina Beach Fla. 32034

PHONE - (Home) 904-261-4950 , (Office) 904-261-3673

D.O.B. - May 6,1925

VEHICLE - Maroon & Silver , Chevy Scottsdale Pick-up
          With silver camper shell .
TAG # - K W M 3 3 E , Nassau county .

PHYSICAL DESCRIPTION

HEIGHT - Approx. 6 FT 2 in.
WEIGHT - Approx. 190 - 210 lbs.
HAIR - Gray , RACE - White , AGE - 68

PERSONAL ACHIEVEMENTS

April 11,1978 - fired from Fernandina's
general hospital after being deemed
unstable.

1981 - charged with ─── prescribing
1,900 Percodan and percocet tablets
to a drug addict. He served two years
probation.

The state medical board has charged
him "with being unable to practice
medicine with reasonable skill and
safety."

CRIMES AGAINST HUMANITY

SHEDDING INNOCENT BLOOD-(Prov.6:16-19)
Britton has MURDERED THOUSANDS of
unborn babies.

NEGLIGENT HOMICIDE- Britton is
directly responsable for the death at
least one woman. Maureen Lyn Tyke, died
at Holms Regional Medical Center on
May 31,1983 from complications stemming
from a "SAFE, LEGAL Abortion" performed
by Britton at the Aware Womens Center
in Melborne Fla. She was a 22 year old
college student.

*** WARNING ***

JOHN BAYARD BRITTON IS CONSIDERED ARMED
AND EXTREMELY DANGEROUS, ESPECIALY TO
WOMEN AND CHILDREN.

The "Unwanted Poster" of abortion doctor John Bayard Britton circulated by anti-abortion activists in Pensacola, Florida. Britton, who began working at The Ladies Center clinic in Pensacola after Dr. David Gunn was killed, was shot to death by Paul Hill on July 29, 1994.

During her trial in 1994, Oregon housewife Rachelle "Shelley" Shannon demonstrates how she shot Wichita, Kansas, abortion doctor George Tiller. Shannon was convicted of attempted first-degree murder and later pleaded guilty to a series of clinic arsons and bombings in the Pacific Northwest. COURTESY OF THE *WICHITA EAGLE*

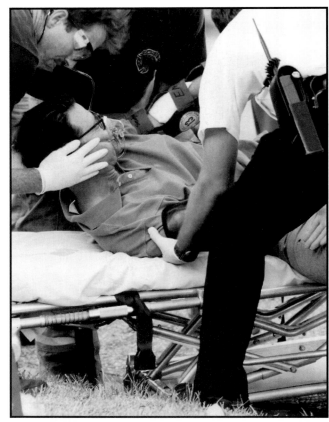

Emergency medical workers lift George Tiller onto a stretcher after he was shot by Shelley Shannon outside his Wichita, Kansas, abortion clinic on August 19, 1993. COURTESY OF THE *WICHITA EAGLE*

national headlines in Atlanta, Andrews was granted clemency and released into Pennsylvania's custody. "We don't want anyone in jail that's attempting to be a martyr," said Brian Ballard, Martinez's chief of staff, happily washing his hands of Joan Andrews.

"I was bitter about their decision to let Joan Andrews out," recalls Patricia Ireland, president of the National Organization for Women. "That just confirmed the belief that she was a martyr, and that this was a civil disobedience movement."

The judge in Pittsburgh immediately released Andrews on probation with the condition that she stay away from the Pittsburgh clinic where she had been arrested years earlier. Andrews refused to agree, but this time the judge gave her probation anyway.

Finally, she was free, and almost immediately she went back to the Pittsburgh clinic for a protest. The judge, furious that she had disobeyed his order so quickly, issued a new warrant for her arrest. Andrews left the state, and she has never been picked up on the warrant.

Once she was out of prison, Joan Andrews's hold on the fundamentalist imagination seemed to dissipate. For a time, she was in demand by anti-abortion groups around the country, and she began a new life of traveling, speaking and protesting in each city she visited. She renewed her secret acts of clinic vandalism as she toured as well.

Andrews never seriously connected with Operation Rescue or with Randall Terry. When she went into prison, "rescue" was still small and Catholic; when she got out, it was big and Protestant fundamentalist. Terry and his cadre of fundamentalist Protestants had taken over, made use of her story, and transformed "rescue" into a mass movement. A free Joan Andrews was a Catholic ghost, someone who, like John Ryan, "made Randy feel uncomfortable," says Andrews's sister Susan Brindle.

Terry ignored Andrews. She joined a handful of Operation Rescue protests, but she never played a role in the organization. For a time, she traveled around the world, taking part in anti-abortion sit-ins overseas, but she soon dropped out of the headlines. She married, settled down in the New York area, and started a family. New York's Cardinal John O'Connor baptized her first child, a daughter. Andrews ended her cycle of protest, arrest, court, and jail. Her story was forgotten even as Randall Terry rushed to notoriety.

Pensacola made national headlines again in the early 1990s, but it was because of Michael Griffin and Paul Hill, not Joan Andrews.

"When I meet people, they have heard of Operation Rescue, but not Joan," says Susan Brindle, still protective of her sister's legend. "And I say to them, 'Operation Rescue started because of Joan Andrews.'"

PART III

OPERATION RESCUE

9

STREET PREACHER
Randall Terry

After following Joe Scheidler from the hotel meeting out into Times Square in his bid to dismiss Scheidler from Operation Rescue, Randall Terry stood alone for a moment in the New York cold. He was on the verge of fame; he could feel it. No one was going to get in his way.

It was March 1988. John O'Keefe was gone, John Ryan was gone, and Joe Scheidler was on his way out the door. The early Catholic activists were giving way to Terry and the fundamentalists, who were about to transform the anti-abortion movement into something that was not only angry and judgmental but also big.

Not yet twenty-nine, Terry had suddenly become the undisputed leader of the movement's activist wing, and he was going to make the most of his position and power. He had privately vowed to the pastor of his small Charismatic church in Binghamton, New York, that the anti-abortion cause would carry him onto nationwide television and make him a celebrity, and Terry could sense that his plans for Operation Rescue were about to make his prediction come true.

Within the year, it happened. By the end of 1988, Terry burst out of obscurity to become one of the most notorious public figures in the United States. He emerged as a strange and fascinating new hybrid, a kind of cross-cultural train wreck—Huey Newton meets Oral Roberts—evoking unalloyed hate from feminists and abortion-rights advocates, universal scorn from politicians and the media, and fierce personal loyalty and love from his fundamentalist supporters. Above all, mainstream America could no longer ignore him or his movement.

He became the most visible symbol of the loud and unapologetic wing of the newly muscular Religious Right, the leader of a youthful Evangelical legion that saw itself as nothing less than an earthly warning of the coming wrath of God. Randall Terry was a kid, mouthy and a little dangerous, and he brought a rock 'n' roll sensibility to Evangelical politics and protest. He believed in heaven, hell, and damnation, and he said so.

With an extraordinary gift for personal theater and impromptu oratory, Terry galvanized Evangelicals by summoning up dark, apocalyptic visions of America. His lurid imagery was foreign and bizarre to the press and public but nothing new to born-again Christians, who heard the same kind of fire and brimstone every Sunday in church. Terry simply brought that loud fundamentalist rhetoric out into the open for all America to see. At heart, he was a street preacher.

Randall Terry and Operation Rescue were products of a great Evangelical surge among young Americans in the late 1970s. Terry was emblematic of a huge generational shift away from mainline denominations to Evangelicalism; he preached his first sermon in an independent Charismatic church when he was eighteen.

As Terry and countless other born-again teenagers of the 1970s came into their own, married, and started families, they created new, bigger churches, and they discovered politics. They could not abide the political isolation accepted by older fundamentalist Protestants, who had come to rely on a mystical, escapist theology—premillennial dispensationalism—to justify their utter noninvolvement in the world.

Young Evangelicals like Terry found dispensationalism hard to swallow. They accepted premillennialism—the idea that Christ was coming back soon—but not the notion that they should stand idly by and allow the world literally to go to hell. Therefore, they eagerly turned to Francis Schaeffer's lectures, books, and films; the "Reformed" Presbyterian minister and author argued that involvement in the world was not heresy but a return to the roots of the Reformation. Schaeffer told Randall Terry's generation to pick up where John Calvin and John Knox had left off four hundred years before. Schaeffer asked them to create St. Augustine's "City on a Hill."

For a time, fundamentalists tried to ignore the inherent contradiction between Schaeffer's teachings and their mystical belief that the coming "rapture" made the world irrelevant. Many Evangelical political figures sought to downplay the conflict for fear of alienating their core supporters. But Randall Terry could not ignore it. He was one of the first major Religious Right political activists to attack premillennial dispensationalism publicly and forcefully as a perversion:

"I became a pro-life activist while I was a fierce premillennial dispensationalist, and for a time I lived an inconsistent life. But I eventually realized this [dispensationalism] is utter nonsense. It has no place in church history. It kept Evangelicals out of politics for fifty years, very successfully. What better way for the demonic to undermine reality?"

Although Randall Terry failed to end abortion, he did play a role in killing off the escapist traditions of American fundamentalists. "The Bible is full of action verbs given in the command form," he reminded Evangelicals. "Rescue, deliver, vindicate, do justice. These commands cannot be fulfilled in the safety of our church pews."

By the early 1990s, dispensationalism was all but dead in the American fundamentalist church, replaced by Schaeffer-style Reformed thinking. Abortion had been the issue of sin and damnation that convinced thousands of Evangelicals to abandon their old theology and move out into the streets.

Jerry Falwell's Moral Majority, founded in 1979, was the first manifestation of the Religious Right's political power, but Operation Rescue was a creation of that young Evangelical generation of the late 1970s. Operation Rescue was a youth movement—right wing, male-dominated, absolutist, and fundamentalist—but a youth movement nonetheless. Later, as those in the 1970s generation entered their late thirties and early forties and burned out on intense, Operation Rescue–style activism, Ralph Reed and the Christian Coalition were there to corral them back into safer, mainstream politics. Later, protest veterans would look back on Operation Rescue as the most intense experience of their lives, the time when "Christians" went to war. "Jerry Falwell provided the political cover; Francis Schaeffer provided the theological cover; but it was Operation Rescue that brought the two together in the street," observes Terry. "There was never a huge street movement of Protestants before that."

Journalists who covered Operation Rescue never understood Terry's religious roots and never accepted the overriding importance of biblical fundamentalism in shaping his life and the movement he led. They looked for hidden agendas and hidden money; they looked everywhere but in his church.

Most feminists who wrote about Terry had no clue about him. They described Terry and other anti-abortion activists in a way that was reassuring to feminists; they were downwardly mobile young baby boomer men lashing out at women in reaction to the recession of the early 1980s. Their hatred of feminism was rooted in their inability to match the living standards of their fathers. Terry became caricatured as a car salesman.

But Randall Terry was never about economics. If he believed in a male-dominated world, it was a concept he learned in his church pew, not in the unemployment line. Through Operation Rescue, Terry believed that God was commanding him to dispel the confusion of premillennial dispensationalism in order to lead fundamentalists back into the world, to the battle against abortion. "You are dealing with sacred history!" Terry warns darkly. "Sacred history!"

Terry revolutionized rescue by making it big. John Ryan recruited handfuls of people; Randall Terry brought out thousands. John O'Keefe could force one clinic owner to close for a few hours; Randall Terry could take on a whole city.

Operation Rescue turned what had been a small, ragtag group of easily ignored protesters into a genuine movement, an aggressive national campaign that put the anti-abortion cause back onto America's Page One. Ryan, O'Keefe, Scheidler, and Joan Andrews had never made a lasting impact on the national consciousness, but Terry and Operation Rescue were noticed. Operation Rescue was news because it was "man bites dog": right-wingers conducting left-wing style civil disobedience. Operation Rescue eventually became the biggest social protest movement since the antiwar and civil rights campaigns of the 1960s, accomplishing more than sixty thousand arrests at protests across the nation before it collapsed in the early 1990s.

Most Americans believed that Randall Terry invented "rescue," to the everlasting chagrin of O'Keefe, Ryan, and Scheidler. In the late 1980s and early 1990s, Randall Terry was the most prominent spokesperson for the entire anti-abortion movement, which left Jack Willke, president of the increasingly irrelevant National Right to Life Committee, fuming in frustration. Willke countered by trying to deny Operation Rescue's existence; like a Soviet commissar who orders the faces of purged officials to be cut out of photographs, Willke refused to allow any stories about the organization to be published in the National Right to Life newspaper.

Terry succeeded where others had failed by following a simple yet powerful strategy. He focused his recruiting efforts almost exclusively on fundamentalist churches, particularly on the pastors of those churches. "I believe in the local church. I think the work of God, the Kingdom of God, is the local church." A Bible school graduate who had fallen under the mesmerizing spell of a Charismatic preacher himself, Terry knew firsthand the influence that Evangelical pastors could wield over their followers. He also knew that fundamentalist pastors were independent of any church bureaucracy and thus free to follow their own politics and push their own causes. Recruit the pastors, Terry knew, and their congregations would follow.

"You men are key," Terry told one small group of pastors on a recruiting mission for Operation Rescue. "I'm speaking today to twelve or thirteen congregations. Your congregations will never go any further than you go, period. What you do, your people will do. If you get out on the picket line, you'll see people get out on picket lines. If you get involved in rescues, your people will get involved in rescues. And if you don't, they won't. It's just that simple."

As Operation Rescue grew, Terry made certain to hire a full-time staffer responsible for ministerial outreach and pastoral liaison; one of his most successful recruiting tools was a cassette tape entitled "Call to the Clergy," which was distributed to Evangelical ministers nationwide.

To recruit the pastors, Terry knew he had to transform "rescue" from a movement that appealed only to handfuls of feverish Catholics like Joan Andrews and John O'Keefe into something that would draw thousands of fundamentalists out of their church pews. He succeeded by changing the rhetoric in ways that few outsiders ever detected. Terry's achievement was to win over his fellow Evangelicals by translating anti-abortion protest into their own Bible-based language of judgment and wrath.

John O'Keefe had tried to recruit veterans of the antiwar movement by appealing to their pacifistic opposition to war and killing. O'Keefe asked them to declare their "solidarity with the child" and to "share the vulnerability" and helplessness of the unborn through their nonviolent protest. But to conservative fundamentalists, O'Keefe's approach had a sixties leftist feel and therefore was alien. It never resonated within the Evangelical community, and Terry swept it aside.

Terry screamed that "the church"—the all-encompassing fundamentalist term for the community of born-again Christians—had blood on its hands. Evangelical Christians had ignored abortion for more than a decade, Terry railed, and so had become accomplices in the murder of millions. By accepting *Roe v. Wade* as the law of the land, Christians had "bowed the knee to Caesar. We have committed idolatry by saying to this government, 'Yes, Caesar, you have the right to kill children; no, Caesar, we won't interfere.'"

The only way to wash away the "blood-guiltiness of the church," Terry said, was for the church and its people to do everything in their power to stop abortion. If "the American church" rose up, ending its acquiescence, abortion would be criminalized once more. Terry saved his most lacerating criticism for church leaders who refused to heed his call. When Operation Rescue finally collapsed, he blamed it on the failure of "the church" to recognize the window of opportunity God had provided. "The pro-life movement," Terry wailed, "is the bastard child of the church."

Unlike Catholics and mainline Protestants, fundamentalists look directly to the Bible for their faith, not to a formal church structure. Few Evangelicals have strong allegiances to any denomination and, instead, tend to move from church to church in search of pastors and congregations who share their views. However, they all share a belief that the Bible holds all the answers and that it is possible to divine God's will by reading biblical passages, even very short ones—and even very short ones out of context.

Terry was fluent in that language. When he told pastors that Proverbs 24:11 trumps Romans 13 and that they should thus feel scripturally free to join Operation Rescue, the pastors knew exactly what he was talking about. When he said his vision of Operation Rescue had come "as men as trees, walking," they knew Terry was drawing on Mark 8:24 to argue subtly that he was not a dangerous freelancer but was submitted to God's plan, a plan that had only slowly been revealed to him. His speeches and writings were almost indecipherable to anyone unfamiliar with the way fundamentalists parse the Bible. But Terry knew the Evangelical shorthand: "Those who still debate the morality of doing so-called illegal things will have to do a lot of explaining when it comes to Acts 5:29." Catholics are not trained to deconstruct the Bible in the same way, so that the early leaders like O'Keefe, Lee, and Ryan had no way of reaching Evangelicals the way Terry could.

Francis Schaeffer's writings and the "higher law" theories of Reformation pioneers like John Knox were always at the heart of Terry's scriptural pitch to fundamentalists. Terry, like Schaeffer, constantly argued that the fact that abortion was legal was of little consequence; there was a higher law, God's law, that said abortion was the work of Satan. Breaking man's law to obey God and stop Satan was not breaking the law at all. Rescue, Terry said, was more than civil disobedience. It was "biblical obedience."

A Christian Manifesto, Schaeffer's 1981 tract that popularized Reformation-era higher law theories for a new generation and also called on Evangelicals to conduct civil disobedience to protest abortion, was the blueprint for Operation Rescue. But Terry took Schaeffer's arguments and gave them a sharper, angrier edge that could resonate with a mass audience. "The anti-Christs in power," Terry wrote, putting his own spin on Schaeffer's teachings, "like nothing better than when pastors proclaim Hell's party line: 'religion and politics don't mix.'"

Michael Terry's fist smashed into Randy Terry's face. A reed-thin sixteen-year-old, a dope-smoking, piano-playing slacker with an enormous white-man's Afro, Randy Terry, a true child of the 1970s, had just told his father that he was dropping out of high school four months shy of graduation: "I want to quit school and travel around the country."

His father, a Rochester, New York, public school teacher, had responded by lashing out with such force that he gave his son matching black eyes. "He just beat the heck out of me," Terry says. It was the worst thrashing his father had ever inflicted on him, and it was a sign of what the Terry household had become. Michael Terry had a drinking problem that worsened with time and that finally led to divorce. Randy Terry stormed out of the house and did not come back for weeks.

Until that day in February 1976, Randy Terry had led an unremarkable suburban life. His parents were married in September 1958, just after Doreen DiPasquale found out she was pregnant. She later told her son she had never considered abortion, which was illegal at the time, over marriage. Randall Terry was born the following April and baptized in the Church of Christ. His Italian mother was from a family of fallen-away Catholics, and as Randy grew up, religion hardly played any role in his home. His parents were Christmas and Easter churchgoers.

His mother was the oldest of four sisters with alliterative names: Doreen, Diane, Dawn, and Dale DiPasquale. His aunts often baby-sat for Randy while his mother tried to finish her education and start her teaching career. Still teenagers at the time they watched over Randy, his aunts went on to become feminist activists; two later became public critics of their nephew as he rose to prominence. (All three of his aunts had unplanned pregnancies, and one nearly died from a botched illegal abortion.)

Terry's parents moved the family to suburban Henrietta when he was five, and his mother finally joined her husband as a full-time teacher in the Rochester public schools when Randy was eight. Terry had one younger brother, Jeff, and only one lifelong friend, his neighbor Eric Michaloski.

Terry inherited his father's love for music, playing both piano and guitar, and focused his teenage energy on his school's stage band and on organizing garage bands with friends. Naturally bright and articulate, Terry earned advanced placement credits that put him close to graduation much earlier than most of his classmates. But by the time Terry entered his junior year in Henrietta's Charles Roth High School, both he and Eric Michaloski had drifted into a crowd of fairly serious drug users and were engaging in bouts of shoplifting and petty thievery. At school, Terry was soon pegged as part of the "doper" crowd, and he began to lose interest in his studies. All that Terry truly cared about was his music; he harbored dreams of becoming a rock star. Rock stars, Terry told himself, don't need high school.

If Terry had any doubts about the wisdom of dropping out, the beating dispelled them. After spending a few days with friends, he asked Eric to quit school and leave town with him. When Eric refused, Terry reluctantly left without him, hitchhiking across the country with another drifting teen from upstate New York whom he met along the road. Terry had a vague notion that he would go to California and have his parents ship him his guitar so he could start a music career, but he never even got close. He ended up in Galveston, Texas, sleeping on the beach, hanging out, and doing drugs.

While he was living on the beach, his backpack and belongings were stolen, including a Bible, which he had just started to read on his own; as a result, he hitchhiked home in time for his seventeenth birthday in April. His mother, concerned but tolerant, bought him a new knapsack; an old minister gave him a new Bible; and he took off again for the road and the beach in Galveston.

On this second trip, he went alone, and along the way he began to meet eccentric, 1970s-style New Age characters, the "kind of people who take a sixteen-year-old doper into their house. People who are into Aquarian gospel, into reincarnation, into astroprojection, into witchcraft. I was just hanging out with some freaky people."

His New Age encounters combined with his increasingly serious Bible readings made for a strange brew. "I was hanging out with wacky people, I was smoking dope, and I was reading the Bible. But it was all this mishmash of spiritualism. I was reading the Book of Revelation. Now, if you want to read a bizarre book while you're under the influence of narcotics, it's the Book of Revelation."

His mother finally contacted Terry in Galveston to tell him his pending workers' compensation claim was coming up for a hearing; he had sliced his thumb while working at a Steak 'n' Brew restaurant in Rochester before he quit school and left home. In June 1976, he returned to Rochester for the hearing, and this time he stayed for good. He won a claim of $450 and used $220 of it to buy his first car, a yellow 1970 Plymouth Duster that already had 200,000 miles on its odometer. Needing money for gas and insurance, he landed a job at the Three Sisters ice cream stand.

Back at home in the summer of 1976, Terry's newfound spiritualism struck his family as bizarre. His aunts later claimed that he made statements that suggested he now thought he was Jesus Christ, and they pointed to such statements to suggest that some traumatic event had occurred to transform Terry while he was living on the beach in Galveston. In fact, he had not been traumatized. What his aunts had seen was a teen in transition; he was still trying to sort out answers from the spiritual "mishmash" he had been exposed to on his travels.

Terry's conversion came in September 1976, just seven months after he dropped out of Charles Roth High. He was reading his Bible and working at the ice cream stand in Henrietta when Mark Saunders stopped for some dessert. Saunders, a bricklayer and student at Elim Bible School, a small, unaccredited, Evangelical Bible college in the area, saw Terry's Bible sitting on the counter and asked Terry if he was a Christian.

The question caught Terry at a critical moment, and it troubled him. "Well," he told Saunders, "it's kind of hard to be [a Christian] with the friends I hang around with."

When Saunders told Terry about his faith—Evangelicals feel obligated to proselytize—Terry realized that Saunders "had something real, something that I did not have." Saunders left thinking, "Oh boy, they can't be any riper than this. This was one of those that the Lord puts in your lap."

That night, Terry went to a party with his old friends and asked them to talk with him about God. "Will you shut up!" his friends scolded. "Be done with it."

Terry had had enough as well. He stubbed out his cigarette and told his friends he was done, not with religion but with smoking dope and his old lifestyle. The next day he called Mark Saunders, who invited him to his house to talk. Saunders quickly took Terry under his wing and "explained how a person becomes a Christian."

On September 6, Saunders picked up Terry and asked him to help him for a few hours on a contracting job he was doing to help pay the bills while he was attending school. Saunders was convinced that Randy was searching for the answers, and he was anxious to have a few hours to talk to him about God and also to have him meet his family and see the Elim Bible College campus.

As they drove to Saunders's home in Lima, Saunders explained his faith; finally, he asked Terry if he was prepared to receive Christ as his savior. "Would you like to do that?" he asked. Terry sat quietly for a few moments, pondering Saunders's question. Finally, he said yes, and Saunders pulled over to the side of the road. Terry was about to go through the most intense experience of his life, a conversion moment that he would never forget. He could still recount every detail twenty years later.

"We pulled over on Route 15A between Rush, New York, and Lima, New York. We pulled over in his van and I said, 'Jesus, I know that I'm a sinner. I know that you are the son of God and that you died for me. Please come into my life. Please forgive me of my sins.' And it was like a thousand pounds taken off my back. I just felt exhilarated."

Recalls Saunders: "It was one of those ordained moments. It was almost absurd how beautifully God worked. He received Christ just about three miles before Lima."

Saunders sat and prayed with him as Terry went through his wrenching experience. Finally, as they began driving to Saunders's house, Saunders picked up a woman who was hitchhiking. She became the first target of the newly converted Randall Terry's religious zeal.

"I preached my guts out to her all the way. I said to her, 'God is real. Jesus is real. You've got to follow him.' It was so awesome for me, because here I was just a brand-new believer, but I knew this Gospel was true. And when she got out of the car, she said, 'You've made more sense to me than any preacher I've listened to my whole life.' And that was it. I never did drugs again."

The next morning Terry went to a chapel service with Mark Saunders at Elim Bible College, and he never looked back. "I felt like God had his hand on me to do something important, to affect the course of history. Literally."

Randall Terry was now "on fire." His religious conversion had an immediate impact on his personality. He straightened himself out; no longer a doper and slacker, he hit the books again and eventually aced the test for a high school equivalency degree. "You could tell he was at peace," recalls Eric Michaloski.

Terry resumed music lessons with classically trained teachers and briefly thought about attending a serious music school like Juilliard. "I apologized to my parents for the heartache I put them through when I quit school and left home." In return, his father apologized for the beating he had inflicted on his son. Yet Terry's unyielding passion for his new religion clearly startled and concerned his family. Indeed, Terry was in the grip of his religion in a way that he has never previously described publicly; at seventeen, he says, he began to have "visions" that he believes foretold his future life as an activist leader:

"I remember praying in my bedroom and all of a sudden I envisioned myself in the middle of a coliseum and I was speaking the truth, but the whole coliseum was filled with hostile people who became enraged at what I said and turned on me and began to rush at me. But then, they all just fell over and they couldn't hurt me. I was seeing this in my mind's eye." Terry was attending church as often as possible, trying to catch up for his years of sin and irreligious ways through remedial Christian reading. He joined a Sunday school program at a mainline Lutheran church, but Terry wanted more energy from his religion than the Lutherans could deliver. Terry's Sunday school teacher, sensing he was anxious for a more passionate form of worship, referred him to a Friday-night prayer group. It met in the home of a young Evangelical named Bill Purves.

Purves was then the assistant pastor at Bushnell Basin Community Church, a suburban Charismatic church with a congregation of about one hundred, which was affiliated with Elim Fellowship and Elim Bible College. In Purves's house, Terry finally found the religious drama he had been seeking.

Purves quickly supplanted Saunders as Terry's spiritual guide. A former drug abuser and alcoholic, Purves was not an ordained minister and had no formal religious education or training. His lack of credentials did not matter in the fundamentalist world of the late 1970s, however, when new, nondenominational churches were literally popping up overnight, setting up in high school gyms or rented halls. People were flocking to Evangelical churches to get away from the rigidity of older, mainline denominations, and the last thing they cared about was ministerial credentials from established seminaries. Although Bushnell Basin Community Church was affiliated with Elim Fellowship, Elim itself was only a small, loose association of fundamentalists, and it had no authority to oversee affiliated churches or to appoint ministers.

Purves made up for his lack of formal training with boundless personal charm and a power of persuasion that few could resist. He was particularly attractive to young people like Terry who were discovering fundamentalism; like them, he had turned his back on the worst society had to offer in order to worship Jesus. The Friday-night prayer service hosted by Bill Purves and his wife became a magnet for stray teens. "Purves had just come out of the drug scene and the alcohol scene, and so he was able to relate and connect with a lot of the people who had been involved in the same things and who were looking to follow the Lord," observes Stacy Cline, dean of nearby Elim Bible College and an old friend of Purves. "He was really being used by the Lord in those early days."

Through Purves, Terry became a devoted, almost obsessive, member of Bushnell Basin Community Church. "Every time the doors opened, I was there." The church's pastor, Philip Miess, was so impressed with

Terry's energy, religious fervor, and remarkable ability to learn and absorb the Scriptures that by June 1977 he decided to let Terry try his hand at preaching. Terry was nervous and stunned: "He invited an eighteen-year-old kid who had been nine months in the Lord to take the pulpit!" Terry won a delay to give himself time to prepare, but to Miess it seemed natural to have a teenager preach to a congregation filled with young "Jesus People and Jesus Freaks." Miess assigned Terry to preach to a Sunday-evening prayer service: "It was a good opportunity for those with budding ministries to try their wings."

Terry chose the New Testament and preached from Paul "about the grace of God." For the first—but hardly the last—time, Randall Terry felt the power of his voice wash over his listeners. "They loved it," he says, and so did he. From then on, Terry preached whenever Miess gave him the opportunity.

Still, it was Bill Purves's outspoken passion for Jesus rather than Phil Miess's more mature form of worship that clicked with Terry. Purves was a full-blown Charismatic, a fiery, self-taught preacher who spoke in tongues and who believed that God had given him the power of prophecy; he was an intimidating and awe-inspiring figure to many at Bushnell Basin.

As young Evangelicals continued to pack the pews at Bushnell Basin, a second, satellite church called The Ark was spun off, founded in an old barn in nearby Canandaigua, New York, to handle the overflow. Bill Purves was named the new church's pastor. Soon, Randall Terry left Bushnell Basin to follow his new mentor to The Ark.

Encouraged by the example of proselytizing set by Bill Purves and other fervent young Evangelicals he had encountered, Terry began to find his voice outside the pulpit as well. He quickly determined that God was calling him to save souls throughout upstate New York. He took a job at McDonalds and began preaching to his co-workers in between taking orders for Big Macs. He switched to a job as a night clerk at a gas station, where he was robbed twice, once at knife-point, but he kept the job because of the freedom it gave him to preach to customers one-on-one throughout the night.

Terry could not abide the fact that his closest friends still had not found Jesus, and he tended to their salvation as well. While his friends sat in neighborhood basements smoking dope and listening to heavy metal music, Terry preached relentlessly. He found a stark, Christian-produced audiotape that dramatized the end of the world and Judgment Day and played it for his wide-eyed, and perhaps stoned, friends, freaking them out. Finally, his best friend, Michaloski, underwent a conversion of his own, bringing the two close once again.

Terry and the newly saved Michaloski began "street preaching" together, evangelizing at the top of their lungs to the passing world. On the streets of Canandaigua and other Rochester suburbs, they would stand for hours at a time, Bibles in hand, exhorting all who heard them to save themselves: "Have you heard the Good News? . . . Jesus Christ died on the cross for your sins. And even though that was two thousand years ago, He's alive, He rose from the dead, and the blood He shed is powerful and can wash away your sins right now, and you can be forgiven!" There were few limits on how far Terry would go to preach to those in need of salvation. Once, he and Michaloski were waiting to go into a movie theater when Terry turned to preach to the rest of the ticket line. Walking along a suburban street, he saw a family picnic under way and began shouting his call to Jesus across their backyard—to cold stares. He evangelized door-to-door, he evangelized at rock concerts, he evangelized at local beaches; he literally gave one listener the shirt off his back. Terry and Michaloski even formed a Christian band so they could get people's attention in order to evangelize some more.

Terry and Michaloski were greeted with jeers, hostility, and apathy, but every once in a while, they would find an anxious listener; sometimes, someone would stop and cry. Randall Terry learned to shrug off the hostile jeers, to wait and listen for the one who might cry. That would serve him well years later, when he switched his focus from street corners to abortion clinics.

Says Michaloski, "What he did outside the abortion mills, that was the same thing. Street preaching. Except street preaching was a lot more radical. More people get mad at you."

By 1978, Terry committed himself more deeply to his new fundamentalist faith by enrolling at Elim Bible College. Terry had by now developed strong connections to Elim; Mark Saunders had studied there, and Bushnell Basin Community Church was an affiliated church.

He arrived at Elim at a critical moment in the school's history. Elim was then drenched in the Charismatic Renewal, a radical, emotional Pentecostalism that marked the rebirth and rapid growth of the old fundamentalist traditions such as speaking in tongues. It was similar to the Charismatic renewal that had swept through the Roman Catholic Church in the late 1960s, attracting John O'Keefe and Sam Lee.

Just one year before Terry enrolled at Elim, in fact, the growing power of the Charismatic Renewal had been on public display for the first time. The landmark Kansas City Charismatic Conference of 1977 brought fifty thousand Charismatic Catholics and Charismatic Protestants of all stripes together to acknowledge their common belief in the living power of the Holy Spirit. The Kansas City Conference was dubbed the "super bowl of the Charismatic movement," and the cross-denominational alliances forged in Kansas City later convinced fundamentalists they could put aside interdenominational theological differences to work together in politics.

Elim Fellowship leader Carlton Spencer, the son of Elim's founder, Ivan Spencer, played a prominent role at the Kansas City Conference; therefore, when Randall Terry walked onto Elim's campus for the first time, the Bible college was fully committed to inculcating its students in Charismatic beliefs.

Elim students were also encouraged to engage in "outreach"—public evangelizing—the kind of street preaching that Terry had already been conducting from gas stations and Canandaigua's intersections. Before long, Michaloski followed Terry and enrolled at Elim as well, and the two often returned to the nearby streets of Rochester to preach alongside other Elim students.

Terry blossomed in Elim's Charismatic climate, and soon he was pegged as the most vocally passionate fundamentalist in a class filled with them. During his freshman year, he was nicknamed "Hallelujah Randy" by classmate Barbara Magera. "He was just on fire for the Lord."

Elim did not provide Terry with a disciplined, secular education; it is a three-year unaccredited school that does not offer a bachelor's degree and does not provide credentials for ministers seeking ordination. What it does offer is a stark, fundamentalist interpretation of the Bible and a worldwide network of contacts and support for would-be fundamentalist missionaries. The college is essentially a feeder school for Elim Fellowship's international missionary program, which consists largely of Elim graduates working to spread fundamentalism throughout the Third World.

Elim's fundamentalist, biblical focus suited Terry's religious ardor, and he thrived. In his second year at Elim, he wrote the script and composed the music for the school's major theater production of the year, a musical he called *Turn Again*. It was a contemporary and perhaps autobiographical version of the story of the Prodigal Son. During his third and final year, Terry was elected student body president, learned Spanish, and focused his life on becoming an Elim missionary in Latin America. As a student, he was sent on brief trips to visit Elim missionaries in Haiti, Costa Rica, and Honduras to get a feel for the life.

It was in an Elim class on "apologetics," the study of the defense and proof of Christianity, that Terry was first exposed to the teachings of Francis Schaeffer. Terry's teacher, Stacy Cline, loaded up his reading list with most of Schaeffer's works and had his class watch Schaeffer and C. Everett Koop's film on abortion, *Whatever Happened to the Human Race?* Cline remembers that Terry wept openly during the film and later told him that it made him realize that "he had to do something" about abortion.

"I just sobbed convulsively," Terry recalls. "I sat there and prayed: God, use me to fight this evil."

Schaeffer's broader views on the role of the Christian in society also deeply influenced him. In an ethics class at Elim, Terry wrote a term paper on the "higher law" theory. As Terry read more, he saw how Schaeffer hammered away at the obligations of Christians to reclaim the rotting culture from "secular humanists." Schaeffer's jeremiads had a profound impact on Terry's thinking; he came to agree with Schaeffer that Christians had to do more than live good lives and wait for the End Times.

"I was entrenched in a separatist, just-preach-the-Gospel theology. Up until that point my theology had been shaped by escapists."

Although one side of Terry was on Elim's quiet campus, there was another side, one that was caught up in the volatility and dark religious passion of Bill Purves. During his Bible school days, Terry broke away from Elim as often as possible to play music and preach at The Ark; his ties to Purves were clearly growing stronger. Soon, Eric Michaloski joined him at The Ark as well.

It was at The Ark that Terry met Cindy Dean, another of Purves's young converts. Dean was a rail-thin woman, slightly older than Terry, who had grown up in nearby Shortville, New York; had attended cooking school in Hyde Park, New York; and then had returned to Rochester for a promising job at a French restaurant before undergoing a conversion experience in 1978. She first encountered Terry a few months after her conversion, and the two quickly became friends. Their friendship only slowly blossomed into romance; they did not start dating until the summer of 1980, and they became engaged on Christmas Eve that year. Cindy began auditing a few courses at Elim along with Randy, absorbing the fundamentalist biblical doctrine that had shaped her fiancé. (Elim adhered to a fundamentalist interpretation of the Bible that emphasized that a wife should submit to the authority of her husband and taught that the concept of pastoral "headship" begins in the home, where the man is the head of the household. Cindy Terry has never expressed any doubts or reservations about those precepts.) They were married in July 1981, just after Terry's graduation from Elim.

Terry had a standing invitation from Elim missionary John Spyker to join him in Mexico; he and Cindy were planning to make missionary work the focus of their new life together. But even with the invitation from Spyker, Terry needed the financial backing of a local church to finance his mission work, and for Terry that meant a reliance on Bill Purves and The Ark.

While he waited for church support to make his dream come true, Terry and his new wife rented an apartment in suburban Victor, New York, and he took a job at a local potato chip company to pay the bills. He moved to another job, as a foreman in a local electronics factory, and was laid off in May 1982.

However, Purves had no interest in supporting Terry, according to Michaloski, or in allowing him to go overseas as a missionary. Purves was growing "darker," more openly self-centered, and was beginning to view The Ark as his personal instrument. Sending one of his acolytes off on a distant mission would be nothing more than a drain on his church and on what Bill Purves wanted to do, Michaloski adds.

Michaloski found that out firsthand when he and his wife briefly went to Haiti as missionaries with The Ark's backing. A month or two after their arrival, Purves cut off their support and yanked them back to Rochester.

"Why didn't Randy become a missionary? The problem for both

Randy and me was that we were tied in with Bill Purves," recalls Michaloski. "Randy had been with Purves for years by then. But Purves wasn't interested in that kind of stuff [sending out missionaries]. He wasn't interested in other people's things. This guy was a loser, he couldn't see anything beyond himself. Nothing was going to happen [at The Ark] unless it was about him. He was completely and totally about himself."

Terry stayed with Purves and The Ark, however. Increasingly, Terry appeared to be ensnared in his relationship with Purves; he seemed to accept Purves's claims that he was "gifted" by God with the voice of a prophet.

"Randy had an addictive relationship with Purves," says Randal Stewart, one of Terry's Elim classmates, who is now assistant director of U.S. ministries for Elim Fellowship. "Bill was a very manipulative guy who was attracting young Bible school graduates to him and getting them to do whatever he wanted. I think Randy was attracted to him because Purves was a nonconformist, and Randy was a nonconformist, too. When you are young and filled with idealism, and someone appears to be such a nonconformist, it's real easy to buy in. You see the traditional religious institutions not working, and you see someone who is such a nonconformist and such a persuasive guy, and you say this is the way."

In 1982, when Purves left Rochester and The Ark for another Elim-affiliated church in rural Montour Falls, a tiny hamlet near Watkins Glen, New York, Terry and his wife followed, moving into a trailer right behind Montour Falls Bethel Church, Purves's new church. Although the Terrys had dropped everything to follow Purves across the state, Purves had not given Terry any formal position with the church. Terry was there to help out with the church's youth and music programs.

By the time Purves and Terry arrived in Montour Falls, Purves was becoming more and more unstable. Purves came to believe that he not only was "gifted" with a prophetic voice but was a real prophet and thus unaccountable to any man or earthly institution. Soon, word began to filter back to Elim that something was going terribly wrong at Montour Falls Bethel Church.

"The rumors coming back to Elim were that Montour Falls was becoming like a cult," says Stacy Cline. "Bill was building his own little kingdom down there."

Eric Michaloski remembers visiting Purves and Terry in Montour

Falls and recalls that Purves "would literally get spastic, angry, and violent if you confronted him on anything."

Eventually, Terry saw through Purves as well. Although he refuses to discuss the details of what happened, Terry left the Montour Falls church in early 1983. Purves's spell over Randall Terry was finally broken.

After Terry left, Purves's activities became even more bizarre; the church in Montour Falls finally collapsed and was later reopened under a new minister. Purves began to roam the Northeast, moving from one fundamentalist congregation to another, until finally Elim Fellowship officials confronted him and withdrew his credentials as an Elim-affiliated minister. He legally changed his name to Micaiah, an Old Testament Prophet who, in the Second Book of Chronicles, has the courage to stand up against four hundred false prophets to tell the truth. Briefly hospitalized for complications from alcohol and drug abuse, Purves, now Micaiah, finally dropped out of sight.

Terry insists that Purves did not prevent him from becoming a missionary and stresses that he was never in a manipulative relationship with Purves:

> I would not qualify our relationship as addictive at all. I know enough about addictive and controlling behavior to know that it wasn't like that. Bill was a man who had had a heroin addiction and who had then developed a great love for the Lord. He was a good preacher, and when he invited us to come down [to Montour Falls] I had just gotten laid off and Cindy and I thought it would be fun. And when we got there, it wasn't what we thought. We got nervous with what was going on with Bill, and we got out of there. The Elim brethren didn't know how bad it was until I brought my concerns with Bill to them. I was able to go on with my life and put it quickly behind me.

Terry insists that the church at Montour Falls did not develop cult-like tendencies until "after I left."

As his relationship with Purves collapsed, Terry began to search for a new direction. Music seemed to offer one. While living in Montour Falls, Terry had become an avid listener of a Christian radio station owned by Pat Robertson's Christian Broadcasting Network (CBN) in nearby Ithaca, New York, and he often called into the station to make musical requests. He struck up a relationship with the local disc jockey, Fred Gauge, who moonlighted as a concert promoter for local Christian musical groups. When CBN sold the station in 1982, Gauge organized a Christian music concert in Ithaca and invited Terry to perform with his keyboard. Gauge saw that what Terry lacked in talent he made up for in his on-stage presence. "He wasn't a professional-quality musician, but he could captivate an audience." Gauge agreed to book more concert dates for Terry in the region.

By then Gauge was living in Owego, New York, and was struggling to start a small Evangelical church in his home with some friends. He invited Terry to join them. With nothing to keep him in Montour Falls, Terry and his wife moved to Owego, just five doors down from Gauge.

The religious services held in Gauge's home were attended by just a few families of young Evangelicals who had left mainline denominations only to find there were virtually no fundamentalist churches nearby to choose from. Terry saw Gauge's home church, named Cornerstone, as a new opportunity. He could become a pastor on his own, free from the influence of Bill Purves. He quickly gained control over the services in Gauge's home and became Cornerstone's unofficial pastor.

Soon, however, Terry's aggressive fundamentalist style and his highly charged and very vocal services began to grate on Gauge and others at Cornerstone. They did not share Terry's Charismatic background, and they were stunned when over the next few months Terry began to transform Cornerstone into a fiery, Elim-style church. Gauge began to have second thoughts not long after Terry arrived in Owego. One day, the two men went to a local convenience store together; Gauge was horrified when Terry suddenly began to "street-preach" at the store clerk, shouting and speaking in tongues.

At Cornerstone, Terry soon proposed the radical Charismatic practice of "prayer closets"; he wanted to order church members to stuff themselves into closets in their homes for at least two hours a day to pray in enforced solitude. "Randy," Gauge told him, "this isn't happening."

Terry's concerns about abortion were gradually becoming more visible at Cornerstone as well; he began to call on Cornerstone members to pray for the unborn. Privately, he started to talk to Gauge about the need for Christians to act. Gauge was shaken when Terry quietly told him that given the right circumstances—and assurances that he would not be caught—he would bomb an abortion clinic.

The last straw for Gauge came in the summer of 1983, when Terry brought Elim minister Michael Cavanaugh to Cornerstone. Cavanaugh began to speak in tongues during the church service and "laid hands" on Terry, loudly proclaiming to Cornerstone's small congregation his prophecy for Terry's life. Terry had been anointed by God for greatness as a leader of men.

Gauge and Steve Worth, another Cornerstone member, were irate that their church had been hijacked. "We didn't want to go that way," they say. Fed up, the two men finally went to Terry's house and told him that he was finished at Cornerstone. Furious, Terry "cursed us biblically," Gauge recalls. "He said we were cursed because we had come against God's anointed." Cornerstone collapsed.

Coming so soon after his break with Purves, Terry's ouster from Cornerstone was a major blow. He drifted for the next few months, once again searching for a new direction.

Terry soon began to attend a regular prayer service held in a flower and garden shop owned by Howard Potts, and there he met Potts' son-in-law, Dan Little, who was working hard to revive a small fundamentalist church in nearby Binghamton called the Church at Pierce Creek. When Terry told him about Cornerstone's collapse in August 1983, Little invited him to join his struggling church.

Pierce Creek was a "praying church"—loud, tongue-speaking, independent, and Charismatic—and a product of the same Evangelical surge that had transformed Randall Terry. Little had been fronting a Christian band when he first heard about the church in the summer of 1980. A guitar-playing son of a Baptist minister, Little had never gone to Bible college or been trained as a minister himself. He was growing tired of both his band and his church and had just quit both when he received a desperate call from one of the few remaining members of Pierce Creek. The church's congregation had almost disappeared, and the church would soon shut its doors if it did not find a new, energetic pastor. Little was asked if he would take to the pulpit and save Pierce Creek.

By the following Sunday, Dan Little was a pastor for the first time in his life, and he quickly set to work reviving Pierce Creek. Under Little, Pierce Creek was soon transformed into a hotbed of Holy Roller fundamentalism; its congregation began to grow as Little attracted new members who hungered for a more vocal celebration of the power of Jesus and the Holy Spirit than they could find in Binghamton's traditional churches. From eight members, the congregation grew to more than one hundred fifty.

It was at Pierce Creek that Terry found his style of Charismatic worship; in Dan Little he found the warm, understanding pastor he needed after his experiences in Montour Falls and Owego. At Pierce Creek, Terry also found that he could no longer ignore the fact that he was being drawn—he believed by God—to protest abortion.

In October 1983, he was attending a Wednesday-evening prayer meeting when a woman who had just watched a television documentary on the issue asked everyone to pray "that God will do something about abortion in America." Terry joined in the prayers, and as he did, he had a vision. Terry told his fellow churchgoers that the vision was ill-focused, like the vision of the blind man who told Jesus that he saw "men as trees, walking" (Mark 8:24)—but a vision nonetheless. He was to lead great numbers of people out to abortion clinics to protest and shut them down. He explains the experience in the following way:

> As I began to pray about abortion in America, I just had these ideas flooding my head about how to fight abortion. To have people in front of abortion mills. To help women place their babies in Christian homes once they were saved from having abortion, to reeducate the public to the value of human life, from a Bible-based perspective. Because only the Bible gives us value. We were praying, and I had all these thoughts rushing through my head and I really thought God was impressing me to do something to fight abortion. It did not fit my theology, it did not fit my plans for my life. We broke up this prayer meeting with this strong sense that I was supposed to do something.

A week or two after the prayer service, he went apple picking with Michael Mrva, a member of Cornerstone in Owego who remained close to Terry, and told him about his vision. "I told him about thousands of people outside abortion mills, and saving babies, and being on TV, and Christians adopting these children."

"He started to share what was on his heart, and I was overwhelmed," recalls Mrva. "He said we need to go to the abortion clinics, we need to talk to the women, and we need to expose what's going on in there. I remember he said some of us may lose everything, but we have to lay our lives down on the line. It became really intense. It was overwhelming."

Says Terry, "Mike thought I was crazy."

Terry was still afraid to say anything to his wife about his vision. The couple still had hopes of becoming missionaries in Mexico, and protesting abortion would once more defer a dream already delayed by Bill Purves. Finally, Randy worked up the nerve to talk to Cindy. "To my happiness, she said, 'Let's pray about it.'" Terry went away over the weekend, and while he was gone, Cindy watched a documentary on abortion; when Randy got home, he found to his surprise that she was equally convinced of the need to fight abortion.

By January 1984, Terry had approached Dan Little to share his vision. Abandoning thoughts of missionary work in Mexico, Terry boldly predicted that he would make his name by leading Christians in anti-abortion protest: "I said to Dan, 'I'm going to be on *Donahue!*'"

Dan Little was a small-town businessman who, despite his lack of ministerial training, had saved Pierce Creek from oblivion. He was to become Randall Terry's religious father figure, developing with him the kind of close, spiritual relationship that Terry had never enjoyed with his real father. Little responded to Terry's giddy predictions like a tolerant father to an overzealous boy.

"Where are you going to start?"

Terry paused only for a moment. "Right here in Binghamton!"

In April 1984, Randy and Cindy Terry left their home in Owego and moved into a small apartment in Binghamton, about one mile from the only abortion clinic in the region, Southern Tier Women's Services. On May 1, on his lunch hour from his job in the tire department at Montgomery Ward, Randall Terry went to the Binghamton Plaza Shopping Center, where Southern Tier had its offices, stood in the parking lot, and started talking to the women going in for abortions. He was street preaching once again. Almost immediately, Cindy joined her husband, spending all her free time in the Binghamton Plaza parking lot.

Liberated from Bill Purves, freed from the distractions of starting a church, Randall Terry had finally become a missionary.

10

BLOOD GUILTINESS

When Randall and Cindy Terry began their vigil outside the Southern Tier clinic in May 1984, anti-abortion militancy was catching fire. John O'Keefe was organizing his biggest sit-in ever, and Michael Bray was about to betray him with violence and lies. Joseph Scheidler was presiding over the first PLAN convention, and John Ryan was relishing his first taste of success after years of obsessive solitary protest. Joan Andrews was gluing locks and invading clinics from St. Louis to Philadelphia. John Burt was picketing Linda Taggart's Ladies Center in Pensacola, and Matthew Goldsby and James Simmons were about to blow it up.

It was the fourth year of the Reagan administration, and the anti-abortion movement was finally beginning to see through White House lip service. There would be 1.57 million abortions in 1984, thousands more than in 1980, the year before Reagan took office; the first "pro-life president" had an abortion "deficit." The Supreme Court was still not willing to reconsider *Roe,* and the Senate's 1983 defeat of a constitutional amendment to ban abortion had left mainstream abortion opponents, both in Congress and at the National Right to Life Committee, dazed and disorganized. Worse, the debate over abortion in the United

States had become frozen and stale. Both sides had staked out uncompromising positions, either abortion on demand or no abortion at all, and their opposing rhetoric had degenerated into agitprop. The 1984 presidential election campaign only reconfirmed the national stalemate on the issue; abortion-rights and anti-abortion sloganeering was becoming the background noise of the 1980s.

Many in the right-to-life mainstream were beginning to despair of the political process. They were both Catholics and Protestants who had started out writing letters to Congress, joining the March for Life in Washington each year on the anniversary of *Roe v. Wade,* and sending money to National Right to Life.

A sense of betrayal by Reagan's Washington was sending mainstream abortion foes into the arms of the militants. Clinic bombings reached a crescendo in 1984; activists unwilling to resort to outright violence were turning instead to civil disobedience, turning to the likes of John O'Keefe, John Ryan, and even John Burt. Nearly half of all abortion providers in the United States—1,250 clinics, hospitals, and other doctors' offices—reported in a 1985 survey by an abortion-rights group that they had become the targets of anti-abortion "harassment," a politically loaded term that clinic personnel and abortion-rights advocates used to describe civil disobedience and even legal protest activity like picketing.

By 1988, Randall Terry was the catalyst, creating a true nationwide protest movement out of the local pockets of militancy and extremism. But in 1984, few activists knew what was going on beyond the horizon; newcomer Randall Terry had not yet heard of Scheidler or of his unfulfilled dreams for PLAN. As he paced across the cracked parking lot of the Binghamton Plaza, a strip shopping center in a blue-collar section of Binghamton, Randall Terry, just barely twenty-five, did not know quite where to begin. "We didn't know anything about anything," remembers his wife.

But Randall Terry did know about street preaching. He had a gift, a relentlessness, that made it possible for him to talk to perfect strangers about their innermost fears and desires; he and Eric Michaloski had done it countless times on the streets of Canandaigua. Speaking to harried, nervous young women, speaking to them of Jesus and the Bible and their bodies and the life they were harboring in their wombs—all in the brief time it took to keep pace from car door to clinic door—came naturally to a grassroots Charismatic. It came especially easily to the compulsive Randall Terry; one fellow Evangelical described him as born with a need to "find where to connect with a person—and then go after it." Historian Gary Wills got it right when he said later that "there are no casual encounters with Randall Terry. He turns them all into contests of some sort, clashes of moral standards, games, probings."

Terry's new missionary work in the Binghamton Plaza was to open the hearts and minds of Southern Tier's patients, open these women to the Holy Spirit and the Lord's miracles so they could recognize sin and understand God's retribution and His power of forgiveness, just as Mark Saunders and Bill Purves had helped Randall Terry discover a Pentecostal God years before.

They were street preaching in front of an abortion clinic. In Chicago, Joseph Scheidler called it "sidewalk counseling," but Randall Terry gave it a new fundamentalist spin, and the clinic staff at Southern Tier had never seen anything like it. "Cindy and Randy Terry," clinic administrator Peg Johnston wrote in an internal memo to Southern Tier's corporate owners in the summer of 1984, have become "a persistent and troublesome presence."

At first, Cindy Terry spent far more time outside the clinic than did her husband. He was still working at Montgomery Ward, and she had no job, no children, and time on her hands. During the spring and summer of 1984, Cindy spent as many as forty hours a week outside Southern Tier's offices whereas Randy appeared only at lunchtime and on weekends.

Because they saw her more frequently, Southern Tier staffers initially thought Cindy was the more committed activist. Later, when Randall Terry gained nationwide fame, Southern Tier spread the word that the protests had been Cindy's idea and that Randall only came after her, seizing the attention and squeezing her out of the picture. That was not true, but it made for good abortion-rights propaganda; it made Randall Terry appear at once both less creative and more domineering.

The clinic's personnel never fully understood Cindy or her relationship with her husband. Alex Aitken, the clinic's assistant administrator and the staffer who had the most direct contact with the Terrys, was the only one at Southern Tier who ever even tried. The two women could not have been more different; Cindy was a committed fundamentalist willing to bend her life to fit her husband's, whereas Aitken was an avowed atheist. But Aitken was fascinated by Cindy Terry, and she finally worked up the courage to call her and arrange a private meeting at a local restaurant. Although their back-channel discussion did not lead to an ongoing relationship, Aitken grudgingly came to accept that Cindy genuinely believed in her religion and her mission—and in her husband.

Cindy Terry was a tall, gaunt woman with the pale, hollowed-out looks of a Dust Bowl farm wife, and she had a special motivation for joining her husband's crusade. After nearly three years of marriage, she was frustrated that she was unable to conceive. Watching other women so easily shed the potential life for which she so desperately yearned filled her with a zeal to stop them and, if necessary, raise their children herself. She soon began telling the passing women of her plight, pleading with them not to go through with their abortions but to give birth and to let her adopt.

The Terrys protested outside the clinic by themselves for the first few weeks, armed with little more than a few posters mounted with graphic photographs of fetal development. Entitled "If Wombs Had Windows," the posters were part of a cache of anti-abortion literature the Terrys had purchased from Last Days Ministries, a Lindale, Texas–based Evangelical group that had become a major distributor of anti-abortion materials within the fundamentalist community. The Terrys held the posters up as they tried to talk to the passing patients, hoping the fetal pictures would shock the women into turning around. But they had no luck during those first weeks. Business was booming at Southern Tier.

Binghamton was a tired old industrial town of fifty thousand laid out awkwardly along the Susquehanna River just above the Pennsylvania border. The town was spared economic oblivion thanks to the New York legislature, which made it home to the most prestigious campus of the state's university system (SUNY), and to the federal government's highway planners, who laid out Interstate 81 so that it snaked through the heart of Binghamton on its way north from Pennsylvania to Syracuse.

Both the SUNY campus and easy highway access made Binghamton an excellent location for an abortion clinic; the clinic served both SUNY coeds and the working-class women from the small, hardscrabble towns in the surrounding region. Operated by an Allentown, Pennsylvania–based chain and specializing in first-trimester abortions, Southern Tier became the only freestanding clinic between Syracuse and the Pennsylvania border when it opened in May 1981.

Occupying rented space on the second floor of the Binghamton Plaza's professional building, Southern Tier had a brisk volume almost from the start. Its experience reflected the growing dominance of free-standing clinics within the abortion industry; more and more hospitals had withdrawn from the business, in part because of community pressures but primarily because they found it difficult to remain cost-competitive with the new chains of clinics. In 1973, more than half of all abortions were performed in hospitals; by 1988, 86 percent of all abortions were being performed in freestanding clinics like Southern Tier and only 10 percent in hospitals. Like other industries in the 1980s, abortion was undergoing a dramatic shakeout and consolidation, which reduced the number of abortion providers while volume remained unchanged, thus increasing profitability. By 1988, 98 percent of all abortions were being performed in urban areas. Whereas abortion-rights advocates argued that the rural counties were being denied local abortion services because of anti-abortion harassment, the truth was that there had never been many clinics in rural areas and the handful that had closed had done so because the abortion volume was not high enough for them to make money. Clinics like Southern Tier had emerged as regional abortion providers, drawing patients into the nation's cities.

After a brief political controversy surrounding Southern Tier's opening, the clinic encountered only scattered protests by a handful of Catholics during its first three years of operation. The biggest headache for administrator Johnston was that local doctors, fearful of controversy, had refused to work at the clinic. Instead, Dr. Salomon Epstein, an abortion doctor from New York City, was flown to Binghamton each week. Johnston also found it impossible to convince any local doctors to serve as a backup for Epstein, and eventually, two other out-of-town doctors—Amy Cousins from Manhattan and Jeffrey Stowe from Philadelphia—agreed to supplement Epstein's work. Southern Tier's experience was hardly unique; a reliance on out-of-town doctors was becoming commonplace at abortion clinics in the nation's small and medium-sized cities, where doctors were most vulnerable to anti-abortion protest and harassment. Big-city "circuit-riding" abortion doctors like Epstein and Cousins were emerging to fill the gap, although anti-abortion activists were just as quickly beginning to target them as the "weak links in the abortion industry."

By the time Randall and Cindy Terry began their vigil, Southern Tier was setting volume records almost every month; the clinic performed nearly a thousand abortions in the first six months of 1984, up sharply from the year before.

Southern Tier's patients were mostly young, blue collar, and politically apathetic, and almost all refused to stop and listen to the Terrys. They were usually accompanied by boyfriends who were openly hostile to last-minute lectures, a fact exploited by administrator Johnston, who later acknowledged that she had "encouraged boyfriends to take out their frustrations" on Randall Terry. At least one man slammed Terry's head against a car window.

As the Terrys brushed up against the edges of accepted protest behavior, the clinic and its customers fought back vigorously, and as a result Terry had almost nothing to show for his efforts. By July, an angry patient filed the first complaint against the Terrys with the Binghamton police, charging that both Randy and Cindy had harassed her; they had stuck a picture of a bloody fetus in her face while trying to block her from entering Southern Tier.

In his first book, *Operation Rescue,* Terry recalled his initial naiveté, how he and his wife rode an emotional roller coaster from elation to depression whenever a woman they had convinced to turn away came back to the clinic a few days later. He acknowledged his humiliation after discovering that one woman who agreed to forestall abortion turned out to be an abortion-rights activist sent by the clinic to find out what he was saying. "It seemed the work that God had called us to," Terry wrote, "was going to be filled with constant hopelessness and despair."

Amateur videos filmed outside the clinic by his friend Gary Leber offer telling proof of just how disorganized and ineffective Randall Terry was in that early summer of 1984. Looking every bit the Montgomery Ward tire salesman, typically wearing polyester slacks, white short-sleeve shirt, and tie [but no sports coat], Terry would loiter in the middle of the shopping center's public parking lot, eyeing women as they got out of their cars, trying to gauge whether they were bound for the abortion clinic or the auto parts store next door. Women would hesitate when he approached and then hurry past, doing their best to ignore him, averting their eyes from his photographs, and refusing his pamphlets. Terry would chatter nonstop in their ears, but he did not yell or scream or block their path. Not yet willing to break the law, he would back away to avoid trespassing as soon as the women had traversed his gauntlet, watching forlornly as they walked through the outer doors of the professional building on their way upstairs to the clinic. A young woman working for Southern Tier was a constant presence, shadowing Terry wherever he walked. She often placed herself between Terry and the clinic patients, making it difficult for him to talk to the women or show them his posters. Terry seemed nothing more than a local oddity, someone to be brushed past without a second thought. Out of the hundreds of women who walked past the Terrys in the summer of 1984, only two or three agreed not to have abortions.

One of the women they succeeded in turning away that first summer agreed to allow the Terrys to take her baby, a girl named Tila, when she was born. In addition, the Terrys took in the woman's two older children for foster care; New York State paid the Terrys $1,200 a month to care for the three children. The Terrys ultimately adopted and raised Tila and one of the older children, a boy named Jamiel. Although the mother, Tina Turner, was white, the two children had black fathers. Terry's critics later ignored the fact that he was the legal father of two mixed-race children when they accused him of being, among many other things, a racist.

Terry's sense of desperation over the futility of his early campaign was evident. In one of Leber's videos, Terry can be seen standing on the sidewalk of the Binghamton Plaza, staring off into space and preaching at the top of his lungs to the air and the sky.

Those early days were "unbelievably intense for them," recalls Michael Mrva, Terry's friend. "Randy and Cindy were exhausted. . . . It was humbling."

Terry was certain that many of the patients were under pressure to have abortions from their boyfriends, husbands, or parents. That was sometimes true, inconveniently so for abortion-rights advocates because it injected ambiguity into the argument that abortion was a women's rights issue. Terry held stubbornly to his image of the waiflike Madonna being led away by the domineering and brutish man, and he refused to walk away and leave the women of Southern Tier alone.

Instead, he vowed to broaden his efforts; he created a group called Project Life, through which he planned to conduct not only street-level protests but also an ambitious array of political and educational anti-abortion activities throughout the Binghamton area.

For a time, Project Life existed only in Randall Terry's vivid imagination, but it was not long before his fortunes turned. Soon, the Church at Pierce Creek gave him shock troops to lead—and financial support to keep Project Life afloat. In the process, Project Life and the Church at Pierce Creek gave life to Francis Schaeffer's dream of the political mobilization of the Evangelical church.

Pierce Creek's pastor, Dan Little, placed a heavy emphasis on weekly prayer groups that gave church members a chance to pray aloud for God's grace and to unburden themselves of their sins. The people of Pierce Creek, Little says, "prayed like they meant it." It was at his Wednesday-evening prayer group in October 1983 that Randall Terry had felt his anti-abortion call; it was through subsequent prayer group sessions that Terry, using all of the innate oratorical and Evangelical skills at his command, recruited the congregation to join him outside Southern Tier. Soon, the talk and prayer at Pierce Creek revolved around the lonely battle being waged by the Terrys and whether the rest of the church should join in. Dan Little was Randall Terry's chief advocate. When Pierce Creek began to pray about the Terrys and abortion, it was almost inevitable that they would take up Randall Terry's crusade.

Breathless reports filtering back to the church that Randy and Cindy were being harassed finally convinced Pierce Creek to act. Gary Leber, a Pierce Creek member, received a panicky phone call from his wife while he was at work, telling him that the Terrys needed his help. Cindy had just been "throttled" by the boyfriend of a Southern Tier patient. "People in the church all had the same feeling—we've got to help Randy and Cindy." By midsummer, Dan Little and fifteen to twenty members of Pierce Creek had joined the protests and were spending much of their free time picketing, marching, and singing in the Binghamton Plaza parking lot behind Randall Terry.

Dan Little and Pierce Creek helped in less visible ways as well. Project Life was established as a "DBA" of Branch Ministries, the same tax-exempt religious organization that was the parent of the Church at Pierce Creek. Dan Little and his father-in-law, Howard Potts, had established Branch Ministries as an umbrella organization that could share its tax-exempt status—and its tax identification number—with the Church at Pierce Creek as well as the Lord Hill Church in Owego, where Potts served as pastor. Once Branch Ministries was established, Potts and Little realized they could extend their new tax-exempt status to sympathetic political-religious organizations established by their friends and supporters, such as Randall Terry's Project Life. Leber, who served as Pierce Creek's financial secretary, says that by making Project Life a unit of Branch Ministries, Terry avoided the legal bills and paperwork costs of incorporating Project Life on its own; more important, Project Life also avoided what could have been a two-year wait for Internal Revenue Service approval for its tax-exempt status. If it had applied on its own, Project Life might not have qualified for tax-exempt status at all, given its involvement in political activity and its later role in law-breaking acts of civil disobedience.

In October 1984, Terry opened his first "crisis pregnancy center" in a storefront near Southern Tier; the center was also established as a tax-exempt unit of Branch Ministries, was staffed by volunteers from the Church at Pierce Creek, and was funded largely by tax-deductible donations from members of Pierce Creek's congregation. The Internal Revenue Service eventually came after Pierce Creek, seeking to withdraw its tax-exempt status because of its involvement in political causes, but it did not do so for another nine years. When Randall Terry began to lead his fellow Charismatics in battle against the U.S. political system, therefore, he was doing so on a tax-free basis.

With Little and the Pierce Creek congregation behind him, Terry could now stage true demonstrations for the first time, complete with picket lines, anti-abortion chants, and music. He and his followers could also pursue Southern Tier's patients more relentlessly, and Terry's "sidewalk counseling" edged closer to actual harassment. Terry's protests began to draw headlines as a result. The local newspaper, the *Binghamton Press & Sun-Bulletin,* published its first article on the Terrys and their lonely protest in late June 1984, and the news coverage quickly expanded as Randall Terry's support grew.

Terry offered an early hint of his media savvy by attempting to exploit the news coverage to expand Project Life's base beyond Pierce Creek. Just after the Binghamton newspaper's first story on his protests, Terry sent a letter to pastors throughout the area, explaining his campaign and asking them to join him. With its heavy reliance on Evangelical rhetoric and biblical references, his letter to the pastors offered an early look at Terry's attempt to translate the language of social protest into the language of Protestant fundamentalism:

> Project Life is a Christ centered, evangelistic, non-political ministry [and its goal is] to be at the abortion clinic every hour it is open, sharing the love of God with young women and their boyfriends/husbands, and telling them the truth about themselves and their babies. . . . We proclaim what God's Word says concerning life in the womb, and what a Christian's responsibility is in this holocaust. Proverbs 24:11 & 12 say Rescue those being led away to death; hold back those staggering toward slaughter. . . . Abortion . . . is an attack on the Word of God and ultimately on the kingdom and Church of God. . . . Abortion is the shedding of innocent blood, which God condemns (Numbers 35:32, Exodus 23:7, Deuteronomy 27:25) and God commands His people to rise in defense of those who cannot defend themselves (Psalms 82:2–4, Proverbs 31:8, 9).

It was months before Evangelicals from other area churches finally joined Terry's campaign, but in the summer of 1984, the backing of his Pierce Creek congregation was enough to keep Terry going. "We will continue to be there," Terry vowed in a letter to the Binghamton newspaper, "with Christ's strength, love and compassion until this country returns to its sanity."

Project Life was starting to become a major headache for Southern Tier. Terry's reliance on biblical quotations could not obscure the fact that he and his followers were conducting a hit-and-run campaign of intimidation and personal harassment against the clinic staff. Internal memos and quarterly reports to Southern Tier's owners in Allentown show just how badly shaken Peg Johnston was becoming by Randall Terry's obsessive campaign.

"Their harassment of patients and staff has escalated," Johnston warned in her September 1984 quarterly report. "On procedure days large numbers (15–50) of aggressive sidewalk counselors and chanting picketers with signs make it difficult to come into the building. . . . The picketers routinely hurl epithets at patients, deliverymen, visitors and staff, calling them murderers, Nazis, savages, blood thirsty, and scum of the earth. . . . The possibility of further escalation of tactics is an active fear for us." In the fall of 1984, soon after the clinic received its first bomb threat, Johnston told a local reporter that Randall Terry had created a "siege atmosphere" at Southern Tier.

The battle at Southern Tier was turning into a bitter duel between two stereotypical figures: Peg Johnston, an openly gay feminist, former director of a rape crisis center, and former antiwar protester, and Randall Terry, a fundamentalist true believer in a male-dominated world, a world governed by biblical law. The Terry-Johnston battle was a microcosm of the abortion wars of the mid-1980s; it personified the hardened edges of America's abortion debate.

In September, Terry launched his most effective campaign against Southern Tier, announcing a boycott of the entire shopping center to put public pressure on the center's owner, John Galesi, to evict the clinic. The boycott not only generated a new round of headlines and local television news stories, it also succeeded for the first time in attracting broad support for Terry from other Evangelical churches.

Prodded by Terry, ministers who had never been active in the anti-abortion cause put pressure on Galesi to oust the clinic. "In view of the sanctity of human life from the moment of conception, I, as the new Pastor of the First Baptist Church in Marathon, N.Y. [28 miles north of Binghamton] plan to encourage our 300 plus members and families to refrain from using the services" at the plaza, wrote the Reverend Robert Bulmer in October.

Unable legally to keep the picketers out of the shopping center's parking lot, Galesi was soon hit with complaints from his other tenants about the impact of the protests and the boycott on their businesses. He clearly had no stomach for the fight with Terry and would have been happy to evict the clinic, but Southern Tier had a lease, and he could not force the clinic out until it expired in 1986.

Galesi finally met with Terry and convinced him that he had no legal recourse; Terry agreed to end the boycott. But the fact that Galesi had taken his boycott so seriously made Terry a legitimate newsmaker; the local media now considered him to be Binghamton's leading spokesperson for the anti-abortion movement.

The publicity also enhanced Terry's stature within the Evangelical community, especially at Pierce Creek, which was now completely enmeshed in his campaign. Pierce Creek members who were not Terry enthusiasts saw little choice but to drift away. The hard core who stayed at Pierce Creek became fiercely devoted to Terry and Project Life.

With $2,000 in donations and volunteers from Pierce Creek, Project Life opened a crisis pregnancy center in October 1984, giving Randall Terry an office from which to do battle. With Dan Little presiding, the center's opening ceremony served as a kind of political-religious rite of passage for Terry. As dozens of supporters and fellow members of the Pierce Creek congregation crowded into the center's storefront, Dan Little "laid hands" on Terry's bowed head, consecrating him as God's chosen leader in the fight against abortion.

A video of the ceremony offers extraordinary insight into the seamless relationship that had so quickly developed between Dan Little's Pierce Creek and Randall Terry's Project Life. "Our Father in heaven," Little prayed aloud, amid a chorus of amens, as he and dozens of others reached out to lay hands on Terry and his wife. "We seek precedent in the Word of God . . . the Church at Antioch which laid hands on Paul and Silas, and sent them out to do the work of God, You sent them out to Macedonia and Thessalonica and Philipi and Corinth and Athens. . . . Lord, you have given us the precedent, where the Church laid hands on the one. So today, afresh and anew, we lay hands on our brother, Randy. We ask in the name of Jesus Christ that the Holy Ghost will fill you with power, Randy. We bless you with a supernatural strength that you have not yet known." Randall Terry's missionary work now had the full sanction of his church.

Terry soon quit his job at Montgomery Ward to devote all his time and energy to Project Life, and by early 1985, he had finally won over a small cadre of local Evangelical ministers willing to back him. "Randall Terry has caused a greater awareness for me and my congregation," one minister told reporters outside Southern Tier. "We hid our heads in the sand for too long. Now . . . church members are coming alive." Fundamentalists were spilling out of Binghamton's churches, and Terry could soon draw more than one hundred people at a time to take part in his pickets.

Even with this larger force behind him, Terry's ability to convince women to abandon their abortion plans was negligible. Project Life claimed that it convinced one woman a day to stop in at the Crisis Pregnancy Center to talk and estimated that as many as one hundred fifty babies had been saved over the first year of its campaign. But Southern Tier still set a new volume record in the first quarter of 1985, and the clinic ended the year having performed almost exactly the same number of abortions as in 1984.

Such statistical measures did not matter; Terry was flushed with his transformation into a public figure, and he was constantly on the look-out for new headline-grabbing initiatives. He expanded his boycott to include local hospitals that performed abortions and made the out-of-town doctors who came to Binghamton to perform abortions a new focus of his ire. He organized a protest outside Stowe's Philadelphia office, rattling him so much that Stowe immediately sent in his resignation to Southern Tier.

Epstein was Terry's favorite target. Terry and other protesters followed Epstein to a restaurant to picket and pray while he ate. Terry met Epstein's plane at the Binghamton airport to harass him as soon as he arrived from New York, forcing Epstein each time to race to Peg Johnston's waiting car. Eventually, Epstein filed harassment charges against Terry.

Johnston and Southern Tier responded by becoming more aggressive as well. Johnston agreed to let a militant group of fifty Young Socialists from SUNY act as clinic escorts. Shoving matches and other confrontations were inevitable, yet neither Terry nor Johnston showed remorse. "One patient punched one of the frequent harassers, much to the delight of the staff," Johnston glibly wrote in a memo in the summer of 1985.

Terry's greatest success was in making it nearly impossible for Southern Tier to renew its lease at the Binghamton Plaza while throwing roadblocks in its efforts to find other office space in town. With the clinic's lease set to expire in early 1986, Johnston looked frantically for a new location throughout 1985, but whenever Randall Terry applied pressure, openly threatening potential landlords with boycotts or harassment, they backed out.

Johnston finally found a new office in suburban Vestal, New York. Although she was forced to take twice as much space as she needed to obtain a lease, the office came with a private parking lot, giving Southern Tier a new measure of security and control over its entrance. Terry and his followers tried everything to pressure Vestal city officials to keep the clinic out; one city official was subjected to an intense campaign of telephone harassment by Terry's supporters, receiving calls at home every hour starting at 7 A.M. and continuing until 1 A.M. each day. But the protests failed, and Johnston moved the clinic into the new office in April 1986.

Without a job, Terry was now completely dependent on Project Life and was scraping by on a salary of about $7,500 in donations. Often, the Terrys did not have enough money to buy groceries. But his hunger, poverty, and unemployment also meant that there was nothing to hold Randall Terry back.

Terry was no longer the naive local activist. He was eager to engage in more militant tactics, and he now knew where to turn for advice. By late 1985 he had heard plenty about Scheidler, Ryan, and PLAN, and he decided it was time to draw on their expertise. He called Ryan in St. Louis and asked how to escalate from picketing and petty harassment to civil disobedience.

Ryan eagerly encouraged Terry to take his protest tactics to the limit. Ryan told him that his group should shut themselves into a procedure room, pound wedges in to jam the doors, chain themselves to a sink or table, and then wait for the police. Because Ryan was accustomed to sympathetic judges in St. Louis, he reassured Terry that he would only suffer a slap on the wrist and "be out of jail in fifteen minutes."

Terry followed Ryan's advice to the letter. On January 8, 1986, the same day that one hundred fifty people jammed Vestal's town hall to protest Southern Tier's planned move, Terry conducted his first sit-in ever, at Southern Tier's Binghamton Plaza office. He and six other protesters, including three women, were arrested after they stormed into the clinic just as it opened, brushed past Alex Aitken, and chained themselves inside one of the procedure rooms.

Leber rushed in with his camera. He followed Terry's every move, filming as the protesters crowded into the procedure room and unfurled the chains they had wrapped around their waists underneath their heavy winter coats, hurriedly locking the door behind them while chaining themselves to the procedure table, sink, and furniture. Ever the media hound, Terry spoke directly into the camera throughout, as he nervously awaited the police. "It's for Jesus and for the least of his brethren! Hallelujah! Thank the Lord. There's not going to be any abortions here today!"

The clinic chain-in made Terry's name and guaranteed that he would forever be transformed from local oddity into one of the most influential anti-abortion activists in the nation. For the first time, Terry had angered the police; it took them forty minutes using bolt cutters to extricate his group from the procedure room, and then they had to carry the protesters down a steep flight of stairs when they went limp.

Terry now had a loyal band of supporters willing to go to jail on his orders, and that was a heady feeling. Their sit-in had generated more news coverage than Terry could ever have imagined, and he quickly became convinced that civil disobedience is the only path to successful protest in modern America. When one gets arrested, reporters listen. When Terry was thrown into the back of a police van after his arrest, reporters gathered around to hear what he would say. He managed to shout out one sound bite before the police drove him away: "It's for the babies!"

Terry and the six others were charged with misdemeanors—criminal trespass and resisting arrest—and were released, confirming John Ryan's prediction of a slap on the wrist and encouraging Terry to keep up the momentum. Before the end of January, Terry and seven others staged a second sit-in at Southern Tier's Binghamton Plaza office; this time both Dan Little and his wife, Judith, were arrested alongside him. In Project Life's next newsletter, Terry's elation at the sudden transformation of his campaign was obvious: "WHAT A MONTH!"

But Terry was already thinking beyond Binghamton. He had connected once with John Ryan, and now he wanted to link up with Scheidler, who had just founded PLAN, recently published his controversial book Closed: 99 Ways to Stop Abortion, and was at the height of his fame. Terry called Scheidler at his office in Chicago, told him what was going on in Binghamton, and invited him to town to speak. Always on the lookout for young recruits to his brand of militancy, Scheidler eagerly accepted.

With Terry by his side, Scheidler roused a lunchtime crowd of one hundred seventy-five outside the Vestal building, picketed the home of the building's owner, and then told a crowd at an evening rally why feminists despised his brand of militancy: "Because they're scared of us, because we take away their right to choose, because we take away their right to fornicate. . . . And they don't like us because we are effective."

Randall Terry soaked it all up and saw in Scheidler what he hoped for himself: national recognition through controversy and acts of extremism. For his part, Scheidler was impressed that such a young man had the oratorical power and the will to foment so much activity so quickly in one town. Scheidler decided that he would take Terry under his wing; he would bring him to PLAN's next convention, to be held in St. Louis that April, and would make Terry a lieutenant in his campaign to create a national activist movement.

Despite the outward signs of a close alliance, their stark religious differences placed early limits on the Terry-Scheidler relationship. Terry, like other fundamentalists, believed that Catholics had not found the true path to Christ, and before long he was trying to save Scheidler's soul. Scheidler sternly informed Terry that claiming one's own salvation was considered a sin in the Catholic Church, "the sin of presumption," and told Terry to mind his own business. For Scheidler, a pragmatist who had rebelled against the restrictions placed on anti-abortion protest by the Catholic Church, religious differences were irrelevant to his work with Protestants in a shared cause, but he failed to grasp that religion was everything for Randall Terry. To Terry, the movement was a militant expression of the church, and Scheidler's blindness to Terry's beliefs ensured that there would always be an unspoken distance between the two men.

Terry's first contacts with Ryan and Scheidler drew him onto the national activist scene but also gave him a greater incentive to intensify his local campaign against Southern Tier. In March, Terry and the six others arrested for the first sit-in went to court and were convicted, but they were merely fined sixty dollars apiece and given a warning by a local judge to stop their sidewalk counseling. Terry, sensing an opportunity to take on the legal system, refused to pay the fine and was sentenced to thirty days in the Broome County Jail as a result.

"I'm just happy to know where Terry is going to be for the next thirty days," retorted Peg Johnston. But Johnston miscalculated; Terry's jailing made him a local martyr. His followers held protest vigils outside the jail, and his acts of civil disobedience were energizing an expanding circle of fundamentalists. In late April, the Reverend Ronald Kesnig of Resurrection Life Fellowship, and Barbara Magera, Randall Terry's old friend and classmate from Elim Bible College, led a dozen members of Brothers and Sisters in Christ (BASIC), a Christian student group from SUNY-Binghamton, in the first sit-in at Southern Tier's new location in

Vestal. Magera was soon hooked on protest; she later became Terry's personal assistant and ultimately Operation Rescue's press secretary.

Terry got out of jail early, setting a pattern that would later come to haunt him. He was freed after ten days when an "anonymous" benefactor paid his sixty-dollar fine; although he still claims that he does not know who paid it, it was almost certainly Dan Little or one of Terry's other friends or fellow church members. Years later, when a similar episode occurred in Atlanta, Terry's actions were taken as a sign of weakness and hypocrisy by his lieutenants, and the incident all but killed Operation Rescue. This time, however, Terry's mysterious release from jail did not affect his reputation; he was riding high.

Terry went to his first national activist event almost immediately on his release, the St. Louis PLAN convention, held in mid-April and hosted by John Ryan. Terry traveled to St. Louis along with Leber and David Long, a young Evangelical he had met at Cornerstone. Long was running a tire wholesale business in Rochester and had briefly hired Terry to serve as his regional salesman for southern New York to help Terry make ends meet.

Inspired by Terry's example, Long was developing a protest organization of his own, Project Life of Rochester, and like Terry was drawing on local Evangelical churches for support. Long had ambitious plans, and he hoped to persuade Terry to return home to Rochester to work for him in his new protest campaign. He had a catchy name that he was considering for one of his Rochester projects: "Operation Rescue."

In St. Louis, Terry was one of 107 arrested in the largest sit-in yet staged in the anti-abortion movement; it was his first act of civil disobedience outside Binghamton, and it opened his eyes to broader possibilities. By the end of the PLAN convention, Terry was calling for the start of a nationwide sit-in campaign, emptying the churches and bringing Evangelicals and Catholics together in massive numbers for the first time. Terry was dismissed by his fellow activists at PLAN; he was restating the obvious. If anyone was going to lead the activists to the promised land, it would be an established star like Joe Scheidler or John Ryan, not some unknown from upstate New York.

Terry's friend David Long did not ignore him, however. In the middle of the sit-in at the PLAN convention, Long leaned over to Terry and whispered "Operation Rescue." Terry turned and asked what he was talking about. The new name for sit-ins, Long replied, a name he had been playing around with in Rochester. Terry smiled.

erry may have been snubbed by the established leaders in St. Louis, but he was nonetheless exhilarated—and radicalized—by the experience. Southern Tier awaited Terry's return with a sense of foreboding.

He was now looking for ways to use his campaign against Southern Tier as a platform from which to launch his own national movement, independent of PLAN. "The burden on my heart," Terry wrote in Project Life's July 1986 newsletter, "is to see Christ-centered activist works like this started and to see abortion confronted by believers everywhere all across the nation."

In late May, Terry was convicted for leading the second sit-in in January, but the prospect of more jail time did not deter him. He began to cash in on his acts of civil disobedience by selling videos that packaged Leber's footage of the Binghamton sit-ins along with lectures encouraging other Evangelicals to follow his lead. In early June, Terry caught Southern Tier off guard with a predawn blockade of the clinic's entrances by a group of seventeen cars, vans, and trucks—locked and empty—jammed up against the clinic's door. While Terry and his followers watched and sang from one hundred yards away, the Vestal police angrily towed the vehicles off.

Terry told reporters that the car blockade was proof that he and his supporters were willing to do anything to stop abortion, anything "except for violence. We are pledged to nonviolence. That's critical to me." In fact, there is no evidence that Terry ever engaged in serious acts of violence against Southern Tier, although Johnston believes he was behind petty acts of vandalism, like the repeated gluing of the clinic's locks. Unlike so many other clinics around the country, however, Southern Tier was never the target of an arson or bombing attack. Although he had secretly told Fred Gauge, his onetime friend at Cornerstone in Owego, that he would bomb a clinic if he could get away with it, Terry either changed his mind or never found the right moment. Even abortion-rights advocates who were longtime observers of Terry never considered him to be violent, charging instead that he fomented violence through his militant rhetoric. Although Terry stubbornly refused to denounce clinic bombings, he eventually did publicly oppose the killing of abortion doctors. "Randy Terry is not *that* crazy," observes Anne Bower, a leading abortion-rights activist in Binghamton.

Terry was emerging as an activist leader at the perfect time: The conditions were finally right for a national campaign. By mid-1986, radical protests were under way from Philadelphia to Portland, Oregon. Whereas Washington was frozen on abortion policy, state-level initiatives, fueled by grassroots protests and activism, were becoming a popular alternative in state after state. Most notably, Missouri enacted the anti-abortion law that St. Louis activist-turned-lobbyist Sam Lee had crafted; the law was quickly challenged in court by Judith Widdicombe's St. Louis clinic, setting the stage for a showdown over abortion rights three years later at the Supreme Court in the case of *Webster v. Reproductive Health Services.*

All that was needed was a leader to unite the isolated pockets of activism. By the fall of 1986, just as it was becoming obvious that Joseph Scheidler was not up to the challenge, Terry was positioning himself to take charge. Terry asked David Long to come to work for him, but Long turned him down. In fact, Long took the request badly, thinking their roles should be reversed, with Terry joining him in Rochester. Long also doubted Terry's leadership and management skills, and he was the first of many to see that Terry's headstrong, autocratic style would lead to organizational disaster. Still, Terry persuaded Long to give him the rights to the name Long had dreamed up, "Operation Rescue."

Terry hired Gary Leber instead of Long as his first staffer, closed down Project Life, and founded Operation Rescue in its place. He established Operation Rescue as a DBA for Randall Terry, dropping the tax-exempt status that Project Life had enjoyed as a DBA of Branch Ministries. Terry was smart enough to know that he could no longer risk keeping his highly questionable tax-exempt status, and he knew that if Operation Rescue was a DBA of Branch Ministries, his law-breaking tactics might bring down all of Dan Little's entities.

Terry began to travel as frequently as possible to link up with other local leaders and sell them on his ideas for nationwide action; his recruiting efforts finally paid off in Pensacola in November 1986, when he won over many of the activist leaders who gathered to rally around the imprisoned Joan Andrews.

By February 1987, Terry was ready to begin serious planning for Operation Rescue, and he invited a select few activists he had met in Pensacola and elsewhere to his home in Binghamton. He was joined by local fundamentalist supporters but also by key activists from other cities, including Michael McMonagle, an Irish Catholic and former naval officer who was then the leading militant in Philadelphia; Joseph Foreman, a young fundamentalist who had joined McMonagle's Philadelphia organization; and Andrew Burnett, an Evangelical from Portland, Oregon. All of them ultimately became key players in Operation Rescue; McMonagle was by far the most experienced protest leader, and he was quick to offer practical advice on planning demonstrations.

For Foreman, one of the only fundamentalists involved in McMonagle's Catholic-dominated anti-abortion campaign in Philadelphia, the meeting at Terry's house was a revelation. "For the first time I was at a pro-life meeting where I was not the token Protestant." Terry and Foreman hit it off almost immediately, and Foreman eventually emerged as Terry's top aide. The son of a Presbyterian missionary, Foreman was an ordained Presbyterian minister and a graduate of Westminster Theological Seminary, Francis Schaeffer's alma mater; he impressed Terry as someone who shared his vision of a biblically based protest movement that could put Schaeffer's ideas into action. Foreman recognized in Terry the galvanizing figure their movement so desperately needed.

The Binghamton conference was steeped in Terry's evangelism; for the first day, the group did nothing but pray. They prayed throughout the next morning as well, and Terry's focus on prayer impressed his guests, suggesting a depth they had not fathomed in the young man before. Finally, on the afternoon of the second day, Terry began to lay out how he planned to recruit his fellow Evangelicals to join his new crusade.

Operation Rescue's message would be directed at the "church": the Evangelical community. If the "world"—those who have not been saved—did not understand the message, that did not matter. What mattered was the repentance of the "church," repentance for ignoring abortion for fifteen years; Terry would sell the church on Operation Rescue as a form of atonement. He planned to use Christian words and imagery that would shame pastors into mobilizing their congregations. He would stress the "blood guiltiness" of the church: his charge that church leaders who ignored abortion had blood on their hands. He would rely on carefully selected biblical passages to make them see their guilt. One critical passage was Deuteronomy 21:7–8: "O Lord, our hands have not shed this blood, and neither did our eyes see it. Forgive O Lord, thy people Israel, whom thou has redeemed, and set not the guilt of innocent blood in our midst, but let the guilt of blood be forgiven them."

The church in America, Terry argued, had no right to pray to God for forgiveness, like the Israelites did in Deuteronomy 21:7–8, because Christians had seen abortion, knew it was taking place, and had done nothing to stop it.

For Terry, the most telling biblical passage, the quotation that spoke directly to the political mobilization of the church in America, was Proverbs 24:11: "Rescue those who are being taken away to death; hold back those who are stumbling to the slaughter." Proverbs 24:11 would become Operation Rescue's rallying cry.

Terry soothed nerves by announcing that he had abandoned the radical tactics he had espoused in Pensacola. To underscore just how completely he had ditched his earlier extremist tactics, Terry said he would limit Operation Rescue to staging sit-ins on the outside of clinic entrances, prohibiting his troops from entering the clinics and swearing off the kind of "clinic invasions" for which Joan Andrews was serving her long prison term in Florida. "We decided we were just going to stay on the outside of the buildings, because when you sit on the outside, no one can accuse you of going in and damaging anything in the clinic," recalls Terry. Staying outside, he recognized, also enhanced the potential for television coverage of his events. "All these grandmas and grandpas and middle-aged people praying and being quiet. It [would be] a great visual to capture people's hearts."

To try to convince the public that Operation Rescue was assuming the mantle of the civil rights movement of the 1960s, Terry also planned to require every activist who joined his organization to sign a written pledge of nonviolence.

The Binghamton conference kicked off nearly a year of nonstop organizing by Terry and his new lieutenants, who returned home to try to coordinate their local efforts with the new national campaign planned by Operation Rescue. Terry spent much of 1987 trying to recruit pastors, relying heavily on the network of ministerial contacts he had developed at Elim Bible College. Terry showed great deference to their authority, emphasizing that Operation Rescue would not be "an alternative structure to the church" but was designed as an extension of it. He recalls his intentions as follows:

> Most of the pro-life movement was built on the false premise that we could do what we were doing outside of the church, without the church, in defiance of the church, while we were

angry at the church. A pastor can smell that attitude a mile off and won't have anything to do with it. So the two things that I brought to the table theologically were, I brought a cohesive body of biblical thought that it was our duty to do something, that God required it of us. The other thing was the theology of church government. I understood that if we were going to have a mass movement then we had to have the proper authority structure and respect for authority. So I would not allow anyone into the inner core of leadership who was not submitted to a local church. You had to be submitted to a church, and you had to have your pastor's blessing, because we wanted the blessing of God.

Few pastors signed on in 1987; Terry was young, brash, and unknown. "The first time he called me to ask me to get involved, I thought he was a psycho," remembers Pat Mahoney, an Evangelical minister who later became national spokesman for Operation Rescue.

Without the pastors, Terry had to rely instead on the activist movement's existing infrastructure for his initial campaign; he began to use PLAN's organization for his own purposes. PLAN's meeting of regional directors scheduled for August 1987 in Washington was hijacked by Terry, who turned the meeting into a planning session for Operation Rescue's first "field test," which he hoped to stage on McMonagle's home turf in Philadelphia in November. The field test in Philadelphia would give Terry and Operation Rescue a chance to try their hand at mass protest tactics without having their inevitable beginner's mistakes exposed for all the world to see in New York, under the glare of network television cameras.

To recruit troops for the Philadelphia experiment, McMonagle, Burnett, and others gave Terry the free use of their mailing lists, and soon the unprecedented response to his mailings and phone appeals convinced Terry that he had tapped into a deep yearning within the movement for coordinated action.

Philadelphia was no stranger to anti-abortion controversy, protest, and harassment. Long before Operation Rescue arrived, McMonagle had been organizing protests there that were the most raucous of any in the nation. The Philadelphia police and local abortion-rights advocates had already grown weary of McMonagle and his blue-collar Irish crowd and now figured Operation Rescue would be more of the same. As soon as they discovered Terry's plans, they mounted an all-out effort to throttle the protest. On the eve of Terry's planned sit-in, clinics all over Philadelphia were ringed with police barricades and escorts.

Frustrated, Terry and McMonagle improvised, moving out of Philadelphia. At a Saturday predawn rally of four hundred people in a Philadelphia shopping center, Terry announced that they would be going across the Delaware River to suburban Cherry Hill, New Jersey, to blockade the Cherry Hill Women's Center. They mounted a caravan of cars, vans, and buses to cross the river, parked at a nearby Catholic church, and by 6 A.M. the four hundred participants, bundled up against the cold and rain, were packed into the small clinic's parking lot and entrance, completely blockading the doors. An enormous banner unfurled across the clinic's outer wall proclaimed the protest to be the work of "Operation Rescue." A lone security guard, trapped inside, watched through the window, resigned to wait out the storm.

C linic administrator Diane Straus was stunned when she arrived an hour later. Terry and McMonagle's last-minute change of plans had worked beyond their wildest expectations; while dozens of Philadelphia police and clinic escorts were waiting to do battle across the river, Cherry Hill was completely unprepared. There were no clinic escorts on guard, and the suburb's tiny police force was overwhelmed. No clinic "rescue" anywhere in the country had ever approached these numbers.

Wearing a crushed tweed walking hat and a cutout plastic bag over his clothes to guard against the rain, Terry presented a ridiculous image for the local television cameras that were rushed over from Philadelphia to cover the protest. But none of that mattered. Terry was elated, and with Foreman by his side, he led the crowd, a mix of local Catholics and out-of-town fundamentalists, in "God Bless America" and "Amazing Grace." Throughout the morning, Catholics knelt and prayed the rosary while fundamentalists outstretched their arms to catch their Pentecostal fire.

After commandeering a school bus to transport the demonstrators, the police finally began making arrests by 10:30, more than four hours after Terry's group had arrived. When the police waded into the crowd, nearly every demonstrator went limp; they had to be dragged or carried to the waiting buses, slowing the arrest process even further. The police were methodical and gentle with each new arrest, which endeared them to the protesters and kept the event low key and peaceful but slowed the arrest process so badly that by noon they had barely made a dent in the crowd in front of the clinic doors. By late afternoon, as the clinic's attorney was filing for an emergency court injunction, the exhausted police finally opened negotiations with Terry.

Terry agreed to end the protest by 4 P.M., once he was convinced that the clinic was closed for the day and after the police agreed to stop making arrests. Only 210 of the 400 on the scene were taken into custody; Terry and his lieutenants were allowed to remain on the scene all day, untouched.

Terry exulted for the local television cameras. "We stopped the killing for an entire day. We choked the legal system!" Unknown to Terry, however, Straus reopened the clinic as soon as the blockade was over, and abortions were performed into the evening for previously scheduled patients. "This is no victory for anyone, one clinic staffer insisted to reporters. "Nothing has changed."

She was wrong. Cherry Hill did change things; it transformed the anti-abortion protest movement. Clinic sit-ins and blockades were no longer small, isolated local events; they had suddenly become the most important form of political expression in the entire national debate over abortion. Terry had managed to do what O'Keefe, Ryan, Scheidler, and the rest had only dreamt of throughout their wilderness years.

Even Peg Johnston, watching in dismay from Binghamton, acknowledged that much. "Our boy Randy," she wrote in an internal memo after Cherry Hill, "is making a national name for himself."

Cherry Hill gave Randall Terry instant credibility in the fundamentalist community. The fact that Terry had kept the protest peaceful, avoiding violent confrontations with abortion-rights advocates and the police, convinced ministers to listen to him.

When Terry began recruiting aggressively for his first major Operation Rescue event, scheduled for New York City in May 1988, the plight of imprisoned Joan Andrews was beginning to make the rounds on the televangelist circuit, introducing a mass audience of fundamentalists to anti-abortion civil disobedience. The publicity generated by

Joan Andrews fit perfectly into Terry's plans. Her story was selling Evangelical pastors and their congregations on "rescue," priming them to act, and motivating them to flock to Randall Terry.

One pastor enthralled by Terry was Jesse Lee, a soft-spoken Southerner living a life as close to the cultural edge of modern America as humanly possible. A failed actor, Lee had become the pastor of the only Charismatic fundamentalist church in New York City's Greenwich Village. Stridently antigay, Lee was pastoring a church just five blocks from Stonewall, the landmark of the homosexual rights movement.

Although Lee had been involved in right-wing political causes in New York City, he had never heard of "rescue" or anti-abortion sit-ins until a friend who had protested at Cherry Hill told him about Randall Terry and Operation Rescue's plans for a big protest in New York City and urged Lee to sign up. Intrigued, Lee went to the annual March for Life in Washington in January, and while there he listened to Terry speak to the crowd on the steps of the Supreme Court as he tried to drum up fresh recruits for the New York action. Terry was preaching his well-honed rhetoric from Binghamton, Pierce Creek, and Project Life, but it was a mixture of religion and politics that was new to Lee. When Terry began talking of Francis Schaeffer's concept of "higher laws," of the Christian's responsibility to break the laws of man when they conflict with the laws of God, Lee was hooked. He joined up and soon began to help recruit other Evangelicals for Terry's New York campaign, scheduled for early May.

The planning for the New York protests was far more careful and detailed than for any other event Terry staged, thanks to Operation Rescue's newly committed group of lieutenants, who were willing to come to Binghamton for meetings whenever Terry wished. However, Cherry Hill and Joan Andrews had generated so much publicity and enthusiasm for "rescue" within the anti-abortion movement that Terry found recruiting for New York remarkably easy. Christian radio stations spread the word, and veteran activists and militants began to flock to his banner. Jayne Bray was one of the first; her husband, Michael Bray, was still in prison for his bombing campaign with Thomas Spinks, but Jayne left behind her children to join Randall Terry in New York. Tom Herlihy, a stalwart from John O'Keefe's sit-ins in Washington, joined up, as did Juli Loesch, the Catholic leftist who had founded Pro-Lifers for Survival along with O'Keefe back in the 1970s. Ann O'Brien, still trying to hold together the remnants of John Ryan's organization, came from St. Louis, despite her misgivings about Randall Terry's snub of John Ryan.

There were new faces as well. Jeff White, the owner of a BMW parts distributorship in California and newly converted Evangelical, flew in for his first sit-in, and Keith Tucci, a former hood turned pastor of a Charismatic church, joined up after hearing Terry's recruiting pitch in Pittsburgh. Jeff White, Keith Tucci, and Jayne Bray quickly joined Jesse Lee, Gary Leber, Joe Foreman, and Michael McMonagle in Terry's inner circle; all but McMonagle were Protestant fundamentalists.

Terry relied heavily on activists who lived in New York, including Jesse Lee and Tom Herlihy, to help him with the daunting logistics of staging a major protest in Manhattan, including housing hundreds of supporters and transporting them through the congested city. Because Terry had never spent much time in New York, he went to the city to practice riding the subways and to scout the locations of Manhattan's abortion clinics. Terry, Lee, Leber, and McMonagle also met privately with a group of senior New York City police officials, who were worried that a clinic blockade in Manhattan's crowded streets could lead to an ugly confrontation. The police did their best to intimidate Terry, but it was clear that what they really wanted from him was the identity of the clinics that Operation Rescue planned to blockade. Terry refused to tell them.

Abortion-rights advocates and clinic owners in New York soon began to prepare as well, but they still did not take Operation Rescue very seriously. A group of New York clinic administrators asked Peg Johnston to come and tell them what she knew about Randall Terry, but when she started describing her long battle with Terry in Binghamton, many in the meeting dismissed her small-town warnings. According to Johnston, "They all said, 'That's never going to happen here.'"

On the eve of Operation Rescue's New York campaign in May, the city's abortion clinics and local feminist groups, sensing that Terry's numbers and power were growing beyond their expectations, finally began to take the threat seriously. They convinced a New York civil court to issue a last-minute temporary restraining order barring demonstrators from blocking clinic entrances in the city. The court order arrived at Terry's office, still in the back of the Crisis Pregnancy Center on Chenango Street in Binghamton, just as he was about to leave for New York. To Terry, it seemed that the clinics and the courts were trying to up the legal ante, escalating the punishment beyond that of trespass charges to large-scale fines and significant jail time.

Terry dismissed the threat, reverting to his Bible. With a flourish, he spread the court papers across the floor of his office, invoking the Old Testament story of Hezekiah. In Second Kings, Hezekiah, King of Israel, defied Sennacherib, the powerful King of Assyria who had laid siege to Jerusalem; Hezekiah took a message from Sennacherib and spread it on the Temple floor, asking for God's divine intervention and protection. In his cramped backroom office on Chenango Street, in front of his young and wide-eyed Evangelical staff members, Terry proclaimed that Hezekiah was crying out across thousands of years. "Lord, you see their threats," Terry intoned. "Don't let them prevent us from saving children."

It was a piece of Charismatic religious theater worthy of Bill Purves.

New York City officials were determined to avoid physical confrontations, and their careful approach to Operation Rescue virtually ensured the success of Terry's first major campaign. When he gathered his forces at 6 A.M. in the lobby of the run-down Times Square Hotel on Monday, May 2, Terry found he had at least six hundred people willing to risk arrest, short of his goal of one thousand but far more than had participated in any anti-abortion sit-in ever conducted.

With police and abortion-rights advocates tracking his every move, Terry still refused to tell his followers where they were going; he needed the element of surprise to be able to get his people in front of the clinic doors. His lieutenants passed out subway tokens and told his supporters to follow marshals carrying small American flags, silently.

They trooped into the Times Square subway station, boarded trains for lower Manhattan to confuse the trailing clinic escorts, and then quickly changed trains and headed uptown once again. "We are just like sheep, and the Lord will protect us on the subway," one woman told a *New York Times* reporter. Actually, it was the New York transit police who protected them, holding the subway doors open to make sure that all of Terry's confused out-of-town followers were able to keep up with their leaders. Without that assistance, Operation Rescue might have ended before it began.

Finally, Terry led them out of the subway and onto the affluent Upper East Side of Manhattan, to the clinic of Dr. Herbert Schwartz, a small walk-up building on 85th Street. Terry's insistence on surprise worked; he had six hundred people sitting, praying, chanting—and blockading— at the clinic's entrance before abortion-rights clinic defenders could stop him. Counterprotesters from the National Organization for Women and the National Abortion Rights Action League could do nothing more than launch chants of their own from across the street.

Like their counterparts in Cherry Hill, the New York police were unusually gentle as they began to make arrests, using stretchers to carry away protesters who refused to walk to waiting police buses. The police succeeded in their primary objective, which was to keep the event as peaceful as possible, but to do so they had to ignore repeated requests from abortion-rights advocates to enforce the court's temporary restraining order quickly. When a NOW leader asked one police officer to clear the entrance for Dr. Schwartz's staff and patients, the officer replied, "How would you expect us to get anyone through that?"

Terry barked out crowd-control orders to lieutenants over radio headsets from Radio Shack. To keep the protesters busy while they awaited arrest, songbooks were passed through the crowd. About half of the demonstrators were fundamentalists and half Catholic, and at least thirty-six clergy were involved, including New York Auxiliary Bishop Austin Vaughan, the highest ranking Catholic leader to join Operation Rescue's ranks. (For celebrity spice, football star Mark Bavaro of the New York Giants joined in as well.)

It took the police until after 1 P.M. to clear the demonstrators; a total of 503 were arrested and taken to New York's police academy grounds, where they were processed, charged with disorderly conduct, and immediately released with small fines to be paid later.

Their first day's easy success kept Terry's troops coming back for more. At an electric rally that night, Terry asked how many would return to get arrested again the next morning, and hundreds cried out. On Tuesday, May 3, 422 were arrested for blockading a clinic in Queens, which closed for the day. Scuffles broke out, however, as clinic escorts and protesters vied for control of the clinic's entrance; abortion-rights activists were stunned when hundreds of police officers moved in to cart them, rather than members of Operation Rescue, away from the doors.

The police had made keeping the peace a higher priority than keeping the clinic open, and that did not go over well with abortion-rights groups or feminist leaders. Their attorneys stormed into court that afternoon, asking that Terry be found in contempt of the earlier temporary restraining order, which had so far been completely ignored both by Operation Rescue and by the police. "The police's actions today were inexcusable," fumed New York City councilwoman Carol Greitzer. Federal district judge Robert Ward quickly ordered Operation Rescue to pay fines of $25,000 for each day they continued to block clinic doors.

Terry ignored the court order, and after one day off, he moved to Long Island, blockading a clinic in Hicksville, New York; this action led to another four hundred arrests, the largest mass arrest on Long Island in memory. In Long Island's conservative suburbs, Operation Rescue found more sympathetic political leaders than in Manhattan; Nassau County district attorney Dennis Dillon, an outspoken opponent of abortion, announced that he could not "in good conscience" prosecute the demonstrators. Nonetheless, Operation Rescue was met by a crowd of one hundred abortion-rights counterdemonstrators and clinic defenders, who were able to get one patient through; NOW and NARAL had finally begun to mobilize their supporters, and it took one hundred fifty Nassau County police to separate the opposing camps.

On Friday, May 6, the last day of the New York campaign, Terry sent his forces back to the same clinic on the East Side of Manhattan that they had blockaded so successfully on Monday. But Terry had overplayed his hand; the New York police had lost their patience and, under mounting political and legal pressure, were no longer willing to play games with Operation Rescue. On a cold, rain-swept morning, the police moved to clear Dr. Schwartz's clinic entrance as quickly as possible and began dragging demonstrators away, rather than carting them gently on stretchers. Terry was able to block the clinic entrance for only two hours this time; the police had arrested 320 people and hauled them away by 9:30 in the morning. Terry had taxed the system's limits.

Still, Terry considered New York to be an overwhelming success; Operation Rescue had logged sixteen hundred arrests in one week, generated national headlines, and injected the anti-abortion cause with a new sense of mission. Randall Terry was now on the network news and on talk shows across the country as the new spokesperson for the anti-abortion movement. Donations began to pour into his Binghamton offices, and Evangelicals who had joined him in New York fanned out to start local branches of Operation Rescue all around the country. Soon, Operation Rescue was adding thousands of new names to its mailing lists, people who were willing to drop everything to heed Terry's call to "rescue" and who were just as willing to oblige Terry's pleas for funds.

By the time Terry returned to Philadelphia in early July to stage Operation Rescue's second series of protests, his staff had ballooned and his bank accounts were beginning to swell. Operation Rescue was still an unincorporated DBA of Randall Terry, which meant that all of its assets were held by Terry personally. On his 1988 personal income tax returns, later put on the public record in a court case brought against Operation Rescue by NOW, Terry reported that Project Life and its successor, Operation Rescue, were his "sole proprietorships" involved in "pro-life activities" and stated that they brought in a total of $471,722 in gross receipts, or donations, for the year. "The receipts and disbursements reflected on Schedule C," Terry wrote to the IRS, "represents the husband/taxpayer's activity with respect to his efforts to have abortion declared illegal under the law of the United States." With a flourish, Terry also bragged to the IRS that "the taxpayer is a nationally known person in the anti-abortion efforts."

Terry's staff quickly learned that its young leader's style was management by chaos; still only twenty-nine, Terry had already begun to let overnight fame rush to his head.

Philadelphia was largely peaceful and nearly as successful as New York; in the first of two days of blockades, July 5 and 6, 1988, 591 people were arrested at a clinic in suburban Paoli, the largest single-day total yet. It took Paoli police from 8 A.M. to 4 P.M. to arrest them all and carry them away on stretchers, and Terry was even able to force the police to back down on a threat to charge the protesters with misdemeanor trespass rather than a lesser, summary offense, equivalent to a traffic ticket.

Despite his success at choking the system in Philadelphia, Terry left the city exhausted and uncertain of his next move. After his rift with Scheidler, Terry had abandoned plans to take Operation Rescue to Chicago, and now he needed to come up with an alternative target before his group lost its sudden burst of momentum. In Philadelphia, Michael Hirsh, a young Evangelical from Atlanta, had pressed Terry to bring Operation Rescue to the Democratic National Convention, scheduled to open in Atlanta later in July. Atlanta was an attractive target; it would give Terry an opportunity to take his new street theater right into the midst of the national media swarm gathered at the convention and put abortion back at the top of the presidential campaign agenda. But Terry had doubts; it had taken him months to plan Cherry Hill, New York, and Philadelphia, and the Democratic convention was only ten days away.

Terry had not yet made up his mind when he appeared on CNN's *Crossfire* immediately after the Philadelphia campaign to discuss Operation Rescue and debate the issue of abortion. As the show was ending, one of hosts asked whether he planned to take his campaign to the upcoming Democratic convention. Impulsively, Terry smiled and said yes, Operation Rescue was going to Atlanta.

Watching the show back in Binghamton, Gary Leber was dumbfounded. Terry had not consulted with anyone, had not made any plans. He had decided the fate of the hottest new protest organization in the nation in a split second on live television. Recalls Leber, "We all told him he was crazy."

11

THE SIEGE OF ATLANTA

The enduring stereotype of the American abortion war—
Evangelical fury crashing against feminist certitude—was
forever fixed into the national consciousness by Operation
Rescue's siege of Atlanta.

When Randall Terry and his fundamentalists poured into Atlanta's
streets in the summer of 1988, America discovered Operation Rescue,
the organization that completed the sudden transformation of anti-
abortion activism from a movement of scattered and easily ignored
pockets of local protest into a national phenomenon. Feminists and
abortion-rights advocates were forced to respond, and the politics of
abortion would never be the same.

Randall Terry's *Crossfire* appearance and his impulsive decision to target
Atlanta and the Democratic National Convention forced Terry's small
but growing staff to shift into overdrive. Logistics for a major protest were
daunting even with months to prepare, but now they had almost no time to
find transportation, lodging, and rally sites and to notify their widely scattered supporters of their new target. Inevitably, things turned chaotic.

New York's success owed much to Terry's willingness to meet quietly with the city's police department in advance, but in Atlanta he was so rushed that he forgot the importance of sitting down with the police himself. Instead, Michael Hirsh, a young and impatient Atlanta activist, met with police on Operation Rescue's behalf. Hirsh's arrogant attitude immediately angered Major Kenneth Burnette, the commander of the midtown Atlanta police precinct where the city's most visible clinics were located, and the meeting turned into a disaster; the bad feelings between Operation Rescue and the Atlanta police never improved. Burnette believed that Hirsh and Operation Rescue were trying to steamroll their way into his city in the midst of the Democratic National Convention with virtually no warning or a good-faith effort to negotiate logistics with the police.

Burnette curtly informed Hirsh that Operation Rescue was not going to have its way on Atlanta's streets. Sgt. Carl Pyrdum was put in charge of the police effort to deal with the protests. Following Burnette's lead, he established a tough, uncompromising approach to Operation Rescue. Pyrdum, a thirty-six-year-old Vietnam veteran who had been shot and badly wounded by a car thief three years earlier, soon found himself in a bare-knuckled test of wills with Randall Terry. By the end of Terry's siege of Atlanta, Pyrdum emerged as the nation's leading law enforcement expert on Operation Rescue and anti-abortion protest.

Before Operation Rescue arrived, Pyrdum contacted police officials in New York to find out about their experiences with the group; he was given the name of Sgt. Joe Ryan, a police officer in Binghamton who knew all about Randall Terry. Ryan sent Pyrdum a package of materials on Terry and his protests, including Project Life literature. The literature, Pyrdum recalls, "confirmed in my mind what I'd already suspected, which was that I was dealing with a very fanatical group of people."

Convinced that Terry was dangerous, Pyrdum met with the local clinic administrators and promised that the Atlanta police would not allow them to be shut down. For the first time, Operation Rescue was about to encounter a hostile police force determined to stop it in its tracks.

Terry also found it difficult on such short notice to round up the huge numbers with which he had swamped New York and Philadelphia; therefore, he prepared for his first Atlanta protest with fewer than two hundred activists behind him. Yet Terry was still determined to "confront the system" in a new way in Atlanta, and on the long drive from Binghamton to Atlanta, he decided that he would announce to his supporters a new tactic: They would not give their names to the police. They would strip themselves of their driver's license and other identification papers and would respond only to the name of "Baby Doe." The tactic would show the world just how committed Operation Rescue was to its cause, Terry told his traveling companions.

After a predawn meeting in the parking lot of a motel in suburban Marietta on the morning of July 19, nearly two hundred supporters piled into chartered buses and vans for the ride down the interstate to Atlanta. Terry had decided to target the Feminist Women's Health Center, one of the most visible clinics in Atlanta's midtown area.

Burnette and the Atlanta police, however, had a surprise waiting for Terry. Knowing that none of the demonstrators would be carrying identification, Burnette established a roadblock at the freeway exit closest to the clinics in the midtown area and ordered his officers to conduct a license check, arresting anyone driving without one.

Burnette's tactic stopped the convoy, but Terry improvised: The protesters piled out and began walking to their target. Because the Feminist clinic was too far away, they headed instead for the Atlanta SurgiCenter, housed in a small hillside office building just a few blocks from the interstate. By 7 A.M., they had crowded into the SurgiCenter doorway and established a relatively small but effective blockade, with Terry, bullhorn in hand, leading them in prayer and chant.

Burnette and Pyrdum moved quickly; by 8:15 A.M., 134 activists had been arrested, and the clinic was open for business. Although the blockade itself was lifted quickly, a brief confrontation between the police and Operation Rescue, with television crews documenting every moment, made it clear that tensions were running higher in Atlanta than they had in New York.

Following Terry's orders, those arrested refused to give their names and were shipped off to Atlanta's Key Road Detention Facility, nicknamed The Farm, until the city could figure out what to do with them. To ensure unity, Terry used peer pressure; written "rules of rescue" handed out to every demonstrator in Atlanta said that Operation Rescue "strongly discourages" its supporters from seeking early release from prison by giving the police their names. Immediately after the arrests, Pyrdum went out to a temporary holding facility to see Hirsh, and the two talked for nearly two hours but to no avail; the battle lines hardened for good.

The media coverage of the first day's clinic blockade was partially diluted by the fact that so many others brandishing causes—from AIDS activists with the organization ACT UP to inner-city community advocates from the group ACORN—were in town at the same time to stage protests of their own outside the Democratic National Convention. Just days before Operation Rescue's first blockade of the Atlanta SurgiCenter, white supremacists and antiracist demonstrators had skirmished with the police, prompting Atlanta mayor Andrew Young to increase the police presence on the city's streets during the remainder of the convention. Pyrdum's quick sweep, and the city's decision to keep the protesters locked up until they gave their names, ensured that Operation Rescue would be out of sight for the remainder of the convention, where the Democrats' wooden candidate, Massachusetts governor Michael Dukakis, was nominated to lead his ill-fated campaign against Vice President George Bush.

Within a few days, local reporters began to notice that although the Democrats had left town, more than one hundred Operation Rescue protesters remained in jail, still refusing to give their names. In addition, they were now calling themselves "martyrs" to a corrupt system.

Segregated from the general prison population and kept intact as a group, the Operation Rescue activists did not even use their real names with each other in jail; instead, they composed outlandish nicknames for each other, which in some cases stuck for years. They were housed in a large dorm at the Key Road facility, where Terry and others led all-day prayer services that merged into protest strategy sessions. Terry's followers, primarily Evangelicals already inclined to see the hand of God working in everyday events, began to view their time together at The Farm in spiritual terms. "Once, I looked down the hallway to see that a cloud of light had descended on a group of people standing there around Randy, their arms all outstretched in prayer . . . it was awe-inspiring," recalls Frank Holby, an assistant pastor at Calvary Temple Baptist Church in suburban Atlanta, who was a prisoner at Key Road.

For at least a few, jail in Atlanta became not only a searing experience but an addictive one, transforming them into full-time activists, regulars who would ultimately develop their own floating subculture of anti-abortion militancy and extremism.

Many of those who later became prominent in the extremist fringe of the anti-abortion movement first came together in jail in Atlanta in 1988: Shelley Shannon, an Oregon housewife later convicted of shooting an abortion doctor in Wichita, Kansas; John Arena, an upstate New York activist later imprisoned for acid attacks against clinics; Father Norman Weslin, who later became the leader of the "Lambs of Christ," a group that took noncooperation with the legal system to radical extremes; and James Kopp, who was nicknamed "Atomic Dog" in jail in Atlanta, a nickname later mentioned prominently in the anonymously written Army of God manual, which shows extremists how to make bombs. Indeed, the preface to the Army of God manual is so full of in-jokes, nicknames, and coded references to people and events known only to those intimately involved in Operation Rescue's Atlanta campaign that it seems almost certain that its author was one of those arrested with Operation Rescue in Atlanta in July 1988.

His experience in Key Road convinced Terry that Operation Rescue should make its stand in Atlanta; it would be the anti-abortion movement's "Selma." After convincing his supporters to stay in jail for at least forty days without giving their names, he got out of jail himself to recruit for a new round of blockades.

Pat Robertson helped immeasurably when he agreed to make a television appeal for Operation Rescue on CBN's 700 Club, devoting as much as twenty minutes at a time to the campaign while also airing extensive interviews with Terry. The national exposure gave Terry and Joseph Foreman greater entree into Evangelical churches, and excited fundamentalist ministers across the Midwest and South agreed to come to Atlanta and to bring their congregations with them.

By mid-August, the response had fallen short of Terry's predictions, although he had attracted several busloads of fundamentalists to Atlanta to pack the city's jails for a new round of clinic blockades. They included a large contingent of fiery Pentecostals from Louisiana who spoke in tongues as they were getting arrested, frightening Atlanta police officers who thought they were mentally unbalanced. "I told my men they were harmless, they were just speaking in tongues," Pyrdum deadpans. "I told them don't worry unless they bring out the snakes."

After a series of smaller blockades, Terry had enough fresh troops by mid-August to stage his largest protest yet in Atlanta, generating 158 arrests. But Terry was finding it difficult to control all of the activists who had flooded into Atlanta. Some staged brief and unauthorized clinic invasions; the first came when Betsy McDonald, John Ryan's one-time friend turned accuser from St. Louis, burst into the Atlanta SurgiCenter clinic by herself. Terry was forced to issue an apology to the Atlanta police for "any instances which even remotely resemble aggressiveness on our part." Yet the apology had an empty ring. It was clear that Michael McMonagle, McDonald, and other veterans of earlier protest campaigns were beginning to inject their own militant tendencies into Operation Rescue, eroding the discipline that Terry had initially imposed on his protests. Before the Atlanta campaign was over, raucous, physical confrontations, often led by McMonagle and Foreman, became the hallmark of Operation Rescue.

By the end of August, 753 arrests had been made by the Atlanta police. Most important, Pat Robertson and Jerry Falwell were now solidly behind Terry, and their televised appeals were leading to both increased visibility for Operation Rescue within the fundamentalist community and a surge of new donations. "The battle lines of the pro-life movement have been clearly drawn," Robertson enthusiastically told his viewers on the 700 Club after the first week of the Atlanta campaign. Falwell came to Atlanta in August to meet with Terry, and in a photo opportunity in front of the Feminist Women's Health Center, he publicly presented Terry with a check for $10,000; he also said he would consider getting arrested with Operation Rescue himself. "Nonviolent civil disobedience," Falwell said, "is the only way to bring an end to the biological holocaust in this country."

Falwell also urged Republican presidential candidate George Bush to endorse Operation Rescue, a gambit to try to hold Bush to a strong anti-abortion stance at a time when Bush seemed determined to downplay the party's Reagan-era ties to the movement. Bush ignored Falwell's entreaties; instead, he complained on the campaign trail that Republicans should not be subjected to an abortion "litmus test." Anti-abortion activists concluded what they had long suspected: that Bush was far less committed to their cause than was Reagan. The 1988 general election campaign marked the first time in eight years that Evangelical Christians did not feel that they had their own candidate, and that alienation from mainstream politics seemed to enhance Operation Rescue's allure among fundamentalists.

Carl Pyrdum and the Atlanta police were handily beating Randall Terry and Operation Rescue in almost daily battles to keep the city's clinics open. Burnette had given Pyrdum extra forces and a helicopter to track Terry's moves, and the police had learned how to clear the blockades within minutes. Abortion-rights advocates, meanwhile, acted as Pyrdum's intelligence agents, sitting in on Operation Rescue's nightly rallies and phoning Pyrdum with news of Terry's plans. Operation Rescue began to practice elaborate, predawn diversionary tactics to counter the police, throw off the other side, and allow its activists to arrive first at an unprotected clinic.

Pyrdum was usually able to establish an interior cordon of police officers around each targeted clinic, preventing most of Terry's activists from getting any closer than the sidewalk, where they would sit down and await arrest. During July and August, Pyrdum and his officers dealt with the protests in a patient, low-key manner, and they won the grudging respect of their adversaries.

Pyrdum could not resist privately taunting Terry whenever he had the chance. After quickly clearing one protest, Pyrdum quietly told him, "This is never going to go the way you want it to go. Every day you come out here, I'm going to be here, and I'm going to put your people in jail just as quickly as I did today."

The clinics also began to rely heavily on volunteer escorts to accompany patients through Operation Rescue's gauntlets. In scenes that would become commonplace around the country over the next few years, the Atlanta escorts took one patient in at a time, covering the women with sheets to protect their identities.

Beth Petzelt, clinic administrator at the Atlanta SurgiCenter, recalls that most of the patients were not so much frightened as they were angry at Operation Rescue. "Southern women are very strong-willed, and they get angry when someone tries to interfere with what they want to do, regardless of whether it's abortion or something else. These women carry guns in their cars. . . . Quite often they'd try to take a punch at the protesters if they got too close."

In fact, Operation Rescue's Atlanta campaign finally convinced the national abortion-rights leadership that it was time for a coordinated response, both through nationwide clinic-defense programs and through renewed legal assaults on the anti-abortion movement's leaders. "They are . . . trying, through tactics of intimidation, to stop women from exercising what is their very basic, a fundamental right," Kate Michelman, executive director of the National Abortion Rights Action League, complained to reporters at the start of the Atlanta campaign. NOW realized that Randall Terry was much more of a problem than Joe Scheidler had ever been, and the organization added Terry and Operation Rescue to its RICO case against Scheidler.

Many clinic administrators around the country were wary of escorts. They feared that the feminist volunteers would add to the noise and chaos outside their clinics, causing as much harm as good, and that they would attempt to turn their escort service into counterdemonstrations. Eventually, some clinic administrators also came to suspect that the national feminist organizations wanted to use their involvement in the abortion battle to benefit their own fund-raising. It took years for NOW and other feminist organizations to win the trust of the abortion industry; in some cities, that trust never came.

Unable to close the city's clinics, Terry switched his focus to choking the judicial system by having his Operation Rescue followers refuse to give their names. Terry's brinksmanship almost worked. Soon after the Democratic National Convention ended, Atlanta officials were on the verge of giving in, agreeing to release the Operation Rescue protesters for time served and washing them out of the system. But the private negotiations with the city's attorneys fell apart after Margie Pitts Hames, an influential feminist attorney for seven Atlanta-area clinics, intervened. Dryly, Pitts Hames told reporters that "withholding their names and staying in jail is a form of First Amendment protest which they have a right to do, and I would not want to interfere with their right to do it."

By early August, the city decided not to cut a deal, and Georgia state court judge Nick Lambros announced he would keep the Operation Rescue prisoners in jail indefinitely by barring their arraignment until they identified themselves. Meanwhile, Pyrdum obtained a court order to search Operation Rescue's motel rooms for identification papers; the police found only a few driver's licenses, but they did discover piles of cash, deepening Pyrdum's suspicions about Terry's motives.

The city's hardening stance reflected growing impatience. Black leaders in Martin Luther King Jr.'s hometown did not accept Operation Rescue's claim to be the successor to the civil rights movement. "Civil rights demonstrators fought for rights—access to jobs, housing, voting booths, schools and public facilities," editorialized the *Atlanta Journal-Constitution* in the opening days of Operation Rescue's Atlanta campaign. "The anti-abortion forces have a much narrower goal: it is to deny women their right to a legal medical procedure of the most personal sort."

Terry tried to escalate the battle, targeting Lambros for harassment. He went on Christian radio to call on fundamentalists to flood the judge's office with phone calls until he relented and agreed to arraign Operation Rescue activists. But in late August and early September, it was Terry and his tired supporters who began to cave in, giving their names to win their freedom. "They didn't have a real strategy for what they were doing, because they started coming out of jail after saying they wouldn't," recalls Robert Fierer, who served as Operation Rescue's attorney in Atlanta. "The system handled them without much trouble."

The worst blow came from "the church." Terry knew that if he could tap into the resources and congregations of mainline churches like the Southern Baptists, Operation Rescue could take thousands, rather than hundreds, into the streets and into the jails. One minister, above all, held the keys to Atlanta's churches: the Reverend Charles Stanley, pastor of the largest Baptist church in the state, former president of the 14.7-million-member Southern Baptist Convention, and the most influential minister in the South.

Terry and his comrades went to great lengths to cultivate Stanley and win his support. Stanley kept them guessing for weeks; he seemed to be gauging which way the wind was blowing, waiting to determine which way to jump. When Falwell came to Atlanta to hand Randall Terry his check in front of the Feminist Women's Health Center, Stanley was there as well, quietly watching from the sidelines. He told reporters that he had not yet made up his mind whether to support Operation Rescue; while he pondered, at least six members of his congregation were arrested alongside Randall Terry.

By the end of August, Stanley finally gave Terry his answer, and it was a devastating one. Stanley not only refused to endorse the protests, he denounced them. He published a leaflet that he read from the pulpit entitled *A Biblical Perspective on Civil Disobedience,* which turned the language of the Bible against Operation Rescue and mocked Terry's efforts to use the Bible as his justification.

Stanley pointed to Romans 13: "Render to all what is due them: tax to whom tax is due; custom to whom custom; fear to whom fear; honor to whom honor." But he also referred to less famous passages such as Titus 3:1: "Remind them to be subject to rules, to authorities, to be obedient, to be ready for every good deed."

The Bible of course allowed for exceptions, Stanley noted; in Exodus, the Hebrew midwives disobeyed Pharaoh's command to kill all male Hebrew babies, and in Acts, Peter and John violated a specific command not to preach the Gospel after they had been told by an angel to do so. But Operation Rescue, Stanley insisted, had failed to meet the criteria for civil disobedience set forth in the Bible. Christians should engage in civil disobedience only when an earthly law "is contrary to God's Word" or when it "prohibits an act which is consistent with God's Word," the leaflet said. Stanley concluded that U.S. law did not compel abortions but merely gave women the choice of whether to have them. *Roe v. Wade* neither requires abortions nor prohibits them but makes them permissible with certain restrictions. American women were thus "free moral agents responsible before Almighty God for their actions." Only if the United States compelled abortion would Operation Rescue be right in blockading clinic entrances.

Finally, Stanley's pamphlet darkly warned that Operation Rescue's tactics led directly down a slippery slope. If women were to be blocked from entering abortion clinics of their own free will, Stanley asked, then "why not physical restraint of those who are trying to enter, or even destruction of those who are performing the procedure?"

Terry was stunned by Stanley's denunciation; years later, he and others saw it as a critical turning point in Operation Rescue's fortunes. Dozens of other Protestant ministers followed Stanley's lead and kept their distance from Operation Rescue, and the organization never won the support of any mainline denomination. Operation Rescue leaders angrily began to compare American Protestant leaders to the German clergy under the Nazis, who had remained silent during the Holocaust.

By early September, it looked like Terry's assault on Atlanta had run out of steam. "Wishful thinking," countered Juli Loesch, the veteran Catholic leftist and old friend of John O'Keefe who was serving as Terry's press secretary. "We're gearing up. . . . If they listened to the *700 Club* they'd already know that."

Carl Pyrdum was the first to sound the alarm in the city government. Listening to Christian radio and television, Pyrdum realized that Loesch was right; Operation Rescue was coming back for what Terry was calling "the siege of Atlanta." Talking to intelligence officers in other police departments, Pyrdum also heard that independent fundamentalist churches around the country were holding huge rallies to recruit for a renewed assault on Atlanta in October.

Pyrdum finally convinced Burnette to arrange a meeting with Atlanta's police chief and other senior police officials, but his warnings did not register. In a second meeting with the police chief and city council members who handled public safety issues, Pyrdum was frustrated that he was being ignored again; this time, he dialed Operation Rescue's hot line number and put the message on speakerphone so the city officials could listen. The taped message candidly laid out Operation Rescue's plans for a massive assault on Atlanta in early October. "They sat there and listened and then said, 'Oh my God, they *are* coming back!'"

In fact, Terry's group had never really left. Operation Rescue had established an office in Atlanta to supplement its headquarters in Binghamton, and donations were pouring in from viewers responding to appeals from the nation's major televangelists. Despite Stanley's denunciation, Operation Rescue still had the strong support of independent fundamentalist churches whose pastors were free from the restraining hands of bishops and clerical bureaucracies.

Terry spent much of September traveling to recruit pastors to come to Atlanta; at least thirty agreed, and they were given a special tour of Atlanta's streets so they would understand what their congregations would be facing.

All of those jailed in July and August were now free, and many were ready to join the new recruits for a second round. One of those was Jayne Bray, who after arrests in both New York and Atlanta was emerging as one of the few fundamentalist women in Operation Rescue's inner circle.

For October's weeklong "siege," Operation Rescue decided that its activists would give their names to the police; the veterans of July and August realized that the "Baby Doe" tactic had been counterproductive, keeping them off the streets and away from the clinics. Operation Rescue was more determined than ever not to let the Atlanta police and clinic escorts frustrate its efforts to establish effective clinic blockades. Terry, Foreman, and the other leaders were now planning to push their tactics to new extremes to prove their militancy to Atlanta and the nation.

Finally accepting Pyrdum's warnings, Atlanta city officials abruptly switched gears and decided to mount a full-court press against Operation Rescue. Armed with new court injunctions against clinic blockades, the police could now erect metal barricades to prevent the demonstrators from reaching clinic doors. To put some muscle behind its new legal powers, the city decided to deploy the police department's special operations team to deal with Operation Rescue, which for the first time would use "pain compliance" techniques to force the demonstrators to get up and follow police orders when they tried to go limp. Meanwhile, the city filed conspiracy charges against Terry for planning to violate the court injunctions. If Terry wanted to raise the stakes in Atlanta, the city was ready to fight back.

When Carl Pyrdum heard that the special operations squads were planning to use "pain compliance," he was horrified. After ignoring his warnings, the city was now overreacting. He went to his superiors to tell them that such tactics were not only unnecessary but certain to cast the city and the police department in a bad light. He knew that Terry's fundamentalist followers would not give in easily; instead, they would embrace the pain as part of their atonement for having so long ignored the unborn. Pyrdum's warnings were dismissed, however, and he became resigned to the fact that Atlanta was about to make martyrs of Randall Terry's Evangelicals.

Atlanta received an unwelcome preview of the heightened tensions the day before Operation Rescue's renewed assault. As Terry emerged from a Catholic church, where he had been conducting a "training session" for new recruits who were about to take part in their first clinic blockades, Terry was arrested and jailed by Atlanta police on conspiracy charges. Terry's arrest prompted cries of outrage from members of Operation Rescue, yet the group managed to stage a massive rally that night, packing a local church with enthusiastic supporters while generating "trash cans full of money," recalls Operation Rescue's Bob Jewitt.

Just as Terry was hauled off, national abortion-rights advocates, who had descended on Atlanta in anticipation of Operation Rescue's assault, were staging their own large counterdemonstrations; they were led by NOW's fiery president, Molly Yard, who loudly proclaimed how disgusted she was that Terry was pretending "to wear the mantle of civil disobedience of the 1960s." To add to the circus atmosphere, Bill Baird, a New York clinic owner who had emerged as one of the strangest renegades in the abortion-rights movement, had arrived in Atlanta carrying a ten-foot cross that he said symbolized "the cross of religious oppression" that Operation Rescue was attempting to impose on American women.

Terry was released from jail early the next morning after a local supporter agreed to put up his house as collateral against a $75,000 bond, and he arrived in time to help lead the first day's protests. Just as it had in New York and Philadelphia, Operation Rescue ignored Atlanta's court injunctions.

Emboldened by thousands of supporters who gathered for a giant rally in a suburban parking lot early on the morning of October 4, Operation Rescue's activists piled into Atlanta's rapid transit system for the trip downtown, avoiding the possibility of another police roadblock on the interstate. Fanning out behind crowd "marshals" who told them where to get off the subway without telling them their targets, hundreds of activists swarmed into the midtown area, only to run headlong into formidable police lines and barricades outside the Atlanta SurgiCenter, Feminist Women's Health Center, and Hillcrest Clinic of Atlanta.

But it was not enough. The police were stunned when, on orders from their leaders, Operation Rescue's activists began to crawl through their legs and underneath or around the barricades and then began a drive for the clinic doors.

Videotapes, shot both by news crews and by Operation Rescue supporters, document the tumult that resulted, as well as the furious and sometimes comic ways in which the police and the protesters responded. At the Hillcrest Clinic, videos show dozens of activists crawling underneath the police barricades and then across the clinic parking lot for the final few yards to the office doors. So many were crawling that the police initially seemed befuddled about how to stop them; each time a frustrated officer dragged one back to the barricade and left to get another, the first would robotically start to crawl toward the doors once again.

Operation Rescue called it the "Atlanta crawl"; Foreman had dreamed up the tactic, thinking it would convey an image of nonviolence while still effectively circumventing police lines. In practice, however, it made the activists look like zombies straight out of *Night of the Living Dead,* blindly following orders, inexorably crawling to their preassigned objectives. A much more positive image would have been conveyed if the protesters had simply knelt down at the police line, a common sight during the antiwar protests of the 1960s.

Instead, the "crawl" led to chaos and infuriated the police, who began imposing pain compliance holds on those who had made it to the clinic doors. Twisting wrists, bending back arms, and applying pressure from the thumb and forefinger on both sides of the neck just below the ear, the police began to elicit loud groans from the men and shrieks of pain from the women while nearby television news cameras recorded it all.

As Pyrdum predicted, few succumbed by volunteering to walk to police vans under their own power. Instead, the police had to drag them by their legs across the parking lot, throwing them into waiting vans and buses. Even a woman who appeared to be pregnant was dragged across the parking lot when she refused to cooperate. Atlanta's "Red Dog" Tactical Narcotics Squad, assigned to the Atlanta SurgiCenter, used pain compliance even more systematically. Burnette, who was at the Hillcrest Clinic to supervise personally the day's arrests, vented his frustration by kicking one protester who refused to heed his demand to stop. Burnette's kick was captured on videotape and broadcast on television news around the country.

A total of 350 activists were arrested, and Operation Rescue was unable to mount effective blockades for very long at any of the three clinics it targeted. But the day could hardly have gone worse for the Atlanta police force, which now faced a barrage of media criticism for its heavy-handed treatment of the demonstrators.

At first, Burnette breezily dismissed the charges of excessive force. He argued that the activists were no longer receiving special handling and, instead, were finally being treated like any other common criminals. "They brought hundreds of people here to the city in an attempt to siege Atlanta," Burnette said. "Somebody's been sieged, but it wasn't Atlanta."

Terry, who had not joined the protests that day, immediately charged police brutality, and Burnette was soon subjected to a city investigation. "I think it is a sad day for the city of Atlanta when a police major is on television kicking a person," said city council member Dozier Smith.

The criticism was enough to convince the police to back off, and by the next day they had reverted to the low-pressure approach that Pyrdum had employed in July and August. Clearly embattled, Burnette told reporters that the police would now bend over backward to "make it obvious that if there is going to be any violence, it's going to be from the Operation Rescue folks, and not from the police." However, the damage had been done. Operation Rescue's activists immediately gained martyr status within the fundamentalist subculture nationwide.

The remainder of the "siege" was anticlimactic; the city was purposefully slow to release those arrested on the first day, limiting the numbers Terry could call on later in the week. On the second day, only thirteen activists were arrested, and three of them were charged with assault for knocking over a woman patient they were trying to prevent from entering the Feminist Women's Health Center with her clinic escorts; once again, Operation Rescue was forced to apologize. Terry's group beat the police to the clinic doors for an effective, if brief, blockade only once more during the siege, leading to fifty-three arrests at Midtown Hospital.

By the time Operation Rescue ended its Atlanta campaign in October, the group had amassed roughly twelve hundred arrests in the city over a three-month span, fewer than it had accumulated in one week in New York. But Terry was still jubilant; he had achieved his main objective. For the first time, he astutely observed, "the nation has seen rescues in their living rooms."

Inadvertently, Terry's decision to delay the second round of his Atlanta campaign until October had given the national media time to prepare extensive coverage, so that the siege had in fact turned into a top national story. Both ABC's *20/20* and CBS's *48 Hours* newsmagazine shows ran long features on Operation Rescue's October siege, and the protests became a constant presence on CNN. If anything, the white-hot visuals of the protests made Operation Rescue an even better story for television than it was for the print media. Terry was now in constant demand for television interviews, and his celebrity status soon meant that he was the first choice of television producers whenever they wanted a spokesperson for the anti-abortion cause. To keep the media coming back for more, Terry was starting to hone his talent for serving up sound bites guaranteed to make the nightly news. By the end of October, he was back on *Crossfire,* this time to debate Planned Parenthood president Faye Wattleton.

Despite the rejection from mainline ministers like Charles Stanley, Terry had become the hottest interview subject in Christian broadcasting, and it was in these interviews that Terry felt comfortable enough to abandon his "sound-bite persona" to employ the kind of biblical language that would have fallen on deaf ears in the mainstream media. He was interviewed repeatedly on Robertson's *700 Club,* and in November Falwell allowed Terry to preach to his television audience. Operation Rescue is "on the cutting edge, perhaps a couple of years ahead of the Evangelical church in America," Falwell enthused, just before Terry delivered a thunderous sermon. It was Terry at his best: "The dynamic behind our movement is not civil disobedience as much as it is biblical obedience. This book commands us to rescue the innocent!"

The experience in Atlanta also led immediately to an explosion of protests and clinic blockades around the nation, as Terry's newly blooded veterans returned home to start local Operation Rescue affiliates. Fund-raising surged, allowing Terry to increase his staff, start a newsletter, and develop a mailing list that was soon the envy of the Religious Right. Meanwhile, increasing numbers of fundamentalist churches started to sponsor "rescuers" and "crisis pregnancy centers" of their own.

Riding the wave of enthusiasm among Evangelicals generated by Atlanta, Terry moved quickly to stage a "National Day of Rescue" on October 29, 1988, leading to at least twenty-two hundred arrests in twenty-seven cities. Operation Rescue jubilantly claimed that eleven thousand people participated in protests in the United States and Canada on those two days and that more than forty-six hundred risked arrest. In some cities, the police clearly were overwhelmed and stopped making arrests.

Terry had long since gone beyond his initial vision of Operation Rescue as a series of protests during the 1988 election campaign, and now he was eager to transform it into a permanent organization. He quickly pushed on after the November elections to launch a series of major events in one city after another. In January 1989, Operation Rescue returned to New York, and during Holy Week 1989, it took on Los Angeles. In each city Terry blithely ignored court injunctions issued to prohibit his blockades. Soon, enormous fines began to mount against the group as well as threats of possible jail time for violating the injunctions. Terry was too hot to stop and consider the consequences.

By the time Operation Rescue arrived in Los Angeles in late March 1989, abortion-rights advocates were prepared for a full counterattack. In fact, California was home to some of the most aggressive abortion-rights groups in the country. The Bay Area Coalition for Our Reproductive Rights (BACORR) had formed to combat local clinic blockades in northern California in 1988, and Eleanor Smeal's Fund for the Feminist Majority had trained thousands of young southern California feminists in clinic defense. Now, for the first time, clinic defenders would far outnumber Operation Rescue activists along the front lines outside abortion clinics. During Operation Rescue's Los Angeles campaign, Smeal's clinic defenders turned the tide. Led by Kathy Spillar, Smeal's hard-edged lieutenant, they used their numerical advantage, spies inside Operation Rescue, and a willingness to fight fire with fire by being as loud and abrasive as Terry's supporters to take the initiative away from Operation Rescue. Spillar's tactics of massive resistance were soon in use by feminist groups across the country.

Just as important, the Los Angeles Police Department took an even more hostile stance against Operation Rescue than had the Atlanta police, turning the three-day "Holy Week" campaign into a disaster for Terry. Jeff White, Operation Rescue's leader in southern California, began to see danger signs the day before the first clinic blockades, when he called to try to negotiate with Los Angeles police chief Daryl Gates. White warned Gates that with so many feminist clinic defenders about to confront Operation Rescue's Evangelicals, there was sure to be trouble. He offered to tell Gates which clinics Operation Rescue planned to target, to give the police time to arrange crowd control and to lower the tension level. White considered it an unprecedented step; Operation Rescue had never before given such advance warning to the police. But Gates casually turned the offer down, telling White that it was "no longer necessary." White quickly understood Gates's message: The police had already decided to use aggressive tactics to convince Operation Rescue to leave town and never come back.

The Holy Week protests generated more than one thousand arrests, including seven hundred fifty on one day alone, but the Los Angeles police made Operation Rescue pay dearly. The police used pain compliance techniques that were far more draconian than anything used in Atlanta; in some cases police officers even used nunchaku (martial-arts sticks) to grab and drag their prisoners, and at least one protester's arm was broken. The police later said Operation Rescue had exaggerated its claims of police brutality, and unlike the experience in Atlanta, police officials were not widely criticized for the crackdown. The police department's public reputation had not yet been tarnished by Rodney King's videotaped beating. Operation Rescue's charges of police brutality during the Holy Week campaign were virtually ignored by the mainstream media, providing further confirmation to suspicious Evangelicals that the journalists covering Operation Rescue were biased against it.

By the end of Holy Week, Terry faced conspiracy charges for leading the protests, and a trial was scheduled for later in the year, one of many court dates around the country that were beginning to fill up his calendar. But first, Terry made a date at the Supreme Court. The Missouri anti-abortion law that St. Louis activist Sam Lee had helped write back in 1986 was now facing its constitutional test in a case known as *Webster v. Reproductive Health Services*, and Terry was determined to be on hand when the Court handed down its ruling. Much to the dismay of Jack Willke, Terry used the Supreme Court steps to cement his new position as the leading spokesperson of the entire anti-abortion movement.

12

BETRAYAL AND BREAKUP

By 1989, Randall Terry and the Protestant fundamentalists of Operation Rescue were at the height of their notoriety and newsmaking power. By coincidence, Operation Rescue's zenith came just as the most serious legal challenge ever mounted against *Roe v. Wade* was about to come before the Supreme Court. The case, *Webster v. Reproductive Health Services,* had its roots in the Catholic-dominated St. Louis sit-in campaign of the late 1970s and early 1980s. But by the time *Webster* came before the nation, Sam Lee and John Ryan were long gone from anti-abortion activism, and instead Randall Terry was there to exploit it for all it was worth.

After Sam Lee left John Ryan and activism behind, the Catholic sit-in leader from St. Louis became the driving force behind a strict new anti-abortion law enacted by Missouri in 1986. Lee drafted the bill with Andy Puzder, a thoughtful young anti-abortion attorney who had represented Lee and other activists arrested during the St. Louis sit-ins, and Louis DeFeo, a lobbyist for the Missouri Catholic Conference.

Their new law sought to answer the basic question of the American abortion debate: When does life begin? Justice Harry Blackmun had sidestepped that question in his *Roe v. Wade* decision, leaving a philosophical opening that a generation of anti-abortion activists sought to exploit.

Working with David Danis and other lawyers for PEACE, Sam Lee's sit-in group, Puzder had successfully defended the protesters in local courts in St. Louis by pointing out the gaping hole in Blackmun's opinion. Sympathetic municipal judges and juries had repeatedly accepted the "necessity defense." In each "necessity defense" case, the protesters testified that they had trespassed to save what they believed to be a human life; a doctor opposed to abortion would then serve as an "expert witness" to state that life begins at conception. Because the Supreme Court had found that it could not determine when life began, Puzder argued, the protesters had the right to decide the issue for themselves.

While doing legal research for "necessity defense" cases, however, Puzder realized there might be a shortcut. What if Missouri law simply stated that life begins at conception? There would then be no need for expert witnesses; the protesters could simply say they were obeying state law by defending the unborn.

Early in the Reagan administration, Senator Jesse Helms, the conservative Republican from North Carolina, had tried and failed to pass a similar "life begins at conception" federal statute, yet Puzder still believed that his language had broad political potential. Puzder saw it as an opportunity to create a "dichotomy in the law" that could ultimately undermine *Roe v. Wade*. An assertion in the state legal code that life begins at conception could not be used to outlaw abortion as long as *Roe* was the law of the land, yet it could be used to protect the rights of fetuses in cases involving issues other than abortion. A man who shoots a pregnant woman in the stomach could be accused of murder for the death of the unborn child; a drunken driver who causes an accident that leads to a woman's miscarriage could be charged with vehicular manslaughter. Puzder calculated that if Missouri protected the rights of a fetus in those circumstances, the legal and philosophical underpinnings for abortion might ultimately give way as well.

Puzder also saw the bill as the key to reinvigorating the anti-abortion movement, especially the mainstream groups that had lost their focus following the 1983 defeat of the constitutional amendment to ban abortion. To Puzder, it seemed that the National Right to Life Committee and Americans United for Life, a well-funded Chicago-based group that spent its time drafting model legislation for anti-abortion organizations, were spinning their wheels. They had grown wary of investing their time and energy in futile frontal assaults on *Roe* and pursued cautious initiatives on the margins of the abortion debate instead. By limiting their legislative goals, they were accepting defeat on the basic argument over whether abortion should be allowed at all; Puzder complained that National Right to Life was "playing in the pro-choice ballpark." The movement had to win legal recognition that the fetus was a life, entitled to the same due process under the United States Constitution as its mother. Otherwise, abortion would always be debated as an issue of whether to expand or restrict the rights of women. The anti-abortion side would lose that battle every time.

Puzder's "life begins at conception" language was grafted onto a bill Lee had written that included a series of specific abortion regulations. But when the two sought the backing of Missouri Citizens for Life, they were astonished that the state's main anti-abortion group was reluctant to support their legislation. The bill was too radical, and it interfered with the cautious legislative strategy favored by the bureaucrats at National Right to Life, of which Missouri Citizens for Life was an affiliate.

Instead, National Right to Life officials in Washington were pressing Kathy Edwards, then president of Missouri Citizens for Life, to back legislation they had crafted for use by their state affiliates that banned abortion for the purpose of sex selection. The NRLC's sex-selection legislation, which would have had virtually no impact on abortion, was a sign to Puzder and Lee of just how badly NRLC had drifted and how it had lost sight of its basic goals.

Finally, Edwards gave in to pressure from Loretto Wagner and other Missouri Citizens for Life leaders and agreed to back the Lee-Puzder legislation. Ultimately, the Lee-Puzder bill was merged with one drafted by DeFeo of the Missouri Catholic Conference, which represented the state's Catholic bishops, and the combined bill was quickly enacted into law. Missouri's Democratic-controlled legislature was dominated by abortion foes, and the state's Republican governor, John Ashcroft, was an ardent abortion opponent as well.

Among its other restrictions, the legislation banned the use of any state property, including hospitals, for performing abortions or counseling women about abortion and also required doctors to perform viability testing on any fetus if the doctor thought it might be at least twenty weeks old. But at heart, Sam Lee and Andy Puzder thought of their legislation as an anti-*Roe* law, and they hoped that it would provide a test case that could make it all the way to the Supreme Court.

They got their wish when the new law was challenged by five doctors and health professionals who worked for the state and by Reproductive Health Services, Judith Widdicombe's St. Louis clinic, which had been one of Lee's sit-in targets. The case soon began a three-year odyssey through the federal judicial system, with Missouri's ambitious attorney general, William Webster, defending it every step of the way.

Just after George Bush's victory in the 1988 presidential election, the Justice Department weighed in, urging the Supreme Court to hear *Webster* and overturn *Roe*. Bush, long pilloried by the Religious Right for his weak support of the anti-abortion movement, was looking for a politically expedient way to win back social conservatives, and *Webster* offered the president-elect an opportunity to do so without suffering the political costs of a bitter battle over abortion with the Democratic-controlled Congress.

The Court soon accepted Bush's challenge, and the new Bush administration filed an amicus brief on Missouri's side. With that, anti-abortion and abortion-rights leaders across the nation suddenly recognized *Webster*'s significance: It was the final exam for the Reagan Court.

The Court had ruled on more than a dozen laws to limit access to abortion since 1973, but *Webster* was the first major test of *Roe* since Anthony Kennedy, Reagan's last Supreme Court appointee, had joined the bench in 1987. Kennedy was seated after the Senate rejected ultra-conservative Robert Bork, and his views on abortion were not clear to the public; therefore, as *Webster* came before the Court, abortion-rights advocates feared that he represented the Court's fifth and deciding vote against *Roe* and that Reagan's long-deferred promise to outlaw abortion might finally come true after he had left the White House.

With so much at stake, feminists and anti-abortion forces scrambled in early 1989 to organize huge rallies and marches in the weeks leading up to oral arguments in the *Webster* case. After having dismissed the Lee-Puzder legislation, National Right to Life now embraced it as its own; *Webster* generated seventy-eight amicus briefs from both sides, more than any other case in the history of the Supreme Court. The nation's media declared that the abortion battle had reached a crossroads.

As the leading symbol of a new and angry Religious Right, Randall Terry was determined to be there when the Supreme Court dealt with

Webster, so that he could steal the show. After the arguments were over, Terry was the first to bound down the Court steps to the waiting crush of reporters, ready with his prefabricated sound bites.

Whereas both sides expected *Webster* to be the ultimate make-or-break test of *Roe,* behind closed doors the Court's nine justices were so badly fragmented on abortion that it soon became clear to Chief Justice William Rehnquist that the votes were not there for a decisive ruling. There was enough support to uphold Missouri's new restrictions on abortion but not to overturn *Roe.* Finessing the issue, the Court upheld the right of Missouri to proclaim that life begins at conception but only by agreeing with Attorney General Webster that the language did not directly regulate or limit abortion. In addition, Sandra Day O'Connor, Reagan's first appointee to the Supreme Court, infuriated abortion foes by refusing to join Rehnquist and other conservatives to form a majority to overturn *Roe.* Although she concurred in the ruling upholding Missouri's abortion regulations, she wrote that "there will be time enough to re-examine Roe," in other cases. "And to do so carefully." Reluctantly, Rehnquist wrote in the majority opinion that *Webster* "affords us no occasion to revisit the holding of *Roe* . . . and we leave it undisturbed. To the extent indicated . . . we would modify and narrow *Roe* and succeeding cases."

There was widespread confusion over the meaning of the Court's ruling in *Webster,* even among the justices themselves. Harry Blackmun, aging but still protective of his most famous decision, warned in his dissent that "a chill wind blows" and that the ruling upholding the Missouri regulations would invite new state regulations designed to provide further test cases for *Roe.* Rehnquist's opinion was "filled with winks, and nods, and knowing glances to those who would do away with *Roe* explicitly," he wrote.

What Blackmun did not realize was that *Webster* was the high-water mark for the anti-abortion cause; O'Connor's hesitancy in joining to overturn *Roe* would become open support to uphold *Roe* three years later in *Planned Parenthood of Southern Pennsylvania v. Casey,* the next major test for *Roe.* In *Casey,* O'Connor, joined by Kennedy and new Bush appointee David Souter, wrote that "liberty finds no refuge in a jurisprudence of doubt" and so ended the guessing game over her own position by stating clearly that "the essential holding of *Roe v. Wade* should be retained."

That kind of clarity was lacking, however, when the *Webster* ruling was handed down on July 3, 1989. The ruling pleased no one. It was so tentative and indecisive that both sides were torn over whether to claim victory or to complain about some aspects of the ruling that had gone against them.

Terry was there again when the ruling was issued, and once again he provided sound bites for the hungry news media. By then, Willke and the National Right to Life Committee were exasperated by Terry's ability to dominate press coverage, and Willke privately asked Representative Chris Smith, a New Jersey Republican and a leading abortion foe in Congress, to intervene. Smith called Terry to ask him not to go on the television talk shows that night as the spokesperson for the anti-abortion movement; let Willke get some airtime, Smith pleaded.

The request astonished Terry and his lieutenants; it was final proof that Operation Rescue had shaken the conservative political establishment to its foundations. The president of the National Right to Life Committee now had to beg Randall Terry to let him act as the figurehead for the anti-abortion movement.

In fact, Jack Willke was standing in the way of a steamroller. Operation Rescue was in high gear; dozens of "rescue" groups, local affiliates of Operation Rescue, had been created around the country by veterans of the New York and Atlanta campaigns, and they were staging countless protests of their own, serving to magnify Operation Rescue's reach. Terry capitalized on the grassroots growth by holding a second "National Day of Rescue," coordinated with the new local affiliates, just three days after oral arguments were heard in *Webster*. Surprisingly, many of the local chapters that participated were springing up in cities where Terry and Operation Rescue had never appeared—from Seattle, Washington, to Charlotte, North Carolina—and even in places that had rarely, if ever, experienced significant anti-abortion protests.

Donations were pouring in. The group took in more than $1 million in 1989, in what turned out to be its peak year, and soon had twenty-four full-time staffers churning out newsletters, pamphlets, and videos. Meanwhile, Terry and other leaders were traveling almost constantly to recruit and promote new clinic blockades. For an outlaw organization, Operation Rescue was taking on all the trappings of a legitimate, and very successful, business.

Operation Rescue's most valuable assets were its mailing lists, which included names of those who had been arrested in its "rescues" as well as of supporters who had participated in rallies or donated money. Staffers had carefully logged the names, addresses, phone numbers, and church affiliations of everyone who had come to Atlanta, and now Operation Rescue had thousands of names of activists who might turn up on short notice. Operation Rescue's mailing lists were never large—combined, they peaked at about twenty-five thousand names—but they included just the sort of highly committed Evangelicals that all the conservative groups in the United States wanted to get their hands on. Operation Rescue records, including hundreds of letters acknowledging donations, show that for the most part, Terry relied on small contributions from those individual supporters. Although James Dobson, Jerry Falwell, and others in the Religious Right made substantial contributions, either to Operation Rescue or to Terry personally, there is no evidence to support feminists' claims made at the time that Operation Rescue was secretly being bankrolled by a shadowy league of right-wing corporate moguls that included the likes of Domino's Pizza founder Tom Monaghan.

Operation Rescue's dramatic growth masked the fact that, underneath the surface, the ground was already shifting against it. Operation Rescue and *Webster* had jarred feminists and abortion-rights groups out of years of complacency. Planned Parenthood was now running abortion-rights advocacy advertisements featuring photos of Randall Terry barking orders to his followers, and NOW and NARAL were mounting large fund-raising campaigns to counter Operation Rescue and clinic blockades.

In addition to their new efforts to train volunteer clinic escorts, NOW and allied groups launched a coordinated legal assault; they used both federal and state courts to blanket Terry in a blizzard of lawsuits and civil fines for his stubborn refusal to heed court injunctions barring clinic blockades, which had been issued in almost every city targeted by Operation Rescue. Local chapters of NOW began to file RICO charges against Operation Rescue, and criminal charges were also building up. By the summer of 1989, Terry faced the prospect of jail in both Los Angeles and Atlanta.

Terry and his aides told themselves and their supporters that martyrs performing God's work had to expect trouble; Jeff White, the leader of Operation Rescue in California, boasted that he never even read the lawsuits and other legal papers sent to him by government prosecutors and attorneys for NOW. That cocky and rebellious air, so reminiscent of the antiwar leaders of the 1960s, hid the fact that their pressure-cooker life was transforming and hardening Operation Rescue's leadership. A tight-knit core of fundamentalist men—Foreman, White, Keith Tucci, and a few others—were part of an inner circle that had formed around Terry. Whereas many of Operation Rescue's grassroots activists were Catholic, Michael McMonagle was the only Catholic in the leadership, and only a handful of women, fundamentalists like Jayne Bray who were willing to submit to male authority, were trusted by Terry. Above all, he demanded that all of his aides submit to his absolute authority; he saw himself as the pastor of a mission church, a pastor who had the final say over his flock.

Those who could not abide by Terry's autocratic style soon began to drift away. Juli Loesch, who had served as Operation Rescue's press spokesperson in 1988, quit after the Atlanta campaign when she saw that everyone except "Randy Terry and his preacher boys" was being excluded from decision making. "In the end, I saw, close up, the way Randy was quite deliberately subordinating women within the movement," recalls Loesch.

The embattled few who remained around Terry came to view their organization in militaristic terms and considered themselves on a war footing with feminists. Foreman once described a revealing incident that took place in Washington in 1989, after he and Jeff White monitored a large abortion-rights rally on the Mall outside the Lincoln Memorial. As Foreman and White were leaving in White's pickup, White "accelerated toward a mob of satisfied feminists crossing the street, and slammed on his brakes—screeching to a halt within inches of the scattering crowd," Foreman later wrote. "Sticking his head out the window, he bellowed, 'If I were pro-choice, you'd be dead now!'"

NOW's legal tactics had the effect of isolating Operation Rescue's leadership even further. NOW began to try to scare off Terry's most prominent supporters by dragging them into lawsuits against Operation Rescue. Most notably, NOW named Jerry Falwell in RICO lawsuits against Terry and Operation Rescue, claiming that his donations to Operation Rescue brought him into Terry's "continuing criminal enterprise." Falwell's attorneys scrambled to have his name removed from the lawsuits, but NOW's tactic worked. Fearful of endangering his Liberty University and his other organizations, Falwell, once Terry's most ardent supporter, gradually began to distance himself from Operation Rescue in 1989 and 1990. Today, Falwell insists that he never had any intention of getting arrested with Operation Rescue and stresses that he finally distanced himself from Terry, not because of the NOW lawsuits, but because of Operation Rescue's increasingly militant tendencies. "I have never been a demonstrator," Falwell insists. "I only appeared with [Operation Rescue] one time. But I am a supporter of all approaches to stop the abortion of the unborn, as long as the effort is nonviolent. As long as Operation Rescue was nonviolent they had my blessing. But after awhile, I would pick up the newspaper and see all the dragging and police confrontations and yelling and shouting, and I thought that hurt our cause. If you remain nonviolent, you will have my prayers and my support, but if it becomes violent or counterproductive, I will withdraw, and that's what I did."

Operation Rescue veterans, however, are still convinced that Falwell pulled back because he was afraid of legal liabilities. Several recall that Falwell told them in a meeting in late 1988 of his postelection decision not to rescue; in the meeting Falwell cited his "fiduciary responsibility" to his university and other holdings.

"Anyone who came near Operation Rescue was sued . . . anyone who gave us money was sued," recalls Pat Mahoney, former national spokesperson for Operation Rescue. "We were a gypsylike organization, and we were all lawsuit-proof and judgment-proof," because all of Operation Rescue's leaders had shifted the titles to their homes and other personal assets to their family members. "But people like Falwell were not."

Terry's public persona—and his penchant for making outrageous statements to generate sound bites and get more airtime—also isolated Operation Rescue from mainline church leaders. Many of them agreed with him when he denounced feminism or homosexuality, but the way he did it confirmed the negative stereotypes of Operation Rescue that were rapidly taking hold in the media.

When Terry told reporters "I despise" feminism because it is "out to destroy, by its own words, the Christian heritage of motherhood and what it means to be alive," he ignored the impact of his words on church leaders as well as the general public. He did not seem to care that his rhetoric was easily turned against him by abortion-rights advocates, who made effective use of his words to make the case with the public that Terry's true agenda was to suppress women. Both he and Operation Rescue were depicted as social pariahs, which forced mainstream ministers to back away. Terry found himself ostracized by the Christian church that had nurtured his movement.

Occasionally, Pat Mahoney, who emerged as Terry's most savvy media adviser, tried to warn him—and tried to get Terry to clean up his ragged personal appearance—but Terry usually either ignored him or told him to shut up. Terry and many of his closest lieutenants had already concluded that the mainstream media were biased against them, and they figured it did not matter what they said. "If I ever run for office," Terry acknowledged, "I'll have to overcome the image the press has created of me, that I'm something close to a monster."

Terry paid scant attention to "how the press coverage was affecting our support," acknowledges Mahoney. In private, Terry was a surprisingly bright and articulate man; he later claimed that his negative public image was designed to attract television cameras and that he could turn it on and off at will. Yet Terry never recognized that the public image had taken a toll.

Rank-and-file demonstrators were also finding it difficult to keep up with the pace of constant arrest and imprisonment that Operation Rescue's strategy required. The middle-class Evangelicals who had heeded Terry's call the previous year—who had followed him into jail for forty days in Atlanta in July 1988 and then faced excruciating pain at the hands of the Atlanta police in October—were burning out. Fresh troops could still be found in each city, but as word spread of the hardening attitudes of the police and the courts in cities like Los Angeles, the ranks began to thin.

By 1990, a hard core of journeyman "rescuers" was almost all that was left. Obsessed by the dream of recapturing the spirit of the early days of rescue, they followed Operation Rescue from city to city, unemployed and living hand to mouth, receiving free food and lodging from sympathizers along the way. Evangelicals who had dropped away from Operation Rescue dismissed them as "professional rescuers." They were developing their own insulated world, the fundamentalist community's version of the Deadheads, who followed the Grateful Dead band from concert to concert. "After a while there wasn't enough new blood coming into the rescue movement," laments Frank Holby, an Evangelical arrested in Atlanta in 1988. "You would watch the news and see the same faces."

Terry made matters worse with his dictatorial approach to dealing with local protest leaders. Whenever Operation Rescue arrived in a city, Terry expected the established local activist organizations to fall into line with his plans, and his arrogance often led to irreparable rifts, especially with local Catholic activists who dated back to the days of PLAN and who remembered when Terry was as obscure as they were. One run-in with Terry was often enough to convince local activists not to go all out to recruit for Operation Rescue the next time it came to town.

Nevertheless, Terry realized there was a need to harness the wild energy he had unleashed within the Evangelical community. He even seemed to sense, through the blinding haze of his own domineering tendencies, that his chaotic leadership style had to be replaced with a more orderly management structure if Operation Rescue was to last. Just before Operation Rescue's second series of sit-ins in New York in January 1989, Terry confided in a few close aides that he had had a "vision" that told him to "let the child go," a metaphor for the decentralization of Operation Rescue and the delegation of authority to his lieutenants.

Terry's vision was prompted by private conversations he was having with Gary North, the head of a small conservative think tank in Texas and a leader in a fringe group of Calvinist fundamentalists known as "Reconstructionists." Cut adrift from the traditional Charismatic theology that preached noninvolvement in the world, Terry was searching for a new theology that interpreted the Bible as he did, as a book filled with "action verbs." He was intrigued by Reconstructionism, whose adherents claimed that Christians were called by God to exercise "dominion" on earth; it was a strange kind of theocracy.

North's first piece of advice was common sense: He told Terry that he had to learn to delegate and decentralize and that he should create a permanent organization that could outlast him. Soon, other conservative advisers began to descend on Terry as well, and they told him the same thing; Paul Weyrich's Free Congress Foundation even sent a consultant to study Operation Rescue's staff to see if it was structured effectively. One consultant pressed Terry to consider costly "video conferencing" to direct Operation Rescue's local affiliates, and another came to tell Mahoney that Terry should "soften his image" by cutting his steel wool hair, improving his wardrobe, and "refocusing his message."

In fact, it became obvious to many inside Operation Rescue that these established groups were mainly interested in finding a way to tap into Operation Rescue's grassroots power. The Moral Majority was dead; the Christian Coalition had not yet been created; and in the interim Operation Rescue was the primary outlet for fundamentalist anger and frustration with the political decline and moral decay of the United States. "Everybody wanted a piece of us," recalls Mahoney.

Terry was flattered and distracted by all of the attention. By the summer of 1989, therefore, he was willing to consider decentralization, and he asked Operation Rescue staffer Art Tomlinson to draft a restructuring plan. Tomlinson had been among the first inside Operation Rescue to recognize that Terry's arbitrary and autocratic leadership style was leading to confusion and costly mismanagement. He believed that the growth of the local affiliates throughout the nation provided an opportunity not only to restructure Operation Rescue but to transform it into a permanent political force.

Tomlinson proposed dividing Operation Rescue into four regions, with directors coordinating the activities of local Operation Rescue affiliates in each region. Terry initially accepted Tomlinson's plan, but it was never implemented, and Terry soon reverted to his capricious and chaotic leadership style. Money ran through his fingers with little accountability, and he began to run up huge bills, launching expensive projects on the side that often caught his lieutenants completely off guard. Late in 1989, his staff was stunned when ten thousand copies of George Grant's latest book arrived unannounced at Operation Rescue's headquarters; Terry had cut a deal to market and distribute the book without notifying his staff. (Grant is the former executive director of Coral Ridge Ministries who has become a leading advocate of Reconstructionist theories.)

Terry's decision to abandon the reorganization plan also reflected his ambivalence about ceding any authority. He recognized the need to delegate yet felt most comfortable following the autocratic leadership model of the fundamentalist church pastor. In addition, Operation Rescue was still a DBA for Randall Terry, and that meant that all of its resources were his personal assets to do with as he pleased. That power was difficult to surrender.

Some former Operation Rescue leaders more modestly spread the blame among themselves; no one in the group had any leadership or management experience, and no one knew how to mold a political movement that had blossomed overnight. In addition, they believe that no management plan could have helped Operation Rescue as it ran from one crisis to another.

Terry did not have time to reflect on long-term strategy. Operation Rescue was beginning to lose the initiative both to the courts and to its abortion-rights opponents, and by the late summer of 1989, the group's worsening legal problems had come to dominate its internal debates. In addition to the mounting civil fines from violations of court injunctions, which Operation Rescue had no intention of paying, Terry and others faced a series of high-profile criminal trials in cities where they had mounted protests in violation of court injunctions.

At first, Terry and his aides sought to turn their court appearances into political theater. One of their first big tests came in August 1989, when Terry, White, and McMonagle were tried on a series of trespass, resisting arrest, and conspiracy charges stemming from the Holy Week protests in Los Angeles. In their five-week trial, the Operation Rescue leaders represented themselves and, to their own astonishment, succeeded in turning the case into the anti-abortion equivalent of the Chicago Seven trial of the antiwar movement.

Outside the courtroom of Los Angeles municipal judge Richard Paez, Operation Rescue supporters noisily demonstrated on Terry's behalf, while inside, Terry, White, and McMonagle managed to drive both Paez and the prosecutors crazy. They engaged in a running psychological battle with the court over such petty issues as whether they could keep their Bibles on their defense table and whether they should be allowed to pray at "strategic moments" while the prosecution was making its arguments to the jury. "The judge threatened us with arrest for contempt of court nearly every day," recalls White.

It was all done for effect, and it worked. Terry and his lieutenants won over the jury with their derisive attitude toward the prosecution's case, while baiting the judge at every opportunity. "Anytime the jury was in the room, we would be polite and calm with the judge," White says, "but when the jury was out of the room, we would gang up on the judge and go after him. He would scream at us. And then Randall would yell at him. And then when the jury came back in, the judge was still keyed up, shouting at people, while we were calm again. We knew how to turn that attitude on and off—we were used to living in that world of screaming and yelling and confrontation—and he wasn't."

In the end, Terry, White, and McMonagle managed to put the Los Angeles police on trial, cross-examining arresting officers and showing videotapes of the Holy Week arrests and the police use of pain compliance techniques. Remarkably, the jury accepted Terry's courtroom dramatics and acquitted all three men on twenty-four of twenty-seven charges; a mistrial was declared in the final three. It was a stunning triumph for Operation Rescue.

"They were trying to save lives and we were for that, too," juror Priscilla Ramos told the *Los Angeles Times*. "I'd love to shake Randall Terry's hand." Reflecting the complex views on abortion of so many Americans, one juror said he was "pro-choice" but had been shocked to learn from the defense testimony in the trial that women could have abortions up to six months into their pregnancies. "I now respect the individuals for standing up for what they believe and I think seeing Mr. Terry in court humanized him a little," said juror Edmund Bleavins.

Courtroom victories were rare for Operation Rescue, however, and Terry had little time to savor his upset win in Los Angeles. Almost immediately, he had to decide how to deal with a September trial on trespass charges stemming from the 1988 siege of Atlanta. Many of the rank-and-file activists who had been arrested in Atlanta the previous fall were finally coming up for trial as well. Burned out by their lengthy time in jail the previous year, almost all of them had decided to dispose quietly of their old charges by paying off their bonds. Their commitment to "confront the system" was now long forgotten.

Terry went through with a jury trial, but unlike his experience in Los Angeles, he was quickly convicted, sentenced to two years' probation, banishment from the Atlanta metropolitan region for two years, and fined $1,000. Terry had avoided a jail sentence, but he was torn over whether to pay the fine and move on or refuse to pay and make one last, lonely stand in Atlanta. In an uncharacteristic move, he turned to a dozen of his most trusted lieutenants and asked them to vote on the issue rather than deciding himself. In the process, he sparked a heated debate over Operation Rescue's strategy and direction.

In internal discussions, McMonagle and Mahoney pushed Terry to pay the fine and put Atlanta behind him; Operation Rescue was in the midst of planning its biggest campaign ever, scheduled for Washington,

D.C., in November 1989, and the group needed Terry to recruit and lead. Stranding Terry in jail and out of the action for an extended period might end any hope that Operation Rescue could regain its momentum. However, a majority of Terry's aides, including Joe Foreman, Jeff White, and Jayne Bray, argued that Operation Rescue's integrity was at stake and that Terry's own martyrdom inside Fulton County Jail would reenergize supporters who were drifting away from rescue.

The debate reflected the unresolved struggle among activists over whether political pragmatism could ever take precedence in their ideological struggle with the "system." Terry sided with the majority, refused to pay the fine, and in October was hit with six months in jail. "I remember sitting out in the hall outside the courtroom with him, and he said, 'I feel God wants me to go to jail,'" recalls Jesse Lee, who had sided with the majority as well. "So I said, 'Praise the Lord. There's going to be good fruit from this.'"

Warming to the task, Terry began to view his decision to enter Fulton County Jail as the anti-abortion equivalent to Martin Luther King Jr.'s time in jail in Birmingham, Alabama. Mimicking King's famous letter from the Birmingham jail, Terry wrote a lengthy jailhouse letter of his own as soon as he was imprisoned, asking Operation Rescue's supporters to rally around him and come back to the cause.

"I am deeply troubled by what I see happening to the rescue movement nationwide," Terry wrote in his letter of October 10, sent out to Operation Rescue's entire mailing list. "In city after city (with a couple of exceptions) the numbers of rescuers are shrinking, and the average number of rescue missions per week is dropping." Terry closed by challenging his supporters to "pray afresh about your part in this battle. I challenge you to read the book of Jeremiah before the Lord and see if your heart does not tremble within you for this country."

To exploit the expected surge of new interest in rescue generated by Terry's martyrdom in jail, Terry named Joe Foreman to run Operation Rescue in his absence. The choice surprised many inside Operation Rescue, but Foreman had gained Terry's trust as his chief aide during the siege of Atlanta, and he appeared to share both Terry's fundamentalist outlook and his views on tactics and strategy. "I know God has prepared you for this hour," Terry wrote confidently to Foreman in a private letter as he turned over the reins of Operation Rescue.

But Terry had badly miscalculated; he and Foreman had almost nothing in common. Terry was a powerful orator and leader with a slightly twisted sense of humor; Foreman was a lackluster speaker and a humorless revolutionary who had come to see Operation Rescue as a dull-edged knife badly in need of sharpening. Although Foreman grudgingly admired Terry's oratorical skills, he had privately begun to doubt Terry's leadership style and his strategic vision.

A Schaeffer-style Reformed Presbyterian and a product of the rough-and-tumble Philadelphia protests of the mid-1980s, Foreman was becoming more and more militant, and he believed it was time for Operation Rescue to demand greater sacrifice from its supporters. He believed activists should become "missionaries to the preborn," willing to give up their lives to block clinic doors. Foreman knew that Terry did not share that vision of total commitment and abnegation.

In fact, Terry had always sought to balance the conflicting goals of rescue: symbolic protest and physical intervention to stop a specific abortion. During the siege of Atlanta, Terry had begun to emphasize the latter, but he had not forgotten that Operation Rescue's success was built on the power of political symbolism. Foreman, by contrast, strongly believed that rescue was not a form of protest, and he wanted to move Operation Rescue much further into acts of extremism. Like Joan Andrews and John Ryan before him, Foreman believed there were few, if any, acceptable limits on "lifesaving" tactics.

"Rescue is not a strategy," Foreman wrote. "The underground railroad was not a strategy to abolish the slavery issue. It is what the serious Christian did to abolish slavery for this slave, then that slave, and then the next slave. They did not look at slavery as an issue. They looked at the slave personally. . . . The underground railroad was not primarily a strategy, it was a way of life, it was rescue."

Privately, in fact, Foreman had little patience for Operation Rescue's middle-class supporters who lacked his purity of commitment. "Operation Rescue came with a beautifully tailored program: die to yourself on the weekend and still make it to work on Monday morning," Foreman later wrote dismissively. "Operation Rescue showed us how we could sacrifice like a hero in a way which fits a busy schedule. . . . The early successes in the 1988 siege of Atlanta . . . showed how ill prepared we were to face up to a world determined to protect legalized murder. At the first sign of resistance we melted and began to turn to the political doors which had crept open a few inches because of our boldness. . . . We still thought of rescue as street-level coercion instead of laying down our lives."

Foreman began to change Operation Rescue's direction almost as soon Terry entered jail. Terry had envisioned Operation Rescue's next major protest campaign—in Washington, D.C., in November—as the start of a new effort to move out of the streets and into conservative politics. It was dubbed "the DC Project," and Terry hoped to use the protests as a platform from which to announce his arrival onto the Washington political scene; he had arranged for Mahoney to open a Washington office that would leverage Operation Rescue's raw grassroots power into legislative influence. Terry had been watching in frustration as mainstream Religious Right groups took advantage of the explosion in Evangelical activism, and he believed it was time for the group that had done so much to unleash that energy to present its own political agenda.

"What we have to do is dispel the myth that we're clinic-bombers or fringe radicals," Mahoney told a reporter at the time, as he sought to set up operations in Washington. "It will take us six to eight months to introduce ourselves to legislators and prove we're not lunatics roaming the streets looking to blow things up. Let's be candid, that's the impression of us out there. A few screws loose."

But Terry never aggressively pursued that dream; he did not take the DC Project seriously enough to stay out of jail in order to lead it. Instead, Foreman took over Operation Rescue one month before the DC Project was scheduled to begin, and he immediately squelched Terry's plans for the group to get involved in political and legislative action.

To Foreman, the political and public relations elements of the DC Project were distractions from hard-edged rescue, and he ended all funding for Mahoney's proposed Washington office. Foreman limited the DC Project to the November clinic blockades and allowed nothing more. Operation Rescue never again attempted to shift gears into politics, leaving a vacuum eventually filled by the Christian Coalition and Ralph Reed.

In jail alone, without the comforting presence of fellow Operation Rescue prisoners, Terry gradually came unwrapped, emotionally and mentally. Terry was facing the longest sentence of his activist career— six months digging ditches and laying sewer pipe on a labor gang in Alpharetta, Georgia—and city prosecutors were threatening him with another six months if he did not give in and comply with the court order. Terry had been arrested at least thirty times in his life, yet he had spent only about ninety days in jail since 1984. Now, he faced the possibility of a year in jail just as Operation Rescue was coming under mounting legal pressures and just as Terry's personal life seemed to be collapsing as well.

In a controversial step taken soon after Terry entered jail, local social services officials in Binghamton launched a high-profile investigation of his family life to determine whether Terry's three foster children should be taken away because he was so often arrested and away from home. The action by Broome County, New York, officials appeared politically motivated and gave Operation Rescue a chance to issue a searing press release underscoring how Terry was suffering the fate of a martyr. Under the glare of the negative publicity, county officials finally backed down.

Privately, however, the foster care investigation rattled Cindy Terry. She had put up with her husband's long absences ever since he began recruiting for Operation Rescue in late 1986, but now she was losing her patience. Tensions rose between Randy and Cindy, and apparently the couple came close to the breaking point. Dan Little, who helped Cindy deal with the foster care investigation while her husband was in jail, recalls that the Terry's marriage faced enormous strains: "It was a difficult time because neither one of them thoroughly understood the pressures that had come to bear."

Allowed out briefly at Thanksgiving to see his wife and children, Terry returned to jail more depressed than ever. "He cried all the time" while he was visiting his family, recalls Foreman. "He was feeling more and more hopeless."

By December, Terry began to hint to Foreman, Jeff White, and other visiting Operation Rescue staffers that he wanted out of jail. Terry knew that meant he would have to compromise with the system that he had vowed to confront through his refusal to pay "blood money," but he secretly proposed a solution to his lieutenants. Someone could pay his $1,000 fine anonymously, he suggested; Terry could swear that he did not know who did it, and he could leave jail without the public humiliation of having folded under the pressure of prison life. It also meant that he could continue to stand tall publicly, before Operation Rescue's rank and file, many of whom had responded to Terry's appeals by sending money both to Operation Rescue and directly to Terry's wife for his personal use. In fact, Terry later said that so much money was sent to his wife by supporters while he was in jail that he was able to buy a farm outside Binghamton. "I always got more money [from donors] when I was in jail," he says.

His secret proposal stunned his aides, who could not believe that after just a couple of months in jail, Terry was willing to sell out his integrity—willing to dissemble his way out from under his public stand against "the system" and against abortion.

Foreman and White grew angry with Terry and told him to his face that they would not lie to save his reputation: "I gave Randy a check and said, if you want out, then let's get out," recalls White. Operation Rescue could pay Terry's $1,000 fine. "But let's do it standing up."

Terry's inability to deal with prison life began to rip apart Operation Rescue and allowed half-buried rivalries and disputes over strategy to come to the surface. In a series of secret meetings and conference calls, carefully kept hidden from both the press and Operation Rescue's rank and file to protect Terry's image as a martyr, Operation Rescue's inner circle agreed to try to pressure Terry to keep his feet to the fire by insisting that he should stay in jail. Led by Foreman, the majority inside Operation Rescue believed that Terry was simply suffering through a dark night of the soul and that it was their responsibility to force him to live up to his word—and to protect Operation Rescue's credibility. Only a few of his closest friends, led by Dan Little, his pastor at Pierce Creek, were sympathetic with Terry's plight, but even they insisted that Terry stick it out.

"He was looking to me, basically asking me to say it was okay for him to get out," recalls Little. "I said, 'I don't want to tell you this, but I think you have to stay. You need to stay with it.'" But the pressure from his lieutenants was backfiring, and Terry was an emotional wreck. Atlanta police sergeant Carl Pyrdum, Terry's adversary during Operation Rescue's siege of Atlanta in 1988, was shocked by the transformation he saw in Terry when he went to serve him with court papers in jail; the strutting, mouthy protest leader he had encountered the year before was now reduced to a passive, shuffling, ghostly figure.

While continuing to drop broad hints about the need for someone to pay his fine anonymously, Terry began to voice doubts about his ability to continue to run Operation Rescue at all. In a moment of despair, Terry told White and Foreman that he thought it was time to shut down Operation Rescue and walk away. Concerned that Terry was ready to abandon Operation Rescue, White asked Terry to give him the Operation Rescue name so that he could continue the fight. Terry was insulted; Operation Rescue was still his DBA, and he had no intention of surrendering it to someone else. "Randy told Jeff he would give it to him when Hell froze over," recalls Foreman. "We always had strong arguments in jail."

At the same time that Operation Rescue's leadership was being ripped apart by the secret debate over Terry's imprisonment, the external pressures were intensifying as well. Operation Rescue had out-run the federal court injunctions as it moved from city to city, but now the slowly grinding legal system was finally catching up. In December 1989, a federal judge in New York got fed up with Operation Rescue's refusal to pay a $100,000 fine stemming from the group's violation of the injunctions against its first major rescue in New York City in May 1988. Federal judge Robert Ward threatened to seize all of Operation Rescue's assets to pay the huge penalty and gave the group an ultimatum: either turn over its financial records to the U.S. attorney or post a $50,000 bond to appeal the case.

From jail, Terry told Foreman to defy Ward, and Foreman moved to notify Operation Rescue's supporters to stop sending donations to Binghamton, where the money was in danger of being seized. Instead, he instructed them to send their donations to Atlanta, where an office had been set up during the 1988 campaign. "Just picture a bounty hunter with all the power of the IRS, and you will begin to understand what a federal prosecutor can do to us," Foreman warned Operation Rescue donors in a letter dated December 5.

Foreman's action kept Operation Rescue one step ahead of the courts. In a high-profile legal move taken just before Christmas, 1989, federal marshals seized two of Operation Rescue's Binghamton bank accounts, but they retrieved only $3,000. The court order, however, had put Operation Rescue in financial limbo; although it could temporarily hide money in new bank accounts, it could not stay in business for long under those conditions. Operation Rescue's staff could not be paid, and those who stayed on board found themselves temporarily working for free.

Art Tomlinson came up with an ingenious, if legally questionable, solution that kept Operation Rescue solvent, at least for a few more months. Tomlinson had been assigned to maintain and expand Operation Rescue's ties to fundamentalist pastors around the country, and in his travels he had come in contact with other conservative groups tapping into fundamentalist anxiety and rage. At one small Washington conference for conservative Presbyterians, Tomlinson met Larry Pratt, founder of a right-wing group called Gun Owners of America. Pratt, an early pioneer in the antigovernment movement that blossomed in the mid-1990s, hated how the government seemed to be cracking down on Operation Rescue, and he responded to Tomlinson's request to help find a way to skirt the court-ordered freeze on Operation Rescue's bank accounts. Pratt had a second organization, called the Committee to Protect the Family Foundation, and he agreed to allow Operation Rescue to funnel its money secretly through the group's bank accounts. In January 1990, Terry wrote a letter to Operation Rescue's donors asking them to send contributions to the Committee to Protect the Family, and whenever Operation Rescue received a bill, Carol Ann Krzykowski, Terry's bookkeeper in Binghamton, sent it to Pratt in Virginia. He then paid the bills with checks written from the committee's accounts. Krzykowski later testified that Pratt's group paid at least eighty thousand dollars of Operation Rescue's bills in the first three months of the covert deal.

Tomlinson's financial alliance with Pratt presaged the links that later emerged between anti-abortion militants and the antigovernment militia movement in the mid-1990s. By 1996, in fact, Pratt became enmeshed in a national controversy when his ties to the militia movement were revealed at the same time that he was serving as a national co-chairman of Pat Buchanan's presidential campaign.

Tomlinson's stopgap measures did little to relieve the pressures building inside Operation Rescue. By January 1990, Terry was going stir-crazy in Fulton County Jail and had come to regret his decision in October to send out the fiery letter that now was holding him hostage. He was also becoming suspicious that Foreman wanted to keep him in jail so that he could remain in charge of Operation Rescue. "I couldn't put my finger on it, but I knew something was amiss. I felt like I was being used as a pawn," recalls Terry. He began to argue every day with Foreman and White about whether he should get out of jail. "I told them I'm a human being, there are problems with my family. I'm a flesh-and-blood man. And they kept giving me this General Patton talk," upbraiding Terry for his weakness and defeatism.

Terry's increasingly vocal doubts paralyzed Operation Rescue. Jesse Lee told others in the inner circle that he feared that Terry was caught in a "demonic stranglehold"—the leader they had once honored as anointed by God was now being tested by Satan. The only way to defeat Satan, Terry's lieutenants believed, was to force Terry to live up to his promise to stay in jail. Within the inner circle, no one argued more strongly that Terry should stay in jail than Foreman. He was unwilling to give up on Atlanta and, Terry suspected, to give up power. Although others in Operation Rescue drifted, Foreman took action and began to look for ways to keep Terry incarcerated.

The best way was to send out another letter to Operation Rescue's supporters, under Terry's signature, reaffirming his original decision to stay in jail as a martyr while the Christian community rallied to the cause. That would make it impossible for Terry to try to finesse his way out of jail. Foreman decided he should use something that already had Terry's name on it, so he started with a letter Terry had written early in his jail term to televangelist James Dobson, in which Terry reaffirmed his initial defiant stance and asked Dobson to come to Atlanta to join a clinic sit-in and risk arrest. Ultimately, Terry had decided not to send the letter for fear of alienating Dobson, who was among his most loyal supporters and who had privately been sending money directly to Cindy Terry. Foreman made a few alterations in the Dobson letter to make it suitable to send out to Operation Rescue's entire mailing list and then faxed a copy to Operation Rescue headquarters in Binghamton to be proofread and printed.

When the letter came in, Operation Rescue staffers Wendy Wright and Mark Lucas were elated. Thinking that it had been written by Terry, they saw the letter as a sign that the old Randall Terry was back, that he had emerged from his private hell. Wright and Lucas, who had been praying for Terry's rehabilitation, eagerly prepared thirty thousand copies.

Foreman insists that he had planned to show the letter to Terry for his approval after it was proofread and typed in Binghamton, before it was mailed to supporters. "My goal was to rehabilitate Randy, not to shut him up in jail," Foreman says. "He was the golden-haired child who made the thing work; we needed him." But when he contacted Wright and Lucas, Foreman was surprised to discover that they were already stuffing envelopes, poised to send the letter out. Lucas told Foreman that Operation Rescue did not have enough money to alter and reprint the letter, and that was enough for Foreman. Foreman went ahead with his power play, and Lucas backed him up. "Randy needs to grow up," Lucas told Foreman.

Hearing another insider echo his own thoughts, Foreman decided that it was God's will that the letter be sent out without Terry's knowledge—that it was God's way of breaking Satan's grip on Terry. "I got Charismatic and I said maybe God wants Randy to know what he should do," Foreman recalls. "That was a mistake, because I'm not Charismatic." Foreman told Lucas and Wright to go ahead, and the letter was sent out on January 22, 1990.

Seeking cover, Foreman quickly called Jeff White to tell him what he had done and pressured him to agree not to tell Terry. "We were unmerciful," admits White. Foreman knew that Terry would be furious after the letter was made public, so he prepared a private letter, to be delivered later, telling Terry to "be a man" and stay in jail. After the forged letter was sent to Operation Rescue's entire mailing list, Foreman gave a copy to Bob Jewitt to take into jail to show to Terry. He also gave Jewitt a sealed envelope containing his private letter to Terry and told Jewitt to give it to Terry only if he seemed upset after reading the first letter.

Terry was enraged on seeing what had gone out under his name without his knowledge, and he came completely unhinged after reading Foreman's private note upbraiding him. "I had been totally betrayed," says Terry, the anger still evident years later. "These guys wanted me in jail for their own purposes, and Joe Foreman was the ringleader."

As soon as he heard how Terry had reacted, Foreman knew he was to be ousted. But he was not alone. When Jeff White confessed to Terry that he had known about the letter for several days before Terry learned of it, Terry coldly told him that he was "dismissed."

Terry was convinced that he had to get out of jail as soon as possible to put down Foreman's rebellion, but he still faced the political problem of how to get out without appearing to have caved in to the city of Atlanta. No one outside Operation Rescue's inner circle knew about Terry's emotional breakdown or Foreman's coup attempt. Operation Rescue's rank-and-file supporters still believed Terry remained steadfast in his defiance of the "system" with the full backing of the rest of Operation Rescue's leadership, and it was important to maintain that illusion.

Days after the Foreman-engineered letter was sent to Operation Rescue's mailing list reaffirming Terry's determination to fight on, therefore, Terry's $1,000 fine was suddenly paid by an "anonymous" donor. Terry was released from jail on January 29. His release surprised almost everyone in Operation Rescue's inner circle, catching most of them when they were secretly meeting to rip power away from him in yet another coup attempt.

Irate over Terry's decision to fire Foreman and White, most of Terry's lieutenants were meeting at Jayne Bray's house outside Washington to draw up a list of demands for greater power sharing within Operation Rescue. The group included virtually all of Operation Rescue's veterans: Michael McMonagle, Gary Leber, Art Tomlinson, Jeff White, Jesse Lee, Mark Lucas, and Jayne Bray. They wanted to force Terry both to take Foreman and White back and to submit all his decisions to a ruling council, made up of them, that would have the final say over Operation Rescue. They wanted to end Terry's autocratic, Charismatic approach to leadership and replace it with the management-by-committee approach favored by Presbyterians like Foreman and White.

When Terry flew directly from Atlanta to Washington to attend the Christian Broadcasters annual convention, many of the coup plotters wanted to confront him immediately with their list of demands. But Terry was so haggard and weak that Keith Tucci, one of the few in the inner circle who remained loyal to Terry, demanded that they wait until Terry had a chance to go home and rest.

The showdown came in February, when Terry, Foreman, and the others held a bitter meeting in a Binghamton motel; the conference was so acrimonious that Dan Little was forced to act as referee. After two days of confused debate interspersed with screamed accusations, Foreman and White took control of Operation Rescue's key asset—its mailing lists—and set off for North Carolina to start a new group they planned to call Operation Rescue National. Still drained from his time in jail, Terry at first acquiesced, but he quickly realized that Foreman and White were effectively taking his organization with them. They were in "insurrection," Terry complained, and he ordered them to return the mailing lists and other assets. Fed up, Terry staged a final confrontation with the rebels in March. At a hotel in Washington, he brought in those who had signed the "list of demands" and, in a series of angry sessions, dismissed them all.

His action gutted Operation Rescue. Terry's lieutenants were just as angry at him as he was with them, and they quickly went their separate ways. "A spiritual and emotional split took place," says Mahoney. "And when the relationships were broken, it was almost impossible to rebuild the organization." But Terry no longer seemed to care; too exhausted to continue the fight, he was thinking about getting out himself. He hoped to move on: to repair the breach with his wife and family and to think about a new future—as a radio talk-show host.

What was left of Operation Rescue, Terry told supporters, would be turned over to the loyal Keith Tucci, and it would be renamed Operation Rescue National, the name that Foreman and White had briefly co-opted. The name change was designed to give Tucci at least a brief respite from the court orders targeting Operation Rescue's bank accounts. In late March 1990, Tucci set up Operation Rescue National in Summerville, South Carolina, and with Terry's blessing, he announced that he was the movement's new leader. Terry assumed the title of Operation Rescue founder and became the movement's "outside man"—its leading spokesperson—and Tucci tried his best to be the inside organizer. But Tucci had inherited an empty shell. No one outside the inner circle was told of the behind-the-scenes feuding that had led to the dramatic shakeup. Even those Terry had shoved aside, including Foreman, kept quiet for years. "All anybody knew was that we had a parting of the ways," says Foreman.

The press failed to get the story of the breakup and, instead, kept covering Operation Rescue events as if nothing had happened. Reporters only occasionally expressed confusion over the fact that Tucci claimed to be running things even as Terry kept a high profile as the movement's spokesperson. For months, however, Terry remained fearful that word of the rebellion might leak out and destroy his reputation. Therefore, he sought to pressure the dissidents to take their names off the list of demands that had been presented to him in February. His former lieutenants refused; they were no longer working for him, and they found his latest demand insulting.

Terry enlisted Dan Little to intervene with the former Operation Rescue staffers who were also members of the Church at Pierce Creek. Quietly, Little agreed to use his leverage as their pastor, telling them that they had sinned and that only by withdrawing their signatures could they cleanse their souls. Little's threats cowed Mark Lucas but backfired on fellow Pierce Creek members Gary Leber and Art Tomlinson, who completed their break with Terry and Operation Rescue.

It took years for Terry to reconcile with many of his former aides. Although he and Jesse Lee both still live in the Binghamton area, they have barely spoken since 1990. Terry has not forgiven Foreman and admits that he has quietly tried to undermine Foreman's efforts to work with other leaders in the anti-abortion movement.

Hardly anyone stayed to help Tucci launch Operation Rescue National. Throughout 1990 and into early 1991, Tucci failed to mount any major protest campaigns that could grab national attention. Local organizations continued to stage their own protests but without national coordination. The press occasionally wrote about Operation Rescue's inability to recapture its past success but otherwise failed to grasp that something had changed.

In October 1990, when a federal judge in Washington threatened to go after the group's donors to find money to pay fines stemming from Operation Rescue's DC Project blockades the previous November, Terry and Tucci told donors to send their contributions to local affiliates. Operation Rescue was all but dead anyway; the group ended 1990 with just twenty thousand dollars to its name. "Operation Rescue went from overnight success to overnight failure," says Tomlinson. "I mean we fell flat and we fell hard."

For militants like Foreman, however, Operation Rescue's breakup was perversely liberating. Freed from Terry's centripetal force, Foreman and other Operation Rescue veterans like Andrew Burnett, who shared his hard-edged vision of anti-abortion activism, could split off to form their own small but uncompromising new organizations. They could abandon all of Operation Rescue's pretenses of trying to appease large numbers of middle-class fundamentalists. Through tiny cells like Foreman's Missionaries to the Preborn and Burnett's Advocates for Life, they would perfect dangerous new tactics, such as attaching bicycle locks to their necks and to the axles of strategically parked cars, all designed to slow police efforts to clear clinic entrances. Gradually, they began to voice their frustration over the failures of civil disobedience and to develop perverse new theories that they claimed showed that the Bible justified the use of violence to end abortion.

Later, insiders traced the origins of the anti-abortion extremism of the 1990s—and the movement's ultimate descent into violence—to the splintering of Operation Rescue's leadership.

Operation Rescue came together for one last stand, in Wichita in the summer of 1991, where members briefly encouraged Terry to work with Tucci to stitch the movement back together. If this event failed to spark a revival, the road would be open for extremists like Joe Foreman, Andrew Burnett, and even Michael Bray, who was now out of prison and eager for a comeback.

PART IV

WRATH

13

WICHITA
Summer of Mercy?

Like so many others who had once been close to Randall Terry, Gary Leber bitterly cut himself off from his old leader after Operation Rescue's acrimonious breakup in the winter of 1990. Terry had dismissed Leber along with most of Operation Rescue's staff following Joe Foreman's attempted coup, and Leber soon started an independent life in Binghamton, far from Terry's orbit. Operation Rescue was all but dead, and like other fundamentalists, Leber figured that anti-abortion activism was dying with it. But as he was going through his mail one day in the summer of 1991, Leber found a recruiting letter from Terry that brought back a flood of memories—and sudden hope for reconciliation and renewal.

Terry was in Wichita, Kansas, helping Operation Rescue's new leader, Keith Tucci, mount the group's first major campaign since the breakup. Tucci had attempted on his own to recapture Operation Rescue's spirit and fire, but the event he had organized in Dobbs Ferry, New York, had come up short. Now Terry was once again engaged, and Operation Rescue seemed poised to score its biggest hit ever.

Come to Wichita, Terry said in the letter. Come back to Operation Rescue. "Our God is the God of second chances," Terry wrote, in words that Leber interpreted as Terry's plea for forgiveness for the cold-hearted way he had dealt with his lieutenants the year before. "God is doing something here we have never seen before, but always hoped and prayed for," the letter continued. "Now it seems God is answering our prayers. He's giving us another chance."

"Randy's back," Leber told himself. He answered the call, as did many of the other dissidents who had been banished just one year earlier: Jeff White, Michael McMonagle, even the discredited Joe Foreman. Along with thousands of grassroots activists who were also undergoing a brief rebirth of enthusiasm, they swarmed into Wichita for what would become Operation Rescue's largest campaign ever: the "Summer of Mercy." Over forty-six days, the Wichita campaign resulted in nearly twenty-seven hundred arrests; long emotional rallies attracted followers from almost every state in the country. Local churches flung open their doors—and their coffers—and Wichita became a fundamentalist Woodstock, a summer happening out of nowhere.

Wichita was also Operation Rescue's last stand, however, and the tense air of desperation that hung over the campaign by the end would serve as a warning of the movement's coming slide into extremism and violence.

Keith Tucci was horribly miscast as Randall Terry's successor and the man tasked with getting Operation Rescue moving again. An earnest Charismatic preacher, Tucci had not been involved with the day-to-day running of Operation Rescue, and he lacked Terry's oratorical skills and charisma. Tucci recognized his own shortcomings and was stunned when Terry asked him to take over.

In addition, Tucci had no base of support in the movement. His only qualification was that he had remained loyal when Terry believed everyone else connected with Operation Rescue had turned against him. However, Tucci's selection as head of Operation Rescue in March 1990 only added to the strains between Terry and the rest of the anti-abortion movement. Terry's former lieutenants, now dispersed, were dismayed that Terry had plucked Tucci out of obscurity to run what remained of the largest organization in the movement. Many were smugly convinced that Tucci would never revive Operation Rescue and turned their backs on him. Foreman and others began to set up small, rival organizations to tap into what was left of activism.

Throughout 1990 and into early 1991, it appeared as though Tucci would prove his doubters right. He tried to pick up the shattered pieces of the organization, now renamed Operation Rescue National, and operate from an office building in Summerville, South Carolina, a sub-urb of Charleston, where he had moved from his hometown of Pittsburgh. Although local Operation Rescue affiliates in some cities remained active, Tucci was unable to generate enthusiasm for any of his efforts at nationally coordinated action. Without the support of Terry's former lieutenants, Tucci's first major event, in Dobbs Ferry in January 1991, was a huge disappointment. "People just didn't show up," Tucci remembers painfully.

With fewer demonstrations came fewer arrests, less media attention, and less money coming in from donors. Tucci's calls for contributions to support the Dobbs Ferry protests were met by a deafening silence; he had to borrow $15,000 just to launch the campaign. He realized that if he did not do something big, and do it fast, Operation Rescue would simply disappear.

Tucci was a born-again product of Pittsburgh's mean streets, and he was just stubborn enough to try to turn things around. He had grown up alongside gang members in Pittsburgh's housing projects, drinking and doing drugs, until at eighteen he encountered a street-preaching former member of the Hells Angels who quite literally put the fear of God into him. Tucci's life was never the same. He got a diploma from a Bible school in Oklahoma and, at twenty-two, became a preacher at a small church in a hardscrabble mining town in western Pennsylvania.

Tucci later moved back to Pittsburgh to preach at a church where, in 1982, a young, single pregnant woman came to him for counseling. The experience marked Tucci and made him think about abortion for the first time. He began working with other pastors to found a network to help pregnant women and girls, and by late 1982 he had formed a coali-tion of local churches that regularly sent volunteers to distribute anti-abortion literature outside Pittsburgh's three abortion clinics.

Tucci was introduced to the tactics of the militant wing of the anti-abortion movement in 1984, after a member of his church suggested that he read Francis Schaeffer's works. When Randall Terry came to Pittsburgh in May 1987 to speak and recruit, Tucci was in the audi-ence; he joined Terry in time for Operation Rescue's first major cam-paign in New York in May 1988, bringing more than one hundred fifty members of his church with him. New York was a searing experience for

Tucci. "I had never seen the contrast between good and evil as crisp and clear as I saw that day. This is the church. This is what we're supposed to be doing."

Tucci had recently moved to South Carolina to become the associate pastor of a new Charismatic church when Terry asked him to take over Operation Rescue. Tucci's greatest attribute as Operation Rescue's new leader was his toughness; unfazed by the failure in Dobbs Ferry, he was soon ready to try again. In the spring of 1991, he called a meeting of activist leaders to select a target for a national summer campaign. Milwaukee was the choice by consensus, but Tucci stunned his supporters when he pushed for Wichita, Kansas, a small and isolated city that experienced occasional protests but had never been a hotbed of anti-abortion activism.

Tucci claims that the idea of going to Wichita came to him through a revelation from God. However, there was another reason for the choice. Tucci had made an astute and pragmatic political decision to focus Operation Rescue for the first time on late-term abortion, long before this became a central issue in Washington. Tucci believed that by targeting a late-term abortion doctor, he could personalize the struggle and generate renewed interest and enthusiasm among fundamentalists who had drifted away from the movement. He found the perfect target in Wichita. Dr. George Tiller, the owner and operator of the Women's Health Care Services clinic, was one of the few doctors in the country willing to perform late-term abortions.

"The nation's most notorious killer practices his demonic trade in Wichita, killing babies until 'birth,'" Tucci wrote in a recruiting pamphlet sent out to fundamentalists, urging them to join the Wichita campaign. "George [Killer] Tiller advertises nationally and internationally to solicit women in their second and third trimesters." Tucci later told reporters that Operation Rescue targeted Wichita because of "Mr. Tiller's operation."

Wichita, a city of only three hundred thousand that was best known as an aircraft manufacturing center, was a tough sell to the activists. In its heyday, Operation Rescue had targeted big cities like New York, Atlanta, and Los Angeles; Tucci was abandoning the nation's major media centers and running the risk that the national press corps might ignore the entire campaign. It was only after Tucci's enthusiasm began to rub off—and after other activists realized that a small Midwestern city might offer a more hospitable reception to their conservative shock troops—that they grudgingly agreed to go along with the idea.

Wichita was about to become the first national Operation Rescue campaign specifically designed to target an individual abortion provider. Tucci's focus on Tiller represented a major shift; Operation Rescue no longer sold itself to fundamentalists primarily as providing a means for personal atonement. Increasingly, Operation Rescue was becoming a way to lash out at the "weak links" in the abortion industry. In Operation Rescue's earliest events, protesters had asked God to wash away their sins for having ignored abortion for fifteen years; by the time of the siege of Atlanta in October 1988, that hunger for repentance had dissipated. Three years later, in Wichita, Operation Rescue was dropping nearly any pretense of soul searching and was ready to point fingers and attack.

Wichita's clinics quickly got word that Operation Rescue was on its way, and by mid-June 1991, local abortion-rights advocates were gearing up to mount a defense. Peggy Jarman, Tiller's spokeswoman and cofounder of a Kansas abortion-rights group, began to train local clinic escorts, and Tiller himself called Midtown Hospital in Atlanta to find out more about its experiences with Operation Rescue.

It was perhaps inevitable that Dr. George Tiller would become a major target of Operation Rescue. His defiant attitude toward anti-abortion protesters made him even more of a lightning rod for the opposition. He had staked out his position on the anti-abortion movement as early as 1986, when a bomb caused one hundred thousand dollars worth of damage at his clinic. Amid the ruins, Tiller draped a hand-lettered sign that loudly proclaimed: "Hell, no. We won't go!" Five years later, when Operation Rescue laid siege to his clinic, Tiller was not afraid to scream back at Randall Terry, "Too bad your mother's abortion failed!"

Abortion was not George Tiller's chosen field of medicine; it was thrust on him only after he began to uncover his father's secrets. As a boy growing up in Wichita, Tiller wanted to be a doctor like his father, Dean Jack Tiller, and he often accompanied his father on house calls. He went on to study at his father's alma mater, the University of Kansas School of Medicine in Kansas City, Kansas, before joining the Navy to serve as a flight surgeon.

Tragedy pulled him back in 1970, when his father, mother, sister, and brother-in-law were all killed when the private plane Dean Tiller was piloting crashed into a rugged mountain slope east of Yellowstone National Park. Tiller received a humanitarian discharge from the Navy and returned to Wichita, where he adopted his dead sister's infant son and began making plans to close down his father's medical practice. His new ambition was to begin his own career in the field of dermatology.

After Tiller began to see some of his father's patients, however, he realized there were not enough doctors in the area to absorb them all. He decided to phase out his father's practice more slowly, over a three-year period. It was during that period that he discovered that Dean Tiller had performed illegal abortions for generations of women in Wichita. His father had kept his abortion business hidden from his son, but now patients began to approach him tentatively to ask if he "was going to do the same thing for them" that his father had done.

Tiller learned that his father had been performing illegal abortions since the late 1940s, a decision prompted by pangs of guilt over the death of a patient he had refused to help. A woman who had given birth to two children came back to him during her third pregnancy and told Dean Tiller she could not handle another pregnancy. He ignored her pleas for an abortion; she later died at the hands of a back-alley abortionist. Haunted by the woman's unanswered cry for help, Dean Tiller secretly began to perform abortions in his office.

George Tiller decided to keep his father's practice and stay on in Wichita, and in 1973 he performed an abortion at a local hospital for the first time, not long after the *Roe v. Wade* decision. Tiller was bothered, however, by the hospital's insensitive handling of abortion patients, who were wheeled right past the nursery filled with newborns on their way to the operating room. He also realized that he could beat the hospital's high price of $1,000 per abortion and began to offer private, outpatient abortions at his office for $250. His medical practice became a magnet for Wichita women seeking inexpensive abortions, and by 1985, he had phased out the majority of his family medical practice to concentrate on abortion.

When Tiller broadened his practice to include more difficult and costly late-term abortions, his clinic began to attract patients from all over the world. Whereas many doctors seldom perform abortions beyond the first trimester, Tiller gained a national reputation for his willingness to perform elective abortions through the second trimester, up to about twenty-six weeks and four days into a normal forty-week pregnancy. He also performed abortions later in the pregnancy in cases of severe fetal abnormalities. (Tiller never performed the controversial procedure that critics call *partial-birth abortion,* which Congress repeatedly tried to ban in the mid-1990s. In fact, Tiller says he opposes that procedure on ethical grounds. He prefers what is called the *induction method,* in which he injects a chemical into the chest of the fetus, stopping the heart. The woman then is induced into labor and delivers a dead fetus.)

Married and the father of four children, Tiller acknowledges that he is a recovering alcohol and drug abuser. In 1984, he was charged with driving while under the influence of alcohol or drugs, and the Kansas Board of Healing Arts placed restrictions on his medical license, allowing him to continue practicing only if he agreed to enter a treatment program. He did, and the license restrictions were soon lifted. Tiller insists that his substance abuse was not brought on by the stress of his career as an abortion provider.

Despite Tiller's defiant stance toward anti-abortion activists, he and his local supporters made a series of critical moves that helped ensure Operation Rescue's success in Wichita. First, Jarman and her ProChoice Action League turned down offers from Eleanor Smeal's Feminist Majority Foundation and other national organizations to deploy veteran clinic-defense teams from around the nation. Jarman believed that bringing in more outsiders, even sympathetic feminists, to deal with Operation Rescue would only add to the tensions in Wichita.

The biggest mistake came when Tiller and the city's other clinic operators agreed to a request from the Wichita police to close down their operations during the first week of the protests. Tucci had originally billed the "Summer of Mercy" as a one-week campaign, and both the police and the clinics agreed they could wait out the storm. They planned to return to business as usual the following week, after Operation Rescue left town.

In effect, Wichita was engaging in unilateral disarmament, and Operation Rescue exploited the city's vulnerabilities to the fullest. With few clinic defenders to battle, Tucci and Terry could use militant tactics to dominate the clinic entrances, and the closing of the city's clinics served as a wonderful recruiting tool for Operation Rescue.

Once they saw that the clinics were closed, Terry and Tucci put out the word that Operation Rescue had turned Wichita into an abortion-free city, and they called on Evangelicals from around the country to flock to Wichita to join a campaign that they claimed was having a rare, direct impact on abortion in America.

The "Summer of Mercy" began quietly in the searing heat on July 15, 1991, and there was not a hint of what was to come. With the clinics closed, the protesters had little to do in the first few days except wait for Tucci and Terry to put out the word for reinforcements. Small groups of picketers marched in front of Tiller's clinic and the Wichita Family Planning clinic three miles away, singing "Jesus Loves the Little Children" and "He's Got the Whole World in His Hands," but there were no clinic blockades or arrests, and there was only sporadic media attention. (Operation Rescue did not know, however, that Tiller had secretly gotten a few patients into the clinic the night before the protests began to perform late-term abortions for previously scheduled patients who could not wait.)

Although the streets remained quiet, a wave of new energy was building, the kind that Operation Rescue leaders had rarely felt since the siege of Atlanta. Tucci was stunned to see that his rallies were drawing nightly crowds of more than one thousand supporters, and cardboard buckets passed through the crowds were overflowing with cash. Operation Rescue brought in an estimated $177,000 during the Wichita campaign; nearly $70,000 was funneled through just one bank account controlled by Wichita's Central Christian Church, a large fundamentalist church that acted as Operation Rescue's banker and bookkeeper.

A religious fervor began to build behind Operation Rescue; American fundamentalists quickly came to see the shutdown of Wichita's clinics as a miracle, a sign from God, and a blessing on Tucci's campaign. Never before had Operation Rescue been able to close all the abortion clinics in a single city for an extended period, and fundamentalists, particularly Charismatics who believed in visible miracles, convinced themselves that the Holy Spirit was moving in Kansas. As word spread through the fundamentalist subculture, sympathizers simply packed up and headed toward Wichita, some to pray and sing, others to risk arrest.

It was "a huge blunder for the clinics not to open," observes Pat Mahoney. "It was the worst mistake ever. At the rallies, people would get up and say, 'No killing today in Wichita.' And everybody would just go wild. People in Wichita got the feeling that 'Dear God, if we've done this for five days, can we do it for six? If we've done it for six, can we do it for seven?' And after nine days, the energy was building so much, there was a feeling that if we can continue on, maybe Tiller will close down altogether."

When Randall Terry arrived in Wichita a few days after the campaign began, he immediately sensed the electric atmosphere, and he decided to stay and exploit it. On his first day in town, Terry held a press conference, which spontaneously turned into an emotional rally in which Operation Rescue supporters far outnumbered reporters; the experience seemed to rejuvenate Terry. That afternoon, Tucci and Mahoney decided that Operation Rescue would stay in Wichita indefinitely, and before long Terry issued his call to Evangelicals around the nation to join the extended protests.

Operation Rescue's call was enthusiastically answered by the fundamentalist community, but Tucci's announcement that the protests would not end as scheduled infuriated both abortion-rights advocates and the Wichita police. Tiller and the other clinic operators were determined to reopen at the start of the second week. Wichita police, who had planned for only one week of protests, felt they had been duped by Operation Rescue and now prepared to back the clinics to the hilt.

The showdown came on July 22, when the clinics were scheduled to reopen for the first time. Wichita police arrived that morning ready to do battle, with some officers in full riot gear and others on horseback, only to find Tiller's front gate already blocked by hundreds of Operation Rescue protesters.

By now the police had lost their patience, and they moved with military precision to regain control of the clinic entrance. First, mounted police moved in, using their horses to force a clearing through the crowd and scattering frightened demonstrators in the process. Next, two dozen officers in riot gear formed a wedge and secured the entrance. Finally, a city van flanked by three police motorcycles rushed in; behind the police cordon, Tiller's staff and patients entered the clinic.

The strong-arm tactics came as a shock to the demonstrators, but by the afternoon, Operation Rescue leaders were ready to respond. Led by Chet Gallagher, a former Las Vegas police officer who had resigned rather than arrest anti-abortion demonstrators, dozens of activists went to the Wichita Family Planning clinic and lay down in the middle of the street, determined to stop traffic. When mounted police tried to clear them away, the protesters refused to be moved. A melee quickly erupted on one of the city's busiest streets as startled horses, screaming protesters, and police brandishing nightsticks and Mace swirled together, until the officers finally began handcuffing protesters and dragging them away.

As he had in Atlanta and Los Angeles, Randall Terry charged that the police had used excessive force. The Wichita police tactics, he told reporters, "are among the worst we've seen. Our people are bleeding." The street battle suddenly transformed the Wichita campaign into a high-pressure, high-visibility confrontation. "The climate changed instantly," recalls Tucci. Wichita mayor Bob Knight, who was an abortion opponent, was the first to flinch under the stress. He quickly decided that he had to reduce the tensions building in the city and that the police would have to ease up.

"Originally, the idea [behind the hard-nosed police tactics] was to get the doctor in, keep the clinic open, and allow him to do business," recalls Mike Watson, a senior police official at the time of the protests and now Wichita's police chief. "I was coming up with novel ways of getting Tiller into the clinic and then keeping it open so the patients could come in." But the besieged mayor gave the police new marching orders that were not as favorable to Tiller. The police would continue to work to clear the clinic entrances, but they were told that it was no longer their responsibility to help doctors and patients run the protest gauntlet.

When Jarman arrived at Tiller's clinic at six the next morning, Operation Rescue already had protesters seven rows deep blocking the entrance. Unlike the previous day, however, there were no mounted police and no city vans available to escort patients and clinic employees. Instead, the police moved slowly throughout the day, and did not even begin making arrests until the afternoon. Even then, they allowed the protesters to take "baby steps" to waiting buses, further delaying the lifting of the blockade.

With the city seemingly cowed by Operation Rescue, Tiller turned to the federal government, and his attorney quickly convinced U.S. District Judge Patrick Kelly to issue a temporary restraining order to prevent further clinic blockades. Kelly's order packed a wallop, calling for fines of $25,000 a day for the first violation and $50,000 after that. It was the start of an ugly legal showdown that neither side would ever forget.

Kelly was a volatile sixty-two-year-old Irish Catholic born and raised in Wichita, a liberal Democrat who had been an early opponent of the Vietnam War and who had run unsuccessfully for Congress in the 1960s. A law school classmate of Senator Bob Dole, he had risen through the ranks of the local legal community and the Democratic Party until he was appointed to the federal bench by President Carter in 1980. On the bench, he had developed a reputation for both tough talk and tough rulings.

Kelly's confrontation with Operation Rescue came just months after he had experienced his own personal crisis over abortion and religion. Kelly had quit his parish church after his priest asked the congregation to sign petitions calling for the impeachment of Supreme Court Justice Harry Blackmun because of his ruling in Roe v. Wade. During Mass, the priest charged that Blackmun was responsible for the murder of millions of children, prompting Kelly to stand up in the middle of his sermon and walk out, never to return. He later told the priest that "if a Roe case comes my way, I certainly will not step aside because I'm a Catholic. I will carry out the law."

When Randall Terry received a copy of Kelly's order on Tuesday afternoon, July 23, he threw it on the ground outside Tiller's clinic. "We have an injunction in the Bible that commands us to rescue innocent children," he said. "We fear God, the supreme judge of the world, more than we fear a federal judge."

Terry's followers dismissed the federal order as well, and more than two hundred were arrested the next day during protests at all three of the city's abortion clinics. Operation Rescue had logged 672 arrests in just three days; because so many protesters were being rapidly released from the city's jails, many had already been arrested two or three times. Under orders to negotiate with Operation Rescue, Wichita police were now allowing the group to dictate the way its activists were taken into custody; during one stretch, Operation Rescue managed to keep Tiller's clinic closed for twenty-six consecutive hours.

Kelly's fury grew when he saw his order first ignored by Operation Rescue and then largely unenforced by the Wichita police. He promptly ordered federal marshals to arrest Terry and two other Operation Rescue leaders on contempt charges. By Wednesday afternoon, when Terry came into court, Kelly warned him that "I watched you on television last night, and I don't need much evidence to tell me what your attitude is," referring to Terry's dismissal of his federal court order. Kelly asked Terry and Pat Mahoney whether they planned to mount more clinic blockades, and when both said yes, he cited them for contempt and ordered them jailed until they agreed to comply with his order. In a private meeting after the hearing, a disgusted Kelly made it clear that he could not comprehend what was driving Operation Rescue or the new Religious Right. "You can't win," he remembers telling them. "Why don't you go home?"

Kelly held Terry but quickly released Mahoney after he promised to leave town by Sunday. After he was released Friday morning, however, Mahoney was out in front of Tiller's clinic once again in the midst of at least one hundred clapping and singing protesters blockading the entrance. While police struggled for hours to clear them away, Mahoney told reporters he had changed his mind and would not abide by his pledge to Kelly to leave town.

At this point, Kelly found it difficult to contain his anger at both Operation Rescue and the city of Wichita, and he began to lash out. He summoned Rick Stone, Wichita's chief of police, for an acrimonious meeting in his chambers Friday night. Kelly demanded that the police do a better job of enforcing his restraining order, but Stone told him that he could not abide his instructions. His job was on the line, Stone said. "He was under a directive" not to enforce the order more effectively, Kelly recalls.

Kelly then called Mayor Knight at his home, and Knight agreed to meet him the next morning. "I said to him, 'Mr. Mayor, you need to clarify this situation with the [police] chief and see to it that my order is in place.' And he said, 'I can't do that.' He said, 'This is a peaceful protest.' And I said to him, 'Bob, I'll tell you this. If it takes United States marshals, I'm going to open that damned gate. And this meeting's over.'"

On Monday morning, July 29, after learning that Operation Rescue was again blocking Tiller's gates, Kelly ordered federal marshals to keep the entrance open. It was the first time federal law enforcement officers had been called out to intervene in an anti-abortion protest.

Despite the federal order, Day 15 of the protests—Tuesday, July 30— quickly turned ugly. At 6:30 A.M., about one hundred protesters crawled into the driveway of Tiller's clinic and pressed two dozen marshals and police officers against a fence. By the end of the day, 214 protesters had been arrested, including some who had already been arrested eight times since the start of the campaign.

Kelly now began to broaden his attacks on Operation Rescue's hierarchy to force compliance with his order, ordering four more leaders arrested, including Tucci and Jeff White. He jailed three of them on contempt charges and released Tucci only after learning he had not been served a copy of his order. The next day, Kelly also released Terry, who had been jailed for eight days, after Terry told him he had no "premeditated" plans to violate his order. "This has been one of the most awkward moments in my entire life," an exasperated Kelly told Terry as he let him go. "In my experience on the bench, I've never handled this problem. I had naively assumed that when an order is issued in court, it will be honored."

Convinced that his get-tough attitude was finally getting through to Terry and other Operation Rescue leaders, a fatigued Kelly went along with Wichita's city officials when they recommended that the police and marshals be withdrawn from the clinics. Inexplicably, they had decided to take Operation Rescue's word that the group would no longer try to block access to Wichita's clinics. They apparently hoped the unilateral action would once again deescalate tensions around the clinics.

Instead, Terry exploited the opening, vowing that rescues would continue; two days later, on August 2, Operation Rescue's blockades resumed. When Tiller tried to navigate his blue Chevy Suburban through the clinic gate at 7:30 that morning, more than one hundred protesters blocked his path. Terry walked up to his car window, shaded his eyes and peered inside. "You can laugh now!" Terry shouted. "But you'll pay some day."

Police arrested 124 protesters that morning, and Police Chief Rick Stone pleaded for an end to a campaign that was ripping the city—and his department—apart. "We had police officers who had to arrest relatives in the crowd," recalls Mike Watson. But the Operation Rescue campaign was now receiving national attention, and conservative political support was growing. In an obvious rebuke to Kelly and his use of federal power, Kansas's Democratic governor, Joan Finney, came to Wichita that afternoon to speak at an Operation Rescue rally, the first governor in the country ever to do so. "I am pro-life," Finney told a cheering crowd of fifteen hundred, gathered in 103-degree heat to support Operation Rescue. "My hope and prayer is that Wichita's expression of support for the right to life for unborn babies will be peaceful, prayerful, and united in purpose. I commend you for the orderly manner in which you have conducted the demonstration." The blockades continued throughout the weekend as fundamentalist pastors and preachers arrived by the busload to get arrested.

On Monday, August 5, the beginning of the fourth week of protests, sixty-six more demonstrators were arrested outside Tiller's clinic. That afternoon, a fist-pounding Kelly expanded his temporary restraining order into a more permanent injunction, calling Operation Rescue leaders hypocrites while also lashing out at Wichita city officials, local clergy, and Finney.

"The full force of the U.S. court is now in place," Kelly fumed after issuing the new order. "This court will do what it must to bring about order in this community." Now, anyone even encouraging a clinic blockade, Kelly said, "will be arrested on the spot by the United States marshal . . . taken away in handcuffs and brought here." Kelly also ordered Operation Rescue leaders to post a $100,000 "peace bond" to cover any financial damages that might result from a lawsuit filed by the clinics. And in an action that intimidated many of the church leaders who had joined the campaign, Kelly warned that any churches or clergy members who violated his order would be held financially responsible as well. The next morning, more than one thousand protesters assembled outside Tiller's clinic, but with a dozen marshals at the gate none tried to block the entrance.

Operation Rescue attorneys filed suit to stop Kelly's court injunction, and to the surprise of both Terry and Kelly, the Bush administration decided to weigh in on the side of Operation Rescue. In a highly controversial move the Justice Department, without checking with the White House, filed an amicus brief calling for Kelly's order to be overturned, arguing that the states, rather than the federal government, should decide issues involving access to abortion clinics. The Justice Department had already filed a similar brief in the *Bray v. Alexandria Women's Health Clinic* case that Operation Rescue had filed following the DC Project in November 1989, arguing that the Ku Klux Klan Act of 1871 should not be used to ban anti-abortion civil disobedience. At the time of the Wichita campaign, the *Bray* case was still pending; therefore, the Justice Department tried, with little success, to argue that its intervention in Wichita was not an effort to help sustain Operation Rescue's latest campaign but an attempt to buttress its support for the constitutional issues raised in the *Bray* case.

In spite of the Bush administration's actions, Kelly's directive still held, and the U.S. marshals were under orders to carry it out. But Kelly now felt besieged from all sides, and he viewed Washington's intervention as a personal betrayal. After an expletive-filled meeting in his chambers, Kelly gave the local U.S. attorney a public tongue-lashing in court: "I am disgusted with this move by the United States, that it would now put an imprimatur on this conduct, and I will ask you to please report that to the attorney general personally."

Burning with anger even after that tirade and needing to vent more steam, Kelly took the inappropriate step of granting an interview about a pending case by agreeing to appear on ABC's *Nightline* to discuss the protests. He said he wanted to send a message directly to Attorney General Richard Thornburgh.

In the live interview, Kelly angrily charged the Justice Department with giving its "imprimatur" to "a license for mayhem" and added that if he had not issued his court injunction, there would be "blood in the streets." In his interview, Kelly had crossed the line of acceptable behavior for a sitting federal judge, and after the protests were over, the Tenth U.S. Circuit Court of Appeals not only overturned his injunction but also admonished him for his television appearance. However, his *Nightline* appeal seemed to bring the public to his defense; on August 11, a survey found that more than 75 percent of those polled in the Wichita area said they approved of Judge Kelly's handling of the case.

The television interview also prompted as many as three hundred hate calls a day for the next several weeks. "They were vicious," Kelly recalls. The judge reluctantly agreed to accept twenty-four-hour protection from the U.S. marshal's service after a protester confronted him while on a walk in his own neighborhood.

Terry and Tucci left Wichita on August 7, promising to return later that month. By August 8, Joe Foreman had arrived, fresh from a five-month jail term in Atlanta, and with him came his penchant for dangerous and extreme tactics. The protests had hit a lull, but he vowed to restart clinic blockades in Wichita as soon as possible. Foreman was now a freelancer with no real authority in Operation Rescue, but with Terry and Tucci briefly out of town and the protest campaign veering from one crisis to the next, he was able temporarily to take the helm once more.

With Foreman in the lead, clinic blockades began again the next day, with ugly results. Shortly before noon, a fifteen-year-old girl and five of her seven brothers and sisters, one as young as ten, ran into the street and sat down in front of a car trying to enter Tiller's clinic. The children's mother, who had brought the family from Ypsilanti, Michigan, sat down with them, angering both the marshals and state welfare officials, who charged that the protests were endangering children.

The tactics seemed to convince authorities once and for all that patience and tolerance did not work with Operation Rescue. Marshals and Wichita police worked together that day to carry off the protesters brusquely and swiftly, clearing Tiller's entrance in just seven minutes. Backed by barricades, a line of U.S. marshals now stood vigil to keep the protesters far from the clinic entrances. However, the hardened approach by the police and marshals seemed only to fuel the protesters' desire. On August 20, their pent-up energy was unleashed when dozens of activists rushed Tiller's gate, more than thirty of them scaling a six-foot fence and pushing past the marshals into the clinic's parking lot.

They were quickly rounded up and arrested, but the invasion was the final straw for Kelly. Through clenched teeth, he declared from the bench that afternoon that "it is over." He ordered Terry, Tucci, Mahoney, and Joseph Slovenec, another Operation Rescue leader, all arrested. Terry and Mahoney had flown to Kennebunkport, Maine, in an unsuccessful bid to see President Bush to gain his support, and Mahoney was arrested when he returned to Wichita. Kelly jailed Tucci, Mahoney, and Slovenec and fined them $10,000 each plus $500 a day for the next ten days. He added that he would order their personal assets and those of Operation Rescue's seized at the end of the ten days if the fines were not paid. Under threat of imminent arrest, Terry did not return to Wichita until September, when Phil Donahue came to town to tape a program about the protests.

On August 24, with Kelly's edict in place and the protest campaign finally beginning to wind down, abortion-rights activists staged a "Speak Out for Choice" rally in downtown Wichita. Eleanor Smeal, head of the Feminist Majority Foundation, was scheduled to speak, as were Patricia Ireland, president-elect of the National Organization for Women, and National Abortion Rights Action League director Kate Michelman. The rally was to begin with remarks by Tiller's spokeswoman, Peggy Jarman, followed by the featured speakers in alphabetical order. An argument erupted, however, when Smeal and Ireland, afraid the media would leave before they got on stage, demanded to be moved up in the program. Jarman did not budge.

The ninety-minute rally drew more than five thousand supporters, who chanted slogans like "Randall Terry, go to jail; we're pro-choice and we'll prevail." During their speeches, both Ireland and Smeal called for confrontations with the protesters in the streets. "We're going to go toe-to-toe with these bullies," Ireland said, something Jarman and her group had been trying to avoid for weeks. In interviews after the rally, the national leaders criticized the way the local abortion-rights groups had handled the protests.

That afternoon, Jarman and Smeal had it out. "She accused me of not caring about women around the country and not taking responsibility for reproductive freedom anywhere except in my own backyard," Jarman said, adding that Smeal told one reporter that "I believe you are required to confront evil or you will allow that evil to flourish." When Jarman heard that, she retorted, "It sounds like a Randall Terry quote to me."

The "Summer of Mercy" ended on Sunday, August 25, with one last flourish, a rally that attracted more than twenty-five thousand people at Wichita State University's football stadium. The featured speaker was Pat Robertson, who had just launched the Christian Coalition, and who was clearly impressed by the passionate support that Operation Rescue had found in Wichita.

"We submit today that we will not rest until every baby in the United States of America is safe in his mother's womb," Robertson told the cheering crowd. "Ladies and gentlemen, we will not rest until this land we love so much is truly, once again, one nation under God."

The three-and-a-half-hour event was a remarkable hybrid: part religious revival, part political rally. As Operation Rescue's supporters filed into the stadium, a plane flew overhead, trailing a sign that read "Go home! Wichita is pro-choice!" The crowd began chanting, "We *are* home! We *are* home!"

Kelly may have ultimately run them out of town, but Operation Rescue's leaders could still claim victory; the energy channeled into Wichita during the protests spilled over into the political arena, at least in Kansas. The Religious Right's biggest victory in Kansas in the 1992 elections was the takeover of the Sedgwick County Republican Party, which began during the protests when Mark Gietzen, head of the Kansas Republican Coalition for Life, went to Operation Rescue rallies to sign up recruits to run for precinct committee positions. Eighty-three percent of the new committee members elected in the 1992 Republican primary were abortion foes. Two weeks after the election, Gietzen's recruits took over the party's central committee leadership, and Gietzen became the party's new county chairman. Conservative Republican Todd Tiahrt also relied heavily on volunteer workers recruited during Operation Rescue rallies to power his 1992 upset win over Wichita's Democratic congressman, Dan Glickman.

More broadly, of course, Wichita put anti-abortion protest back into the national headlines for the first time in nearly two years, thanks to a new cadre of fundamentalist supporters. Terry appeared engaged in Operation Rescue once again, and he and Tucci soon announced plans to target a string of cities for "Wichita-style" protest campaigns. Operation Rescue found, however, that Wichita could not be repeated. When it tried to do so in Buffalo, New York, in April 1992, billing its "Spring of Life" campaign as "bigger than Wichita," Operation Rescue was defeated.

The action in Buffalo was met not only by another federal court injunction, but also by a police force with strict and consistent orders to keep the city's clinics open and by hundreds of militant clinic defenders from all over the country who had come to Buffalo to prevent a repeat of the Wichita debacle. This time, the clinic defenders did not ask for permission from local clinic administrators as they had in Wichita. Instead, Kathy Spillar, the clinic-defense leader for Smeal's Feminist Majority Foundation, simply showed up and deployed her forces. Clinic defenders in Buffalo used the most aggressive tactics ever employed to thwart Operation Rescue, including forming human circles around Operation Rescue leaders while following them and screaming in their faces. But it was effective. "Wichita sent the lesson that you can't give an inch or they will take a mile," a satisfied Smeal told reporters in Buffalo. "We're going to be wherever Operation Rescue is, in bigger numbers."

Buffalo's failed "Spring of Life" was followed by a string of unsuccessful Operation Rescue campaigns in cities like Baton Rouge and Houston. Unable to keep up the momentum gained from Wichita, Terry lost interest again and began to focus his attention on launching a radio talk show. Under Tucci, Operation Rescue slowly crumbled.

In hindsight, Terry now acknowledges that Wichita was Operation

Rescue's last chance, and that anti-abortion activism was doomed after the movement failed to exploit its brief success in Wichita to win over more churches and church leaders. The turning point came, Terry believes, when Kelly threatened to target churches and their pastors in Wichita for legal action if they continued to support Operation Rescue; after that, fundamentalist church leaders backed off from the protests, and Operation Rescue never won them over again.

"We [fundamentalists] lost our nerve," Terry says now. "And the game was over. The window of opportunity was closed. . . . It was in my mind that we must somehow harness this [energy] and turn it into a political movement, and for whatever reasons, we did not do that and others did." Political compromisers, such as the Christian Coalition's Ralph Reed, whom Terry has publicly vilified, took control of the Religious Right in the mid-1990s and directed fundamentalists into mainstream Republican politics. Terry's hopes for a "Christian" revolution were dashed. "I believe that some of those who did [harness the energy] have polluted the message, diluted the message, compromised the message, and are raising up bureaucrats," he adds.

Just two months after Operation Rescue's disappointment in Buffalo, the Supreme Court dealt what turned out to be a final blow to the anti-abortion movement in its landmark decision in *Planned Parenthood of Southeastern Pennsylvania v. Casey*. The *Casey* ruling ended any lingering public doubts about whether *Roe* would be overturned, and brought to a close the twelve-year struggle throughout the Reagan and Bush eras over the Supreme Court's position on abortion.

Casey stemmed from a law enacted in Pennsylvania after the Supreme Court's *Webster* ruling in 1989 gave states greater latitude to regulate and restrict abortion. Pennsylvania was one of a handful of states to take advantage of *Webster* to impose new restrictions. Its tough new law came with a blizzard of new regulations, requiring, among other things, that abortion providers counsel women on the risks of abortion and then obtain patients' written consent to perform the abortion; that women wait twenty-four hours after giving written consent before obtaining an abortion; that minors obtain the consent of at least one parent or a judge; that married women, except in certain circumstances, notify their husbands; and that abortion providers file state reports on all abortions performed.

Planned Parenthood promptly sued to stop the law, and the case began a lengthy journey through the federal courts. For very different reasons, abortion-rights advocates, the state of Pennsylvania, and the Bush administration all urged the Supreme Court to make a decisive ruling in *Casey* that would end the uncertainty over abortion in a way that *Webster* had failed to do.

As it had in *Webster*, the Bush administration again filed an amicus brief asking the Court to use *Casey* to overturn *Roe,* and anti-abortion forces seemed to have good reason to hope that *Casey* might go their way. Since *Webster*, two Bush appointees had joined the Court: David Souter and Clarence Thomas. Also, in a 1991 decision in the case of *Rust v. Sullivan*, Souter had sided with the conservative majority led by Chief Justice William Rehnquist to uphold a federal "gag rule" preventing personnel at family planning clinics receiving federal funds from counseling on abortion.

When the ruling on *Casey* came out on the last day of the Court's term, June 29, 1992, it was instead a devastating blow to the anti-abortion movement. Three Reagan-Bush appointees—Sandra Day O'Connor, Anthony Kennedy, and Souter—formed a decisive centrist coalition and issued a strong endorsement of *Roe*. Although they upheld almost all of Pennsylvania's regulations (striking down only the spousal notification provision), O'Connor, Kennedy, and Souter used *Casey* to state forcefully that "the essential holding of *Roe v. Wade* should be retained and once again reaffirmed."

Stating that doubt and uncertainty over a critical issue like abortion undermined the Court's credibility, the three issued a ruling that offered clear parameters for legal abortion in the United States. Their plurality opinion recognized "the right of the woman to choose to have an abortion before viability and to obtain it without undue interference from the State. Before viability, the State's interests are not strong enough to support a prohibition of abortion or the imposition of a substantial obstacle to the woman's effective right to elect the procedure."

Their opinion went on to restate the limits placed on abortion after viability that were included in *Roe*. Although the ruling did not try to determine the point at which viability occurs, it did help clarify *Roe* by stating that the Court would grant great flexibility in efforts to regulate postviability abortions. The opinion provided "confirmation of the State's power to restrict abortions after fetal viability, if the law contains exceptions for pregnancies which endanger a woman's life or health," adding that a final tenet of their decision was "the principle that the State has legitimate interests from the outset of the pregnancy in protecting the health of the woman and the life of the fetus that may become a child. These principles do not contradict one another; and we adhere to each."

Harry Blackmun, nearing the end of his long career on the bench and always protective of his most famous decision, praised O'Connor, Souter, and Kennedy for their "act of personal courage and constitutional principle." Most abortion-rights advocates were more critical, however, focusing on the trio's broad acceptance of state abortion regulation and their construction of a new standard of review that allowed restrictions on abortion prior to viability as long as they did not constitute an "undue burden" on the woman.

Such criticism missed the point. O'Connor, Kennedy, and Souter had accomplished a rare judicial feat: They had placed the Supreme Court in sync with the rough national consensus. By the early 1990s, that consensus was more clearly defined than ever before: Abortion should be legal and available upon demand, but the government should be able to regulate the procedure and severely restrict its use for minors and in late-term pregnancies, when the fetus might be able to live outside the womb. If *Casey* imposed new restrictions, it could be argued that the ruling was merely filling in the blanks left by *Roe*, because Blackmun's decision had been structured to allow state regulation after viability.

Anti-abortion leaders certainly had no illusions about *Casey*'s impact, and a sense of betrayal by the Reagan-Bush appointees quickly ran through the movement. That anger was soon overtaken by a sense of foreboding at the prospect of a liberal Democrat in the White House, following Arkansas governor Bill Clinton's defeat of Bush in the 1992 presidential election. Bush had never been considered a reliable ally by anti-abortion leaders, but Clinton was the first strong abortion-rights advocate ever elected to the presidency. Coming just months after *Casey*, Clinton's election seemed to underscore the degree to which the nation had come to terms with *Roe*. Clinton seemed to give voice to the new national consensus when he told voters he wanted to keep abortion "safe, legal, and rare."

Once in office, Clinton began to roll back Reagan-Bush anti-abortion policies almost immediately. Two days after his inauguration in January 1993, he signed executive orders repealing the Title X "gag rule" on abortion counseling, a ban on fetal tissue research, and a ban on performing abortions at overseas military bases.

That same month, the Supreme Court finally issued a ruling in Operation Rescue's long-pending challenge to federal court injunctions prohibiting clinic blockades. In *Bray v. Alexandria Women's Health Clinic*, the case stemming from the DC Project of November 1989, the Court surprisingly ruled in Operation Rescue's favor, saying that the Ku Klux Klan Act of 1871 could not be used by federal judges, as it had been in Wichita, to stop abortion protesters from blocking clinic access. The Court held that the Klan Act, a product of the Reconstruction Era, when Congress was trying to prevent Southern whites from terrorizing newly freed blacks, did not protect women seeking abortions as a class. In the *Bray* case, the Court held in a 6–3 decision that Operation Rescue was not motivated by "discriminatory animus" against women but rather by concern for "the innocent victims" of abortion.

Randall Terry was briefly elated by Operation Rescue's first Supreme Court victory: "I feel like I've won the Super Bowl," he told a reporter in Binghamton. But the *Bray* decision came too late; court orders, fines, and injunctions had long since taken their toll, and by 1993 the movement was once again badly fragmented. Wichita marked the last time that anti-abortion activists successfully united to work in a nationally coordinated event. With Clinton's election, anti-abortion militants now felt disenfranchised and increasingly were willing to follow extremists like Foreman into radical fringe groups. Within two years of Wichita, what was left of the movement was dominated by extremists who refused to place any limits on direct action to stop abortion.

The seeds for this virulent new form of anti-abortion extremism had, of course, been sewn in Wichita, thanks to Tucci's decision to personalize the battle and target Tiller for harassment. Before long, fringe groups were publishing "wanted posters" for doctors. After Wichita, abortion doctors everywhere became targets of similar, organized campaigns of personal harassment. And, as Tucci and other activist leaders cited biblical passages describing the punishment deserved by Tiller and other "murderers" they had identified by name, their followers soon began to draw their own conclusions.

14

A TIME TO KILL

Michael Griffin fervently believed that his accidental encounter with abortion doctor David Gunn was a sign from God. On the morning of March 5, 1993, Griffin, a thirty-one-year-old factory worker in Pensacola, Florida, and a zealous follower of local anti-abortion leader John Burt, pulled into a Pensacola Exxon station, and there was Gunn. The doctor, well known to anti-abortion activists in the area, was sitting in his car drinking coffee and reading a newspaper before heading to work at The Ladies Center, the local clinic that had so often served as ground zero for the anti-abortion movement in the South. The clinic, run by the headstrong Linda Taggart, had in earlier years been invaded by Burt and Joan Andrews and bombed by Matthew Goldsby and James Simmons.

"I thought it was Providence," Griffin now says, revealing his meeting with Gunn for the first time in an exclusive prison interview. "I knew he was getting ready to go kill children that day. I asked the Lord what he wanted me to do. And he told me to tell him that he had one more chance."

Griffin walked over to Gunn's car and tapped on the window. "I said, 'Are you David Gunn?' and he told me to go away. I went back to my car, but I felt the Lord told me to warn him. So I walked back and knocked on his window. And I looked him right in the face and said, 'David Gunn, the Lord told me to tell you that you have one more chance.' He just looked at me."

For five hours that afternoon, Griffin stood outside The Ladies Center waiting for Gunn to leave. "As soon as he came out," Griffin recalls, "I felt like I had another word from the Lord for him: that he was accused and convicted of murder and that his sentence was Genesis 9:6. Then, right before he got in his car, I said, 'David Gunn, are you going to kill children next week?'" Griffin claims that Gunn replied by saying, "Yeah. Probably."

Five days later, Griffin fired three .38-caliber bullets into Gunn's back as the doctor got out of his car in the parking lot behind the offices of the city's other abortion clinic, Pensacola Women's Medical Services. The Bible verse Griffin had relayed to him the Friday before: "Whosoever sheds man's blood, by man his blood shall be shed."

Michael Griffin's murder of David Gunn was to have a swift and terrible impact on America's abortion war.

Nothing in Michael Griffin's past suggested he would become enmeshed in the violence-soaked anti-abortion fringe. Born and raised in Pensacola, Griffin was the youngest child of a prominent local dentist; a mainline Methodist, he grew up believing that abortion was a rational option for women. After his parents divorced, Griffin attended Pensacola Junior College; in 1981 he joined the Navy, with his girlfriend, Patricia Presley, pregnant. Griffin considered abortion—acquaintances say he and his family were leaning toward that option—but the couple decided to get married five weeks before their daughter Ashley was born. A second daughter, Bethany, was born in 1984.

In the Navy, Griffin was assigned to submarine duty, and he consistently received good reviews from his supervisors, according to Navy personnel records later attached to police files in his criminal case. By the time of his 1987 discharge, Griffin was a nuclear power plant supervisor on the USS *Whale*. In 1989, he was hired at Monsanto's Pensacola plant and by 1992 was earning a comfortable $40,000 a year.

It was not until the late 1980s that Griffin became immersed in fundamentalism and began attending the Brownsville Assembly of God Church in Pensacola, which later became the scene of the largest fundamentalist revival in recent U.S. history. A church shopper, Griffin later switched to the smaller Charity Chapel of Pensacola. Despite his new and intense interest in religion, Griffin was clearly becoming emotionally troubled. In April 1991, Patricia Griffin left Michael and, alleging abuse, won a restraining order against him.

On August 12, 1991, police were sent to the home of Patricia Griffin's parents on a family disturbance call. According to their report, Michael Griffin had gone there to pick up his daughters and had called police to complain that Patricia's parents were taking care of the children. He accused his wife of taking drugs without a prescription and demanded that police go into the house and get his children. The report said that Griffin battered his mother-in-law during the altercation, pushing her down as he attempted to take the children. Police issued Griffin a trespassing warning. Patricia's mother filed a complaint against Griffin, but the charges were later dropped at her request. Two days after the incident at his in-laws' home, Griffin filed for divorce, asking for joint custody of his daughters, then ages eleven and eight. Patricia Griffin filed a counterpetition asking for sole custody. The following March, however, the couple got back together and their divorce case was dismissed.

In late 1992, the Griffins heard about Our Father's House, John Burt's home for troubled and pregnant girls, and Patricia Griffin called to volunteer her husband's services. On January 9, 1993, while Griffin was doing some handyman jobs at Our Father's House, Burt and fellow activist Donnie Gratton arrived with a big-screen television. They set it up in the living room, where Michael, Patricia, and the Griffins' two children—who were visiting that day—could watch, and inserted *The Hard Truth,* a graphic video that depicts an abortion.

The video had a profound impact on Griffin. "I never really thought about abortion after we had decided to have Ashley. But this was an injection of the truth. It slapped me in the face." Burt gave Griffin copies of that video and another, called *Who Will Cry for Me: A Song for David,* which showed a woman preparing an aborted fetus for a funeral. Burt also showed the Griffins some aborted fetuses he kept in a jar of saline solution in his office.

Twelve days later, the Griffins took a five-hour weapons training program conducted by the Pensacola Police Department. Both received top marks. That same week, on the twentieth anniversary of the *Roe v. Wade* decision, Burt conducted a burial and memorial service for what he claimed were two aborted fetuses. Griffin attended the service and, deeply affected, decided he needed to do something; he soon joined Burt and other protesters outside The Ladies Center. One of Burt's props for his protests was an effigy of David Gunn. Almost life-size, the effigy depicted Gunn wearing scrubs and bloody gloves. Inscribed on it was a Bible verse: Genesis 9:6.

The real David Gunn was a slight man of forty-seven from Kentucky who had walked with a limp ever since his leg was crippled by polio as a child. A graduate of the medical school of the University of Kentucky, Gunn was an obstetrician who had been delivering babies at a hospital in Brewton, Alabama, before deciding to devote his practice to abortion.

Anti-abortion harassment, the relatively low pay, and the social stigma attached to abortion medicine had by the early 1990s led to a worsening shortage of abortion doctors around the nation; therefore, David Gunn's services were in demand throughout the South. He had become a "circuit rider," a doctor who scurried from one clinic to another in small and medium-sized cities throughout the region; he performed abortions in Georgia, Alabama, and Florida, sometimes covering two cities in one day. In Pensacola, he was the sole doctor for both of the city's clinics.

Despite the escalating harassment from the anti-abortion movement, Gunn tried hard to lead a normal life, refusing to wear a bulletproof vest or even carry a cellular phone. Gunn felt so strongly about a woman's right to have an abortion that he lectured patients about the importance of registering to vote. "He had seen, before the laws changed, all these women ending up in the emergency rooms, and he'd seen too many die from botched abortions," recalls The Ladies Center administrator Linda Taggart. "He just couldn't stand it. He just felt that this had to be done right."

By the time Gunn became the target of Pensacola's anti-abortion activists, John Burt, the local movement's leader and Michael Griffin's mentor, had become an old hand at stirring up trouble. After being placed on four years' probation for his role in the 1986 invasion of The Ladies Center with Joan Andrews, Burt was arrested again in May 1988 for his alleged involvement in a clinic-bombing plot. In that case, anti-abortion extremist John Brockhoeft of Hebron, Kentucky, who had been visiting Burt, was arrested near The Ladies Center with explosives in his car after his alarmed wife informed law enforcement officials of his intentions. Brockhoeft was convicted on bomb charges and was later tied to a string of previously unsolved clinic bombings and arsons in Ohio. Burt, meanwhile, was sentenced to two years of house arrest for violating his probation by showing Brockhoeft the clinic's location, although he has steadfastly denied any knowledge of Brockhoeft's bombing plans.

After his house arrest was over, Burt went right back to targeting The Ladies Center. In 1991, he purchased a horseshoe-shaped piece of land that encircled the clinic's parking lot, which allowed his followers to talk to—or shout at—clinic patients without trespassing on clinic property. The clinic responded by erecting an eight-foot fence, but Burt retaliated by building scaffolding on which he set up a wide-screen television and videocassette recorder that constantly and loudly ran anti-abortion tapes.

By early 1993, Burt and other abortion foes were planning their first protest at the new offices of the city's other abortion clinic, Pensacola Women's Medical Services in Cordova Square. Michael Griffin was one of Burt's newest acolytes, and he had even begun to attend Burt's fundamentalist church, Whitfield Assembly of God. On Sunday, March 7, Griffin sat in the front row during church services. When the call went out for prayer requests, according to Burt, Griffin stood up and said, "Would you agree with me in prayer that David Gunn should get saved and stop killing babies?" The congregation then joined Griffin in a prayer for David Gunn's soul.

Three mornings later, David Gunn was dead. The only doctor who performed abortions regularly in Escambia County, Florida, had just become a martyr in America's abortion war.

B y drawing blood, Michael Griffin changed forever the shape and direction of the anti-abortion movement, prompting the first open debate among activists over whether the use of violence was justified. Ironically, only two months earlier, the Supreme Court had finally issued a landmark decision that expanded the movement's right to use nonviolent civil disobedience. In January 1993, the Supreme Court ruled in favor of Operation Rescue in the *Bray* case, striking down the ability of federal judges to impose federal court injunctions against Operation Rescue–style clinic blockades and banning the use of the old

Ku Klux Klan Act as the legal basis for those preemptive orders. It was the most significant legal victory in the history of anti-abortion activism, yet it came too late. Operation Rescue was by then no longer a powerful force and so could not exploit the ruling. Griffin's murder of Gunn in March 1993 ended all hope that the movement could regain credibility or influence through nonviolent civil disobedience.

After Gunn's murder, activists became frustrated by the collapse of Operation Rescue and the rise of Bill Clinton and a national consensus in favor of abortion rights; they were increasingly willing to say yes to "justifiable" violence and to say it in public. Within hours of Gunn's shooting, Rescue America, a Houston-based anti-abortion group run by Don Treshman, a longtime ally of Joseph Scheidler, issued a press release that set the tone for the movement's response to Gunn's killing. Rescue America asked that donations to Griffin's family, not Gunn's, be sent to John Burt's post office box. Other anti-abortion groups across the country, including Operation Rescue, issued only tepid statements of opposition to Griffin's action, severely damaging the credibility of anti-abortion activism. "While we grieve for [Gunn] and for his widow and for his children, we must also grieve for the thousands of children that he has murdered," said Randall Terry.

After Gunn's killing, Operation Rescue veteran Andrew Burnett wrote that "the death of an abortionist has caused me to re-examine my own convictions. Was his life really more valuable than the lives of his thousands of victims?" Griffin had ripped back the curtain to reveal the dark side of the movement's soul, and with pacifists like John O'Keefe and Sam Lee long gone from the leadership ranks, there were no counter-balancing forces within the movement pushing for peace.

Griffin flushed the extremist fringe out into the open; inevitably, Michael Bray reemerged, assuming the role of national spokesperson for violence and retribution. Soon, Bray's *A Time to Kill,* a book advocating the murder of doctors, became must reading among extremists. John O'Keefe's *A Peaceful Presence* was forgotten, shoved to the back of bookshelves to gather dust.

Bray and former Operation Rescue leaders Joe Foreman and Burnett joined forces, envisioning the creation of a national extremist network, while doing their best to stay out of jail themselves. Their new network began to take shape at the 1993 annual convention of Joseph Scheidler's old group, the Pro-Life Action Network, which in the wake of Operation Rescue's collapse was finding new life as a refuge for extremists. Bray and Burnett were the featured speakers at the convention; Burnett opened by discussing Gunn's shooting and explaining that his earlier opposition to the killing of abortion doctors may have been wrong. Bray, referring to Gunn's murder, told those attending that "churches are afraid to proclaim the truth." Gunn's death resulted in life for his intended "victims," Bray said. Then he cited a Bible verse that was becoming a familiar one among supporters of justifiable homicide: Genesis 9:6.

The day after the Gunn shooting, two U.S. representatives and several abortion-rights groups called for an immediate FBI probe into clinic violence; that same day, shortly after she was confirmed by the Senate in a 98–0 vote, incoming attorney general Janet Reno said the federal government would look into the shooting. But on March 19, after seventeen U.S. senators asked the FBI to investigate a "pattern of harassment" by abortion opponents at clinics across the country, the FBI, still reluctant to become embroiled in what its leaders saw as a political controversy, said it could do nothing under current law. To force a broad response by federal law enforcement officers, abortion-rights supporters in Congress would have to pass a new law to give the FBI the legal cover it demanded. Soon, frightened doctors around the country were wearing bulletproof vests, packing guns, and hiring bodyguards. Within ten days of Gunn's murder, three abortion doctors quit their practices.

Paul Hill, a fundamentalist preacher with a fixed and eerie smile, was so excited by Michael Griffin's actions that he was bursting with desire to talk about it. On March 12, he walked to a pay phone, and within twenty minutes he had a producer from *Donahue* on the line. Hill was not a prominent leader in the anti-abortion movement at the time, but his pro-Griffin zeal was apparently just what the *Donahue* producers wanted for a show on anti-abortion violence. *Donahue* eagerly and irresponsibly jumped at the chance to put Hill on the air, and on March 15, he appeared on the show with an abortion doctor, two abortion-rights activists, and David Gunn's son. Hill proclaimed on national television that the murder of David Gunn was "as good as Doctor Mengele being killed."

It's not too strong to say that *Donahue* created Paul Hill as a national symbol of anti-abortion extremism. Hill soon realized that the more outrageous his statements, the more attention he could garner both from the media and within the anti-abortion movement, and he became associated with slogans like "execute murderers, abortionists, accessories." It was not long before he was being asked by interviewers and by other activists the inevitable question: If you believe so strongly in killing doctors, why don't you do it yourself? At first, Hill's cautious response was that he was called to "minister" to those who killed, not to kill himself. But the baiting questions, asked repeatedly in both public and private, clearly gnawed at Hill.

In Chicago, Joe Scheidler was initially suspicious of Hill, but he soon began to offer quiet encouragement. On April 29, 1993, Scheidler wrote to Hill, telling him that "it took guts" to defend Gunn's shooting. "Your arguments are strong and from a biblical perspective quite convincing, but you can be sure they won't be accepted in a U.S. Court of Law," Scheidler told him.

Operation Rescue and local activist leaders in Pensacola feared that Hill was either an FBI plant or mentally unbalanced, and they sought to distance themselves from him. Many insisted that there was no evidence that Hill had any prior involvement in the movement. But research shows that in 1987, Hill had received Mississippi Right to Life's Friend of the Year Award for being "the first and most active Jackson area pro-lifer who protested the evil of abortion at the abortion facilities of this city." Mason Swinney, president of the Jackson Right to Life chapter, said that Hill "paved the way; he was the pathfinder of our present day rescue missions." If others in the movement claimed they knew nothing of Hill, that was not the case with Scheidler; at the banquet in Jackson where Hill was honored, Scheidler had been the guest speaker.

Born in 1954, Paul Hill was the youngest son of an airline flight engineer and was raised in one of south Florida's most affluent enclaves, Coral Gables. He proved to be trouble for his parents, however; at seventeen, he was arrested for assaulting his father, and his parents filed charges in order to get their son treatment for a drug problem. Later that year, Hill says now, he had a born-again experience, "and from that moment on, my life went through a dramatic change."

After high school, Hill enrolled at Belhaven College, a Presbyterian school in Jackson, Mississippi, where he majored in Bible studies. He went on to the Reformed Theological Seminary, also in Jackson, studying under Greg Bahnsen, a leader in the radical new Reconstructionist movement. Hill now considers himself a Reconstructionist.

Hill's anti-abortion fervor was fueled during his time at the seminary. After viewing Francis Schaeffer and C. Everett Koop's *Whatever Happened to the Human Race?* film series, he began picketing and sidewalk counseling in Jackson. By 1984, Hill had been ordained in the Presbyterian Church in America before switching to the more conservative Orthodox Presbyterian Church, serving in churches in South Carolina and Florida. His ministerial career came to a halt, however, when he had a falling-out with his Florida church congregation after he decided that infants should receive Communion, something almost unheard of in Reformed Presbyterian churches. In 1991, he moved his wife, Karen, and their three children to Pensacola, and he began attending a small church in nearby Valparaiso that accepted his beliefs.

By October 1992, Hill was running a small auto-detailing business, and his family was able to move from an apartment into a comfortable white-brick ranch-style house in Pensacola. Hill was soon earning enough that he could afford to spend time outside the city's abortion clinics. Just six weeks before Gunn was killed, Hill began picketing for the first time.

After Gunn's death, Hill began working on a paper in defense of justifiable homicide. Following his appearance on *Donahue,* he became embroiled in an angry debate with his church elders over his violent views, and by May 1993, he was excommunicated. The rejection by his church did not stop Hill; he was now obsessed with anti-abortion violence, and he soon circulated his first paper, "Should We Defend Born and Unborn Children with Force?" Andrew Burnett's extremist publication in Portland, Oregon, *Life Advocate* magazine, helped spread Hill's views by printing a shortened version of his paper and telling readers how to contact Hill.

As Hill's radical reputation spread, he attracted the attention of Foreman, Bray, and Burnett, and he was soon serving as a kind of figurehead to propagate their extremist ideas. In fact, both Foreman and Bray quietly helped Hill write his "Defensive Action" petition endorsing violence. In an interview, Foreman revealed that he had helped Hill draft the statement, but said that after giving Hill the go-ahead to include his name on the petition, he realized that it would "take on a life of its own," so he carefully withdrew his signature.

About thirty other activists did sign the statement, including the Reverend David Trosch, a Catholic priest in Alabama whose involvement in the new extremism was to become a source of embarrassment for the American Catholic Church.

As soon as she returned from Gunn's funeral in Tennessee, Linda Taggart faced the difficult task of finding a new abortion doctor for The Ladies Center. Nearly two dozen doctors turned her down before Taggart finally found John Britton, a sixty-eight-year-old doctor from Jacksonville, Florida. Britton's record was blemished—he had been disciplined over the years by his hospital and by Florida medical authorities for conduct that included improper prescription of painkillers—but many of his patients described him as a competent, compassionate doctor who made house calls and treated poor people for free. Britton was performing abortions in the Jacksonville area and still operating his small medical practice when he began filling in at The Ladies Center. He showed up for work in a homemade bulletproof vest.

Hill, Burt, and other local activists, undeterred by Gunn's murder, spent the next four months working to "out" the tall, gaunt man who answered to "Bayard" and "Doc" and drove to work in a beat-up pickup. Britton's identity remained a tightly guarded secret, however, until August 6, 1993, when Burt, Hill, Donnie Gratton, Mike and Vicky Conroy, and Floyd Murray decided to try to identify the new doctor so they could issue a "wanted poster" for him. They stayed outside the clinic all afternoon, sitting in the driveway with their cameras. Somehow, the doctor slipped away unnoticed.

On his way home, however, Murray pulled into a highway rest stop and saw Britton in the parking lot; Britton had stopped to pull off his bulletproof vest and store his gun in the back of his truck. Murray quickly wrote down Britton's license plate number, and activist Mike Conroy fed the number into the publicly available database of the Florida motor vehicle department; out popped Britton's name and his address near Jacksonville.

Burt and Gratton then drove to Britton's home to let him know his secret was out. On his doorstep, they left a pamphlet entitled *What Would You Do If You Had Five Minutes Left to Live?* When they returned to Pensacola, they made an "unwanted poster," naming Britton as the new doctor. The poster included Britton's home and office addresses and phone numbers, a picture of Britton's house, a description of his pickup, and his license plate number.

After he was "outed," Britton stopped driving back and forth to Pensacola and began flying. On the fourth Friday of each month, he was met at the airport by Jim and June Barrett, members of a local Unitarian church that had begun a clinic escort service at The Ladies Center after Gunn's shooting. Jim Barrett was a seventy-four-year-old retired lieutenant colonel in the Air Force, and June, sixty-eight, was a former nurse and retired U.S. Public Health Service captain.

It did not take long for others to heed Hill's call to launch "justifiable" attacks on abortion providers. In August 1993, Rachelle Ranae (Shelley) Shannon, an impressionable thirty-seven-year-old Oregon housewife who had joined in Operation Rescue's "Summer of Mercy" protests in Wichita in 1991, boarded a bus in her hometown of Grants Pass, Oregon. Shannon told her nineteen-year-old daughter, Angi, that she was heading for an out-of-town protest and would be home in a few days. There was nothing out of the ordinary about that; Shannon had by then become enmeshed in the small, floating "rescue" subculture that had been created in Operation Rescue's wake. But it was a subculture that was just beginning to provide the shock troops for a dangerous new brand of anti-abortion extremism advocated by Michael Bray, Andrew Burnett, and Joseph Foreman. The next time Shannon's family saw her was on television four days later, a towel covering her head as she was escorted to jail, charged with attempted first-degree murder in the August 19 shooting of Wichita abortion doctor George Tiller.

Shannon's transformation from a housewife participating in mainstream protest to a radical member of a violent new underground was, in many ways, a metaphor for the decline and fall of the anti-abortion movement itself.

Born in Wisconsin in 1956, Rachelle Ranae Pauli was the second of seven children in a nomadic blue-collar family; her parents divorced in 1969. While just a junior in high school, Shelley became pregnant by a boyfriend and gave birth to Angela. After graduating, Shelley loaded her car and headed for Bellingham, Washington, to start a new life with her baby. Near Wenatchee, Washington, she stopped to pick up a hitchhiker. Her passenger, David Shannon, would soon become her husband. After marriage, David joined the Marines, and it was while living at Camp Lejeune in North Carolina that Shelley found and read a Gideon Bible and had a "born again" experience.

Over the next decade, Shelley and David were just as nomadic as her parents had been; they were constantly on the move from state to state, stopping wherever both David and Shelley could find work. They finally settled down in Grants Pass, and it was there in 1988 that Shelley discovered the anti-abortion cause; a friend had sent her a newsletter from Melody Green's Last Days Ministries in Texas, the same fundamentalist group that had provided Randall Terry with his graphic, anti-abortion literature when he started Project Life in Binghamton, New York. The materials made such an impact on Shannon that she immediately contacted the local Right to Life chapter and began attending its meetings. At her first meeting, Shannon watched an Operation Rescue recruiting video. Afterward, plans for an upcoming clinic blockade in Portland were announced, and Shannon eagerly signed up. She had found her cause.

Shannon and Angi, who was fourteen at the time, were arrested for the first time in February 1988 in the blockade of Portland's Lovejoy Surgicenter. The experience was an exhilarating one, allowing Shannon to escape her mundane personal life, and she soon became a regular at clinic blockades across the country, including Operation Rescue's "siege of Atlanta" in October 1988. Her husband and children did not seem to mind her new obsession or her constant travels. Her son, David Jr., said in an interview that he was happy whenever his mother left town. It gave him a break from her Christian-based home schooling lessons. "When she was gone, I would go to the library and read about what *really* happened," recalls David.

In July 1991, Shannon arrived in Wichita for the "Summer of Mercy" in a caravan of activists from the Pacific Northwest led by Andrew Burnett. On the trip, she had discussed the use of force with Burnett and other activists and had decided that she "was all for it." When extremists like Burnett and Foreman began to drift away from Operation Rescue, Shannon drifted with them; she was arrested in protests staged by Burnett's Advocates for Life in Portland as well as Foreman's Missionaries to the Preborn in Milwaukee.

Shannon also found inspiration from Michael Bray's memoirs, *When Bricks Bleed, I'll Cry*. She found instruction in the art of violence in the

Army of God manual, which describes dozens of illegal activities ranging from how to obtain and use butyric acid to vandalize abortion clinics to how to make and detonate bombs, including the kind used in the Oklahoma City bombing. The manual, which federal law enforcement officials believe first surfaced within activist circles during the "Summer of Mercy" in Wichita, included an ominous warning of violence: "We, the remnant of God-fearing men and women of the United States of Amerika, do officially declare war on the entire child killing industry. . . . Our Most Dread Sovereign Lord God requires that whoso-ever sheds man's blood, by man shall his blood be shed." By the time the third edition of the manual was published, Shannon was helping to edit it on behalf of its anonymous author.

Shannon soon began to correspond regularly with jailed clinic bombers and kidnappers like Curt Beseda, John Brockhoeft, and Don Benny Anderson; receiving their letters in return became the highlight of Shannon's life. According to a 1992 entry in her private diary, which has been under seal in a federal court but which the authors have obtained, she wrote, "GREAT mail! Cards from Curt, Don B. Anderson. . . . Don asked for my phone # to call!! Wow!"

In their letters, the activists explained to Shannon how they had made the transition from peaceful protest to extremism, and they grad-ually began to encourage her to follow the same path. Shannon received special encouragement from convicted clinic arsonist Marjorie Reed. In a March 1992 letter, Reed wrote, "It is going to get a whole lot worse. Blood will be shed, not just the babies' blood either."

Finally, Shannon was ready to act. On April 11, 1992, she secretly set fire to the Catalina Medical Center in Ashland, Oregon, not only caus-ing damages of $379,000 to Dr. Willard Brown's office but damaging adjacent businesses as well. The clinic never reopened. "Ashland art-work," Shannon wrote that day in her diary, referring to the code name she and Marjorie Reed used for clinic arsons.

In a computer document she called "Join the Army," Shannon, using the pseudonym "Shaggy West, A.O.G.," described her crude but effec-tive methods. "I made two little torches by putting four candles with a rubber band on the end of each of two small sticks." She drove to the clinic and threw a jar of gas and two gas-filled milk cartons inside. Then she lit both torches and tossed them in. Nothing happened. She lit a birthday candle and tossed it in. Still nothing. She lit the last candle, "Praying, 'Lord, if you want that fire going, you're going to have to light it.'" The candle landed in a pool of gas and the fire took off. "Praised God all the way home," Shannon wrote. "It was a very powerful religious experience."

Shannon then anonymously distributed her "Join the Army" document to encourage other activists to commit violence against clinics. At the top, she wrote, "Please re-type or photocopy this and burn the copy you were given, with the fingerprints thereof." Less than four months later, on August 1, 1992, Shannon set fire to the Lovejoy Surgicenter in Portland, where she had participated in her first Operation Rescue clinic blockade four years earlier. She described the crime, along with several others, in a computer file she called "Adventures."

Her plan was to throw a jug of gas on the clinic roof, then toss fireworks on top to light it. On July 19, she prepared by reading the *Army of God* manual and received further encouragement in a letter from Marjorie Reed, in whom she had confided. "So you are going on a mission," Reed wrote. "I'll keep you in prayer. I know how you feel when engaging in a life-saving mission, the awe and excitement and some fear and apprehension all at the same time. God Bless. I just pray that there are a lot more."

Shannon's diary and computer files indicate that she drew others into her plans as well. Someone with the code name "A.C." provided her with maps and directions, and her alibi for one arson was to be at the home of "W.P." Anti-abortion activist John Bell later told a grand jury that he was "W.P." and that Shannon often stopped at his home. Bell and his wife, Elaine, were never charged, however, because they had been granted immunity for their testimony.

"Getting ready," Shannon wrote in her dairy just before her attack on the Lovejoy clinic. "Help, God! If I die doing this, I die in Christ, walking obediently in a work He gave me."

Disguised in men's clothes, Shannon carried out the attack on the Lovejoy clinic by throwing jugs filled with gasoline onto the clinic roof, lighting some fireworks, and then throwing them on top of the gasoline. After stopping to spend the night with her friends the Bells, Shannon was disappointed the next morning to learn the fire caused damages of just twenty-five hundred dollars.

"Why no results?" an exasperated Shannon wrote to her friend Michael Bray. Bray responded in a postcard: "Thanks for the good news! Don't be discouraged. 'Little strokes fell mighty oaks,' said Ben Franklin."

Now Shannon was on a roll. David Shannon was working in California for six weeks in August and September, leaving her the car and giving her more freedom than ever. (There is no evidence that Shannon's husband ever knew about her violent activities.) In a letter of August 16, Marjorie Reed wrote from prison, "I would give my right arm to be in that situation—a car, time, money, ideas. . . . What an opportunity. Get certain of us together with the above. What wonders could happen!!"

Shannon decided to hit two clinics at once. On August 17, she drove to Redding and got maps, gas, and jugs from the Bells and then proceeded to Sacramento. Early in the hours of August 18, she used homemade napalm to try and firebomb an office complex that housed the Feminist Women's Health Center of Sacramento. The fire caused damages of about five thousand dollars, but not to the clinic. Shannon later learned that she had instead firebombed the offices of the California Board of Chiropractic Examiners next door.

But Shannon refused to stop. She headed to Reno the same day, where she hit the city's West End Women's Health Group. She tossed jars at the window, but they bounced off. "Plexiglass again!" So she hurled a jug into some wood chips by a window, lit them, and took off, again stopping at the Bells' house on her way home. To Shannon's dismay, damage to the Reno clinic was also minimal.

On September 16, with her husband still working in California, Shannon drove to Eugene, Oregon, where she firebombed the Feminist Women's Health Center with napalm. The fire melted an outdoor plastic water pipe, but the blaze was extinguished before it caused any major damage.

Shannon then drove on to Reno, taking along butyric acid she'd purchased with money from the Bells. Pretending to be a patient, she went into a rest room at the West End Women's Health Group and, using a method identical to one described in the *Army of God* manual, injected butyric acid into the wall with a horse syringe. The noxious fumes spread quickly through the clinic, shutting it down and causing damages of five hundred dollars. Shannon spent the night at a rest stop, then drove to the Feminist Women's Health Center in Chico, California, where she performed a similar acid attack on September 17. The incident caused damages of twenty thousand dollars and closed the clinic for several days.

Shannon returned to Sacramento on November 28, 1992, for her next arson. The fire at the Pregnancy Consultation Center resulted in damages of $175,000 to the clinic and minor injuries to a firefighter. "Glorious, glorious trip," Shannon later wrote in a computer file. "Didn't even care if I made it back, or care so much about getting caught or killed, just wanted to close the place. . . . It was supposed to be a birthday present to Jesus, early for expediency, but I found it was He who gave me a gift."

On the way home, Shannon "kept praying God would burn the place to the ground. Very joyous, worshipful trip back with much singing, prayer and thanksgiving. . . . At rest stops I kicked back and rested in a glorious state of worship, so full of praise. So good. God is so good."

In a letter to Burnett's *Life Advocate* magazine in January 1993, Shannon wrote, "I'm sure the bombers are acting in the will of God, and doubt they would or should stop if a guilty bystander or innocent person is hurt. If they don't act, a lot of people will be killed. Let's pray no one gets hurt, but this is a war and we have to be realistic."

By early 1993, Shannon had evolved into an advocate of what she and others on the fringe called "u.d.r."—ultimate determined rescue— the killing of abortion doctors. "I've met several more who feel u.d.r. is the way to go, including two who have convinced me that God is calling them to that," she wrote in a computer file called "Next Advent."

Shannon continued to join in clinic blockades, but she now used them as intelligence-gathering missions, just as Michael Bray had done when he joined John O'Keefe's protests in the early 1980s. In February 1993, Shannon and Angi joined a clinic blockade with Foreman's Missionaries to the Preborn in Milwaukee. (Foreman acknowledged in an interview that he discussed the issue of anti-abortion violence with Shannon before she shot George Tiller in August 1993.) While in Milwaukee, Shannon gathered information on local abortion doctor George Woodward, and in early March, she wrote an anonymous death threat to him:

"I'm writing this letter to give you your final warning," she said. "I'm coming into Milwalkie [*sic*] March 16. If you have stopped killing by then, I'll leave you and your family alone. If not I'll stalk you down. I know everything about you. . . . I will hunt you down like any other wild beast and kill you." Shannon later confessed to writing the letter, and in 1996, Angi was convicted and sentenced to four years in prison for mailing it.

Just days after Shannon sent the death threat to Woodward, Griffin killed Gunn in Pensacola. Almost immediately, Shannon began writing and sending money to Griffin, contributing $160 to the fund John Burt had set up. "I know you did the right thing," she wrote Griffin in an April 10 letter. "It was not murder. You shot a murderer. It was more like anti-murder. I believe in you and what you did, and really want to help if possible. I wish I could trade places with you."

On April 25, Griffin called Shannon from prison, prompting Shannon to write him that he was "the awesomest, greatest hero of our time." She found another hero in John Brockhoeft. In March, she began editing and distributing Brockhoeft's newsletter, the *Brockhoeft Report*. In his July 1993 report, Brockhoeft wrote, "Why, oh why do so many who profess Christ fail to see their responsibility?"

At the end of July, Shannon flew to Ashland, Kentucky, to visit Brockhoeft in prison. She drove from there to Chillicothe, Ohio, to visit Ray Streicher, who was serving time for clinic vandalism and burglary. Shannon met with Brockhoeft over two days, describing the visits as "awesome" and saying Brockhoeft "told me some of his great adventures." When it was time to leave, she broke down in tears. Upon returning to Grants Pass on August 2, Shannon began making preparations for her next mission: going after George Tiller.

"This morning in bed it seemed God asked, Is there any doubt?" Shannon wrote in a computer file. "No, Lord. Please help me do it right."

S hannon obtained a .25-caliber handgun and practiced shooting it with another anti-abortion activist in Grants Pass, Howard Romano. By August 14, it was clear that Shannon had decided to go through with her mission. In her diary, she wrote, "I love my kids. David too (the poor guy—having a wife like me!) I'm sad about going. Will I get to come back this time? I love you, Jesus."

She arrived at Oklahoma City's Union Bus Station at 6:30 P.M. on August 18 and, after renting a car at Will Rogers World Airport, headed for Wichita, stopping to sleep at a rest area on the way. Shannon arrived at Tiller's clinic early on the morning of August 19 and, with the loaded gun in her purse, went inside, pretending to be a patient. Although she had planned to shoot Tiller inside the clinic, she could not find him; she left and drove to a nearby park. There, she changed her appearance and returned to the clinic, where she stood with other local activists all afternoon, identifying herself to the other demonstrators as "Ann" from Sacramento.

Tiller finally left the clinic shortly after 7 P.M., driving out of the parking lot in his 1989 Chevy Suburban. As Shannon moved toward him, Tiller thought she was going to hand him some anti-abortion literature, and he "gave her the finger," Tiller recalls. "Then I remember hearing six shots . . ." Tiller was stunned. "I looked down and there's glass and blood every place, and I said, 'She shot me. She can't do that.'"

Furious, Tiller started driving after Shannon, but he had second thoughts when he saw her stop and reach into her pocket. He turned back to the clinic and stumbled out of his Suburban, bullet wounds in both arms. In the ambulance on the way to the hospital, Tiller refused to let the paramedics start an intravenous transfusion. His years of drug use had left him with only one good vein in his arm, and he did not want to compromise it.

Meanwhile, Tiller's nurse-assistant, Stacey Pack, chased Shannon down the street and was able to write down most of Shannon's license plate number. Police used the number to track Shannon down as she returned the car in Oklahoma City several hours later. Shannon was arrested at about 11 P.M., and she quickly implicated herself. "If there ever was a justifiable homicide, that would have been it," she told police. Included among Shannon's possessions were anti-abortion pamphlets, a New Testament Bible, and three *Life Advocate* magazines. A September 1991 issue was opened to an article about Tiller called "The Wichita Killer."

When Shannon was booked into jail in Wichita the next day, police found a bizarre letter she had written to her daughter, Angi, describing in detail what had happened. "I'm not denying I shot Tiller," she said. "But I deny that it was wrong. It was the most holy, most righteous thing I've ever done. I have no regrets." Then Shannon added, "Oh! Do not dig up my stuff under any circumstances. Don't keep anything incriminating in the house. It will most likely get ransacked before long."

Five weeks after Shannon's arrest, authorities finally did dig up her backyard, and they were astounded at what they found: Shannon's 1992 diary, books and manuals about bomb making, letters from other anti-abortion activists, and several *Army of God* manuals. Inside the house, investigators confiscated Shannon's computer files describing arsons and acid attacks she had committed. The evidence painted a picture of

Shannon's evolution from mainstream abortion foe to radical extremist and triggered one of the first federal investigations into the existence of a national conspiracy of anti-abortion terrorists whose aim was to shut down clinics and kill doctors.

First Griffin, now Shannon; by the fall of 1993, the violence had devastated the anti-abortion cause. The shootings prompted Congress to pass the Freedom of Access to Clinic Entrances Act, making it a federal crime to block access to clinics or to commit acts aimed at denying a woman access to an abortion. The Supreme Court followed suit, abruptly changing the direction it had set so recently in the *Bray* case. The Court issued rulings allowing law enforcement officials to use racketeering investigations against anti-abortion groups and provided lower courts the freedom to establish protest-free "buffer zones" around clinics to protect doctors and patients. With clear-cut laws and jurisdiction, the Justice Department, which had been reluctant to intervene in what the FBI and other federal officials had long viewed as a partisan political issue, established a new task force aimed at cracking down on anti-abortion extremists. The investigation focused on supporters of Paul Hill's violent philosophy and on the *Army of God* manual.

Meanwhile, Keith Tucci was struggling to stave off the final collapse of Operation Rescue, which by then was only a shell of its former organization. In September 1993, he called about sixty activists together in Melbourne, Florida, in a desperate effort to keep the civil disobedience movement afloat. Tucci thought the only way to save what was left of the group was to make a clean and public break with the new violent fringe; in the September conference, therefore, he tried to draw a line in the sand on the issue of violence. Tucci proclaimed that Operation Rescue was to be nonviolent and said that anyone who refused to pledge to condemn violence would have to leave the organization.

The Melbourne meeting quickly turned into a disaster for Tucci and for what remained of Operation Rescue. Jeff White, the head of an independent group he called Operation Rescue–California, was disgusted with Tucci's stance; White and other militants in Operation Rescue's leadership claimed that although they would not commit violence themselves, they were unwilling to condemn those who did attack doctors. In Melbourne, White tried to shout Tucci down: "You are about to do something that is going to tear this movement apart!" White yelled.

Tucci soon realized he had lost control; his uncompromising stand against violence was now the minority view within the activist ranks. The Melbourne conference broke up in disarray. In early 1994, Tucci resigned from Operation Rescue's leadership and turned over what was left to Flip Benham, a Dallas fundamentalist preacher with only limited experience in the movement.

Keith Tucci stepped down just as Michael Griffin's trial was gearing up in Pensacola. Michael Bray and Paul Hill were constant presences at the trial; both used it as a soapbox to spread their theories on violence. "Michael Griffin acted legally, morally, and heroically in defending the innocent," Bray told reporters on the steps of the courthouse.

Much of the defense's case focused on John Burt, who had been leading a protest outside the clinic the morning Gunn was killed. Griffin's attorney contended that Burt, by exposing Griffin to graphic anti-abortion videos, aborted fetuses, and the effigy of Gunn, was largely responsible for poisoning Griffin's mind. It was a weak defense, and jurors did not buy it; they deliberated less than three hours before finding Griffin guilty, and he was sentenced to life in prison with no chance of parole for twenty-five years. Burt was not charged in the criminal case, but he soon became the target of a wrongful death civil suit filed by David Gunn's estate.

Meanwhile, prosecutors in Wichita were preparing for Shannon's trial on attempted murder charges. In October 1993, Shannon had begun talking to *Wichita Eagle* reporter Judy Thomas, first in jail, then in long telephone conversations. On November 2, the *Eagle* ran a front-page story saying that Shannon had confessed to shooting Tiller. "I'll always know I did the right thing," Shannon told Thomas. In the interview, Shannon also said her diary contained enough evidence about other anti-abortion activities to put her behind bars for years. But that did not bother Shannon. "Even if I spend the rest of my life in prison, I did the right thing." Over the next five months, Shannon continued to stay in touch with Thomas through phone calls and letters. During their conversations, Shannon provided details that indicated her involvement in the earlier abortion clinic arsons. In December 1993, federal authorities in Oregon subpoenaed Angi Shannon as a grand jury began looking into her mother's activities. In Kentucky, ATF agents raided John Brockhoeft's prison cell with a search warrant to seize any information relating to Shannon.

By February 1994, the federal investigation into a possible conspiracy was going strong. Several leaders of Advocates for Life Ministries in Portland, as well as other friends of Shannon's, had been subpoenaed to testify before the grand jury, and a confidential FBI teletype confirmed that investigating abortion clinic violence had become a priority for the federal government. The document, sent to all FBI field offices, directed agents to pay particular attention to two activists: John Burt and John Brockhoeft.

The directive marked a significant policy change. During the Reagan-Bush era, when the White House supported the anti-abortion cause, the FBI had resisted outside demands that it investigate abortion-related violence. Saying that it lacked jurisdiction, the agency had left investigations up to the Bureau of Alcohol, Tobacco and Firearms. But with violence now flaring across the nation and Bill Clinton, an abortion-rights advocate, in the White House, the FBI suddenly became more aggressive. "Under Reagan and Bush, those guys [the FBI] wouldn't come within a hundred feet of an abortion clinic," observed one bemused ATF supervisor.

Even as federal law enforcement officials were beginning to investigate Burt, he became involved in another bizarre incident. On February 26, 1994, with Griffin's trial under way, Houston cabdriver and anti-abortion activist Daniel Ware arrived in Pensacola and, according to Burt, told Burt that he was planning a suicide assault against abortion doctors who were in town to attend a meeting of the National Coalition for Abortion Providers and a memorial service for David Gunn.

In Ware's Pensacola hotel room, Burt saw that Ware was not bluffing: He had arrived in town with a high-powered rifle, a .357-magnum handgun, and about five hundred rounds of ammunition. Ware "started talking about doing this suicide thing, where he'd go in and kill as many doctors as he could," Burt recalled in an interview. Frightened, Burt called Don Treshman in Houston, the leader of a fringe group he called Rescue America. Treshman asked Burt to put Ware on a bus and send him back to Houston. By the time Burt told authorities what had happened, Ware had already returned to Houston. Federal officials arrested Ware on weapons charges, but he was later acquitted. Burt's decision to notify law enforcement officials about Ware led to denunciations from other extremists, who accused Burt of being a government informant.

Ten days after Ware's arrest, Shannon's trial began in Wichita. Hill attended and held a press conference in the courthouse to defend Shannon's actions. On the final day of the weeklong event, Shannon took the stand. Although her public defender tried to convince the jury that Shannon did not intend to kill Tiller, Shannon told the district attorney, "I think it's irrelevant whether or not I was trying to kill him . . . because it would have been right either way, to try to stop what he's doing." Shannon was found guilty after the jury deliberated for just one hour and twenty-two minutes.

The following month, Joe Foreman, Andrew Burnett, and the new Operation Rescue leader, Flip Benham, gathered anti-abortion leaders for another round of meetings in Chicago in a last-ditch effort to close their rift over the issue of violence. On April 30, 1994, about eighty activists gathered at the Radisson Lincolnwood Hotel in Chicago, but the conference was just as big a failure as the conference held the previous September. Benham was just as uncompromising—and just as unsuccessful—as Keith Tucci had been in Melbourne.

In fact, the extremists were now more committed to violence than ever before. Scheidler, who attended the Chicago conference as an elder statesman, was "genuinely shocked" that support for violence had become so widespread. "It scared me to death," he says.

As the meeting disbanded, Burnett and Foreman realized that if they wanted to continue working at the national level, they were going to have to do it through a forum other than Operation Rescue. Over the next few months, they quietly founded a new group to bring together like-minded extremists: the American Coalition of Life Activists (ACLA). It quickly began to supplant Operation Rescue as the dominant new force in anti-abortion activism.

"ACLA's goal is to find those abortionists who are hiding out from public scrutiny and expose them," Foreman said in a letter addressed "to all Christian pro-life activists." Half of ACLA's new regional directors had signed Paul Hill's "justifiable homicide" declaration. The group soon launched a campaign to target individual doctors around the country, issuing a list of abortion providers it called "the deadly dozen," distributing wanted posters listing some of their home addresses, and offering a $5,000 reward for information leading to their arrest, conviction, or license revocation. In what they called the "No Place to Hide Campaign," ACLA leaders also vowed to leaflet physicians' neighborhoods and picket their homes and workplaces to publicize their role in providing abortions.

The ACLA's actions prompted Planned Parenthood and other abortion-rights groups to file a class-action lawsuit against members of the group and members of Burnett's Portland-based Advocates for Life Ministries, seeking at least $200 million in damages. The lawsuit, which is still in progress, seeks to link the two groups to the killings of abortion doctors.

By 1994, the fallout from the shootings had drastically changed the political climate surrounding the abortion debate. In January, the Supreme Court ruled in the *NOW v. Scheidler* case that demonstrators who blocked access to clinics or tried to stop women from having abortions could be sued under the conspiracy section of the federal racketeering, or RICO, statute. The decision allowed the National Organization for Women to proceed with its long-stalled RICO lawsuit against Scheidler, Operation Rescue, and others.

In the meantime, Congress passed the Freedom of Access to Clinic Entrances Act (called the FACE bill), which President Clinton signed into law in May. That was followed in late June 1994 by a Supreme Court ruling in *Madsen v. Women's Health Center,* in which justices decided to allow lower courts to establish protest-free buffer zones around clinics. In that case, which forced the Court to weigh the First Amendment rights of anti-abortion groups against the rights of women seeking abortions, justices upheld a state judge's order barring anti-abortion protesters from getting within thirty-six feet of the Aware Woman Center for Choice clinic in Melbourne, Florida. The order had been issued a month after Gunn's murder in Pensacola. Clinic owner Patricia Baird Windle sought the order because abortion protesters, through so-called impact teams, had launched intensive campaigns to shut down the clinic.

On June 10, 1994, two weeks after President Clinton signed the FACE bill into law, Paul Hill put the legislation to a test outside The Ladies Center of Pensacola. As Linda Taggart tried to perform a sonogram, Hill stood outside and screamed, "Mommy, mommy, don't murder me." Pensacola police told Taggart she could have Hill arrested for violating the local noise ordinance, but she wanted him charged with violating the new FACE law instead. When an FBI agent came to look into the matter, however, the agent refused to arrest Hill. Irate, Taggart got on the phone and contacted the Justice Department. "We're real familiar with Paul Hill and we're familiar with your clinic, but this is not the time to make an arrest," Taggart was told by a Justice Department official. The Justice Department apparently did not want to have its first court test of FACE in a conservative Southern state like Florida.

Hill returned to the clinic a week later, screaming so loudly that the staff again had difficulty performing sonograms. This time, Pensacola police arrested Hill for disorderly conduct and for violating the noise ordinance. Again, the new federal law was not brought to bear, and Hill was released. An FBI spokesperson later said that the Bureau had investigated Hill but dropped the case because there was no direct threat of violence against any particular person.

On July 12, 1994, Hill mailed a letter to supporters in which he called on the biblical concept of "blood guiltiness" that years earlier had motivated Randall Terry to found Operation Rescue: "Our tiny planet is saturated with the blood of the innocent. The blood guilt that hangs over our head is unspeakably staggering. Yet few seem to notice and fewer still take a stand."

Later that week, Hill went to Kansas City to attend a three-day seminar on how to become a full-time anti-abortion activist. He stayed at the home of Regina Dinwiddie, a longtime local protester and advocate of justifiable homicide. The seminar was conducted by the Center for Bio-Ethical Reform, a California organization run by anti-abortion activist Gregg Cunningham, a former member of the Pennsylvania House of Representatives who served in both the Reagan and Bush administration Justice Departments. After returning home from Kansas City in mid-July 1994, everything began to click into place for Hill.

"I was thinking about who might take action next," Hill recalled in an exclusive death row interview in the Florida State Prison. "And then I began to think, 'Well, what would happen if I did it?' And the more I thought about it, it seemed like a reasonable thing to do." Hill went back to The Ladies Center and learned Dr. Britton's schedule from one of the regular protesters. "I was thinking in terms of logistics and what I might do."

Hill continued to think about his mission for the next few days; after fasting, he says, "I decided that I was going to do it." He insists that he did not tell anyone of his plans, not even his wife, Karen, who was preparing to leave town to take their son to church camp near Atlanta. With the house to himself, "I realized I had a window of opportunity." As soon as his wife and children left, Hill took his shotgun to a gun range to practice. When the gun jammed on him, he bought a replacement: a solid black 12-gauge Mossberg pump shotgun with an extended magazine and a short barrel.

In the solitude of his empty house, Hill prepared for his attack by loading and reloading his new gun. While practicing his assault, his shotgun accidentally went off in the house, blowing a hole in the wall. Hill was afraid the shot would alert his neighbors, but the blast apparently went unnoticed.

Early on the morning of Friday, July 29, Hill finally put his plan into motion. He arrived at the clinic at about 6:45 A.M., concealing his shotgun in a large tube that normally contained the posters he used for his protests. Outside the weathered two-story building, he slid the gun into the grass. He then placed about twenty white wooden crosses in the ground and stood at the clinic entrance with an anti-abortion pamphlet, waiting for the doctor to arrive. Strapped to both of his ankles were extra rounds of ammunition. "Like a good Boy Scout, I wanted to be prepared."

Shortly after Hill's arrival, a police officer pulled up and told him to take the crosses down, saying they were in the city's right-of-way. Hill complied, stacking them in a pile next to the clinic driveway, and the officer left. At 7:27 A.M., Hill's wait was over. John Bayard Britton arrived at the clinic, a passenger in James Barrett's blue Nissan pickup. Barrett's wife, June, was sitting behind Britton in the jump seat of the club cab. As they pulled into the clinic drive, James Barrett grumbled, "Paul Hill, get out of my way. You know who this car belongs to."

Hill calmly recalls the chilling details of those few seconds: "They pulled in past me, and I stepped over to where the gun was in the grass, which put the fence between me and them. Then I picked up the weapon and stepped out from behind the fence and fired three times directly at the truck. I aimed directly at the abortionist, but the driver was directly between me and him, so their heads were almost blocking one another." The shotgun blasts moved James Barrett out of the way; he fell out of the pickup and onto the ground, "and so the abortionist was unprotected," recalls Hill. He reloaded. During the brief respite, Britton turned toward June Barrett. "Does Jim have his gun today?" he asked, referring to the .38-caliber pistol James Barrett sometimes carried in a locked box in the truck. "No." June Barrett ducked down on the floor of the truck and closed her eyes as the shots came again.

"I fired directly into him, five rounds, and then laid the shotgun down and walked away, slowly with my hands down to my side," Hill said.

When the shooting stopped, June Barrett began to stir. Clinic employee Dorothy Dunaway came cautiously outside, then bent down to take Jim Barrett's pulse. Realizing that he was dead, she went to the passenger side of the truck to check on Britton. "He was slumped over toward the middle and his head was all bloody and his right arm was partially blown away," she told police. "I could see the bone. Nothing but bone." She did not need to take his pulse.

Britton and Barrett were pronounced dead at the scene. Britton's bulletproof vest was useless; both he and Barrett had been shot in the head. June Barrett was struck in the forearm and breast. She later recalled the horror of getting out of the truck and having to step over her husband's body crumpled on the ground. "I knew he was dead."

Hill now says that although he intended to kill Britton, he knew James Barrett could pose a problem. "And so I realized that if I was going to have any assurance of killing the abortionist, I was probably going to have to kill him, too." Hill said he had no idea June Barrett would be in the pickup that day, but he felt no remorse over shooting her: "She was part of the movement. She was there to protect him and to support and lend aid and encouragement to him. So it would certainly be justified if she had been killed. I wasn't going to turn aside from my intent to save those children from them."

Witnesses said that after the shooting, Hill began jogging south from the clinic, then slowed to a walk. Police arrested him a few hundred feet away. As Officer Mark Holmes searched Hill, he found a black nylon and elastic shell holder containing five 12-gauge shotgun shells strapped to Hill's right ankle and another holder with two 12-gauge shotgun shells attached to Hill's left ankle. He found five more shotgun shells in Hill's left rear pocket and two in Hill's left front pocket. Hill also had a small plastic fetus in one pocket, along with a copy of his essay, "Should We Defend Born and Unborn Children with Force?" Holmes said that as officers escorted Hill to a police car, he said, "I know one thing. No innocent babies are going to be killed in that clinic today."

Linda Taggart, who had arrived just minutes after the shootings, closed the clinic for an indefinite period. "I couldn't deal with anything that day. I couldn't stop crying. It was awful. I said I would never again ask a doctor to work for me." When the shock wore off, Taggart was furious that Hill had not been stopped before. "I called the Justice Department back and said, 'Now is it the time to make an arrest? Now?'"

Later that day, a maintenance man told police he had seen Hill at about 7:30 the night before the shooting at a garbage dumpster that belonged to a 140-unit apartment complex across the alley behind Hill's home. The man said Hill was either placing something in the dumpster or taking something out. A search of the dumpster found a cardboard box and an owner's manual for a 12-gauge shotgun. The maintenance man also said that at about 9:30 that night, he saw Hill talking outside his house to a heavyset man in a blue Datsun with Texas license plates. When they saw him, he said, they drove away, with Hill leading in his pickup and the man in the Datsun following him. The identity of the person Hill was seen talking to remains a mystery.

The reaction to the latest murders was decisive. In Washington, President Clinton called the shootings a form of domestic terrorism and encouraged "a quick and thorough investigation into this tragic incident." Operation Rescue spokesman Pat Mahoney called it "a crushing blow" for the movement. "Nothing could be worse for the pro-life movement than what happened," he said. "In terms of political lobbying, in terms of public opinion."

Yet a handful of activists vocally supported Hill, just as they had supported Griffin and Shannon. Within a week, Michael Bray's sister-in-law, Donna Bray, wrote a letter from her group, Defenders of the Defenders of Life, asking for prayers and money for Hill and his family. The group also issued a declaration similar to Hill's Defensive Action statement, saying that Hill's actions were morally justified. Among the twenty-eight signers were Michael Bray, Andrew Burnett, Regina Dinwiddie, and Shelley Shannon.

Hill's crime provided the coup de grâce to anti-abortion activism. The press and public no longer accepted the arguments of moderate activists like new Operation Rescue leader Flip Benham who tried to distance themselves from the violence; tarred with a broad brush, Operation Rescue was now publicly perceived as little more than a violence-prone cult. America's tolerance for clinic blockades and other forms of anti-abortion civil disobedience abruptly ended, and Attorney General Janet Reno was finally prodded into creating a Justice Department task force to investigate whether there was a nationwide conspiracy behind the violence.

Within a day of Hill's crime, Reno ordered U.S. marshal's deputies to guard clinics in a dozen cities in an effort to head off further violence. Reno also formed an interagency anti-abortion violence task force to intensify the yearlong investigation into clinic violence that she had ordered when Griffin shot Gunn. Sources said Reno was disturbed that so little had been accomplished in the investigation to that point.

The beefed-up investigation began focusing on extremists who had signed Hill's Defensive Action statement, as well as those with connections to the anonymously published *Army of God* manual. A new FBI teletype went out listing half a dozen militants who might be conspiring to use force—among them Michael Bray. Although he was an obvious target of the investigation, Bray refused to stop speaking out in favor of justifiable homicide.

In October 1994, Hill became the first person in the country to be tried on FACE charges in federal court. Acting as his own lawyer and barred from using the necessity defense—the argument that he had killed to prevent the greater evil of abortion—Hill called no witnesses, cross-examined none of the prosecution's witnesses, and presented no evidence. The jury deliberated just over two hours before convicting him, and he was sentenced to two life sentences in federal prison.

That same month, Shelley Shannon was indicted for eight arsons and two acid attacks at clinics in the Northwest. She later pleaded guilty to six of the arsons and both acid attacks and was sentenced to twenty years. In prison, Shannon capitalized on her celebrity status among a small group of extremists, trying to incite from her jail cell the same violent acts she had once committed herself. She also attempted to warn and protect others who had been involved in clinic violence and even tried to take credit for acts committed by others.

Following his federal conviction on FACE charges, Hill went on trial on state murder charges in a Florida court in November 1994. Again acting as his own lawyer and again denied the use of the necessity defense, he offered no defense during the trial and refused to make any statement or question any witness. The jury deliberated just twenty minutes before convicting him. In December 1994, Circuit Judge Frank Bell sentenced Hill to die in Florida's electric chair. Although Hill was silent, Regina Dinwiddie, the radical activist from Kansas City, was escorted out of the courtroom when she jumped up and shouted at Bell, "This man is innocent, and his blood will be on your hands and the hands of the jury!"

By the end of 1994, a federal grand jury in Alexandria, Virginia, working in conjunction with the Justice Department's new anti-abortion violence task force, began issuing subpoenas to activists around the country. John Burt was one of the first to be summoned. When authorities learned Burt had an *Army of God* manual, they flew with him back to Pensacola to get it; Burt's willingness to cooperate with the federal authorities by turning over the manual again angered extremists, who thought Burt had sold them out.

Just as the federal investigation was gaining momentum, violence erupted again on December 30, 1994, when John C. Salvi III burst into the waiting room of a Planned Parenthood clinic in the Boston suburb of Brookline, Massachusetts, and opened fire with a .22-caliber rifle, killing a receptionist and wounding three others. Salvi then drove two miles to Brookline's Preterm Health Services clinic and began shooting again, killing another receptionist and injuring two more. He was arrested the next day, but only after he had fled south and attacked again, firing nearly two dozen shots at a building housing a Norfolk, Virginia, abortion clinic.

Abortion foes said Salvi, a twenty-two-year-old apprentice hairdresser and former altar boy who quoted Scripture and displayed color photos of aborted fetuses in the rear window of his pickup, was a mentally unbalanced loner who had no association with any group. But abortion-rights activists believed otherwise; Eleanor Smeal of the Feminist Majority Foundation noted that Salvi had driven more than five hundred miles and bypassed 180 other abortion clinics before zeroing in on the Hillcrest Clinic in Norfolk, a clinic that had long been the target of activists, including Michael Bray, who was convicted in 1984 of bombing it. Their suspicions intensified after authorities found the name and unlisted phone number of Donald Spitz, a Norfolk anti-abortion extremist, in Salvi's possession after his arrest. Although Spitz was one of the few anti-abortion extremists to hail Salvi publicly as a hero, he denied knowing him.

After the shootings, Cardinal Bernard Law of Boston shocked abortion foes by calling for a moratorium on all demonstrations outside the city's abortion clinics to prevent further violence. The action infuriated Catholic anti-abortion radicals like Joe Scheidler, who called his niece, Elsa Scheidler, in Boston and ordered her to defy the cardinal's request and picket at the clinics. She complied.

While in U.S. marshal's custody awaiting trial for the clinic bombings, Shannon wrote a letter to supporters, saying,

> For the ARMY OF GOD, 1994 was a pretty great year. Paul Hill performed a termination procedure on an abortionist and his accomplice, and may be put to death for his obedience to God, a most honorable way for a Christian to die. . . . The year ended with a big bang thanks to John Salvi III. I have to admire his determination. . . . God, please help and bless him.

Salvi was found guilty and sentenced to two consecutive life terms. Clearly a man plagued by inner demons, he committed suicide in his jail cell in November 1996.

The Justice Department's conspiracy investigation slogged on throughout 1995, as authorities called dozens of activists to testify before the grand jury. The list of those subpoenaed read like a who's who of anti-abortion extremists: Andrew Burnett; Michael Bray; Don Treshman; David Crane, a leader of the ACLA; and Don Spitz, head of Pro-Life Virginia. One abortion foe, Cheryl Richardson, was jailed for refusing to testify before the federal grand jury about the activities of her former fiancé, who had endorsed clinic violence. Richardson, a member of Michael Bray's church, said she had committed no crimes but feared that if she testified, prosecutors would twist her statements to indict innocent associates.

No indictments were issued, and the violence continued. The number of clinic arsons doubled from five in 1994 to ten in 1995; the number of bomb threats increased from fourteen to twenty-eight, according to National Abortion Federation statistics. In August 1995, a Wisconsin anti-abortion extremist, Robert Eugene Cook, who had said he planned a bloody revolution to save the unborn, was arrested in Chicago just days before he was planning to kill an abortion doctor. Inside Cook's storage locker, authorities found a cache of weapons and ammunition, including an assault rifle, handguns, and a pistol-type crossbow. Cook was also charged in connection with a September 1994 armored car burglary in Kenosha, Wisconsin, which authorities believe he committed to fund his anti-abortion campaign. Cook had been a part-time security guard for the armored car company at the time of the heist, in which $260,000 in cash was stolen.

Cook had picketed at clinics in Pensacola during the November trial of Paul Hill, and in January 1995 he allegedly appeared at The Ladies Center and at nearby businesses, stating, "You'd better get bulletproof glass" and "soon it's going to look like the Fourth of July around here." Just two weeks before his arrest, Cook had attended an ACLA conference in St. Louis. He had also been to Portland the week before that and had sent a contribution to Advocates for Life Ministries there. Leaders of those groups denied any knowledge of his plans.

Despite the connections among extremists and the terrorism described in the *Army of God* manual that circulated among them, authorities were unable to prove that there was a national conspiracy behind the violence. "Unless there's specific knowledge that someone's going to commit a crime, you don't have a criminal conspiracy," observes Cheryl Glenn, a special agent with the ATF in Portland and lead investigator in the Shelley Shannon case. "Paul Hill's Defensive Action statement created a national community of support for people who were willing to shoot doctors and gave them the rationale and emotional justification for actually acting it out, but there's a difference between having a common purpose and having an actual criminal conspiracy."

Some of those involved in the investigation said privately they were not surprised that a conspiracy was never found, in part because the two agencies working the case—the ATF and FBI—have a notoriously poor relationship. ATF agents, who had been investigating clinic arsons for years, resented the Justice Department's decision to send in the FBI to search for a conspiracy that they did not believe existed. After the FBI failed to find enough evidence of a conspiracy, they said, some agents became increasingly disgruntled with the Justice Department's efforts to build a case. Playing off the investigation's code name VAAP-CON, for Violence Against Abortion Providers Conspiracy, they nicknamed the probe "Crapcon." The federal grand jury in Alexandria was finally disbanded in January 1996, and Cheryl Richardson, who had stubbornly refused to testify, was released from prison.

Justice Department officials stressed, however, that the investigation was not necessarily over. Just because they had not found a national conspiracy did not mean there were not smaller, regional cells of extremists who were conspiring to commit violence. Instead of searching for a national underground, therefore, the Justice Department began to take the evidence gathered by the Alexandria grand jury and parcel it out to other grand juries around the nation for use in regional prosecutions. That new strategy soon led to the conviction of two protesters in Norfolk, Virginia, for arsons committed at clinics there.

Meanwhile, Bray continued to taunt authorities. In January 1996, as the Alexandria grand jury was disbanding and while mainstream anti-abortion groups were gathering for their annual march on Washington, Bray's church sponsored a "White Rose Banquet" in Arlington, Virginia, to honor comrades imprisoned for committing clinic violence. About one hundred extremists attended the banquet at a Best Western hotel, where they jokingly referred to each other as "coconspirators" and officers in the Army of God. Just outside the banquet hall, Bray had filled a table with anti-abortion literature and merchandise, including bumper stickers that said: "EXECUTE Murderers/Abortionists." Before the end of the dinner, Bray asked for a show of hands of all those who had been subpoenaed by the federal grand jury; dozens raised their hands.

The banquet featured letters from Shelley Shannon and Paul Hill that brought tears to those in attendance. Shannon encouraged activists not to give up. "I happen to know that if they lock up every single person they've subpoenaed to the Virginia grand jury, they won't stop anything," Shannon wrote. Her words generated hearty applause and murmurs of "amen."

Hill's letter was read last. "Now is the time to arise in the strength of the Lord that his enemies may be scattered," he wrote. "What shall we say if one of us who puts a hundred to flight receives a mortal wound? Is it not better for one to fall while causing hundreds to flee than for any man to cause his brother's heart to faint by his cowardly example?" Many wept and prayed as the letter was read. In a death row interview later, Hill said he still hopes his actions will inspire others. "There's no question that one of the greatest teachers is an example."

John O'Keefe, the long-forgotten father of rescue, could only look with horror on the state of the movement he had helped found. Michael Bray, the man who had betrayed him so many years before, was now the movement's de facto spokesman and leader.

"The direction of the movement?" O'Keefe wonders aloud. "I think it is a disaster."

Epilogue

The violence of the 1990s spelled the end of anti-abortion activism as a significant political and cultural force in American society. The killings of abortion providers, coupled with a renewed wave of bombings and arsons, finally forced a federal response.

With the FACE bill, Congress handed the Justice Department and the FBI the legal basis for an all-out assault on anti-abortion violence as well as activism. Not only did the law provide the FBI with the federal jurisdiction it had demanded to investigate clinic violence, but the new legal power allowed the government to stamp out clinic blockades and other forms of anti-abortion civil disobedience as well. Because "rescues" impeded clinic access, those who conducted them could now be prosecuted on federal charges under FACE rather than under local trespassing ordinances. Once FACE was the law of the land, the potential punishment for conducting a clinic blockade went from a few days in jail to years in a federal prison; "rescue" quickly ended as a result.

FACE withstood repeated constitutional challenges by activists in federal courts, but it clearly played a significant—and troubling—role in snuffing out an entire category of civil disobedience. The American Civil Liberties Union and other liberal groups normally concerned with free speech issues supported FACE and its use as a tool to quash anti-abortion activism. (Oddly, Norma McCorvey, the Roe of *Roe v. Wade,* had a born-again experience in 1995 and switched sides to join Flip Benham and the remnants of Operation Rescue just as large-scale anti-abortion activism was ending.)

Although the Supreme Court refused to overturn FACE, the Court did offer one last legal victory to the all but defunct Operation Rescue.

The Court struck down the legality of so-called floating buffer zones that had been imposed years before to prevent Operation Rescue's "sidewalk counselors" from talking to or harassing patients walking to and from abortion clinics. In *Schenk v. Pro-Choice Network of Western New York*, a case that had its roots in Operation Rescue's 1992 Buffalo campaign, the Court ruled that such "floating" zones created around clinic patients represented an unconstitutional infringement of the free speech rights of the protesters. Because the ruling did nothing to erode the power of FACE, however, *Schenk* was largely irrelevant.

By the time of the Supreme Court's *Schenk* ruling, in fact, all that was left of activism was a handful of extremists. Michael Bray and a few others were still preaching violence, but they were doing so only to tiny cells of radical supporters. Increasingly, their extremism extended to opposition to many forms of artificial contraception as well as abortion. More ominously, the extremists were beginning to draw support from the ranks of the new right-wing militia organizations. That volatile mix of anti-abortion extremism and antigovernment hate, in fact, appears to have boiled over in a series of bombings in Atlanta in 1996 and early 1997.

Horrified by the movement's plunge into extremism and violence, an eclectic group of anti-abortion veterans joined forces with a few of their onetime abortion-rights adversaries to try to find ways to end their mutual distrust and hold civilized discussions. Known as the Common Ground Network for Life and Choice, the alliance had its roots in the St. Louis abortion battles of the 1980s. Loretto Wagner, the St. Louis anti-abortion activist, and B. J. Isaacson, the former director of Reproductive Health Services, St. Louis's largest clinic and the plaintiff in *Webster*, founded the group after they decided to try to coexist without compromising their core beliefs about abortion. By 1996, Common Ground was large enough to hold its first annual conference; the group met in Madison, Wisconsin, bringing together activists in an attempt to reach across the no-man's-land of the abortion war. Of course Common Ground was handicapped by the fact that there was no way the activists could resolve their differences over abortion. Also, those from both sides who joined Common Ground often found their involvement was met by suspicion by others on their own side.

Although Common Ground found it difficult to make much of an impact, the end of large-scale, Operation Rescue–style protest did allow the right-to-life mainstream to return to the forefront of the movement for the first time in nearly a generation. Most notably, the National Right to Life Committee, long overshadowed by Operation Rescue, finally found a winning political issue when it began a campaign to ban a late-term abortion procedure that they and other critics had labeled *partial-birth abortion*. It was a marginal issue, like so many others that National Right to Life had emphasized in the past, but the debate over partial-birth abortion struck a surprising chord with the American public; even many abortion-rights supporters believed that this late-term procedure went too far.

Although the legislation that would have banned the so-called partial-birth abortion procedure was vetoed by President Clinton, the controversy helped shape a new and more sophisticated national consensus concerning the acceptable limits of abortion rights. After the partial-birth debate, that national consensus seemed remarkably close to the limits expressed by Justice Sandra Day O'Connor and her allies in *Casey*: freedom for adult women seeking early abortions, coupled with the right of the state to regulate more closely abortions performed on minors and those performed on all women who sought abortions late in their pregnancies.

This new, more subtle consensus represented an important change from the public attitude that held sway throughout the 1970s and 1980s. Opinion polls had long showed a consensus in favor of *Roe v. Wade*, yet those statistics had masked a deeper national ambivalence. In the broadest terms, Americans in the 1980s accepted abortion as a fact of life, but even many supporters told pollsters they believed abortion was the killing of a human life; Americans did not believe the abortion argument was settled.

A complex jumble of beliefs and emotions led to remarkable volatility in polling on abortion throughout the 1980s, and survey results fluctuated wildly with even the slightest alterations in the wording of poll questions. Anomalies cropped up throughout the polling data; blacks said they opposed abortion more strongly than whites, yet black women were nearly three times as likely to have abortions. Catholic women were more likely to have abortions than Protestant women, despite the Vatican's pronouncements. Polls showed that Americans most strongly supported a woman's right to an abortion under circumstances that were the most rare: in cases of rape, incest, or birth defects, or when the health of the pregnant woman was at stake. They were far more evenly divided over abortion in situations that most commonly prevailed: abortions performed to ease the social or economic burdens of young, unmarried working-class women. The irony was that most abortions took place "for precisely the reasons most Americans disapprove: financial or psychological reasons or convenience," noted Barbara Hinkson Craig and David M. O'Brien in *Abortion and American Politics,* a 1993 study of the issue.

Such ambivalence had created an opening for Operation Rescue's "in-your-face" approach; there was room to shake things up, to arouse old passions—to force America to think twice. That was what Randall Terry had had in mind when he told his followers that Operation Rescue's mission was to create "social tension." But once American public opinion began to coalesce around *Casey's* parameters in the 1990s, anti-abortion activism inevitably began to wane. The eventual introduction into the United States of mifepristone, the abortion pill also known as RU–486, could finally make anti-abortion activism obsolete.

In hindsight, there is little evidence that Operation Rescue made any significant inroads into abortion in the United States. In 1988, Operation Rescue's first full year, the number of abortions hit an all-time high of 1,590,750, a record broken just two years later, when abortions peaked at an estimated 1,608,600, according to the Alan Guttmacher Institute.

A gradual decline began in 1991, and by 1994, abortions fell to an estimated 1.43 million, the lowest level since 1978. That downward trend was the result of a complex set of demographic, economic, social, and political factors that analysts are still trying to sort out. But nonpartisan experts dismiss the notion that anti-abortion activity was a major factor.

To be sure, community pressures on doctors and hospitals, including protest and harassment like that targeted against Dr. George Tiller in Wichita, began to play a role by the early 1990s in the decline in the number of doctors willing to perform abortions. Those pressures, coupled with the relatively low pay earned by abortion doctors compared with their counterparts in other medical fields, had a ripple effect back into the nation's medical schools, where fewer and fewer students were willing to consider abortion as their specialty. The percentage of medical residency programs in obstetrics and gynecology providing routine training in first-trimester abortions decreased from 23 percent in 1985 to 12 percent in 1991, and the declining numbers of doctors soon became the abortion industry's biggest concern. By 1995, the medical profession was so worried about the shortage that the Accreditation Council for Graduate Medical Education, which oversees medical education in the United States, declared that residents in obstetrics and gynecology would be required to learn about abortion procedures in their hospital training unless they had moral or religious objections.

Nevertheless, experts believe the decline in the nation's abortion rate in the 1990s has little to do with either anti-abortion activity or the doctor shortage.

Instead, experts say that the decline is due to fundamental changes in the American way of reproduction. Above all, they believe that contraception is finally coming into "better use" in the United States. Contraception is becoming more automatic, partly through the growing acceptance of both male and female sterilization, reducing the number of unplanned pregnancies, and bringing America more in line with Western Europe, where "effective" contraceptive use is much higher and abortion rates far lower. "We may be catching up" to Western Europe, says Jeannie Rosoff, president of the Alan Guttmacher Institute. Constant, habitual use of contraception, she adds, "is a learned habit, and it takes a couple of generations to be fully internalized in a culture."

Still, the generation-long battle over abortion has forever changed the way Americans view social protest movements. The American abortion war also transformed Protestant fundamentalism; it served as the catalyst for the political mobilization of Evangelical Christians. And so even as Operation Rescue and anti-abortion activism died out, the Religious Right that they helped create remained one of the most potent forces on the American political landscape.

Bibliography

Abortion in 19th Century America, An Anthology of 19th Century Speeches and Writings on Abortion. New York: Arno Press, 1974.

Andrews, Joan, with John Cavanaugh-O'Keefe. *I Will Never Forget You: The Rescue Movement in the Life of Joan Andrews*. San Francisco: Ignatius Press, 1989.

Andrews, Joan, edited by Richard Cowden-Guido. *You Reject Them, You Reject Me: The Prison Letters of Joan Andrews*. Manassas, VA: Trinity Communications, 1988.

Aquinas, Thomas. *Selected Philosophical Writings*. Oxford, England: Oxford University Press, 1993.

Bainton, Roland H. *The Reformation of the Sixteenth Century*. Boston: Beacon Press, 1952.

Bellant, Russ. *The Coors Connection*. Boston: South End Press, 1988.

The Holy Bible. Revised Standard Version, Catholic edition. London: Catholic Truth Society, 1966.

The Holy Bible. Revised Standard Version. New York: Thomas Nelson & Sons, 1952.

Blanchard, Dallas A. *The Anti-Abortion Movement and the Rise of the Religious Right: From Polite to Fiery Protest*. New York: Twayne, 1994.

Blanchard, Dallas A., and Terry J. Pruitt. *Religious Violence and Abortion: The Gideon Project*. Gainesville, FL: University Press of Florida, 1993.

Branch, Taylor. *Parting the Waters: America in the King Years, 1954–1963*. New York: Touchstone, 1988.

Bray, Michael. *A Time to Kill: A Study Concerning the Use of Force and Abortion*. Portland, OR: Advocates for Life Publications, 1994.

Brown, Judie. *It Is I Who Have Chosen You*. Stafford, VA: American Life League, 1992.

Byrnes, Timothy A. *Catholic Bishops in American Politics*. Princeton, NJ: Princeton University Press, 1991.

Calderone, Mary S., ed. *Abortion in the United States*. New York: Hoeber, 1958.

Casey, William Van Etten. *The Berrigans*. New York: Avon, 1971.

Clabaugh, Gary K. *Thunder on the Right*. Chicago: Nelson-Hall, 1974.

Connery, John. *Abortion: The Development of the Roman Catholic Perspective*. Chicago: Loyola University Press, 1977.

Craig, Barbara Hinkson, and David M. O'Brien. *Abortion and American Politics*. Chatham, NJ: Chatham House, 1993.

Cruden's Handy Concordance, edited and adapted by Charles H. H. Wright. Grand Rapids, MI: Zondervan, 1963.

DeParrie, Paul. *The Rescuers*. Brentwood, TN: Wolgemuth & Hyatt, 1989.

Devereux, George. *A Study of Abortion in Primitive Societies*. New York: International Universities Press, 1955.

Diamond, Sara. *Spiritual Warfare: The Politics of the Christian Right*. Boston: South End Press, 1989.

Dobson, Ed, and Ed Hindson, with Jerry Falwell. *The Fundamentalist Phenomenon*. Garden City, NY: Doubleday, 1981.

D'souza, Dinesh. *Falwell: Before the Millennium*. Chicago: Regnery Gateway, 1984.

Ely, John Hart. "The Wages of Crying Wolf: A Comment on *Roe v. Wade*." *Yale Law Journal* 82 (April-July 1973).

Fager, Charles. *Selma: 1965*. New York: Scribner, 1974.

Faludi, Susan. *Backlash: The Undeclared War Against American Women*. New York: Crown, 1991.

Falwell, Jerry. *If I Should Die Before I Wake*. Nashville, TN: Thomas Nelson, 1986.

———. *Listen, America!* Garden City, NY: Doubleday, 1980.

———. *Strength for the Journey*. New York: Simon & Schuster, 1987.

Faux, Marian. *Crusaders: Voices from the Abortion Front*. New York: Carol Publishing Group, 1990.

———. *Roe v. Wade*. New York: Macmillan, 1988.

Foreman, Joseph Lapsley. *Shattering the Darkness: The Crisis of the Cross in the Church Today*. Montreat, NC: Cooling Spring Press, 1992.

Fowler, Robert Booth, and Allen D. Hertzke. *Religion and Politics in America: Faith, Culture and Strategic Choices*. Boulder, CO: Westview Press, 1995.

Friedan, Betty. *The Feminine Mystique*. New York: Norton, 1963.

Garrow, David J. *Liberty and Sexuality: The Right to Privacy and the Making of Roe v. Wade*. New York: Macmillan, 1994.

Ginsburg, Faye D. *Contested Lives*. Berkeley: University of California Press, 1989.

Gold, Rachel Benson. *Abortion and Women's Health: A Turning Point for America?* New York: The Alan Guttmacher Institute, 1990.

———. *Abortion Factbook, 1992 Edition*. New York: The Alan Guttmacher Institute, 1990.

Grant, George. *Third Time Around: A History of the Pro-Life Movement from the First Century to the Present*. Brentwood, TN: Wolgemuth & Hyatt, 1991.

Guitton, Stephanie, and Peter Irons, eds. *May It Please the Court: Arguments on Abortion*. New York: New Press, 1995.

Guttmacher, Alan F., ed. *The Case for Legalized Abortion Now*. Berkeley, CA: Diablo, 1967.

The Alan Guttmacher Institute. *Abortion Services in the United States, Each State & Metropolitan Area*. Editions of 1976–1977, 1977–1979, 1979–1980, 1981–1982, 1984–1985. New York: The Alan Guttmacher Institute.

Hertz, Sue. *Caught in the Crossfire: A Year on Abortion's Front Line*. New York: Prentice-Hall, 1991.

Hill, Paul. *Shall We Defend Born and Unborn Children with Force?* Pensacola, FL: 1993.

Ireland, Patricia. *What Women Want*. New York: Dutton, 1996.

Jarman, Peggy. *The Siege of Wichita*. Wichita, KS: 1994.

Jeffries, John C. II. *Justice Lewis F. Powell Jr.* New York: Scribner, 1994.

Kaplan, Laura. *The Story of Jane: The Legendary Underground Feminist Abortion Service*. New York: Pantheon Books, 1995.

The Joseph P. Kennedy Jr. Foundation. *The Terrible Choice: The Abortion Dilemma*. New York: Bantam Books, 1968.

Keown, John. *Abortion, Doctors and the Law: Some Aspects of the Legal Regulation of Abortion in England from 1803 to 1982*. Cambridge, England: Cambridge University Press, 1988.

King, Martin Luther, Jr. *Strength to Love*. Philadelphia: Fortress Press, 1963, 1981.

Koop, C. Everett. *Koop: The Memoirs of America's Family Doctor*. New York: Random House, 1991.

Korn, Peter. *Lovejoy: A Year in the Life of an Abortion Clinic*. New York: Atlantic Monthly Press, 1996.

Lader, Lawrence. *A Private Matter: RU 486 and the Abortion Crisis*. Amherst, NY: Prometheus Books, 1995.

———. *Abortion*. New York: Bobbs-Merrill, 1966.

———. *Abortion II: Making the Revolution*. Boston: Beacon Press, 1973.

Library of Congress. William J. Brennan Jr. Papers. Boxes 281, 417, 420A.

———. Thurgood Marshall Papers.

Lord, Captain Leslie. *The Cincinnati Police Division's Response to Anti-Abortion Demonstrations: Case Studies in Police Decision-Making*. Police Executive Research Forum, 1994.

Luker, Kristin. *Abortion and the Politics of Motherhood*. Berkeley: University of California Press, 1984.

Maloy, Kate. *Birth or Abortion: Private Struggles in a Political World*. New York: Plenum Press, 1992.

Marsden, George M. *Understanding Fundamentalism and Evangelicalism*. Grand Rapids, MI: Eerdmans, 1991.

Martin, Ralph. *The Catholic Church at the End of an Age: What Is the Spirit Saying?* San Francisco: Ignatius Press, 1994.

Martin, William. *With God on Our Side: The Rise of the Religious Right in America*. New York: Broadway Books, 1996.

Marty, Martin E., and R. Scott Appleby. *Fundamentalisms Observed: The Fundamentalism Project*. Chicago: University of Chicago Press, 1991.

———. *The Glory and the Power: The Fundamentalist Challenge to the Modern World*. Boston: Beacon Press, 1992.

Maxwell, Carol. *Meaning and Motivation in Pro-Life Direct Action* (unpublished doctoral dissertation). St Louis, MO: Washington University, 1994.

McCorvey, Norma, with Andy Meisler. *I Am Roe: My Life, Roe v. Wade, and Freedom of Choice*. New York: HarperCollins, 1994.

McDonnell, Kilian, and George T. Montague. *Fanning the Flame: What Does Baptism in the Holy Spirit Have to Do with Christian Initiation?* Collegeville, MN: Liturgical Press, 1991.

McGrath, Alister et al., eds. *Roman Catholicism: Evangelical Protestants Analyze What Divides and Unites Us*. Chicago: Moody Press, 1994.

McHugh, James T. *The Relationship of Moral Principles to Civil Laws with Special Application to Abortion Legislation in the United States of America, 1968–1978* (unpublished doctoral dissertation). Rome: In Facultate S. Theologiae Apud Pontificiam Universitatem S. Thomae De Urbe Rome, 1981.

McKeegan, Michele. *Abortion Politics: Mutiny in the Ranks of the Right.* New York: Free Press, 1992.

McNeill, John T. *The History and Character of Calvinism.* London: Oxford University Press, 1954.

Meloon, Marion. *Ivan Spencer: Willow in the Wind.* Plainfield, NJ: Logos International, 1974.

Merton, Andrew. *Enemies of Choice: The Right-to-Life Movement and Its Threat to Abortion.* Boston: Beacon Press, 1981.

Merton, Thomas. *New Seeds of Contemplation.* New York: New Directions, 1961.

———. *Passion for Peace: The Social Essays,* edited by William H. Shannon. New York: Crossroad, 1995.

———. *The Seven Storey Mountain.* New York: Harcourt, Brace, 1948.

Mohr, James. *Abortion in America: The Origins and Evolutions of National Policy.* New York: Oxford University Press, 1978.

Moore, James. *Very Special Agents.* New York: Pocket Books, 1997.

Nathanson, Bernard N., with Richard Ostling. *Aborting America.* New York: Doubleday, 1989.

National Abortion Rights Action League. *Who Decides? A State-by-State Review of Abortion and Reproductive Rights.* Washington, DC: NARAL, 1995.

O'Brien, David M. *Storm Center: The Supreme Court in America.* New York: Norton, 1986.

O'Keefe, John Cavanaugh. *No Cheap Solutions.* Gaithersburg, MD: Pro-Life Nonviolent Action Project, 1984.

———. *Non-Violence Is an Adverb.* Gaithersburg, MD: Pro-Life Nonviolent Action Project, 1985.

———. *A Peaceful Presence.* Gaithersburg, MD: Pro-Life Nonviolent Action Project, 1978.

Olasky, Marvin W. *Abortion Rites: A Social History of Abortion in America.* Wheaton, IL: Crossway Books, 1992.

Paige, Connie. *The Right to Lifers: Who They Are, How They Operate, Where They Get Their Money.* New York: Summit Books, 1983.

Parker, Thomas Henry Lewis. *Calvin: An Introduction to His Thought.* Louisville, KY: Westminster/John Knox Press, 1995.

Parkhurst, Louis Gifford, Jr. *Francis Schaeffer: The Man and His Message.* Wheaton, IL: Tyndale House, 1985.

Petchesky, Rosalind P. *Abortion and Woman's Choice: The State, Sexuality, and Reproductive Freedom.* New York: Longman, 1984.

Ramey, Cathy. *In Defense of Others: A Biblical Analysis and Apologetic on the Use of Force to Save Lives.* Portland, OR: Advocates for Life Publications, 1995.

Reagan, Leslie J. *When Abortion Was a Crime.* Berkeley: University of California Press, 1997.

Reagan, Ronald. *Abortion and the Conscience of the Nation.* Nashville, TN: T. Nelson, 1984.

Reed, James W. "The Birth Control Movement Before *Roe v. Wade.*" *Journal of Policy History* 7, no. 1 (1995): pp. 22–52.

Reed, Ralph. *Active Faith.* New York: Free Press, 1996.

———. *Politically Incorrect: The Emerging Faith Factor in American Politics.* Dallas, TX: Word Publishing, 1994.

Rosten, Leo, ed. *Religions of America.* New York: Touchstone, 1975.

Sarvis, Betty, and Hyman Rodman. *The Abortion Controversy*. New York: Columbia University Press, 1973.

Schaeffer, Edith. *The Tapestry: The Life and Times of Francis and Edith Schaeffer*. Waco, TX: Word Books, 1981.

Schaeffer, Francis A. *A Christian Manifesto*. Westchester, IL: Crossway Books, 1981.

———. *The God Who Is There*. Downers Grove, IL: InterVarsity Press, 1968.

———. *He Is There and He Is Not Silent*. Wheaton, IL: Tyndale House, 1972.

———. *How Should We Then Live?* Old Tappan, NJ: Fleming H. Revell, 1976.

——— *True Spirituality*. Wheaton, IL: Tyndale House, 1971.

Schaeffer, Francis A., and C. Everett Koop. *Whatever Happened to the Human Race?* Old Tappan, NJ: Fleming H. Revell, 1979.

Scheidler, Joseph M. *Closed: 99 Ways to Stop Abortion*. Westchester, IL: Crossway Books, 1985.

Shofner, Myra Sims. *Protectors of the Code*. Pensacola, FL: Author, 1989.

Supreme Court of the United States. *Decisions, Opinions, Briefs*. Library of the Supreme Court of the United States.

Synan, Vinson. *In the Latter Days: The Outpouring of the Holy Spirit in the Twentieth Century*. Ann Arbor, MI: Servant Publications, 1984.

Terry, Randall A. *Accessory to Murder: The Enemies, Allies, and Accomplices to the Death of Our Culture*. Brentwood, TN: Wolgemuth & Hyatt, 1990.

———. *The Judgment of God: Terrorism . . . Floods . . . Droughts . . . Disasters*. Windsor, NY: Reformer Library, 1995.

———. *Operation Rescue*. Springdale, PA: Whitaker House, 1988.

———. *The Sword: The Blessing of Righteous Government and the Overthrow of Tyrants*. Windsor, NY: Reformer Library, 1995.

———. *Why Does a Nice Guy Like Me Keep Getting Thrown in Jail?* Lafayette, LA: Huntington House Publishers.

Tribe, Laurence H. *Abortion: The Clash of Absolutes*. New York: Norton, 1990.

Walbert, David F. *Abortion, Society and the Law*. Cleveland, OH: Cleveland Press, Case Western Reserve University, 1973.

Wattleton, Faye. *Life on the Line*. New York: Ballantine Books, 1996.

Weddington, Sarah. *A Question of Choice*, 2nd ed. New York: Penguin Books, 1993.

Whitney, Catherine. *Whose Life?* New York: Morrow, 1991.

Wilcox, Fred. *Uncommon Martyrs*. Reading, MA: Addison-Wesley, 1991.

Wills, Gary. *Under God*. New York: Simon & Schuster, 1990.

Woodward, Bob, and Scott Armstrong. *The Brethren: Inside the Supreme Court*. New York: Simon & Schuster, 1979.

NEWSPAPERS AND PERIODICALS

The Atlanta Journal-Constitution
The Binghamton Press & Sun-Bulletin
The Chicago Sun-Times
The Chicago Tribune
The City Paper
The Dallas Morning News
The Fort Worth Star-Telegram
The Kansas City Star
The Los Angeles Times
The Miami Herald

Newsweek
The New York Post
The New York Review of Books
The New York Times
The Pensacola News Journal
The Philadelphia Inquirer
The St. Louis Post-Dispatch
Time
The Washington Post
The Wichita Eagle

OTHER MATERIALS

The *Army of God* manual
The Human Life Review
Research articles, the Alan Guttmacher Institute
Private journal and documents of Anne Bower
Private papers and videotape collection of Robert Jewitt
Videotape collection of Gary Leber
Letters, private papers, and videotapes of Joseph Scheidler
Diary of Shelley Shannon
Videotape collection of Diane Straus
Private papers of Wendy Wright
Documents from the Feminist Majority Foundation
Documents from the National Abortion Rights Action League
Documents from the National Abortion Federation
Documents from the National Center for the Pro-Choice Majority
Life Advocate magazine
Capitol Area Christian News
Prayer & Action Weekly News
The Body Politic magazine
Miscellaneous court documents
Wisconsin State Historical Society Archives on Social Protest, Madison, WI.

Sources

Alex Aitken
Joan Andrews
Earl Appleby
Ann Baker
Burke Balch
Brian Ballard
Jerram Barrs
Mark Belz
Flip Benham
Father Daniel Berrigan
Randall Bezanson
Harry Biltz
Dallas Blanchard
Fred Blumer
James Bopp
Anne Bower
John Brandt
Jayne Bray
Michael Bray
Susan Brindle
John Broderick
Patricia Brous
Judie Brown
Father Edward Bryce
Andrew Burnett
John Burt
William Caplinger
Michael Cavanaugh
John Cavanaugh-O'Keefe
Sherri Chessen
Joan Clark
Fay Clayton
Stacy Cline

Mary Jean Collins
Mike Conroy
Vicky Conroy
Dr. Robert Cook
Bill Cotter
Richard Cowden-Guido
John Cowles
Mary Kay Culp
David Danis
Ignatius DeBlasi
Paul deParrie
Vivian Diener
Regina Dinwiddie
Michael Dodds
Richard Doerflinger
Tim Dreste
Barb Magera Duffy
Laura Dunn
Phil Eck
The Reverend Al Ericksen
Pat Erwin
Bernard Evans
The Reverend Jerry Falwell
Robert Fierer
Joseph Foreman
Gail Frances
Wanda Franz
David Gaetano
Kip Gannett
Allan Gates
Fred Gauge
Carolyn Gerster
Ann Glazier

Cheryl Glenn
Judy Goldsmith
Donnie Gratton
Carole Griffin
Michael Griffin
Judy Hager
Lucy O'Keefe-Hancock
Harry Hand
Dan Heidelmeyer
Karen Ryan Heidelmeyer
Paul Hill
Susan Hill
Michael Hirsh
Frank Holby
Mary Holby
Tom Horkan
Jerry Horn
Karyn Hudson
The Reverend Henry Irby
Patricia Ireland
Peggy Jarman
Mildred Jefferson
Bob Jewitt
Paul Johansson
Harold Johnson
Peg Johnston
Judge Patrick F. Kelly
Kenneth Kimball
Allene Klass
Dr. C. Everett Koop
Edward Korb
Lawrence Lader
Gary Leber
Jesse Lee
Sam Lee
The Reverend Dan Little
Jan Lockridge
David Long
Mark Lucas
Pat Mahoney
Father Francis Martin
Robert Mathias
Carol Maxwell
Norma McCorvey
Gary McCullough
Claire McCurdy
The Reverend Robert McCurry
Betsy McDonald
Bishop James McHugh

Michael McMonagle
Mary Meehan
Roxann Meyer
Eric Michaloski
The Reverend Philip Miess
Jeanne Miller
Monica Migliorino Miller
Gerald Mitchell
Captain Gerald Mizell
Forrest Montgomery
The Reverend Howard Moody
Michael Mrva
Tim Murphy
Robert Muse
Glen Halva-Neubauer
Ann O'Brien
Kathy O'Keefe
Martha O'Keefe
John O'Keefe Sr.
Karye Ortman
David O'Steen
Stephen Peifer
Beth Petzelt
Assistant Police Chief Jerry Potts
Andy Puzder
Carl Pyrdum
Cathy Ramey
Lynne Randall
Joseph Reilly Jr.
Pat Robertson
Tom Roeser
Ann Rose
Jeannie Rosoff
Dr. Alan Ross
John Ryan
Linda Ryan
Vicki Saporta
Mark Saunders
Father Michael Scanlon
Edith Schaeffer
Ann Scheidler
Jim Scheidler
Joseph Scheidler
Paul Schenk
Rob Schenk
Andy Scholberg
Dorothy Schonhorst
Michael Schwartz
Jay Sekulow

Myrna Shaneyfelt
Shelley Shannon
David Shannon Jr.
Gina Shaw
Sandra Sheldon
Mary Ann Sheridan
The Reverend David Shofner
Joe Slovenec
Eleanor Smeal
Jennifer Sperle
Kathy Spillar
Randal Stewart
Diane Straus
Leszek Syski
Marilyn Szewczk
Linda Taggart
Michael Taylor
Cindy Terry
Randall Terry
Susan Tew

Dr. George Tiller
Art Tomlinson
Don Treshman
Keith Tucci
Eric Tyson
Helen Wagner
Loretto Wagner
Joe Wall
Chief Mike Watson
Sarah Weddington
Jeff White
Judith Widdicombe
Juli Loesch Wiley
Geline Williams
Dr. John Willke
Patricia Baird Windle
Linda Wolfe
Wendy Wright
Terry Wycoff
Leonard Zeskind

Index